ACCOUNTING
DESK BOOK

FIFTH EDITION

The Accountant's Everyday
Instant Answer Book

**Adapted from the first four editions
by William J. Casey and the IBP Research
and Editorial Staff. Completely revised
Fifth Edition by Stephen R. Novak, CPA**

INSTITUTE for BUSINESS PLANNING, Inc.
IBP Plaza • Englewood Cliffs, N.J. 07632

Fifth Edition
© 1977 *by*

Institute for Business Planning, Inc.
IBP Plaza, Englewood Cliffs, N.J. 07632

Library of Congress Catalog Card Number 76-52197

This publication is designed to provide accurate and authoritative information in regard to the subject matter covered. It is sold with the understanding that the publisher is not engaged in rendering legal, accounting
or other professional service. If legal advice or other expert assistance is
required, the services of a competent professional person should be
sought.

> — *From a Declaration of Principles jointly adopted by a*
> *Committee of the American Bar Association and a Committee*
> *of Publishers and Associations.*

Printed in the United States of America
ISBN 0-87624   008-2

About the Author

Stephen R. Novak is a CPA in the State of New Jersey and a member of the American Institute of Certified Public Accountants and the Passaic County chapter of the state society.

He is a graduate of Pace University and of Lehigh University. From 1969 to 1974, Mr. Novak worked for Hauser, O'Connor and Hylind, CPAs, a public accounting firm in Paterson, New Jersey, and New York City. He served as a managing senior in field audits.

In 1974, Mr. Novak decided to devote his entire career to professional writing. Since leaving active field work, he has had several major writing successes. In accounting literature, he has been published by *The National Public Accountant*, and, in addition to doing this Fifth Edition of *The Accounting Desk Book*, he is working on a *Field Auditors Manual and Guide*, to be published by IBP. In poetry, he has won several small magazine contests. In fiction, he is a member of the Mystery Writers of America, Inc., and one of his short stories, which appeared in *Alfred Hitchcock's Mystery Magazine*, was also recently published in the 1976 Mystery Writers Anthology, *Tricks and Treats* (Doubleday). He is also now working on a political mystery novel.

INTRODUCTION

Following the concepts established in the prior four editions, this Fifth Edition of the *Accounting Desk Book* is designed primarily as a handy portable reference for the latest financial accounting and reporting standards and principles, together with some discussion and illustrations of their practical applicability.

Because of the copious changes in recording and reporting guidelines, this author has found it necessary to revamp most of the entire content of the prior edition, beefing up and solidifying the body of accounting regulations, mostly in thorough, highlighting, outline format — easy-to-find and read — conveniently referenced for further research if desired. Separate sections on taxes and management considerations are also presented in a style offering brief, but inclusive, coverage, to make easy supplemental comparison with the accounting aspects of similar topics.

Practitioners, teachers and students will find, among other things, the following useful outlines:

What are the "official" as opposed to "unofficial" standards?

GAAP (Generally Accepted Accounting Principles).

What disclosures are required?

When are restatements required?

A listing of timing differences.

A listing of permanent differences

Over 100 sample journal entries.

The balance sheet and income statement sequence-format used in both the accounting and tax sections.

The nature of accounting is such that it often invites discussion and disagreement. This author encourages comments, suggestions, disputations (or compliments) and promises personal reply.

A book such as this involves not only the craftsmanship of all who participate in its production, but also those personal, immeasurable factors of encouragement and confidence. It is my privilege to single out one of the many people who were responsible for helping me bring this edition to fruition, William M. Doremus, CPA, colleague and friend.

Stephen R. Novak, CPA

FOREWORD

Most accounting books and articles, in quoting or referencing the AICPA standards, mention as a source the original number of the APB, ARB, SAS, FASB, etc. Reference to those individual pronouncements often involves the further trace to a prior announcement, which amended a prior one, which amended ... and so on. Also, every opinion, by itself, is dated and pinpointed in time and cannot in itself indicate *subsequent* changes thereafter. Unless one makes manual changes and references to the opinions as they are amended by later pronouncements, he may be working with a provision which is outdated or voided by a later one.

There is only one adequate timely publication which constantly updates the standards — paragraph by paragraph — as changes occur. This is the four-volume *"Professional Standards"* loose-leaf service published by the AICPA, with the cooperation of Commerce Clearing House, Inc. (A fifth volume, *"Technical Aids,"* is an important adjunct to the series.) In this service, the APB's, FASB's, etc. are codified, indexed and arranged for systematic additions, modifications and deletions, so that one always has the latest, applicable information.

Periodically, the AICPA also publishes paperback updates (also codified in the same manner), as it has twice now since the new FASB was formed in 1973. These, also, are immediately outdated to some extent by subsequent pronouncements.

All parenthetical references in this Fifth Edition of the Accounting Desk Book (in the Accounting Section) are geared to this loose-leaf service (and also to the paperback publications to the extent provisions remain unchanged by subsequent pronouncements). The references in this Desk Book cover the updated standards through December 15, 1976.

The following letter-prefix abbreviations, as used in the Accounting Section of this Desk Book, are from the loose-leaf volumes indicated:

AU	— Vol. 1	— PROFESSIONAL STANDARDS — Auditing
ET	— Vol. 2	— PROFESSIONAL STANDARDS — Ethics
BL	— Vol. 2	— PROFESSIONAL STANDARDS — Bylaws
AC	— Vols. 3 & 4	— PROFESSIONAL STANDARDS — Accounting
AC U	— Vol. 4	— PROFESSIONAL STANDARDS — Accounting Interpretations
TA	— Vol. 5	— TECHNICAL AIDS

Appendix H (at the end of this book) has been provided as a cross-reference from the AC (Accounting) references to the original pronouncements and opinions (APB's, FASB's, etc.)

The Accounting Interpretations (AC U references), in the codification, conveniently carry the same numbers as the opinion paragraph to which they pertain.

We express our appreciation to the Financial Accounting Standards Board (the FASB) and the American Institute of Accountants (the AICPA) for the permission granted for quoting from and referencing the above volumes as well as their other publications mentioned in the text and in the bibliography.

Contents

SECTION ONE — ACCOUNTING

SECTION TWO — TAXES

SECTION THREE — MANAGEMENT

SECTION FOUR — APPENDIXES

SECTION ONE

ACCOUNTING

1

The Accountant and Accounting

[¶101]

In 1941, the Committee on Terminology of the American Institute of Accountants defined and explained the term "accounting":

> Accounting is the art of recording, classifying and summarizing in a significant manner and in terms of money, transactions and events which are, in part at least, of a financial character, and interpreting the results thereof. ... careful attention to the significant words, 'the art of recording, classifying and summarizing' will rule out any interpretation that no more is indicated than bookkeeping. The recording and classifying of data in account books constitute an accounting function, but so also and on a higher level do the summarizing and interpreting of such data in a significant manner, whether in reports to management, to stockholders, or to credit grantors, or in income tax returns, or in reports for renegotiation or other regulatory purposes." (Accounting Terminology Bulletin No. 1, August 1953)

In the AICPA Professional Standards for Accounting (Volume 3), Section AC 1023, ("The Environment of Financial Accounting") that definition was superseded as follows (October 1970):

> Accounting is a service activity. Its function is to provide quantitative information, primarily financial in nature, about economic entities that is intended to be useful in making economic decisions, in making reasoned choices among alternative courses of action. Accounting includes several branches, for example,
>
> Financial Accounting
Managerial Accounting
Governmental Accounting

Financial Accounting is, therefore, only one branch of accounting — and the one with which this book is concerned.

Financial accounting provides: "A continual history quantified in money terms of economic resources and obligations of a business enterprise and of economic activities that change those resources and obligations." (AC 1023.02)

2

Standing alone, the term "Financial Accounting" merely indicates the providing of that continual history — the recording function. The coexisting corollary of *financial reporting* must be included to complete the full concept of the function and purpose of financial accounting. This all-inclusive concept is applicable to the coverage in this section of the book.

Before outlining "who determines the standards," "what the standards are," and "how they apply to financial accounting (and financial reporting)," it is appropriate to point out *why* the standards are important, *why* they prevail in the accounting profession, *why* they should *not* be ignored by the financial accountant, whoever he or she is and in whatever capacity he or she serves.

[¶102] THE ACCOUNTANT

What is an accountant? Simply and best-described, perhaps, an accountant is one who has *been trained* in accounting. This training may have been obtained in educational institutions or in practical experience, or in both.

There are practicing accountants; non-practicing accountants.

There are private accountants; public accountants.

There are experienced field accountants; non-experienced ones.

There are accountants who are teachers, writers, advisors, etc.

There are accountants who, having met state requirements for education, experience and examination, are granted certificates authorizing them to practice public accounting within that state, "certifying" them as qualified under that state's law. One of the qualifications to be met for certification, which has been universally accepted by all the states, is the getting of passing grades on all the following examinations prepared for each semi-annual sitting by the AICPA:

1. Accounting Practice (in two parts)

2. Auditing

3. Accounting Theory

4. Business Law

The time for the exams is set by the AICPA uniformly for all states (and territories, etc.). The questions on each exam are changed from sitting to sitting, seldom, if ever, being repeated verbatim. The exams contain both objective questions (multiple-choice) and questions requiring essay-type written answers or mathematical solutions in accounting formats. Most states have imposed time-frames within which all the exams must be passed in order for all of them to remain valid toward certification.

Having qualified as a certified public accountant under state law, the new CPA is immediately offered the opportunity of becoming a member of:

1. The American Institute of Certified Public Accountants (the AICPA).

2. The respective state society of Certified Public Accountants (locally in a county chapter of the same).

For CPAs who are members of the AICPA, the "standards" are mandatory (with the penalty being reprimand or possibly expulsion for non-conformance). The standards have also been adopted (sometimes enlarged) by most state societies.

This text does not in any way seek to appear to be approving or disapproving these standards, nor does it wish to reflect in any manner on the abilities or qualifications of *any* accountant, regardless of certification or non-certification, or his status or non-status in public, private (profit or not-for-profit organizations), governmental, teaching or other accounting capacity.

What is important is the *existence of these standards*. The *fact* of their existence coupled with the widespread *recognition* given them (by owners and the investing public, lending institutions, stock markets, governmental regulatory bodies and others) makes the *knowledge* of them imperative for those who do not wish to be held legally or professionally liable for *divergencies* from what are called, "Generally Accepted Accounting Standards and Principles." Moreover, proof of rigid adherence to professional accounting standards may be a valid legal defense in a court of law for a non-member, as well as for a member, or for a non-certified public or private accountant as well as for a certified one. Alternatively, deviations from these standards may, in court, preclude an accountant from leaning on the profession as a defense.

How these standards are set is discussed briefly later.

The observant reader may have noted that the term "auditing" has not yet been used — with a purpose. *Management* is responsible for the function of financial accounting (and reporting). The *auditor* is an independent who examines management's financial accounting (and reporting) and *attests* to its conformance with, or deviations from, "generally accepted accounting principles." In an "opinion" which accompanies the management-prepared financial statements (impliedly and in actuality adjusted to conform with the auditor's detailed error-findings during extensive testing of the system and records), the auditor puts his professional stamp of *relative* approval to the statements presented as well as to the methods used in arriving at the figures presented. In addition, the auditor attests to certain information (financial notes) which is now mandatory or advisable for certain disclosures.

The wording of attestations ("opinions"), as well as the auditing process itself, has been fairly well-defined and prescribed by the AICPA in "auditing standards" which are separate from, but based upon "financial accounting" standards.

This text is *not* concerned with the auditor's function or the attestation he must make after the examination of management's records and report.

This text *is* concerned with pointing out the *techniques* and *standards* to be followed which, hopefully, would result in an unqualified or "clean" opinion from that independent auditor. The *knowledge* of these factors is important to *both* management and auditor — management (internal or private accountants), to assure proper preparatory and running procedures per the standards; the auditor, to examine management's conformance to those standards. The closer both are to the knowledge of the guidelines, the less likely will be significant divergence from those guidelines.

[¶102.1] Rules of Conduct for the Profession

There is one aspect of the accounting profession which is perhaps more important than skill in the eyes of the outside observer — *Integrity*. The integrity of the individual and the profession of which he is a member — uprightness, honesty, sincerity, soundness.

For CPAs who are in public accounting, the AICPA has developed, through historical evolution, specific rules of conduct which constitute the standards of ethics for the membership.

The affirmative ethical principles toward which CPAs should strive are embodied in these five broad concepts of conduct: (ET 51.07)

1. Independence, integrity and objectivity
2. Competence and technical standards
3. Responsibilities to clients
4. Responsibilities to colleagues
5. Other responsibilities and practices for conduct which will enhance the stature of the profession and its ability to serve the public.

CPA members of the AICPA who are *not* engaged in *public* accounting must observe only the following specific rules: (ET 92.04)

1. The rule of integrity and objectivity. (ET 102.01)
2. The acts discreditable rule. (ET 501.01)

Other public accounting organizations also specify rules of conduct geared to the same goal of the highest possible ethical standard.

[¶102.2] Legal Liability

Despite the high standards of conduct and performance demanded within the profession, despite precautions taken for near-perfect performance, even the most dedicated accounting professional, public or private, individual or firm, is always faced with the risk of a lawsuit over some engagement or work in which he participated or supervised.

Some of the charges against which an accountant may have to defend himself against clients or third parties are:

Negligence (especially failure to detect fraud)

Breach of confidentiality

Misleading, misrepresented, insufficient or incorrect reports issued under the accountant's attestation

Charges brought by the Securities and Exchange Commission (or other regulatory agency) for improprieties, negligence or fraud, or lack of proper disclosure-in connection with registration statements or periodic reports filed.

The accountant may face monetary damage suits or criminal fraud charges.

Professional liability insurance, to some extent, mitigates the risk of monetary loss. High capitalization of the firm also helps.

But the decision may ultimately rest with judges or juries and be predicated upon the adequacy of the defense offered by the accountant. The strongest defense would undoubtedly be proof of rigid adherence to professional standards, documented by thorough proofs of work and reasonable effort.

To support the "reasonable effort" concept, many accountants are now using statistical sampling for certain phases of proof-testing. Because the use of sampling techniques has gained such wide acceptance in many other fields, judges and juries may more readily accept conclusions based on what some consider "scientific" principles which are more generally known than are accounting techniques which may or may not impress the layman.

The AICPA rules of conduct (ET 505.01 and Appendix C) and most states now permit members to practice as "professional corporations or associations" (primarily for tax benefits), with the stockholders jointly and severally liable for acts of the organization or its employees. Incorporation is thus prohibited for the avoidance of personal liability.

2

Who Determines the Standards?

[¶201]

In society at large, citizens are not praised for *upholding* laws; they are condemned or punished for *breaking* laws or *failure* to conform to the laws. On a smaller scale, the professional accountant is not applauded for adhering to standards; he is, or may be, criticized, reprimanded, ostracized or faced with monetary or criminal penalties for *breaking* with standards or for *failure* to conform with accounting standards.

Most professional accountants will agree that, despite criticism for certain actions or nonactions, the AICPA is the one dominant organization of accountants which speaks with recognized authority for the *entire* profession of accounting (for members and nonmembers alike).

When the AICPA speaks "officially," on-the-record so to speak, adherence is compulsory for members.

When the AICPA speaks "unofficially," off-the-record, adherence is *not* compulsory. BUT — (and to emphasize it) — *but* — a member who violates an *unofficial* pronouncement had better prepare a good defense for his alternate position if it conflicts even with this *unofficial* AICPA position.

The AICPA is the national organization of certified public accountants in the United States. Its membership is made up multi-thousands of certified public accountants engaged in one or more of every conceivable phase of the accountant's function in society.

There are only two requirements for membership: (BL 220.01)

1. The possession of a valid certified public accountant certificate issued by a state, territory or territorial possession of the United States or the District of Columbia, and
2. Passing an examination in accounting and other related subjects, satisfactory to the Board of Directors (of the AICPA).

Members are governed by *four* sets of standards:

1. The Bylaws of the AICPA; (not discussed)
2. The Code of Professional Ethics; (discussed briefly)
3. Auditing Standards; (discussed briefly)
4. Financial Accounting Standards (discussed and enlarged in this entire section of the book).

[¶202]   AUDITING STANDARDS

Auditing Standards (which are *not* the subject of this book) are divided into three parts:

1. Generally Accepted Auditing Standards (AU 150)
2. Statements on Auditing Standards
3. Auditing Interpretations.

The first category of Generally Accepted Auditing Standards consists of : General standards, standards of field work and standards of reporting.

The *Generally Accepted Auditing Standards* (GAAS) are *compulsory*. They were approved and adopted by the membership of the AICPA.

The *Statements on Auditing Standards* are determined by the Auditing Standards Executive Committee, the senior technical committee of the Institute. Rule 202 of the Institute's Code of Professional Ethics recognizes these statements as interpretations of GAAS and considers them pronouncements requiring members to be prepared to justify departures. (Preface to AU 100)

Auditing Interpretations are prepared by the *staff* of the auditing standards division and reviewed by members of the executive committee. An interpretation is *not* as authoritative as a "statement." But here too, members should be prepared to justify departures if the quality of their work is questioned. (Preface to AU 9000)

The major foundation upon which generally accepted *auditing* standards is built is found in the first standard of reporting of those auditing standards:

> The report shall state whether the financial statements are presented in accordance with generally accepted accounting principles. (AU 410.01)

It is these "generally accepted accounting principles" which underlie the Financial Accounting Standards.

[¶203]   FINANCIAL ACCOUNTING STANDARDS

Financial accounting standards, since May 7, 1973, have been determined by the Financial Accounting Standards Board (the FASB), which, by action of the Council of the AICPA, was designated to replace the old Accounting Principles Board (the APB): (ET 203.03)

Status of FASB interpretations. Council is authorized under Rule 203 to designate a body to establish accounting principles and has designated the Financial Accounting Standards Board as such body. Council also has resolved that FASB Statements of Financial Accounting Standards, together with those Accounting Research Bulletins and APB Opinions which are not superseded by actions of the FASB consitute accounting principles as contemplated in Rule 203.

In determining the existence of a departure from an accounting principle established by a Statement of Financial Accounting Standards, Accounting Research Bulletin or APB Opinion encompassed by Rule 203, the division of professional ethics will construe such Statement, Bulletin or Opinion in the light of any interpretations thereof issued by the FASB.

The FASB is *not* a division of the AICPA or a committee thereof. It is an autonomous organization in which the AICPA has representation. It is one of a three-part rule-making process, with each part performing important and distinct functions in the process of setting accounting standards:

The Financial Accounting Foundation is governed by a nine-member board of trustees comprised of five CPAs, two financial executives, one financial analyst, and one accounting educator. The president of the AICPA is a trustee. The trustee's primary duties are to appoint members of the Standards Board and the Advisory Council, to arrange financing, to approve budgets and periodically to review the structure of the organization.

The Financial Accounting Standards Board (FASB) is an independent body with seven full-time, salaried members, at least four of whom are CPAs drawn from public practice; the other members are persons well versed in financial reporting. The FASB's primary duty is to issue statements on financial accounting standards, including interpretations of those standards.

The Financial Accounting Standards Advisory Council comprises not less than 20 members who are experts in the field. The Council works closely with the FASB in an advisory capacity, consulting with the Board to identify problems, set agenda priorities, establish task forces, and react to proposed financial accounting standards.

The net result of the recognition of the new FASB was to make the following designated pronouncements the *official,* binding standards to be observed:

Those *prior* pronouncements of the *old* Accounting Principles Board (the APB) which were *not* changed by the new FASB:

1. APB Opinions
2. APB Statements
3. Accounting Research Bulletins;

Plus the new pronouncements of the FASB:

4. FASB Statements
5. FASB Interpretations

[¶203.1]   An Important Distinction

The (old) ''Accounting Interpretations'' (that is the terminology used) were prepared by the AICPA staff and were *not,* when issued, considered to be official. They were answers to practitioners' questions. These "Accounting Interpretations" are *still* in effect, still unofficial, but recommended for use, with the burden of departures on the individual accountant. There will no longer be any new "Accounting Interpretations," — at least not under that title.

The new terminology for these unofficial answers to practitioners' questions (since June 1973) is *"Technical Practice Aids."* These have been added to the body of *unofficial* interpretations of standards.

Note that the "interpretations" issued by the FASB, however, carry the title, "FASB Interpretations" and, under Rule 203 cited previously, *are official* pronouncements.

[¶203.2]   Unofficial Pronouncements

The following are the unofficial pronouncements which are issued by the AICPA as guidance for members (who might have to explain departures therefrom):

> The Accounting Interpretations (up to June 1973)
>
> The Technical Practice Aids (from June 1973 on)
>
> Terminology Bulletins
>
> Guides on Management Advisory Services
>
> Statements on Responsibility in Tax Practice
>
> Statements of Position of the Accounting Standards Division
>
> Accounting Research Studies (these are different from "Accounting Research Bulletins" which *are* official)
>
> Industry Audit Guides
>
> Most other publications of the AICPA, unless clearly specifying their official nature. (Reference here is to *accounting* publications.)

Reiterating the concept of the first paragraph of this chapter, failure to know the standards and to follow them rests with the individual accountant.

The whole body of compulsory rules and the interpretations thereof (though some are unofficial) is surprisingly small in terms of printed material. As explained in the foreword of this book, the five-volume loose-leaf series published by the AICPA with the cooperation of Commerce Clearing House is readily securable and available to all practitioners and serious students at reasonable investment. The volumes are also updated periodically in a continuing service. The pronouncements, official and unofficial, are also available in other piecemeal publications.

There are other areas of accounting specialization, such as: income taxes, cost accounting, SEC work, statistical sampling, computers, mathematical "decision-making," etc., which require unique education and research. Though peripheral and adjunct, they are guided by the main body of standards, but not explicitly spelled out by them.

Before turning to the detailed outline of "what the standards are" (GAAP) in Chapter 6, a broad canvas of various tints and colors is presented in Chapters 3, 4 and 5 of the environment of accounting — the paints and brushes used — and the artists who participate.

3

Business Structures

[¶301]

Any business enterprise is internally composed of two distinct human elements:

Employers — the owners of the business;

Employees — those employed by the oners.

(Sometimes, an owner is an employee of his own firm, but his classification as an owner is unaffected.)

The owner (employer) of a business may be the founder — the one who initially organized and funded the operation — or he is a successor to that original founder. The founder, in starting the business, has several, but limited, options as to the *type* of legal business-structure format to be used for the operation. (Also, the founder or his successor may choose to change the structure from one type to another at a subsequent date.)

His two primary considerations are:

1. The extent of personal liability should the business fail;

2. The comparative tax advantages offered by different methods of organization.

And the choices which are available to him are:

1. Sole proprietorship

2. Partnership — in combination with one or more other owners

3. Corporation — in combination with others for legal formation, but he might in fact be subsequently the sole owner

4. Sub-chapter S Corporation — with others, or alone

5. Professional Corporation or Association — with others, or alone.

(A Joint Venture is merely a stop-gap entity from which profits flow to one of the above types of entity.)

11

If the owner places a priority on *tax-savings,* any format would be chosen in preference to the corporation format, which historically has been taxed on both the *earnings* and the *distribution* of those same earnings. The Sub-S corporation and the Professional corporation (if electing the Sub-S option) do eliminate the double-taxation feature (and also offer the advantage of full corporate deductions for executive salaries, if paid timely), but they also involve personal taxation on all the undistributed earnings, which pass through to the individuals (with certain exceptions) effectively as in a partnership.

If the owner places priority on the *limitation* of personal liability, he will choose the corporate form (possibly with the Sub-S option). But he cannot choose the Professional corporation to limit liability, since most states prohibit this limitation by law (as for doctors, accountants, etc.).

Once the legal format is set, the method of financial accounting and reporting for that particular type of business comes into play.

Most accounting textbooks and guidelines seem to be directed toward the corporation's method of accounting. The standards of maintaining records for most assets, liabilities and items of income and expense are generally applicable to any type of business structure. Whatever guidelines apply to the corporation also apply to all other forms of business entity, *except* in these areas:

1. The Capital or Equity section:
   A. Initial investment
   B. The sharing of profits/losses
2. Salaries/Drawings of owners
3. Income tax on the entity's profit
4. How to account for investments in subsidiaries or controlled non-subsidiaries
5. Dissolution of the entity.

Here, in brief, are the major differences to recall or research for those various structures:

Clearly distinguish between *personal* expenditures and business expenditures. In proprietorships and partnerships, personal items are to be treated as drawings or withdrawals or as loans. In a corporation, treat as a loan or dividend.

In partnerships, the partnership *agreement* takes precedence and establishes all the rules, especially of distribution. The agreement should spell out: Capital contributions requirements and bases of assets or liabilities assumed, duties of partners, time to be spent in the business, limitations on drawings, the ratio of sharing profits and losses, death provisions, insurance protection, loans and interest on loans. Salaries might, for example, be alloted each working partner before the ratio-splitting of profits; but the salary plus the split-share of the remaining profit effectually go into that partner's capital account and are reduced by *actual drawings* (salary plus profit-withdrawal).

In *dissolution* of partnerships, liabilities to/from partners are paid before distribution, and *no* distribution is made in excess of each partner's just share needed for liquidation of liabilities.

Death usually dissolves a *partnership,* unless the agreement makes specific contingent provisions.

Financial statements for either proprietorship or partnership should provide a "Statement of Capital Changes" (similar to a corporate's "Changes in Retained Earnings").

The valuation of assets (and/or liabilities) at original investment should be stated at fair value, in any structure. Goodwill is set up, if pertinent, and the Capital or Capital Stock section credited for the agreed ownership portion. (Law requires corporations sometimes to distinguish betwen "par value" and "excess of par.") "Negative goodwill" should be used to write down non-current (fixed) assets in an immediate proportion. Goodwill, if any, should be amortized for financial purposes over 40 years unless there is proof of a shorter benefit period. Goodwill is not ordinarily deductible for tax purposes.

The *trade name,* if any, should be used on proprietorship or partnership statements, with disclosure of the type of business structure.

The "cash basis" of accounting is *not* a generally accepted accounting principle, and proper financial statements, when carrying an independent auditor's opinion, are either qualified ("subject to") or with a disclaimer, depending on the materiality of the difference had the accrual method been used. (TA 1600.01)

Financial accounting for proprietors and partnerships *should not* book accruals or deductions for the income tax which that owner or co-owner must pay on his respective share of the earnings. However, financial footnotes should make such a disclosure if the funds for such payment may deplete those belonging to the entity (as future "withdrawals").

Sub-S corporations have 2½ months from year-end to distribute salary accruals or the expense is disallowed to the corporation by the IRS. Thus, Sub-S corporations often find themselves in tight working capital situations. Sometimes, the owners will pay out the accrual, and then, as a loan, put most of it back.

The *equity method* of accounting for investments in subsidiaries or controlled non-subsidiaries is *not* permitted for sole proprietors, trusts or estates (AC 5131.02). Proprietors should carry investments *at cost.* Partnerships and joint-ventures should use cost adjusted for accumulated undistributed earnings. (TA 1600.02)

Deferred taxes on undistributed earnings of subsidiaries or non-subsidiaries should *not* be set up for partnerships, because of the factor of "personal taxing" mentioned above.

Financial statements for sole proprietorships may show a "reasonable" salary allowance for the owner to arrive at a financial operating income. But the salary is still a withdrawal.

Sub-S corporations should show *earnings per share*, but computed without income tax (AC U-2011.081).

Consolidations are permitted a proprietorship (over 50% ownership) (TA 1400.02):

1. If owning 100%, the investment is eliminated against equity;
2. If less than 100%, the minority interest is shown on the income statement before extraordinary items, and on the balance sheet between liabilities and net worth.

Other eliminations should be as in consolidations.

Joint Ventures are usually not majority-controlled by any of the participants. Hence, consolidation is not in order. The equity method is used by partnerships or corporations that participate in a joint venture. Proprietors should use the cost method of investment. Sometimes, however, upon proper disclosure, "proportionate" consolidation is used. Here, a pro-rata share of assets, liabilities and income is consolidated.

4

Systems

THE FLOW OF DOCUMENTS

Paper. The forest primeval — milled and pressed to industrial use.

Contracts, certificates, invoices, correspondence, memos, rules, ledgers, machine-tapes, flow charts, advertising catalogs, computer runs, time-cards, checks, statements, tags, cards, sheets, rolls — scratch paper — envelopes, boxes, cartons. Unused paper supplies; paper-in-process; paper filed. Microfilm. Tax returns. Tape and red tape.

An avalanche, if uncontrolled.

Logic, purpose and usefulness, when held in check. A systematized schematic designed to control the economic current which generates the power of the business entity. Periodically to be monitored and tested for resistance, weakness, stability and storage capacity.

The aim — the goal — is to focus all paper into a group picture — one still-life, the photo at a given moment in time — the year-end for the financial statements, as posed by the figures in the general ledger, adjusted and dressed for that split-second closing moment. The numerical characters in a tableau, arranged and described in narration in conformity with professional standards.

Throughout the year, the numerical characters which will ultimately be stilled for one moment — to be counted and accounted for — to be placed in proper perspective for that financial statement group photograph — these characters keep moving, refusing to stand still, adding, accumulating, building, sometimes detracting and withdrawing — darting in and out of the books of account.

A firm hand is needed to guide these figures, to direct their movements, to prevent the inanimate from taking on life of its own, stop the machine before it becomes the master.

The chart of the anatomical business blood-line, in terms of recorded circulation, must be clearly directed, delineated and controlled:

15

The veins: through which information flows to the heart —
The books of original entry:

1. General Journal
2. Cash Receipts Book
3. Cash Disbursements Book
4. Sales Book with its corollary Accounts Receivable sub-ledger
5. Purchases Book with its corollary Accounts Payable sub-ledger
6. Payroll Register and Summaries.

The heart: which stores and pumps out the information —
The general ledger (with its associated valves):

7. General Ledger and
   Subsidiaries:
         Inventory Control
         Fixed Assets Ledger
         Cost Sub-Ledger Control
         Schedules to supplement.

The arteries: which take that flow for digestion to the body and members of the community — owners, bankers, creditors, government, the general public—
The financial statements:

8. Balance Sheet
9. Income Statement
10. Statement of Changes in Financial Position
11. Statement of Changes in Retained Earnings (or Capital interests)
12. Financial notes.

[¶402]   SUB-LEDGERS AND SCHEDULES

Some accounts in the general ledger are, by their very nature *summaries* of important supplemental data which, because of bulk alone, would, if not entered in summary form, make the physical ledger too huge to handle. Items such as individual accounts receivable and payable, inventory units, machinery and equipment — though each represents an individual asset or liability — are best displayed in one or more summary accounts, with full details being maintained in a separate book or ledger, individually tended, the total of which ties to the control account.

Some, like accounts receivable and accounts payable, are automatic products of the internal system. (The computer updates the accounts receivable file with sales and with payments received, with the monthly summaries of changes going to the general ledger control account). Sometimes, a one-write system updates subsidiaries simultaneously. Others must be maintained manually, like the fixed asset ledger or the manual inventory control card-system. Others may be generated by outside sources, like payroll records and summaries. Others are as basic as a petty cash summary.

[¶403]   **SYSTEMS — MANUAL,
            MECHANIZED OR COMPUTERIZED**

The variety of methods used for keeping records is almost as varied as the personalities of the people designing, operating and maintaining the system. With the exception of those larger entities where work is so divided that each employee performs only one small function in a huge system overviewed by few, except top management and outside auditors — few businesses use a standard text-book approach.

Most private systems are the result of accumulations of changing bit-by-bit adaptations to the needs and demands of the business itself and outside influences (taxes, AICPA and SEC guides and requirements, state and federal laws, competitive practices, advanced technology, market conditions, good-bad sales/profit results, etc.). Except where the availability of funds and skills is unlimited (practically nowhere), most systems in use today are evolvements and combinations of good old basic hand-written techniques, now partitioned into piecemeal refinements, combining mechanical, electronic and manual skills.

Complete automation of the *entire* accounting process is a rarity.

Ultimately, the nature of the system used depends upon one or more of these factors:

Time and expediency

Skill required

Cost

Facilities and space available

The degree of in-depth coverage *wanted* by owners/management.

Note the emphasis on the word "wanted." Many weaknesses need correction for better tax-review backup or for more efficient reporting, but management, in weighing the costs involved, wisely chooses not to refine. For example, the *cost* of instituting a highly complex standard costing system outweighs the advantages to be gained from it, so management chooses to continue with its current, less complex, less specific costing system, which has understandable, but controllable tolerances of error.

[¶403.1]   **The Evolutionary Process of the Machine**

The evolutionary process of systematized accounting record maintenance might follow something like the following piecemeal add-on progression:

[¶403.2]   **All Manual System**

1. The *"shoebox" system.* The owner transacts all business in cash —

buying, selling, paying expenses — and tosses invoices, documents, receipts into a box.

2. *The check book.* The owner stops paying bills with cash, now pays by check. Still uses shoebox for receipts for sales. Notes deposits in checkbook.

3. *Cash disbursements book.* Has now hired someone to do his payroll tax reporting. Lists each check in a book, from which he can obtain a columnar breakout distribution of each type of expense.

4. *Payroll register.* Supplements the above by transferring the weekly payroll items to separate sheets for each employee where total earnings and deductions are accumulated as required for payroll tax reports.

5. *Cash receipts book.* Owner now lists each day's receipts separately and distributes to columns by type of sale or income.

6. *General ledger.* Owner sets up a ledger sheet for each column category in his disbursements and receipts book. "Posts" summary totals periodically.

7. *General ledger expanded.* The owner goes back to the old shoebox and digs out the cost information needed to set up the value of permanent items bought then (assets: equipment, fixtures, etc.). Sets up asset accounts, long-term liabilities and a balancing net worth account.

8. *Sales book/accounts receivable ledger.* To get more sales, owner finds he must start giving credit. He uses sequentially numbered invoices, lists charge sales daily in numerical order in Sales Book. Makes a separate page for each customer in an accounts receivable subsidiary ledger. For this, he uses a car-bonized two-part preprinted statement, which he updates manually every day or so.

In the Cash Receipts Book, he adds a column for "received on account" from customers. Line-by-line, these credits are posted to the above subsidiary ledger-statement. Also, he includes a column for cash discounts and allowances taken by customers. At month-end, he mails original to customer and keeps the copy of the statement as his ledger sheet and starts a new sheet for the new month with the balance from the old sheet.

9. *Periodic financial statements.* Owner now wishes to see how he progresses. Finds he needs further information for an accurate statement. He must, in a side computation, compute or estimate:

Any unpaid bills to creditors

Inventory on hand

Taxes due to date on payrolls, etc.

Possible bad debts among his stated receivables

Depreciate his equipment.

At this point, he probably seeks outside assistance.

10. *Purchase book/accounts payable ledger.* As business expands, his debts accumulate, and he wants to know the exact status of when and to whom payments are due. He adds these books to the system. In the Cash Disbursements

Book, he puts a column for payment on account to accounts payable and another for cash discounts taken.

11. *Perpetual inventory cards.* His on-hand stock of unsold items grows daily, and he can no longer trust his memory to recall the exact cost of items in stock, nor the quantities on hand. He sets up one card for each type of merchandise on hand, goes to the storage area, counts and lists everything, checks his purchase invoices and assigns a cost to each item. On the card, he provides all the details pertaining to that item, so that he knows what's on hand and what cost it represents. Periodically, he takes a physical count to verify the perpetual cards.

12. *General journal.* He rounds off the system by putting in here any entry which does not appropriately go in the other books of original entry. He posts from here and the other books directly to the General Ledger.

13. *Worksheet entries and worksheet trial balance.* As an adjunct to the preparation of the now monthly financial statements, accruals, recurrent adjustments and accrual reversals (when necessary) are made to the balances taken from the ledger — all on workpapers — to determine monthly position and progress.

14. *Imprest petty cash system.* Adds this to tighten up on loose expenditures.

15. *Fixed asset subsidiary ledger.* To better detail them for depreciation, investment tax credit, gains or losses on dispositions, bases on trade-ins.

[¶403.3]   Mechanizing

16. *A one-write system for check disbursements.* Here, he combines the old check book and his Cash Disbursements Book into one writing process, instead of two. He also opens a separate bank account for the payroll and uses a one-write system for it also. At month-end, he summary posts to the General Ledger.

17. *A billing machine.* Rented or bought. Mechanizes his invoices, customer statements, sales book and subsidiary receivable ledger.

18. *Service bureau.* He assigns numbers to his general ledger accounts in an ascending series covering assets, liabilities, equity, income, costs and expenses in that order. He is assisted in setting up framework numbers for captioning and totaling functions so the computer-produced financial statement conforms with the special format he wants. Monthly, he sends to the service bureau:

> A copy of his one-write check listing, with account numbers assigned for the debiting (in lieu of the columnar distribution spread);
>
> Manual summary entries for each other book of original entry;
>
> Manual entries for accruals, adjustments, recurrent monthly entries, reversals of accruals.

All this is submitted in simple debit/credit style with account numbers indicated. He adds each page, gets totals for debits, credits and *account numbers,* gets an overall batch control total for each. The Service Bureau cross-checks the inputting to the batch totals, and posting to wrong accounts is virtually eliminated.

He receives from the Service Bureau a printed Cash Disbursements listing, a General Ledger with alpha description (brief, as inputted), and financial statements with detailed supporting schedules.

19. *Computer terminal.* A typewriter-like console, which is hooked via telephone lines into an outside-owned computer. He may put his sales and receivables on it, his check-processing and disbursements run, his purchase-vendor invoices and purchase book, his inventory, the payroll, or general ledger — practically anything desired, depending upon the programming availability and the costs. The techniques used are compatible with those learned in the use of the service bureau, with the addition of a few typewriter-input techniques.

20. *Video scope.* May supplement the above terminal, so he can call for almost instantaneous display of that off-premises storage in the central processor's electronic file. He may request a printout for later delivery.

21. *The in-house computer.* The final decision is made. He rents or buys a computer for total in-house use. The extent of options available is vast. Basically, the type of in-house computer obtained should depend upon the more important of the following features:

The output wanted.

The capacity of the central processing unit for permanent program storage.

The additional adjunct program storage possibilities.

The type of storage — cassette, disc, tape and on down to magnetic cards or punched-paper tape, with each having advantages in terms of cost or access.

The type of input — punched cards, direct input from console, intermediate from console-to-tape-to computer, etc.

The extent of printout capabilities and demands (speed, size of paper, etc.).

The adaptation of video screens at the console or remote locations — branches, warehouse.

The cost factor — initial investment, machine and programs, maintenance, personnel needed, space necessitated.

The extent of skill needed.

The imagination of the owner or management — willingness to learn, try, develop new methods, new talents.

[¶404]   PAYROLLS AND PAYROLL TAXES

Legal requirements have made the maintenance of accurate earnings records a mandatory function of any financial accounting system. The preparation of payrolls is now, in many companies, a segregated division of duty. Regular periodic summary information from detailed payroll records is needed for entry into the general ledger.

Details of each payroll are usually summarized monthly in a general journal entry and posted to the general ledger with distribution of the debits going to various salary-expense areas (for the gross salary) and the credits going to various withholding accounts (sometimes netted against corresponding employer-expense accounts, such as unemployment insurance) and the cash account upon which the net payroll checks are drawn.

The employer later pays the amounts withheld (hopefully as due) to the various taxing or other authorities, including his employer's added share (expense) as determined in the preparation of the required form for filing.

To support the filings, each payroll item must be isolated and collated for *each* individual employee to accumulate that individual's record of earnings as required for these quarterly, semi-annual and annual reports to federal, state and city taxing arms. The Fair Labor Standards Act and state law also set standards of minimum pay for work hours and overtime for some or all employees.

Many payrolls are now prepared by outside processors, such as banks and service bureaus. Controls should be as strong as possible to assure accurate, protected input and output. All voided checks, for example, should be surrendered to the employer and accounted for in bank reconciliations.

Individual personnel permanent files should be maintained and would probably include:

> Name and address, Social Security number, date of birth, date hired, occupation, work-week, regular and overtime rates, basis of pay (day, week, month), authorized increases, vacation time, bonuses, injuries and compensation claims and settlements, pension and profit-sharing information (deductions, rights and vested interests), W-4 and other withholding authorizations, references and correspondence, educational transcripts, unemployment claims and reports, medical records, health claims, expense-account authorizations, separation information (date, circumstances, etc.) and other information.

Time cards are usually filed separately and tied to specific payrolls by reference identification.

Payroll tax reports usually required are:

Federal:

Card-form 501 for payroll tax deposits with local bank

Quarterly 941 for withholding and FICA

W-2's

W-3

Annual 940 (Federal Unemployment)

1099 — information returns with summary 1096;

State:

Withholding tax — interim and annual

Unemployment insurance — usually quarterly

Disability insurance — usually quarterly, sometimes combined with unemployment report

Annual reports covering individual earnings; possibly annual information returns also.

The entire process of payroll preparation is an area which is conducive to effective statistical sampling techniques. Management (as well as outside auditors) should periodically sample all phases of the payroll routine, from initial authorizations through to the canceled-check returns. The discovery of one flaw might prove significant.

[¶405]   THE GENERAL LEDGER, CHART OF ACCOUNTS AND TRIAL BALANCE

On the human level, the word ''uniformity'' is anathema. We deplore classification of our individual traits, characteristics, personalities and choices.

But in the world of mechanical figures, uniformity offers many advantages, especially the one of eliminating hard-knock costly errors experienced by forerunners in the field of experimentation.

One such area of ''uniformity'' in standard usage, which is most beneficial, is the conventional layout of the general ledger.

As shown below, accounts in the general ledger are most useful if arranged and numbered in the order sequence indicated. Any firm which has gone to an outside computer service or installed its own in-house computer for the generation of machined financial statements will attest to the necessity for this format. The machines, unthinking as they are, can easily be programmed to add, subtract, combine, sub-total, total, balance and print these accounts according to numerically sequential instructions each step of the way down the line-by-line financial balance sheet and income statement. (Moreover, sub-ledgers can be added as needed.)

Assets:
    Current
    Non-current
    Other

Liabilities:
    Current
    Long-term

Equity:
    Capital stock
    Retained earnings

Income — revenue from operations

Cost of sales items

Expenses:
    Selling
    Administrative

Non-operating income and expense

Federal income tax

Extraordinary items:
    Less applicable income tax
        Net income.

Limitations and definitions of what should go into each account should be spelled out for anyone with responsibility for booking entries into the general ledger. Most large firms have drawn up internal "charts of accounts" which pinpoint exactly what should be debited or credited to each account and the sources from which the entry might come. At the least, someone should be charged with the responsibility of making the decision, and written authorizations (sometimes, voucher-type general journal entries) should be prepared and signed by that authority.

Many modern systems call for the manual booking of summaries of all the books of original entry, recurrent monthly journal entries, adjustments, accruals and reversals onto loose-leaf-type numbered journal sheets, batch-totaled, with a copy going to the computer department for processing to monthly hard-copy ledger cards. Sometimes, a yearly re-run is made showing all the action in each account for the entire year. A trial balance is usually a by-product of the computer-run general ledger.

Summary entries may be by-passed for cash disbursements, sales or purchases, if the input of this material is programmed for direct summation of monthly activity, being stored and posted to the general ledger when run with the other input from the summary general journal sheets.

Some systems in use today even by-pass the use of a general ledger, producing all the same pertinent information and references in comprehensive, detailed financial statements. Controls here should assure proper input, output and traceable audit trails.

[¶406] LONG-TERM CONSTRUCTION CONTRACTS

Revenue is usually recognized at the time of exchanges in which cash is received or new claims arise against other entities. However, exceptions are made, for example ... for long-term construction-type contracts. (AC 1027.07 M-1F)

There are two methods available to commercial organizations engaged wholly or partly in the contracting business for handling long-term construction contracts: (AC 4031.03)

1. The completed-contract method;

2. The percentage-of-completion method.

These contracts generally entail the construction of a specific project.

[407] THE COMPLETED-CONTRACT METHOD

The completed-contract method recognizes income only when the contract is completed or substantially completed. Costs of contracts in process and current billings are accumulated, but there are no charges or credits to income except for provisions for losses. If remaining costs are not significant in amount, a contract may be regarded as substantially completed. (AC 4031.09)

General and administrative expenses are not charged off to periodic income but are allocated to the contract. This is especially important when no contracts are completed in a year in which there are general and administrative expenses. It is not as important when there are numerous contracts. In such circumstances it may even be preferable to charge general and administrative expenses to periodic income. However, there should be no excessive deferring of overhead costs which might occur if total overhead was assigned to few or small contracts in process. (AC 4031.10)

Even though the completed-contract method does not permit recording any income before completion, provision should be made for expected losses. Any excess of accumulated costs over related billings should be shown in the balance sheet as a current asset. Excess of accumulated billings over related costs should be shown in most cases as a current liability. Where there are many contracts and costs exceed billings on some and billings exceed costs on others, the contracts should be segregated so that the figures on the asset side include only those contracts in which costs exceed billings and on the liability side, only those in which billings exceed costs. The assets should be described as "costs of uncompleted contracts in excess of related billings" rather than as inventory or work in process. On the liability side the item should be described as "billings and uncompleted contracts in excess of related costs." (AC 4031.11-.12)

The advantage of the completed-contract method is that since it is based on results as finally determined, it is generally more accurate than if it were based on estimates for unperformed work which could involve unforeseen costs or other possible loses. It is generally used for contracts lasting less than one year. But where accurate estimates of completion costs aren't available, it may be used for longer term contracts. The disadvantage of the completed-contract method is that in a period where no contract has been completed, current performance is not reflected. This results in showing high profits one year and little or no profits in other years. (AC 4031.13-.14)

[¶407.1]   Percentage-of-Completion Method

The percentage-of-completion method recognizes income as work on a contract goes along. Recognized income should be *that percentage of estimated total income* that either (a) incurred costs to date *bear to total costs* after giving effect to estimates of costs to complete based upon most recent information or (b) which may be indicated by such other measures of progress to completion as may be appropriate (see illustration). Under the percentage-of-completion method current assets may include costs and recognized income not yet billed for certain contracts, and liabilities (usually current liabilities) may include billings in excess of costs and recognized income with regard to other contracts, (AC 4031.04-.05)

The principal advantages of the percentage-of-completion method are (1) periodic recognition of income instead of the irregular recognition of income on completed contracts, and (2) the reflection of the status of the uncompleted contracts through the current estimates of costs to complete or of progress toward completion. (AC 4031.07) In the *completed-contract method* there is no reflection of status of uncompleted contracts.

The chief disadvantage of the percentage-of-completion method is that it depends upon estimates of ultimate costs and consequently of currently accruing income which is subject to uncertainties inherent in long-term contracts. (AC 4031.08)

ILLUSTRATION

Income reflected under percent-of-completion method:

	Accumulated Percent Completed (1)	Expenses allocable to contract (2)	Year's assigned portion of contract (1)	Net income to report
Year 1	30%	$ 305,000	$ 300,000	$ (5,000)
Year 2	75%	385,000	450,000	65,000
Year 3	100%	210,000	250,000	40,000
Totals		$ 900,000	$ 1,000,000	$ 100,000

Total contract price is $1,000,000.

(1) Percentage of completion is a certified percentage furnished by the architect. The percent increases each year until 100% is completed. The difference between one year and the next is that year's completed portion.

(2) Includes supplies used during year, with consideration given to opening and closing inventories. Expenses are those ascertainable as incurred to bring the contract to the stage of completion.

Note that *billings* are not shown because reportable income is *not* predicated on them, though in some cases billings may coincide with the percentage completed.

[¶407.2]   Income Under the "Completed Contract" Method

Using the same example above, the net income of $100,000 would be reported only in the final year (Year 3), together with details. No reflection of partial completion is shown on the income statement for the first and second year. (See Tax Section of this book also.)

[¶408]   INSTALLMENT, COST RECOVERY AND RETAIL METHODS

"Recognizing revenue and expenses if proceeds are collectible over a long period without reasonable assurance of collection: The terms of an exchange transaction or other conditions related to receivables collectible

over a long period may preclude a reasonable estimate of the collectibility of the receivables. Either an installment method or a cost recovery method of recognizing revenue may be used as long as collectibility is not reasonably assured." (AC 1027.07 S-1F-1)

[¶408.1]   Installment Method

If there is no basis for estimating the *degree* of collectibility because of a contract running over an extended period of time, the installment method or cost recovery method may be used (as opposed to booking the entire sales figure combined with a provision for bad debts). (Footnote to AC 4020.01)

However, at the time of sale, if collectibility is assured and there is no question of recovery, the installment method is unacceptable. (AC 4020.01)

[¶408.2]   Cost Recovery Method

Under the same logic which permits the use of the installment method, the cost recovery method is also permitted. Here, equal amounts of revenue and expense are recognized as collections are made until all costs have been recovered, postponing recognition of all profit until all costs have been recovered. (Footnote to AC 4020.01)

(See Timing Differences and Appendix)

[¶408.3]   Retail Method

The terminology, "retail method," is properly used only in connection with the pricing of retail store inventories, not with the method of accounting practiced by retail stores, which is properly called "the installment sales method," as described previously.

For more discussion of the "Retail Method" for inventory, see this text's chapter on Current Assets (Inventory).

[¶409]   THE NOT-FOR-PROFIT ORGANIZATION

Most not-for-profit organizations derive their funds from the public-at-large. Gifts, donations, bequests and endowments (in most cases tax deductible to the donor) are the main source of income for non-profit organizations, which are organized under special state and federal laws for the purpose of accomplishing a specific goal — education (colleges), research (foundations), hospitals and child-care.

Sometimes, government provides grants and aid for these institutions.

In general, the tax laws and other statutes endeavor to limit these institutions from encroaching on the profit-making activities which are characteristic of the business enterprise. Under current law, certain gains and profits on *unrelated-to-function* activities are now taxable to the not-for-profit organization (such as publishing revenue, security income — interest and capital gains).

The chief accounting characteristic which differentiates the non-profit organization from the profit organization is the strict distinction which must be made and accountability provided for each donation or grant received and disbursed.

There are two broad types of delineation:

1. *Unrestricted funds* — monies received with no restrictive use specified by the giver — to be used for the current continuing operation of the organization in fulfilling the general purpose for which it was organized; and •

2. *Restricted funds* — monies received and spent for *specific* purposes with designated strings attached — such as government funds provided for student loans, or endowment portfolios where the principal is not to be touched but the income thereof may be used for current or designated purposes.

   In addition, permanent property acquisitions are segregated into a "plant fund." Rules for capitalization and writeoff usually depend upon government's participation or non-participation in its funding.

Because of the public and governmental accountability required and the right-to-know how the donated funds are being used, it is imperative that *each fund* (each restrictive gift/grant and the non-restricted fund) be explained, both as to the status of assets, liabilities and fund balance, as well as detailing the income and expenses generated by or in that fund during the period. Moreover, an overall summary of changes in fund balance is also prepared.

The AICPA has guideline recommendations in industry audit guides for many of these institutions, such as: Colleges and Universities, Hospitals, State and Local Governmental Units, Voluntary Health and Welfare Organizations and Medicare Facilities.

[¶409.1]   Tips on Fund Accounting

Maintain complete and adequate files for the initial documentation which established or restricted the fund, together with any special reporting requirements demanded.

Keep separate detailed books of entry for each fund, separate bank account for that fund, separate identification of all property and securities.

Under *no* circumstances should assets of separate funds be co-mingled. Transfers between funds should not be permitted without documentary authorization, and inter-fund receivables and payables should, in contra-effect, be equal and clearly identified, always maintaining the original integrity of each fund.

Interest accruals, cooperative-share funding (example: government 80% — college 20% in Work Study Program), expense allowances or allocations — all should be made timely.

Federal, state and local reporting requirements should be studied, met and reported as due to avoid stringent penalties, interest and possible loss of tax-exempt status. Options may exist regarding the handling of payroll and unemployment taxes; they should be studied and explored for money-saving possibilities.

Independently audited annual financial statements by fund are usually required both by organizational charter and governmental departments (especially where grant-participation is involved). Publication of the availability of these statements is sometimes mandatory (foundations).

One new area of discussion and dispute is the "compliance" feature of audits involving certain governmental agency grants. Here, the independent auditor is called upon to measure the agency's compliance with certain non-accounting rules, such as eligibility of money-recipients, internal controls and other matters not ordinarily associated with a financial audit. The integrity of the auditor's financial opinion should never be compromised by peripheral compliance requirements. In most cases, he should qualify his opinion indicating the results and *extent of tests* made for compliance. The AICPA, to some extent, has spelled out guidelines for "compliance" opinions in Section 9641 of its "Statements on Auditing Standards." (AU 9641)

Municipal accounting techniques, format and demands are not discussed here. Their overall application involves the use of fund accounting. The main distinction is the entering of the budget — the anticipated revenues and the appropriations thereof — directly on and as part of the books of account. Progress reports then show how actual compares with anticipated. The estimates are then zeroed out at year-end. The meaning and use of "encumbrances" should also be understood. Reports for some local subdivisions, such as school-boards, usually involve a strict accounting of each receipt and disbursement, including the detailing of outstanding checks.

5

Internal Control

Internal control, according to the Professional Auditing Standards (AU 320.10), is subdivided as follows:

(a) Accounting control, which comprises the plan of organization and all methods and procedures that are concerned mainly with, and relate directly to, safeguarding assets and the reliability of the financial records.

(b) Administrative control, which comprises the plan of organization and all methods and procedures that are concerned mainly with operational efficiency and adherence to managerial policies, such as sales policies, employee training and production quality control, and usually relates only indirectly to the financial records. (AU 320.27)

Administrative control includes, but is not limited to, the plan of organization and the procedures and records that are concerned with the decision processes leading to management's authorization of transactions. Such authorization is a management function directly associated with the responsibility for achieving the objectives of the organization and is the starting point for establishing account control of transactions.

Accounting control comprises the plan of organization and procedures and records that are concerned with safeguarding assets and the reliability of financial records and consequently are designed to provide reasonable assurance that: (AU 320.28)

(a) Transactions are executed in accordance with management's general or specific authorization.

(b) Transactions are recorded as necessary (1) to permit preparation of financial statements in conformity with generally accepted accounting principles or any other criteria applicable to such statements and (2) to maintain accountability for assets.

(c) Access to assets is permitted only in accordance with management's authorization.

29

(d) The recorded accountability for assets is compared with the existing assets at reasonable intervals and appropriate action taken with respect to any differences.

[¶501.1] Fundamentals of a System of Internal Accounting Control

(1) **Responsibility:** There should be a plan or an organizational chart which places the responsibility for specific functions squarely on specific individuals in the organization.

The responsibility for establishing and maintaining a system of internal accounting control rests with management. The system should be continuously supervised, tested and modified as necessary to provide reasonable (but not absolute) assurance that objectives are being accomplished, all at costs not exceeding benefits. (AU 320.31-.32)

(2) **Division of Duties:** The idea here is to remove the handling and recording of any one transaction from beginning to end from the control of any one employee. Further, making different employees responsible for different functions of a transaction actually serves as a cross-check which facilitates the detection of errors, accidental or deliberate.

(3) **Use of Appropriate Forms and Documents:** Efficient design of forms and documents aids in the administration of the internal control system. Mechanical or electronic equipment can also be used to expedite the process of checking. Both these methods provide control over accounting data.

(4) **Internal Auditors:** Periodic review of all the above elements of the internal control system should be carried out by an internal audit staff. The function of this staff would be to periodically check the effectiveness of above items (1), (2), and (3).

There is a relationship between the size of an organization and the degree of development of its system of internal control. Complete separation of functions and internal auditing department may not exist in smaller companies. The objective in these smaller companies is to divide the duties in the way that creates the greatest amount of internal check.

[¶501.2] Elements of a Satisfactory System of Internal Accounting Control:

The elements of a satisfactory system of internal control include:

(1) A plan of organization which provides appropriate segregation of functional responsibilities.

(2) A system of authorization and record procedures adequate to provide reasonable accounting control of assets, liabilities, revenues and expenses.

(3) Sound practices which are to be followed in the performance of duties and functions of each of the organizational departments.

(4) Personnel of a quality commensurate with responsibilities.

One important element in the system of internal control is the independence of the operating, custodial, accounting and internal auditing functions. There should be a separation of duties in such a way that records exist outside each department to serve as controls over the activities within that department. Responsibilities for various functions and delegation of authority should be clearly defined and spelled out in organizational charts and manuals. Conflicting and dual responsibility is to be avoided. The function of initiation and authorization of an activity should be separate from the accounting for it. Custody of assets should be separated from the accounting for them.

[¶501.3] Relationship of Your Internal Control System to Your Outside Accountants

The efficiency of your internal control system becomes important to your outside, independent auditors. Before determining how much of an audit they should make, they must review the internal control. An efficient system may do away with certain audit procedures which might otherwise be necessary. A poor internal control system may necessitate greater checking on the part of the auditor with a consequent larger cost for the audit.

[¶502] INTERNAL CONTROL FOR INVENTORIES

Some internal control procedures that can be used in conjunction with different types of inventories — finished goods, work in process, materials, goods for resale — are detailed in the paragraphs that follow.

[¶502.1] Inventories of Merchandise Purchased for Resale and Supplies

(1) The purchasing department approves the purchase orders for merchandise to be bought. In a small company, the owner or manager may be the one to approve these purchase orders. Purchase orders should be sequentially numbered and traced to final disposition.

(2) After okays from purchasing manager have been received, requests for price quotations are usually sent out. These requests should go to various companies, and the company quoting the lowest price will be the one from which the purchases are made, unless there are other overriding considerations.

(3) In the selling department, an updated individual quantity record for each type of unit is kept on perpetual inventory stock cards. It is usually the responsibility of inventory clerks to keep these cards up to date. These stock cards indicate the need for reorders and they should be checked against purchase requisition by the manager of the selling department or other person in control of the merchandise stock. In a business too small to have a separate selling department, the owner or manager is the one to perform these functions. The number of

units of merchandise ordered is then entered on the inventory stock cards by one clerk. The number actually received is entered from the receiving list by another clerk. The number sold or used is entered on the stock cards by still another clerk from sales lists or salesmen's orders. After giving effect to the number ordered, received and issued on the inventory stock records the balance represents the number of units actually on hand. A well-rounded perpetual card system usually includes detailed unit costs for ready computation under either LIFO, FIFO, or average methods.

(4) In the receiving department, the receiving clerk should not be allowed to see purchase order records or purchase requisitions. Receiving reports are checked against the perpetual inventory stock records and a notation is made on these stock record cards indicating the date, order number and quantity received. Even where a business is too small to have a perpetual inventory, a receiving report should be made, which should then be checked against the purchase orders and a notation as to the day and quantity received made on those purchase orders.

(5) In the accounts payable department, the receiving report is checked against the merchandise stock record, then sent to the accounts payable department where it is verified against the seller's invoice. The purchasing agent should have approved the price on the seller's invoice before that invoice was sent to the accounts payable department. A clerk in the accounts payable department should verify all extension totals on the invoice. If the vendor's invoice and receiving report are in agreement the invoice is then entered into a purchase journal or voucher register for future payment. Any discrepancy between quantity received and quantity on the seller's invoice will hold up payment until an adjustment is made by the seller.

The departments involved in internal control in merchandise and supplies inventories are purchasing, sales, receiving, accounts receivable and accounts payable.

[¶502.2] Finished Goods Inventories

(1) Ascertain the quantity of units which have been completed from the production record and transferred to the shipping department or warehouse. The daily report of finished goods units transferred to the warehouse or shipping department indicates the number of finished units available to the sales department.

(2) Compute the unit cost of finished goods delivered to the sales department. This information is obtained from the unit cost sheet (for a process cost accounting system) or from the job-order cost card (in a job order cost accounting system).

(3) Set up finished goods inventory cards and for each item record the quantity received at the warehouse, the quantity shipped on orders and the balance remaining at specified unit costs. The number of finished goods units in the warehouse or stockroom should tie in with this finished goods inventory file.

(4) Periodically, physically count the finished goods inventory and see that it ties in with the finished goods inventory file.

The departments involved in internal control of finished goods inventories are manufacturing, cost accounting, accounts receivable and sales.

[¶502.3] Raw Materials and Supplies Inventories

(1) In the stores department, the storekeeper must safeguard the raw materials and supplies inventories — both physically and by accounting control. No raw materials or supplies can leave without a stores requisition. Quantity control at minimum levels is also the responsibility of the storekeeper.

The storekeeper should keep a stores record for each item, listing the maximum and minimum quantities, quantity ordered and number, quantity received, quantity issued, and balance on hand. When stores cards show minimum quantities, a stores ledger clerk pulls those cards from the file to make sure that materials or supplies are ordered to cover the minimum needs. Quantities shown on the stores record should be verified by making an actual count of the stores items which are to be ordered; then a purchase requisition is filled out from the stores records. The quantity of each item ordered is approved by the storekeeper. He knows the average monthly consumption of each item. The ordering of special equipment by department heads also goes through the storeroom after having the necessary executive approval. The purchase requisition is then sent to the purchasing agent.

In the stores department, a receiving report is prepared in triplicate by the receiving clerk. One copy goes to the stores ledger clerk, another to the accounts payable department; the third is kept by the receiving clerk. The receiving clerk puts the stores items in proper places within the storeroom after preparing his receiving report. Sometimes, location numbers are used to facilitate ready accessing.

The stores ledger clerk gets a copy of the receiving report and makes a record of the quantity and the order number on the stores ledger card affected by the items received.

(2) In the purchasing department, the purchase agent places the order for the quantity needed on the quantity requisition. If he feels the quantity ordered is excessive, he may look into the storekeeper's purchase requisition. He then requests price quotations from various supply companies, placing his order with the lowest bidder. The purchase agent also verifies the prices on the seller's invoices by comparing them with the price quotations.

(3) In the accounts payable department, no bill should be approved for payment until materials ordered have actually been received, are in good condition, and the prices of the seller's invoice match his quotations.

(4) In the manufacturing department, only highly trusted individuals have authority to sign stores requisitions to withdraw materials from the storeroom. Usually, a foreman prepares a stores requisition where raw materials or supplies are needed in any of the manufacturing departments. This requisition contains the account name and number, department name and number, job order number, quantity of material issued, the stores item name and classification symbol, the name of the person to withdraw materials from the storeroom, the unit price of the item and the total cost of items withdrawn from the storeroom.

The departments involved in internal control for raw materials and supplies inventory are stores, purchasing, accounts payable and manufacturing.

[¶502.4] Work-in-Process Inventory

(1) In the manufacturing department, stores requisitions are prepared by shop foremen for materials which are to be charged to the work-in-process inventory account. Quantities of materials are obtained from engineering or administrative departments. Specifications for raw materials are usually shown on a bill of materials (a list of different items required to complete an order). The stores requisition will specify the quantity, price, cost of each item of raw material requisitioned and the job order number.

Time tickets are prepared by the workmen and approved by a foreman in the department in which work is performed before it is charged to the work-in-process inventory account. Each labor operation may have a standard time to perform a certain operation which has been predetermined by the engineering department. There also may be a predetermined standard wage rate, determined by the head of the manufacturing department and known by the payroll department. The cost accounting department is responsible for the amount of manufacturing expense charged to the work-in-process inventory account.

(2) In the cost department, raw material cost is computed from sales requisitions, direct labor costs from time tickets, and manufacturing expense is estimated from prevailing overhead rates.

Internal control methods for the work-in-process inventory account depend on whether the firm has a process cost accounting or job-order cost accounting system.

The chief point of internal control for work-in-process inventories is computing costs. Product costs are analyzed by operations, departments and cost elements. This permits measurement of the cost of products at different stages of completion. The number of partly finished units when multiplied by a cost at a particular stage should come close to the value in the work-in-process inventory account.

The departments involved in internal control of work-in-process inventories are manufacturing and cost accounting.

[¶503] TAKING COUNT — THE PHYSICAL INVENTORY

The two most significant factors of inventory control are:

1. Knowing what *should* be on hand, based on paper controls; and

2. Verifying *what actually is on hand*; by a physical count.

[¶503.1] The Perpetual System — Knowing What Should Be on Hand

In many firms, not enough effort and emphasis are put into the timely keeping of detailed perpetual inventory stock records, thus ignoring the most basic control available.

The nature and extent of the records to maintain vary from company to company. At the least, there should be a constant updated record of the *units* handled — a card or a loose-leaf sheet to which are posted the "ins" and "outs" always showing the new morning's balance on hand — or rather, the balance which *should* be on hand. If expanded to the fullest, the system would also include unit-costs of acquisitions (or, in manufacturing, detailed material, labor and overhead costs assigned), unit-sales deleted at cost (based on the company's "flow-of-cost" assumption of LIFO, FIFO or average costs) and balance on hand extended at cost. Also, the individual record would show back-order positions, write-downs, destructions, and, most importantly, locations in the storage area (by location number or description). Also, it may show the total sales income for that particular unit, displaying unit gross profits. Retail stores using the gross profit method of valuing inventories usually maintain controls over entire departments, or sections of departments, rather than by individual units, and extended values are at retail, showing markups and markdowns, as well as bulk cost figures.

The general ledger summary inventory asset account should (where the system provides cost-flowing movement) always tie to the total of the subsidiary perpetual system (at least monthly). They should be matched as often as possible and all differences traced to eliminate any weaknesses in the system.

The point is — know what *should be on hand!*

[¶503.2] The Physical Count — Verifying What Is Actually on Hand

At least once a year, as everyone presumes, a physical count of the entire inventory should be taken, usually as of the balance sheet date. Management, not the auditor, is responsible for taking this physical inventory. The auditor is an *observer* of methods, count and valuation, but he may help establish the system of counting, the tags to use, the methods of assuring a full count, the cutoff procedures, the pricing, etc., so as to satisfy himself of the reasonability of the total value he can accept for his attestation.

The method of tagging, counting, weighing or measuring, locating, recounting — the assignment of personnel — all the procedures should be set in advance and followed (unless properly authorized changes develop).

The auditor should familiarize himself with the nature of the products handled, the terminology, the packaging, the principles of measurement. His "education" in the client's processes should not be obtained at the sacrifice of counting-time.

The auditor is concerned with the final evaluation of that *physical* inventory. The perpetual records, as such, and errors therein are not a necessary part of the audit process, though weaknesses should be commented upon in the management letter.

However, a history of *accurate* internal paper control of inventory can substantially reduce the extent of testing by the auditor. When it can be expected that variations from perpetual inventories will be small and within tolerable limits, the auditor may choose to use statistical random sampling in testing either an immediately prior physical count or in counting only those items *drawn by the auditor* (without advance notice) for random selection. If the sample then indicates a rate of error unacceptable to the auditor, he may request another (or full) physical count, or he may, with management's consent, adjust the overall value of the inventory to an amount indicated by the sample (see Journal Entries in Appendix), with management promising to investigate the error in the ensuing fiscal year.

When an effective perpetual inventory control is in use, management usually "cycle" counts the inventory once, or several times over, during the year, testing bits and pieces throughout the year, covering it entirely at least once.

There are often *portions* of an inventory which may require more time and effort to physically count than the relative merit of those portions warrants. Such items may be *reasonably* estimated (with joint approval of management and auditor), based on such elements as: last year's value, movement during the year, space occupied, weight, or, considering sales and purchases, using an estimated gross profit method.

[¶503.3] Summary Thoughts

The accuracy of a physical inventory may always be in doubt if there is *no* perpetual record for comparison. A perpetual inventory is meaningless unless tested periodically to a physical count. A history of accurate perpetual records can be justification for an auditor's using statistical sampling for year-end evaluation. Moreover, management itself can use statistical sampling techniques for cycle counting. Tie-in to the general ledger asset account should be made regularly by management. The financial statement value of the inventory must be at cost or market, whichever is lower. Standards are *not* acceptable, unless approximating cost.

[¶504]   INTERNAL CONTROL FOR EXPENSES

The internal control procedures for various types of expenses are taken up in the following paragraphs.

[¶504.1] Manufacturing Expenses

(1) In the manufacturing service and producing department, small tools which are not constantly being used should be kept in the toolroom. Each workman requiring such tools is given metal checks, each stamped with his number. The toolroom attendant will release a tool to a workman in exchange for a metal check bearing the workman's number. The check is kept in the toolroom until the tool is returned, at which time the check is returned to the workman.

The department foreman has the responsibility for approving a store's requisition for a new tool should the old one be worn out.

(2) Charges for freight and shipping on incoming supplies should be charged to the account to which the supplies are charged. Copies of the freight or shipping bills should be attached to supply invoices. Supplies inventory is, therefore, charged for these freight and shipping charges instead of an expense account.

(3) Numerous types of shop supplies, such as brooms, oil, waste, solder, wire, are part of the raw materials and supplies inventory. They should be kept in the storeroom and issued only by a stores requisition, signed by an authorized individual. The individual who indicates the need for such supplies (usually a foreman) should indicate the job order number or departmental expense account number to which the material is to be charged on the stores requisition.

(4) Workmen categorized as indirect laborers should have an identification number when they work in a specific department. A time clock card should be kept and verified by a foreman or timekeeper.

The departments involved in internal control of manufacturing expenses are factory production, factory service and accounts payable.

[¶504.2] Selling Expenses

(1) Salesmen's salaries should be okayed by the sales department manager before a summary is sent to the payroll department. The basis for the summary is the salesmen's daily report. Commissions earned by salesmen are verified from duplicate sales invoices mailed to the customer. These are computed in the sales department and approved by the sales department manager.

(2) To prevent padding of travel expenses, many companies allow flat rates or maximum amounts for each day of the week. Unusual amounts should require an explanation from the salesman.

(3) The office manager retains control over outgoing mail and postage. A mail clerk usually affixes the postage. A point to keep in mind as a control of postage expenses is not to permit every office worker access to stamps or a postage meter.

(4) Telephone expenses can be controlled by having the switchboard operator record all outgoing calls by departments on a call report sheet. Long distance calls should be reported on a special form indicating the party making the call and where the call is going to. From the long distance call record, telephone expenses are distributed by departments.

(5) Subscriptions to publications and dues of various organizations and professional societies should be approved by the sales manager before a voucher is prepared for them.

(6) All bills approved by the sales manager are sent to the accounting department for payment.

The departments involved for internal control of selling expenses are sales and accounts payable.

[¶504.3] Administrative Expenses

Internal control for administrative expenses is very similar to the material for the sales department. Bills for adminstrative expense items should be approved by an administrative department executive before they are sent to the accounts payable department for payment.

The departments involved in internal control of administrative expenses are administrative and accounts payable.

[¶504.4] Financial and Other Expenses

In corporations which have special departments to control financial problems in the company, a treasury department or similar department will handle expenses in the nature of interest, discount and dividends and may even supervise handling of cash. The financial department may also have the responsibility for authorizing credit extended to customers.

(1) A credit manager in the financial department should have the responsibility for approving sales orders above a specific amount. To do this he should be in constant touch with the accounts receivable department to determine whether or not a customer has been regular in his payments. The treasurer has the responsibility for authorizing bad debt writeoffs. The writeoff itself should be made by someone in the accounts receivable department on the authority of the financial department executive — not the sales manager.

(2) The financial department executive or office manager approves expenditures such as interest and bank discounts, office expenses and supplies. After approval of these items, invoices are sent to the accounts payable department.

The departments involved in internal control for factory payrolls are timekeeping, payroll, accounts payable and the particular manufacturing division.

[¶504.5] Salaries and Wages

(1) In the timekeeping department each workman is given an identifying number which will serve to identify the department within which he works. A badge with this number indentifies him when his presence within the factory is checked each day.

(2) It is the duty of a time clerk to check the presence of each workman once or twice a day, every day. This is to eliminate the possibility of one man punching the time clock for another workman who is absent. Absences are noted in a time book. These are then checked against the employee's time ticket, time clock card or payroll sheet at the end of each specific pay period.

(3) Care should be taken to prevent one worker punching another worker's time clock card. The time clock card indicates the number of hours the workman is present each day in the plant. The time clock card can be used to verify the hours shown on daily time tickets. This may be done daily or weekly.

(4) In the manufacturing department, a time ticket which lists the workman's name, number of hours worked on different jobs and labor operations

and total hours worked is prepared. It must be approved by the foreman of the department in which work is performed.

(5) In the payroll department, time tickets are verified against the time clock cards and the time keeper's time clock book. The time ticket is then given to a clerk who inserts the hourly or piece-work rate of each workman. Another clerk computes the earnings.The time tickets are then used for working up the payroll sheet. Then, the time tickets are sent to the cost accounting department to prepare a payroll distribution sheet. The payroll sheet becomes the record by which the workman is paid. After the payroll sheet has been completely okayed, it is sent to the accounts payable department for payment. Payment to each worker, either by check or cash, should be receipted.

In the accounts payable department the payroll sheet serves as the basis for payment.

The departments involved in internal control for factory payrolls are time-keeping, payroll, accounts payable and the particular manufacturing division.

[¶504.6] Office Payroll

(1) In the sales department, the sales manager approves salesmen's daily reports. Using these reports, a clerk prepares a record of the salesman's day's work. The record is sent to the payroll department after approval by the sales manager. The manager in the sales department similarly approves the records of work performed by the sales office force before they are sent to payroll.

(2) In the administrative department, the office manager approves time worked by the office force and then sends it to the payroll department. Salaries of top executives are often placed on a special payroll. Their salaries are usually known by the paymaster who prepares their checks and sends them directly to the executives' offices.

(3) The treasurer or financial department office manager similarly approves the work performed by the clerical personnel in his department.

(4) Upon receiving these authorized reports from the various departments, the paymaster sets them up on a payroll sheet and after computing the applicable salary for each office worker, takes all applicable deductions and indicates a net salary for each employee.

(5) In the accounts payable department, payment for these office workers' salaries is prepared from the payroll sheets.

[¶505]   INTERNAL CONTROL FOR CASH

Where currency is available, internal control is needed the most. Incoming checks may be used in manipulating accounts receivable and must be controlled. Accounts receivable control becomes part of cash control, and vice versa. Cash disbursements and petty cash also need special internal controls. The details on internal control for these cash or cash-connected items follow.

[¶505.1] Cash Receipts

(1) In the selling department, cash sales should be recorded in a register. A numbered sales slip should be made up for each sale. These slips should be used in numerical order.

(2) In the cashier's department, an employee should count the cash in each register at the end of the day. Except for a small amount left to make change, all cash should be removed. The total daily cash receipts should be recorded on slips and placed in the same pouch as the cash itself. The pouch should then be turned over to a clerk (a different employee from the one who counted the cash in the register) who will make out a bank deposit slip. Still another clerk in the cashier's department should read the cash register totals of the day or remove the cash sales slips. The cash removed from the register must agree with the tape and the total of cash slips which are numbered sequentially (all numbers must have been accounted for). The sales readings are then compared with the amount of cash removed from the registers by the cashier. Small discrepancies are charged to a cash, short or over account. Larger discrepancies call for an explanation.

(3) In the accounts receivable department, incoming mail should be opened by a trusted clerk (who should be bonded). All checks, currency, money orders are listed by this clerk on a cash-received record. The cash-received record lists date of receipt, name of sender and amount. The record and totals are then sent to the accounts receivable department to be properly applied to the customers' accounts. The cash is sent to the cashier's office and subsequently given to the deposit clerk.

(4) In the accounts receivable department, the record of cash received is used to credit against customers' accounts. This record then goes to the general accounting department where it is compared with daily deposit slips of cash received from customers before it is entered on the books.

The departments involved in internal control of cash receipts are selling, treasury or cashier's and accounts receivable.

[¶505.2] Cash Disbursements

In the accounts payable department, purchase of any item must have prior approval from the authorized person in charge of the department in which the expenditure originates before it comes to the accounts payable department. Where a voucher system is in operation, vouchers are prepared for each expenditure. Information on the voucher matches that shown on the seller's invoice. Vouchers are entered in the voucher register after having been approved by the head of the voucher department and then placed in a pending file for future payments.

The departments involved in the internal control of cash disbursements are accounts payable and voucher.

[¶505.3] Petty Cash

In any department where it is necessary to have a petty cash fund, at least two individuals should have the responsibility for handling petty cash. One individual inspects and approves the item for payment. The other has charge of the petty cash fund and pays the vouchers as they are presented. Each petty cash voucher should list the date, amount paid and name of the account to be charged. A bill or other receipt, if there is one, should be attached to the voucher. The employee who controls the petty cash fund should compare the receipts attached to the petty cash vouchers with the vouchers.

When the petty cash fund needs reimbursement, the person who controls the fund totals those petty cash vouchers which have been paid out and presents them to the accounts payable department, which then arranges for the necessary reimbursement.

The departments involved in the internal control of petty cash are selling, administrative, or others in which there is a need for such petty cash funds, and accounts payable.

[¶505.4] Accounts Receivable

Copies of sales slips from the sales department are used to charge customers' accounts. Copies of any credits due customers come from the sales department. These records are sent to the accounts receivable department, where, if possible, one clerk should have the responsibility for entering only debits to customers' accounts and another for posting credits for returned merchandise, receipt of a note, etc. Still a third employee should enter the credit in the customers's account for cash received.

Sending statements at the end of each month is a good way to check the accuracy of the customers' accounts.

The departments responsible for internal control of accounts receivable are the accounts receivable and sales.

[¶505.5] Notes Receivable

In the treasury department, a record of notes held from customers is made. A record is then sent to the accounts receivable division where a clerk makes the proper credits. A copy is sent to the general accounting department to reflect the charge to the control account — notes receivable. The treasurer keeps the notes until maturity date or until discounted with the bank. A subsidiary note register should be kept if the company receives a large number of such notes.

The departments responsible for internal control of notes receivable are treasury and accounts receivable.

[¶505.6] Cash and Bank Reconciliations:

Cash is the lifeblood of the company. It is the center upon which the whole circle of business activity is pivoted. Here is the reservoir into which all flows — in and out.

It is surprising to find that tests of cash receipts and cash disbursements are usually limited by management (through intermediaries) to monthly bank reconciliations.

Nothing is more effective than unannounced, non-routine, spot-tests of the cash-handling procedure (for that matter, *any* business procedure) by the highest working or non-working authority within the company. Think of the impact made on an employee when he *knows* he may be facing an impromptu test of his work by the president of the company — at any time! Called in, for example, to explain the purpose of a canceled check he now holds; imagine the psychological impact if this is done periodically, but irregularly? A test of application of payments on account — receivables and payables — almost any awareness of constant high-level review has an alerting effect. Peak, more honest, performance is encouraged.

Bank reconciliations by and of themselves can not stand alone as proof of cash authenticity. They prove only the activity *within* that one period and serve to lend to prior reconciliations substantiation of then-listed outstanding checks. The current reconciliation is technically unproved until the outstanding checks and uncredited deposits in transit appear.

Reconciliations should be tested by someone other than the original preparer.

Block-proofs of cash should also be used occasionally to test an entire year's transactions. Here, all deposits are matched to all receipts booked (in total); and all recorded disbursements are matched to total bank charges for cleared checks and minor items, with consideration, of course, given to opening and closing transit items.

The theory behind the mechanics of the bank reconciliation is to *update* the *bank* figures (on a worksheet) to reflect all transit items which have not yet cleared the bank, as follows:

Bank shows a balance of	$ 10,500
Add deposits in transit	2,000
	12,500
Less checks outstanding (itemized)	600
Adjusted bank balance	$ 11,900
Balance per books shows	$ 11,909
Difference	$ 9 (more on books)

Having taken the preliminary steps of determining the deposits in transit (by checking the bank credits against booked receipts) and the outstanding checks (by checking off all returned canceled checks against the listing of those issued or carried over), we note a remaining difference of $ 9.

In *order,* the following are the *most expedient* ways of finding this difference:

[¶506]

1. Look at the bank statement for any bank charge (D/M's) — or combination — not yet booked in the general ledger;

2. Look at the books for any $9 debit (or combination) on the books and not on the statement;

3. $9 may be indicative of a transposition. Match the bank's opening pickup balance to the closing one on the last statement;
Match deposits to receipts booked;
Check general ledger footings and subtraction;
Check summary postings into the general ledger from the original source;
Check footings in the books of original entry (Receipts, Disbursements, General Journal);

4. Having exhausted the above possibilities and still not found the difference, check now the face amount of each check to the amount charged by the bank (each check is canceled with a clearance date).

5. Now match your own listing of the check to the actual check. (Steps 4 and 5 are interchangeable)

6. Not yet? Prove the bank's additions.

7. If still elusive, you've probably missed it above or made a transposition error in listing transit checks or deposits; or, it may be an error made last month which was missed.

[¶507]   FILE MAINTENANCE

One of the most important, yet least emphasized, facets of the business enterprise is the establishment and proper maintenance of an effective, accurate filing system. How costly is the time wasted in frustrating searches for misfiled data, when initial precautions and firm rules might have assured quick access to and retrieval of needed documents by competent, authorized personnel!

[¶507.1] Suggestions

Establish firm rules for filing,.
Provide adequate accessible filing space for current files.
Pinpoint responsibilities for filing and accessing files.
Follow legal requirements for record retention. Establish an annual policy of destroying old, non-needed files.
Flowchart when appropriate.
Documents, such as purchase orders, sales shipping papers — all such which are ultimately tied to either a sales invoice or a vendor's invoice — should have sufficient copies to allow for a complete numerical file of each document.

[¶507.2] A List of File Categories

Sales invoices to customers — both alphabetic and numeric files;

Vendor invoices — alphabetic, sometimes with copy of paid voucher check or numbered voucher. Some firms keep invoices segregated in an "unpaid" file until paid;

Canceled checks — keep by month in reconciled batches. Do not intermingle different batches;

Correspondence files — for customers, vendors, others;

Permanent files — organizational information, legal documents, leases, minutes, deeds, etc. Usually in fireproof areas, accessibility limited.

Other:

Tax files
Payroll and personnel files
Backup for journal entries
Investment files — security transactions
Petty cash voucher files
Purchasing department files — suppliers, bids, etc. (costs)
Credit department files
Prior years' books of entry
Data from subsidiary companies owned
Advertising programs, literature, etc.

[¶507.3] Computer Files — Considerations

1. Security protection — access, codes, permanent tapes/discs of programs, updated balance files for accounts receivables, payables, general ledger, payrolls. Keep enough of these changing files for re-runs or accumulation runs, as needed for emergencies.

2. Keep hard copy until sure replacement hard copy is accurate, or as necessary for continuous file.

3. Be prepared for manual emergency work, if computer goes down suddenly.

4. Pinpoint responsibility for keeping logs, storage, etc.

[¶507.4] Typical Auditor's File (for clients)

Client's permanent file: Basic information on structure, ownership, location, personnel functions, retirement plans, copies of minutes; sometimes the fixed asset cost and depreciation information, other information pertaining to long-term assets, liabilities, capital stock and retained earnings; copy of client's chart of accounts; initial computer programming information; IRS and state tax audits; other data which might require perennial referencing.

Client's current and prior years' audit files: One file for each year, containing all worksheets and data supporting the audit. Interim work also goes here.

Client's tax files: One for each year; copies of all tax returns prepared by the auditor, with makeup sheets and workups; copies of tax returns prepared by client.

Client's correspondence file: All correspondence in one file usually not segregated by years, unless bulky.

Due-date index: A master card-index file which indicates in date order when tax returns and financial statements are due for all clients.

Cross-index file: Alphabetical listing of clients, showing the auditor-assigned client number.

Telephone file: Alphabetic indexing of clients' phone numbers, names of executives and extension numbers.

The custom in most firms is to keep the current year's file for all clients in one numerical or alphabetical sequence, sometimes having a separate location for the current tax files. Prior years' files are also held in this manner. Different colored file-folders are usually used to designate the type of file; white for current, orange for taxes, blue for permanent file. Latest material should always be put in front.

6

What Are The Standards?

PRELUDE TO GAAP OUTLINE

The outline which follows covers those sections of the American Institute's (AICPA) Professional Standards for Accounting which are *specifically titled* with the caption "Generally Accepted Accounting Principles."

Specifically, they are:

> Section AC 1026: "Generally Accepted Accounting
>   Principles — Pervasive Principles."
> Section AC 1027: "Generally Accepted Accounting
>   Principles — Broad Operating Principles."

The outline does *not* cover Section AC 1028, "Generally Accepted Accounting Principles — Detailed Operating Principles," *because there are no detailed* principles in that Section. The section merely points out *why* detailed principles are *not* enumerated.

No other sections in the published accounting standards carry that "GAAP" prefix. (But they are still mandatory)

As a preliminary to the above statements on GAAP, the lead-in Sections AC 1010 through AC 1025 set the scenario detailed for that presentation of GAAP by the development of the following outline:

I. OBJECTIVES OF FINANCIAL ACCOUNTING

II. BASIC FEATURES AND BASIC ELEMENTS OF
   FINANCIAL ACCOUNTING

> A. Basic Features — The Environment
> B. Basic Elements — The Individual Company
>> 1. Economic resources, obligations and residual interests
>> 2. Changes in those resources — events that cause them to increase or decrease

46

> *3. GAAP — for recording and reporting them:
>> *A) The Pervasive Principles
>> *B) The Broad Operating Principles
>>> *1) Selection and measurement
>>> *2) Financial statement presentation
>> C) Detailed Operating Principles.

*3 (A) and 3 (B) (1) & (2) are covered in the outline next following. They pertain to the practical application of the principles, which are described in more theoretical and historical-development terms in the prior sections of the outline.

A reading of those prior sections (not discussed here) provides an invaluable aid for a complete understanding of the nature and development of accounting standards. The accountant's education is incomplete without reference to them.

GAAP

(Generally Accepted Accounting Principles)

[¶602] THE PERVASIVE MEASUREMENT PRINCIPLES

Six of them establish the basis for implementing *accrual* accounting:

1. *Initial Recording:* of assets and liabilities, income determination, revenue and realization.

2. *Realization:*
   - Revenue — when earning process is complete.
     - — when an exchange has taken place.
   - Expenses — gross decreases in assets.
     - — gross increases in liabilities.
   - Classes of expenses:
   - Costs of assets used to produce revenue — cost of goods sold, selling — administrative expense, interest expense.
   - Expenses from non-reciprocal transfers — taxes, thefts, floods.
   - Costs of assets other than product disposed of — plant, equipment.
   - Costs of unsuccessful efforts.
   - Declines in market prices of inventories.
   - Does *not* include repayments of borrowings, expenditures to acquire assets, distributions to owners (including treasury stock) or adjusting prior period expenses.

3. *Associating Cause and Effect*

4. *Systematic and Rational Allocation*

5. *Immediate Recognition*

   Costs of the current period which provide no future benefits (those which have been incurred *now* or *prior*) or when allocating serves no useful purpose.

Measurement is based on its own exchanges: contracts not recorded until *one* party fulfills commitment; not all changes are recorded, not internal increases and not price changes in productive resources.

Assets usually are recorded at cost, or unexpired portion of it. When sold, difference increases or decreases the firm's net assets. The cost principle: use acquisition price (historical cost). Cost also refers to how asset was originally recorded, regardless of how determined.

6. *The Unit of Measure* — is U.S. Dollar — no change is recognized for change in general purchasing power of the dollar.

[¶602.1]   THE PERVASIVE PRINCIPLES — MODIFYING CONVENTIONS

Modifying conventions are applied because too rigid adherence to the measurement principles might produce results not desirable; exclude other important events; or may be sometimes impractical.

The modifying conventions are:

1. *Conservatism*
2. *Emphasis on the importance of income* (LIFO is example)
3. *Judgment of the accounting profession as a whole* with regard to:
    The usual revenue recognition rule— recognition of contracts in progress.

    Segregation of extraordinary items.

    Avoiding undue effect on net income in one single period (installment sales).

[¶603]   BROAD OPERATING PRINCIPLES

Two broad principles:

1. The Principles of Selection and Measurement
2. The Principles of Financial Statement Presentation.

[¶603.1]   THE PRINCIPLES OF SELECTION AND MEASUREMENT

These principles guide the selection of the *events* to be accounted for; they determine *how* the selected *events* affect items; and they guide the *assignment of dollars* to the effect of the *events*.

The types of *events,* classified, are:

1. External Events
    A. *Transfers* to or from *other* entities

    (1) Exchanges (reciprocal transfers)
    (2) Non-reciprocal transfers
       (A) With owners
       (B) With outsiders
  B. *Other-than-transfers*

2. Internal Events
  A. Production of goods or services
  B. Casualties

The outline presented next breaks down each of the types of events above and briefly highlights, where appropriate:

When to record the transaction
How it is *measured* — what value to use
Some *discussion* and/or *examples*

In that order: when to record, how to *value, discussion, examples.*

In *addition to the events* themselves (above), there are:

3. *Additional* principles which relate to the *changes* in events, which determine their effects.

4. Principles governing assets and liabilities that are not resources or obligations (such as deferred taxes).

[¶604] 1A — EXTERNAL EVENTS — TRANSFERS TO OR FROM OTHER ENTITIES

(1) Exchanges (reciprocal transfers)

Assets — Acquisitions: Record as acquired (some not carried forward are expenses); cost, face amount, sometimes discounted value; sometimes fair value in non-cash exchanges (allocate fair values for individual assets in group) — excess is goodwill. Cash, accounts receivable, short-term receivables at discounted amount when no or low interest stated.

Assets — Dispositions: When disposed of, at cost adjusted for amortization and other changes; in partial dispositions value is based on detailed principles (FIFO, LIFO, average).

Liabilities — Increases: When obligation to transfer assets or provide services is incurred in exchanges; value is established in the exchange, sometimes discounted (long-term) — pension obligations, loans under capitalized long-term leases, bonds, notes bearing little or no interest (the difference is amortized over period to maturity).

Liabilities — Decreases: When discharged through payments or otherwise; use recorded amounts. If partial, may·have to apportion to recorded amount.

Commitments — *Not* recorded when unfulfilled on both sides, unless: one party fulfills its part; some leases are recorded; *losses* on firm commitments are recorded. Long-term leases are recorded as assets by the lessee, with the corresponding liability.

Revenue from Exchanges — When product is sold, service performed, resource used by others, and when asset is sold producing gain (or loss); recorded at price in the exchange, sometimes reduced for discounts or allowances. Exceptions: long-term construction contracts, revenue not recognized on purchases, certain products with an *assured* selling price — sometimes recorded over long periods without reasonable assurance of collection (installment method; cost recovery method). (Under the installment method, proceeds collected measure the revenue, but expense is measured by multiplying cost by ratio of collection to sales price. In cost recovery method, use all proceeds collected until all costs are recovered.)

Expenses — Directly associated with revenue from exchanges — use costs of assets sold or services provided, recorded when related revenue is recognized. If other than a product, the remaining *undepreciated* cost is subtracted from the revenue obtained.

(2) Non-reciprocal transfers:

(A) *With owners*: Investments and withdrawals recorded as they occur:
Increases — by amount of cash received; the discounted value of money claims received or liabilities canceled; fair value of non-cash assets received (often, the fair value of *stock issued*).
Decreases — cash paid; recorded amount of non-cash assets transferred; discounted present value of liabilities incurred.

In "pooling" assets and liabilities are combined as on books (no change); "purchase" method entails use of fair value.

Investments of non-cash assets recorded when made; sometimes measured at cost to founder (rather than fair value).

(B) *With outsiders:* assets, when acquired, when disposed of, when discovered; for non-cash assets given, usually use fair value; liabilities, at face value, sometimes discounted.

[¶605]   **1B — EXTERNAL EVENTS —
OTHER-THAN-TRANSFERS**

Examples are: Changes in prices of assets, changes in interest rates, technological changes, damage caused by outside influences.

Favorable events — Generally not recorded, except at time of later exchange. Retained on books at recorded amounts until exchanged (assets) or until satisfied (liabilities). Exceptions are: When using the equity method; foreign currency translations; marketable securities under new rules, written down to market, up to cost, as fluctuates; obligations under warranties.

Unfavorable events — Decreasing market price or utility of asset, adjusted to lower market price or recoverable cost, usually governed by specific rules such as cost or market for inventories. A loss is recognized when utility is no longer as great as its cost, obsolescence; adjust write-offs or write-off entirely currently if it is completely worthless, or down to recoverable cost. Damage caused by others, record when occurs or discovered — to recoverable cost. Increases in amounts currently payable because of higher interest rates only generally not recorded until liquidated. Increases in non-U.S. Dollar liabilities are recorded in terms of U.S. Dollar because of currency translation.

[¶606] 2A — INTERNAL EVENTS — PRODUCTION OF GOODS OR SERVICES

Production is the input of goods and services combined to produce an output of product which may be goods or services. It includes: Manufacturing, merchandising, transporting and holding goods.

Recorded at historical or acquisition costs (previously recorded) as used in the production process during the period; deducted from revenue to which related in the period sold. Costs are usually shifted or allocated from initially recorded asset accounts to other accounts in a *systematic* and *rational* manner.

Costs of manufacturing or providing services — Costs of assets completely used plus allocated portions of assets partially used; allocations are assumed, based on relationship between assets and activities; note that "costs" refers to amounts charged initially to assets — they become "expenses" when allocated to expense as follows:
If benefit only one period — expense then.
If benefit several periods — expense over periods involved (depreciation, depletion, amortization).

Expenses — Some items are recognized as expenses immediately and charged directly thereto. Enterprises never "acquire" expenses, they acquire assets. Costs may be charged as expenses immediately under the principle of immediate recognition when they pertain to the period involved and cannot be associated with any other period, such as officer salaries and advertising.

Revenue — Under certain conditions and special standards, may be recognized at completion of production or as production progresses (precious metals industry; long-term construction contracts). Ratio of performance to date must be capable of being reasonably estimated and collection *reasonably* assured. Take losses *immediately*. Revenue is measured by an allocated portion of a predetermined selling price, less product or service costs as progresses.

[¶607]   2B — INTERNAL EVENTS — CASUALTIES

Sudden, substantial, unanticipated reductions in assets *not* caused by other entities, such as:

Fires, floods, abnormal spoilage.

Recorded when they occur or when they are discovered.

Measured by writing them down to recoverable costs and a *loss* is recorded.

[¶608]   3 — ADDITIONAL PRINCIPLES WHICH RELATE TO THE CHANGES IN EVENTS, WHICH DETERMINE THEIR EFFECTS

Dual effect — Every recorded event affects at least *two* items in the records. *The double-entry system is based on this principle.*

Increases in assets arise from:
  A. Exchanges in which assets are acquired
  B. Investments of assets by owners
  C. Non-reciprocal transfers of assets by outsiders
  D. Shifts of costs during production
  E. From external events (equity method)
  F. Increases ascribed to produced assets.
      with *opposite effect* of:
  1. Decrease in other assets
  2. Increase in liability
  3. Revenue recognition
  4. Sometimes, neutral effect — production costs shifted.

Decreases in assets arise from:
  A. Exchanges in which assets are disposed of
  B. Withdrawals of assets by owners
  C. Non-reciprocal transfers to outsiders
  D. External events which reduce market price
  E. Shifts and allocations
  F. Casualties
      with *opposite effect* of:
  1. Increase in other assets
  2. Decrease in liabilities

3. Increases in expenses:
   Immediately, if used up;
   Or if future benefit cannot be determined.

Increases in liabilities arise from:
   A. Exchanges in which liabilities are incurred
   B. Transfers with owner (dividend declaration)
   C. Non-reciprocal transfers with outsiders
      with *opposite effect* of:
   1. Decrease in other liabilities
   2. Increase in assets
   3. An expense.

Decreases in liabilities arise from:
   A. Exchanges in which liabilities are reduced
   B. Transfers with owners
   C. Non-reciprocal transfers with outsiders
      (forgiveness of indebtedness)
      with *opposite effect* of:
   1. Increases in other liabilities
   2. Decreases in assets
   3. Revenue.

Increases in owners' equity arise from:
   A. Investments in enterprise
   B. *Net* result of all revenue and expenses in a period
   C. Non-reciprocal transfers with outsiders (gifts)
   D. Prior period adjustments.

Decreases in owners' equity arise from:
   A. Transfers to owners (dividends)
   B. Net losses for a period
   C. Prior period adjustments.

Revenue arises:
   A. Primarily from exchanges
   B. Occasionally from production
   C. Rarely from transfers or external events
      with *opposite* effect of:
   1. Usually an asset increase
   2. Decrease in liability (called "unearned revenue").

Expenses arise from:
   A. Exchanges — costs directly associated with revenue are recognized
      when assets are sold or services provided.
   B. Non-reciprocal transfers with outsiders
   C. External events other than transfers
   D. Production:
      1) Costs of manufacturing products and providing services *not*
         included in product costs (example — overhead)
      2) Expenses from systematic and rational allocation, excluding
         those assigned to product costs of manufacturing
      3) Expenses recognized immediately on the acquisition of goods or
         services
      4) Costs of products for which revenue is recognized at *completion*
         of production or as *production* progresses (precious
         metals, percent-of-completion contracts).

[¶609] 4 — PRINCIPLES GOVERNING ASSETS AND LIABILITIES THAT ARE NOT RESOURCES OR OBLIGATIONS:

Certain items are shown as assets which are not in reality resources, such as deferred charges for income taxes; and certain items are shown as liabilities which are not in reality liabilities, such as deferred credits for income taxes.

Accounting for them is governed by detailed principles, such as accounting for deferred federal income taxes in AC 4091.

> The effect of recording these items is an increase or a decrease in assets or liabilities, with a corresponding decrease or increase in expenses on the income statement.

[¶610] THE PRINCIPLES OF FINANCIAL STATEMENT PRESENTATION*

The general objective is to provide reliable information on resources, obligations and progress. The information should be useful for comparability, completeness and understandability. The basic features involved in financial accounting are: the individual accounting entity, the use of approximation and the preparation of fundamentally related financial statements.

[¶610.1] "Fair Presentation In Conformity with GAAP"

1. GAAP applicable in the circumstances have been applied in accumulating and processing the accounting information; and
2. Changes from period to period in GAAP have been properly disclosed; and
3. The information in the *underlying* records is properly *reflected* and *described* in the financial statements in conformity with GAAP; and
4. A proper balance has been achieved between:
   A. The conflicting needs to disclose the important aspects of financial position and results of operation in conformance with conventional concepts, and to
   B. Summarize the voluminous underlying data with a limited number of financial statement captions and supporting notes.

[¶610.2] There Are 12 Principles of Financial Statement Presentation

(Principles are conventions and are subject to change the same as principles of selection and management)

---

* On December 2, 1976, the FASB issued for comments, a discussion memorandum on "Conceptual Framework for Financial Accounting and Reporting: Elements of Financial Statements and Their Measurement."

1. Basic Financial Statements — minimum requirements:
   A. Balance Sheet
   B. Statement of Income
   C. Statement of Changes in Retained Earnings
   D. Statement of Changes in Financial Position
   E. Disclosure of Accounting Policies
   F. Disclosure of Related Notes
   Usually presented for two or more periods.
   Other information may be presented, but not required: Revenue by lines of business; price-level statements; information on physical output; historical summaries.

2. A Complete Balance Sheet (or "Statement of Financial Position")
   A. All Assets
   B. All Liabilities
   C. All classes of owners' Equity.

3. A Complete Income Statement
   A. All Revenues
   B. All Expenses.

4. A Complete Statement of Changes in Financial Position
   Includes and describes all important aspects of the company's financing and investing activities.

5. Accounting Period
   Basic time period is one year
   An interim statement is for less than one year.

6. Consolidated Financial Statements
   They are presumed to be more meaningful than separate statements of the component legal entities

   They are *usually* necessary when one of the group owns (directly or indirectly) *over 50%* of the outstanding voting stock

   The information is presented as if it were *a single enterprise*.

7. The Equity Basis
   For unconsolidated subsidiaries (where over 50% is owned) *and for investments in 50% or less* of the voting stock of companies in which investor has significant influence over investees. 20% or more ownership presumes this influence, unless proved otherwise

   The investor's share of the net income reported by the investee is picked up and shown as income and an adjustment of the investment account — for all earnings subsequent to the acquistion. Dividends are treated as an adjustment of the investment account.

8. Translation of Foreign Branches
   Translated into U.S. Dollars by conventional translation procedures involving foreign exchange rates.

9. Classification and Segregation:
   (Must separately disclose these important components)

   A. *Income Statement* — Sales (or other source of revenue); Cost of Sales; Depreciation; Selling and Administration Expenses; Interest Expense; Income Taxes.

   B. *Balance Sheet* — Cash; Receivables; Inventories; Plant and Equipment; Payables; and Categories of Owners Equity:
   Par or stated amount of capital stock; Additional paid-in capital

Retained earnings: (affected by —
Net income or loss
Prior period adjustments
Dividends
Transfers to other categories of equity).

Working Capital — current assets and current liabilities should be classified as such to be able to determine working capital — useful for enterprises in: manufacturing, trading, some service enterprises.

Current assets — include cash and other assets that can reasonably be expected to be realized in cash in one year or a shorter business cycle.

Current liabilities — include those that are expected to be satisfied by the use of those assets shown as current; or the creation of other current liabilities; or expected to be satisfied in one year.

Assets and liabilities should *not* be offset against each other unless a *legal* right to do so exists.

Gains and losses — arise from other than products or services, may be combined and shown as one item. Examples: write-downs of inventories, receivables, capitalized research and development costs, *all sizable*. Also, gains and losses on: temporary investments, non-monetary transactions, currency devaluations. These are typical items.

Extraordinary items of gain or loss — should be shown separately under its own title, distinguished by unusual nature and infrequent occurrence — should be shown net of taxes.

Net Income — should be separately disclosed and clearly identified on the income statement.

10. Other Disclosures: (Accounting policies and notes)

    A. Customary or Routine Disclosures:
       1. Measurement bases of important assets
       2. Restrictions on assets
       3. Restriction on owners' equity
       4. Contingent liabilities
       5. Contingent assets
       6. Important long-term commitments not in the body of the statements
       7. Information on terms of equity of owners
       8. Information on terms of long-term debt
       9. Other disclosures required by AICPA

    B. Disclosure of Changes in Accounting Policies.
    C. Disclosure of important subsequent events —
       between balance sheet date and date of the opinion.
    D. Disclosure of accounting policies ("Summary of Significant ...").

11. Form of Financial Statement Presentation:

    No particular form is presumed better than all others for all purposes. Several are used.

12. Earnings Per Share:

    Must be disclosed on the *face of the Income Statement*. Should be disclosed for:
    A. Income before extraordinary items
    B. Net Income.
    Should consider:
    A. Changes in number of shares outstanding

B. Contingent changes
C. Possible dilution from potential conversion of:
    Convertible debentures
    Preferred stock
    Options
    Warrants.

END OF GAAP OUTLINE

7

Current Assets

[¶701]

Classification of current assets is important since the more the current assets exceed the current liabilities, the higher becomes the working capital. There is considerable variation and inconsistency among companies in the way assets are classified in financial statements.

For accounting purposes, the term "current assets" is used to designate cash and other assets or resources which are reasonably expected to be realized in cash, sold or consumed during the normal operating cycle of the business. (AC 1027.25)

Here are some examples: (AC 2031.04)

Cash available for current operations and items which are the equivalent of cash; (2) inventories of merchandise, raw materials, goods in process, finished goods, operating supplies, and ordinary maintenance materials and parts; (3) trade accounts, notes and acceptances receivable; (4) receivables from officers, employees, affiliates and others if they are collectible in the ordinary course of the business within one year; (5) installment or deferred accounts and notes receivable if they conform generally to normal trade practices and business terms; (6) marketable securities representing the investment of cash available for current operation; and (7) prepaid expenses, such as insurance, rent, taxes, unused royalties, current paid advertising services not yet received, and operating supplies.

Prepaid expenses are not current assets in that they will be converted into cash, but in the sense that, if not paid in advance, they would require the use of current assets otherwise available during the operating cycle.

The operating cycle is defined as the average time between the acquisition of materials or services until the time that cash is finally realized on sale of the materials or services. Where there are several operating cycles occurring within a year, a one-year time period is used as the criterion for a current asset. Where the operating cycle is more than 12 months (i.e., in the tobacco, distillery, and lumber businesses), a longer period is used. Where a business has no clearly defined operating cycle, a one-year period is used. (AC 2031.05)

[¶701.1]   Assets Excluded From "Current Assets"

The following types of items are to be excluded from the current asset classification: (AC 2031.06)

(1) Cash and claims for cash which are (a) restricted as to withdrawal or use for other than current operations, (b) earmarked for expenditure in the acquisition or construction of noncurrent assets, or (c) segregated for the liquidation of long-term debts. Even though funds may not actually be set aside in separate accounts, funds that are clearly to be used in the near future for the liquidation of long-term debt, sinking fund payments, or other similar purposes should be excluded from current assets, unless the maturing portion of debt is being shown as a current liability. (AC 2033.09 Footnote)

(2) Investments in securities (marketable or not) (or advances) which have been made for the purposes of control, affiliation, or other continuing business advantage.

(3) Receivables arising from unusual transactions (e.g., sale of capital assets, loans or advances to affiliate companies, officers or employees) not expected to be collected within a one-year period.

(4) Cash surrender value of life insurance policies.

(5) Land and other natural resources.

(6) Depreciable assets.

(7) Long-term prepayments which are chargeable to the operations of several years or deferred charges, such as bonus payments under a long-term lease and costs of rearranging a factory or removal to a new location.

Accounts and notes receivable due from officers, employees or affiliated companies should not be included under the general heading "Accounts Receivable." They should be shown separately. The basic reasoning behind this is that accounts receivable are classified as a current asset presuming they will be converted into cash within one year. Except in the case where goods have actually been sold to them on account, for collection according to the regular credit terms, amounts due from officers, directors and stockholders are not likely to be collected within one year. Therefore, they should be shown under some noncurrent caption.

The same is true of accounts receivable from affiliated companies. These amounts are not likely to be paid off currently and are usually of a more permanent nature. Showing them as current assets is misleading. Also, there is an overstatement of current assets and consequently of working capital.

[¶701.2]   Valuation of Current Assets

Sometimes current assets are carried at values which do not represent realizable values. (AC 2031.09). For example, accounts receivable should be net of allowances for uncollectible accounts or net of earned discounts when discounts are expected to give an *estimated* receivable value.

Also, some current assets should now reflect *unrealized* gains or losses. (See Both Marketable Securities and Foreign Currency Translations in this Accounting Section.)

Assets and liabilities in the balance sheet should not be offset unless a legal right of setoff exists. (AC 1027.25 R-9B)

Inventory is valued at cost unless its utility value has diminished to a lower market replacement cost. Standard costing is acceptable, if reasonably approximating actual cost. The flow of costs may be predicated upon FIFO, LIFO or average assumptions. (See further discussion next.)

[¶702]   INVENTORY

The term "inventory" is used to designate tangible personal property which is: (1) held for sale in the ordinary course of business, (2) in the process of being produced for later sale, or (3) currently consumed directly or indirectly in the production of goods or services to be available for sale. (AC 5121.03-.04)

Manufacturing firms have many types of inventory; for example, finished goods, work in process, raw materials and manufacturing supplies. Finished goods of a manufacturing company are comparable to the merchandise of a non-manufacturing company. Excluded from inventory are long-term assets subject to depreciation and depreciable fixed assets retired from regular use and held for sale. Raw materials which become part of a finished product become part of that inventory cost. Trade practices and materiality are usually the determinant factors in either inventorying production supplies on hand or expensing them as part of product costs. (AC 5121.03)

In accounting for inventories we try to match appropriate costs against revenues. This gives us a proper determination of realized income. Another way of putting it is to say that by applying the best method of costing inventory, we are measuring our "cost of goods sold," by associating cause and effect.

Inclusion of goods in inventory should follow the legal rule of title. Inventory should include all those goods which are legally owned by the company, whatever their location. If title to the goods has passed to a customer, they should not be included in inventory; whereas, if title has not passed, they should be included.

[¶702.1]   Cost of Inventory

The primary basis of accounting for inventories is cost. This means the sum of the expenditures and charges directly or indirectly incurred in bringing the inventory to its existing condition and location. (AC 5121.04)

As applied to inventories, costs mean acquisition and production costs. Even so, as a practical matter, there are many items which, although applicable to inventory, are not included in the cost of the inventory; for example, idle facility expense, excessive spoilage, double freight, rehandling costs. If these costs are abnormal, they should be treated as expenses of the current period rather than be carried forward as part of the inventory cost. General and administrative expenses should be treated as expenses of the period. Likewise, selling expenses should not be included in inventory. The cost of inventory, however, should include an applicable portion of manufacturing overhead. The exclusion of *all* overhead from inventory cost is not an acceptable accounting procedure (AC 5121.05)

Cost, however, *must not* be used when the *market* value of inventory items is lower than the cost. (AC 5121.08)

[¶702.2] Flow of Cost Assumptions

Costs for inventory may be determined under any one of several assumptions as to the flow of costs; for example, FIFO, average and LIFO. The method selected should be the one which most clearly reflects periodic income.

The "flow of costs" and "flow of goods" are usually not the same. But we use a "flow of cost" — such as FIFO, average or LIFO — because to identify the cost of a specific item sold is often impossible, impractical, or even misleading. Where similar goods are purchased at different prices at different times, it would be difficult to identify specific goods sold except in a case of valuable jewelry, automobiles, pianos or other large items. Even perpetual inventory records would not make identification possible. Therefore, an assumption is made with respect to the flow of costs in order to provide a practical basis for measuring period income.

LIFO is considered an appropriate method for pricing inventory during extended inflationary periods, when costs continue accelerating. When the economy is deflationary or relatively stable, the FIFO or average methods are usually preferred by management. Practices of the other companies in the same industry should also be considered. Financial statements would be more useful if all companies within a given industry used uniform methods of inventory pricing. (AC 5121.07)

The method used must be consistently applied and disclosed in financial statements. (See Disclosures and Restatements in this text)

[¶702.3]   First-In, First-Out (FIFO)

This is probably the most common method of valuing inventories. The latest costs are assigned to the goods on hand; thus, the earliest costs become the costs of the goods sold. The theory here is that goods are disposed of in the same order as acquired.

Here is a simple illustration of FIFO. Opening inventory and purchases during the year were as follows:

Opening inventory	1,000 units at $10, or	$10,000
First purchase	800 units at $11, or	8,800
Second purchase	500 units at $14, or	7,000
Third purchase	400 units at $12, or	4,800
Fourth purchase	300 units at $13, or	3,900
Totals	3,000	$34,500

The closing inventory consists of 1,100 units. Under the FIFO method of costing, the closing inventory is considered to be made up of:

300 units of the fourth purchase (at $13) .... $ 3,900
400 units of the third purchase (at $12) 4,800
400 units of the second purchase (at $14) 5,600
Cost of 1,100 units in closing inventory $14,300

[¶702.4]   Last-In, First-Out (LIFO)

In recent years, this has become a very popular method. In years of rising prices and high taxes, the LIFO method keeps profits (and taxes) down. It has the virtue of applying the current price structure to the cost of goods sold — thus matching the high price structure of the sales with the high price structure of costs.

The basic approach to LIFO costing is to assign the *earliest* costs to the *closing* inventory, as if the latest-acquired items were the first sold. For example, if we use the figures set forth above in the FIFO illustration, the costs of our closing inventory of 1,100 units under the LIFO costing approach would be:

1,000 units of the opening inventory (at $10) $10,000
100 units of the first purchase (at $11) 1,100
Cost of 1,100 units in closing inventory $11,100

Note that the 100-unit incremental increase over the inventory might, in the LIFO method, have been valued under *any* one of the following four options:

1. In the order of acquisition (as illustrated)
2. At the most recent purchase cost
3. At an average cost for the year
4. At the "dollar-value" method which converts the incremental increase by means of an index based on the LIFO base year prices.

The IRS will *disallow* a change to the LIFO method for tax purposes *if the financial statements are not prepared using the same LIFO method*.

[¶702.5]   Average Costs

A weighted average is sometimes used to determine the cost of the closing inventory. This method is generally not approved for tax purposes. Under the weighted average method, you determine an average unit cost and then multiply that average unit cost by the number of units in the closing inventory. To get the weighted average, the number of units in each purchase is multiplied by the unit price for that purchase. And the total units purchased and the total of all purchase costs are added to the units and costs in the opening inventory. Then the total of all the costs is divided by the total of all the units. The resulting figure is the average cost per unit.

For example, in the FIFO illustration above, the total number of units involved in the opening inventory plus the four purchases was 3,000. The total cost of the 3,000 units was $34,500. Dividing $34,500 by 3,000, we come up with an average cost per unit of $11.50. Since our closing inventory consisted of 1,100 units, if we priced it at average cost (1,100 x $11.50), the cost of our closing inventory would be $12,650.

Thus, depending on the method of cost used, our closing inventory could have been $11,100, $12,650, or $14,300.

[¶702.6]   The Retail Inventory Method

This method of inventory pricing is sometimes most practical and appropriate. (AC 5121.06). It is used by most all major retail establishments. This inventory valuation has as its initial starting point the retail or selling price of the merchandise rather than the cost. It arrives finally at the cost valuation entirely on the basis of average relationships of retail and cost figures over the period involved.

When merchandise is purchased, the retail selling price is placed on the price tag attached. At inventory time; the inventory is taken at the selling price. The cost is then arrived at by multiplying the inventory by the cost complement percentage which is the difference between the mark-on % and 100%. It is arrived at as follows:

	Cost	Retail	Mark On	Mark-On %	Cost Complement %
Beginning inventory	$ 50,000	$ 75,000	$25,000	33⅓%	66⅔%
Purchases	72,000	120,000	48,000	40 %	60 %
Total to Date	122,000	195,000	73,000	37.4%	62.6%
Markdowns		3,000	3,000		
Total to Date	$122,000	192,000	$70,000	36.5%	63.5%
Sale for period		95,000			
Ending inventory		$ 97,000			

At the end of the period the retail inventory of $97,000 will be reduced to cost by applying the cost complement percent of 63.5. Thus the inventory figure at cost is $61,595.

The gross margin tabulation follows:

Sales		$ 95,000
Opening inventory	$ 50,000	
Purchases	72,000	
	122,000	
Closing inventory	61,595	
Cost of sales		60,405
Gross margin		$ 34,595

[¶702.7]   Lower of Cost or Market

A departure from cost basis of pricing inventory is *required* when the disposal of the goods in the ordinary course of business will be at less than cost. This calls for valuing the inventory at the lower of cost or market. (AC 5121.07)

As used in the phrase, "lower of cost or market," market means current replacement cost (by purchase or reproduction) with the exception that: (1) market is not to exceed the net realizable value which is the estimated selling price in the ordinary course of business less reasonably predictable costs of completion and disposal and (2) market should not be less than net realizable value reduced by an allowance for a normal profit margin. (AC 5121.08) Here, for example are the prices to be used in carrying out the lower of cost or market concept (the price to be used in each case is the one in bold face):

	1	2	3	4	5
(a) Cost	**.82**	.95	.95	**.78**	.94
(b) Market — cost to replace at inventory date	.86	**.90**	.80	.75	.94
(c) Selling price less estimated cost to complete and sell	.92	.92	.92	.92	**.92**
(d) Selling price less estimated cost to complete and sell and normal profit margin	.83	.83	**.83**	.83	.83

In applying the cost or market rule, no loss should be recognized unless the evidence indicates clearly that a loss has been sustained. Where evidence indicates that cost will be recovered with a normal profit margin upon the sale of merchandise, no loss should be recognized even though replacement cost is lower. It should also be remembered that pricing goods at the lower of cost or market is not to be followed literally in all cases. Rather, it is to be applied realistically with regard to the form, content, and composition of the inventory.

There are three ways of applying the lower-of-cost-or-market rule: The rule may be applied on (1) each item in the inventory, (2) the total cost of the major categories in the inventory or (3) the cost of entire inventory.

Each of these methods would produce different results, and all of them are considered acceptable for financial statement purposes. The method used should be the one which most clearly reflects periodic income. (AC 5121.10) So, for example, if there is only one product, rule (3) would seem to have the greatest significance. Where there is more than one major product, rule (2) would seem to be the most useful. Rule (1), application of the lower of cost or market to each item of inventory, is the most common in practice.

When substantial and unusual losses result under the cost or market rule, it is desirable to disclose them separately from normal cost of goods sold. (AC 5121.14)

Any procedure adopted for the treatment of inventory items should be applied consistently and disclosed in the financial statement. Without such consistency there is no basis with which to compare the results of one year with another. Any change in the basis of stating inventories will probably have an important effect on the statements, and full disclosure of such a change should be made. (AC 5121.15)

There are some instances when inventories are properly stated above cost. Exceptions are made in the case of precious metals (e.g., gold and silver), agricultural or mineral products or the packing industry. (AC 5121.16)

Where a company has firm purchase commitments for goods in inventory, losses which are expected to arise from such uncancellable and unhedged commitments for future purchase of inventory should be reflected in the current period in the same way as losses on inventory. (AC 5121.17)

[¶703]   MARKETABLE SECURITIES

The traditional precept of stating assets at historical cost has, in the area of marketable securities, been changed by the AICPA. (AC 5132) Effective for statements ending on or after December 31, 1975, marketable securities are to be shown at the *lower* of historical cost or current market value (statement date). Also, *unrealized* losses (or subsequent gains) are recognized.

There are several ramifications to be considered in accomplishing this periodic write-down (or possibly write-up) of historical cost:

1. If the security portfolios are shown as *current assets,* the write-down offset should be charged to *current income* on the income statement as an unrealized loss.

2. If security portfolios are shown as *noncurrent* assets (or displayed separately), the write-down offset should be charged directly against retained earnings (by-passing the income statement) and shown separately as a component thereof as ''unrealized ....''

3. Entire portfolios should be considered as *one unit* for purpose of determining the overall lump-sum value to be shown. This entails an item-by-item comparison between cost and market price for each share held. If the market price of any one security is *higher* than cost, this unrealized gain is also to be recognized to the extent of offsetting unrealized losses within that *entire* portfolio.

4. For subsequent years, the last-used market price then becomes the basis for matching to subsequent yearend market prices for determination of unrealized gain or loss for the year under examination.

5. When securities are sold (or disposed of), the effect on current income depends upon the current vs. non-current asset classification:

   A. If current asset, the difference between the booked unrealized loss/gain and the actual gain/loss (historical cost to selling price) is the amount to be shown on the income statement.

   B. If non-current asset, the *entire* gain/loss (historical cost to selling price) is shown on the income statement, zeroing out the applicable unrealized equity amount with the difference, if any, going back into retained earnings.

6. When reclassifying portfolios from one category to another (current to non-current or vice-versa), permanent entries should be made to reflect the change as of the date of reclassification.

7. Disclosure is required.

8. *No* restatement of prior year is necessary.

9. *Not* mandatory for not-for-profit organizations.

8

Non-Current Assets

**EQUIPMENT AND PLANT —
ACQUISITIONS AND DISPOSITIONS**

[¶801.1]   Acquisitions

Assets acquired in exchanges are measured at the exchange price, that is, acquisition cost. Money and money claims are measured at their face amount or sometimes at their discount amount. (AC 1027.07 M-1A)

In exchanges in which neither money nor promises to pay money are exchanged, the assets acquired are generally measured at the fair value of the assets given up. However, if the fair value of the assets received is more clearly evident, the assets acquired are measured at that amount. (AC 1027.07 M-1A-1)

Under the above standards, equipment and plant are therefore valued:

1. At cost, if purchased for cash or its equivalent.

2. If an exchange of non-cash property is involved (wholly or partially), preferably at the fair value of the asset acquired, or, if that is not clearly evident, of the asset surrendered. (An example of the latter would be the use of the market price of the company's own stock given in exchange for an asset whose fair value cannot reasonably be determined.)

3. If a group of assets is acquired in one exchange, the total price is allocated to the individual assets based on their relative fair values. Excess paid over fair value is treated as goodwill. In the opposite case, any excess of fair value of the assets acquired over the exchange price is used to reduce the value of the non-current assets (except investment securities) proportionately.

[¶801.2]   Dispositions

Decreases in assets are recorded when assets are disposed of in exchanges. (AC 1027.07 S-1B)

Decreases in assets are measured by the recorded amounts that relate to the assets. The amounts are usually the historical or acquisition costs of the assets (as adjusted for amortization and other charges). (AC 1027.07 M-1B)

The disposing of equipment and plant assets usually results in a gain or loss and is reported as such on the financial statements. In an exchange, for financial purposes, losses should be recognized, but gains should be used to adjust the basis of the new acquisition.

On straight dispositions, depreciation is usually calculated to the date of disposal (approximately) and both the accumulated depreciation and the asset account are then netted to the amount recovered to arrive at the gain or loss, which, for tax purposes, may require special consideration, such as recapture of depreciation and investment tax credit recapture.

[¶801.3]   Other Considerations

Self-constructed assets should not be depreciated while under construction. The cost basis should be determined not only by material and labor expended, but also by apportionment of overhead items, such as depreciation on any fixed assets used in that construction process (which application in turn reduces the depreciation expense for that particular fixed asset).

Detailed sub-ledgers or worksheets should be maintained for all fixed assets, showing date acquired, cost or basis, investment tax credit, estimated life, salvage value (if any), depreciation taken by year, accumulated depreciation and gains or losses on dispositions or trade-in information.

Appraisal write-ups are contrary to generally accepted accounting principles, but when circumstances necessitate write-ups, the offset goes to "appraisal surplus" and becomes part of the equity capital. Depreciation then must be based on the higher, appraisal values.

[¶802]   ACCOUNTING TREATMENT OF INVESTMENT TAX CREDIT

Two methods of accounting for investment tax credit are suggested for use:

1. *The deferred method* — in which the credit is reflected in income over the depreciable useful life of the acquisition. (AC 4094.11) The deferred credit unused may be shown as either deferred income or as a reduction of the asset value. (AC 4094.19)

2. *The flow-through method* — in which the credit is used entirely in the year of acquisition and is reflected as a reduction of the income tax expense (as on the tax return). (AC 4094.17)

A carryback of unused investment tax credit may be set up as a refund claim receivable with the corresponding reduction of tax expense shown separately on the income statement (but *not* as an extraordinary item — AC U4091.108) Carryforwards ordinarily are not recognized until they become allowable and available per the tax rules. (AC 4094.21)

The effect of investment tax credits must also be determined, if relevant, in computing and disclosing timing differences pertaining to deferred taxes. (AC U4091.109)

[¶803]   DEPRECIATION

> If an asset provides benefit for several periods, its cost is allocated to the periods in a systematic and rational manner in the absence of a more direct basis for associating cause and effect. ... This form of expense recognition always involves assumptions about the pattern of 'matching costs to benefits' because neither can be conclusively demonstrated. (AC 1026.23)

Depreciation is the term applied to the allocation of a fixed asset's cost over its beneficial useful life. It is a method of accounting which aims to distribute the cost or other value of tangible or capital assets, less salvage (if any), over the estimated useful life of the asset (which may be a single asset or a group of assets in a single account) in a systematic and rational manner. It is a process of allocation, not of valuation, applied on a consistent basis.

Rather than increasing expenses immediately, depreciation might also *increase* other asset values temporarily, such as in the application of overhead depreciation to inventory or to self-constructed assets.

From a tax viewpoint, the deduction for depreciation (which requires no annual cash outlay) reduces the amount of tax we have to pay. This has the effect of increasing the accumulation of cash at our disposal — i.e., the "cash flow."

Before we can determine the amount of our depreciation deductions, we have to know the following three elements: (1) the method of depreciation that we will use, (2) the amount we can recover (depreciable basis), and (3) the period over which we can take deductions (useful life).

The depreciation is usually applicable only to property which approaches, by wear and tear, business ineffectiveness. "Depreciation" and "repairs and maintenance" are not the same. It is necessary to distinguish between repairs and maintenance costs to keep the asset in operation and repairs which increase the life of the asset. The former are expense deductions in the year incurred; the latter must be amortized over the life of the asset. What repairs increase the life of the asset and what repairs are necessary for its operation is often a matter of judgment.

The determination, or estimation of useful life, may be based on: (1) IRS guidelines, such as in Bulletin F or ADR rules, basically determined by estimated physical durability, longevity or unit-productive capability; (2) statutory law, as in the case of a patent; (3) contract, as in the case of some leases; (4) utility, as in the case of an airport built for military training during war.

Although write-up of fixed assets to reflect appraisal, market or current values is not in accordance with GAAP, where such appreciation has been recorded, depreciation should be based on the written up amounts for financial statement purposes. (AC 4072.01)

[¶803.1]   Methods of depreciation

Following the passage of the Internal Revenue Act of 1954, which permitted the use of the declining-balance and similar accelerated methods of depreciation, the AICPA stated such methods met the requirement of being systematic and rational and, could be used for general accounting purposes, with appropriate disclosure to be made of any change in method when depreciation is a significant factor in determining net income. (AC 4074.06)

The declining-balance and the sum-of-the-year-digits methods of depreciation are appropriate and most used in those cases where the expected productivity or revenue-earning power of an asset is greater during the earlier years of life or when maintenance charges tend to increase during later years.

Accounting methods of depreciating assets may differ from tax methods used. It is the practice of many firms to use straight-line depreciation for accounting purposes and an accelerated one for tax purposes. When this happens, disclosure should be made of the timing differences. (See Appendix for illustration of Methods of Depreciation. Also, see Tax Section.)

[¶804] BASIS

Normally, the basis for depreciation (i.e., the capital amount on which you figure your depreciation deductions) is what you paid for property. To the cost of the property itself is added the cost of transporting the property to your premises, the cost of installation, and other costs as in ¶ 805.

For tax purposes, the basis for depreciation can be different from the basis used for financial reporting purposes. This difference often arises when there are trade-ins involved. According to GAAP, the entity paying any monetary consideration on a trade-in should recognize losses immediately, but, for gains, should adjust the basis of the acquisition to the extent of the gain. (AC 1041.22). For tax purposes, neither gain nor loss is usually recognized, with either serving to adjust the basis of the new acquisition. Hence, there may be a timing difference with respect to the different bases used for depreciation.

[¶804.1] Allocation of Basis

When property is acquired, it is often necessary to allocate basis. Here are the instances when allocation is necessary:

(1) When improved real estate is purchased, there must be an allocation made as to land (nondepreciable) and buildings;

(2) When more than one asset is purchased for a lump sum;

(3) When a group of assets (or possibly a business) is purchased for a single sum involving depreciable and nondepreciable assets.

Improved real estate: Whenever you acquire a piece of improved real property, you have an immediate need for an allocation. Land is not depreciable; and in order to determine your basis for depreciating the building, you have to reduce your overall basis by an amount whch represents a reasonable basis for the land. The usual method of making the allocation is in proportion to the respective fair market values.

If you have in fact paid proportionately more for the building for some special reason and can establish the fact, you can use the higher amount as your depreciation basis. The best way to secure such an advantage, however, is by a specific allocation in the contract which spells it out in detail.

If any of the contents of the building are included in the purchase transaction, you need a further allocation between the structure and the contents. Then the amount allocated to the contents must be further broken down among the various items which are included in the sale.

This latter allocation may require all parties to consider the investment credit and depreciation recapture provisions of the tax law.

Acquisition of more than one asset: The purchase of more than one asset (mixed assets) calls into play the same rules which have been discussed above. The cost of a group of assets which is stated as a single sum must be broken down and allocated among the separate items or groups. This permits the proper allocation of useful lives to different assets or groups and separates depreciable from nondepreciable assets. Again, the possible effects of the investment credit and depreciation recapture provisions must be watched.

[¶804.2]   Acquisition of a Going Business

Generally, in the acquisition of the assets of another entity in a business combination, the fair market value at acquisition is used for the assets acquired. (See Business Combinations later in this text.)

[¶804.3]   Allocation in the Purchase Agreement

An allocation made at the time of the agreement and reduced to writing will ordinarily be accepted for tax purposes where it was bargained for at arm's length and in good faith.

[¶804.4]   Goodwill

> The cost of an intangible asset including goodwill acquired in a business combination may not be written off as a lump sum to capital surplus or to retained earnings nor be reduced to a nominal amount at or immediately after acquisition. (AC 5141.13)

Goodwill, which may be either an amount specified in a contract or determined to be that portion of cost applicable to unidentifiable assets, should be amortized over a period of forty years. (AC 5141.29). However, if a lesser period of benefit can be definitely evidenced, that shorter period may be used.

Amortization of goodwill recorded for accounting purposes creates a permanent difference, since it is generally not allowable as a tax deduction. (AC U4091.050)

[¶805]   ACQUISITION-RELATED COSTS

The following is a listing (though not necessarily all-inclusive) of acquisition-related expenditures which *should be capitalized,* according to the

AICPA publication, *Accounting For Depreciable Assets* (Accounting Research Monograph #1), by Charles W. Lamden, CPA, Ph.D.; Dale L. Gerboth, CPA; and Thomas W. McRae, CPA, 1975, 189 pages: (page 54).

1. Buildings:
   a. Original contract price or cost of construction.
   b. Expenses incurred in remodeling, reconditioning, or altering a purchased building to make it available for the purpose for which it was acquired.
   c. Cost of excavation or grading or filling of land for the specific building.
   d. Expenses incurred for the preparation of plans, specifications, blueprints, and so on.
   e. Cost of building permits.
   f. Payment of noncurrent taxes accrued on the building, at date of purchase if payable by the purchaser.
   g. Architects' and engineers' fees for design and supervision.
   h. Other costs, such as temporary buildings used during the construction period.
2. Machinery, equipment, and furniture and fixtures:
   a. Original contract or invoice cost.
   b. Freight and drayage in, cartage, import duties, handling and storage costs.
   c. Specific in-transit insurance charges.
   d. Sales, use, and other taxes imposed on the purchase.
   e. Costs of preparation of foundations and other costs in connection with making a proper *situs* for the asset.
   f. Installation charges.
   g. Charges for testing and preparation for use.
   h. Costs for reconditioning used equipment when purchased.

And, from the same source above, the following is a list of acquisition-related expenditures which *should not* be capitalized (pages 54 and 55):

1. Expenditures for facilities and the renovation of buildings required in connection with specific contracts, which would not have been incurred except for such contracts and which are therefore specifically included in contract costs.
2. Repair of existing equipment, including replacement of component parts, reconstruction, or alteration except as outlined above.
3. Expenditures incurred in demolishing or dismantling equipment, including those related to the replacement of units or systems and the removal of parts in connection with a rebuilding or replacement project.
4. Expenditures incurred in connection with the rearrangement, transfer or moving of equipment within a plant or from one location to another.
5. Special test equipment, fixtures, cutting tools, shaping tools, and boring tools having a comparatively short term of effective life.
6. Extraordinary costs incidental to the erection of a building, such as those due to strike, flood, fire, or other casualty (although unanticipated ex-

penditures, such as rock blasting, piling, or relocation of the channel of an underground stream, *should* be capitalized).

7. Cost of abandoned construction.

8. Cost incurred for bonus payments to contractors, temporary construction because of shortages of material for permanent construction, and so on, for the purpose of hastening completion. Extra payments, such as premium time to take advantage of management operating decisions, should be expensed.

The guiding principle is that "all incidental payments necessary to put the asset in condition and location for use" should be capitalized.

[¶806]   SALVAGE VALUE

Before applying depreciation rates to basis to determine how much we can deduct, we first have to consider salvage.

Salvage value is the amount which it is estimated will be realized upon sale or other disposition of an asset when it is no longer useful in your trade or business or in the production of your income and is to be retired.

What the salvage value will be depends on the asset and the way you handle such an asset. If it is your policy to dispose of assets while they are still in good shape, your salvage value will be a relatively large proportion of your basis. On the other hand, you may customarily use assets until their inherent useful life has been substantially exhausted, and the salvage value may represent no more than junk value. Salvage has been held to be what you reasonably expect to sell the asset for at the time you normally dispose of it.

Removal costs, if material are usually added to the salvage value of the old unit on disposition. Sometimes, a portion of the removal cost is assigned to the new replacement unit. The choice is arbitrary and acceptable.

In actual practice, contrary to both financial and taxing requirements, salvage value is generally ignored because of immateriality rather than strict adherence to theoretical requirements.

[¶807]   LEASES

In November, 1976, the FASB issued a new Statement (#13), *Accounting for Leases,* which supersedes all prior opinions. The new Statement encompasses the requirements for *both lessor and lessee,* and it endeavors to insure the basic theme that the treatment of a lease as a *purchase* by one party (capitalization by the lessee) is contra-treated as a *sale* by the other party (reduction of assets by the lessor).

Section AC 4053 of the codified standards, dated November 1976, covers and illustrates all the new requirements (AC 4053.001 —.123).

In outline form, these standards now require:

THE CRITERIA

[¶807.1]   For Lessees (who pay the rentals):

A lease *must be capitalized* and shown as an *asset* with a contra liability on the balance sheet, when *only one* of these four criteria exists:

.007 A. Ownership is transferred to the lessee (in the lease) by the end of the lease term; or

.007 B. A bargain price option to buy the property is in the lease; or

.007 C. The lease term is 75% or more of the estimated economic life of the property; or

.007 D. The present value of the rentals (as defined) is 90% or more of the fair value of the leased property (minus investment tax credit if retained by the lessor).

(If the lease *does not* meet any one of the above four criteria, it is to be treated as an *operating lease* and *not* as an asset acquisition.)

[¶807.2]   For Lessors (who receive the rentals):

The lease must be treated as a *sale* (if sales profit is involved) or as a direct-financing lease (when no sales profit involved):

.008 If the lease meets *any one* of the four criteria stated above (for the lessee) *plus both* of the following *additional* criteria:

.008 A. Collectibility of the minimum lease payments is reasonably predicted; *and*

.008 B. No important uncertainties surround the amount of unreimbursable costs yet to be incurred by the lessor under the lease.

(If the lease *does not* meet the above criteria, it is to be treated as an *operating lease,* and *not* as a sale or direct-financing lease.)

[¶807.3]   Disclosure Requirements Are:

FOR THE LESSEE:

.016 A. Capitalized lease assets (gross amount — major classes by nature or function)

B. Future minimum lease payments for each of the five succeeding years:
   1. Separately for capital leases
   2. In total for operating leases

C. Rental expense for each income statement period presented showing minimal, contingent and sublease rentals

    D. A general description of the leasing arrangements including rental contingencies, options and escalations, and any restrictions imposed by the lease arrangements.

FOR THE LESSOR:

.023 A. Future minimum lease payments to be received:
1. Separately for sales-type leases
2. Separately for direct-financing leases
3. Separately for operating leases

    B. Other items such as, estimated residual values and unearned income in sales-type and direct-financing leases

    C. Contingent rentals in income for each period

    D. Also for operating leases — the cost (or carrying amount) of property on lease or held for leasing (major classes by nature or function) and the accumulated depreciation

    E. A general description of the lessor's leasing arrangements.

[¶807.4]   Classification of Leases

FROM LESSEE STANDPOINT:

.006A A CAPITAL LEASE is defined as a lease meeting one or more of the criteria in .007.

AN OPERATING LEASE is all other leases.

FROM LESSOR STANDPOINT:

.006B A SALES-TYPE LEASE gives rise to a (manufacturing, dealer, or not a dealer) profit or loss, based on fair value over cost (or carrying amount) at the lease inception.

A DIRECT-FINANCING LEASE — leases (other than leveraged leases) which *do not* give rise to a profit or loss, with the fair value being the cost (or carrying amount) at lease inception.

OPERATING LEASE — all other leases.

[¶807.5]   Recording Aspects — Lessee

CAPITAL LEASES:

.010 Record as an asset *and* an obligation at the *present value* of the lease payments (up to, but not exceeding fair value)

.011 Asset amortization:

    A. If the lease transfers ownership by the end of the lease or contains a bargain purchase option, follow lessee's *normal* depreciation policy over *useful life* of the asset

    B. Otherwise, use the *term of the lease,* following lessee's normal depreciation policy

.012 Allocate lease payments to:

A. Reduction of the obligation, *and*

B. Interest expense (so as to produce a constant periodic rate of interest on the remaining obligation).

OPERATING LEASES:

.015 Normally, rentals are expensed as they become payable, unless a different basis of systematic and rational apportionment is more representative of derived benefits.

[¶807.6] Recording Aspects — Lessor

SALES-TYPE LEASES:

.017 A. Minimum lease payments *plus* unguaranteed residual values are calculated as GROSS INVESTMENT in the lease

B. The gross investment (as determined above) *minus* the *present values of that same gross investment* is recorded as UNEARNED INCOME

1. The net investment is the gross investment minus the unearned income

2. The unearned income is amortized to income over the lease-term to produce a constant rate

C. The SALES PRICE is the present value of the minimum lease payments — and is credited to income

The COST (or carrying amount) of the leased property (asset value on the books) — *plus* any initial direct costs and *minus* the present value of any unguaranteed residual values — is charged against income.

DIRECT-FINANCING LEASES

.018 A. GROSS INVESTMENT is the minimum lease payments plus unguaranteed residual value

B. UNEARNED INCOME is the difference between above and the cost (or carrying amount) of the leased property

1. The net investment is the gross investment minus the unearned income

2. The unearned income is amortized to income over the lease term to produce a constant rate

3. Initial direct costs are charged to income as incurred and offset by an exact portion pulled from the unearned income above

FOR BOTH TYPES:

The residual value must be reviewed annually and adjusted to income if the change is not temporary.

Renewals and residual guarantees or penalties require additional considerations under the standards.

Display of asset on the balance sheet — follow the same considerations as for the other assets classified as current or noncurrent assets in that firm's classified balance sheet.

OPERATING LEASES:

.019 A. The leased property (asset) is displayed with or near property, plant or equipment on the balance sheet at its cost or carrying investment value

B. Depreciation is taken according to the lessor's normal depreciation policy and the accumulated depreciation is deducted from the investment value

Rent is ordinarily reported as income over the lease-term as receivable unless a different benefit-diminishing basis is more representative of the time pattern

C. Initial direct costs are deferred and allocated over the least-term, proportionate to the recognition of rentals.

[¶808]   **OTHER LEASES**

LEASES INVOLVING REAL ESTATE:

.024 Four categories:

1. Involving land only
2. Involving land and building
3. Involving equipment as well as real estate
4. Involving only part of a building

[¶808.1]   **Land Only:**

.025 *For Lessee:*

A. As a CAPITAL LEASE if *either* .007A or .007B is met; otherwise treat as an OPERATING LEASE.

For Lessor:

B. As SALES-TYPE or DIRECT-FINANCING LEASE whichever is appropriate; if .008 is fully met *as well as either* .007A or .007B; otherwise, treat as an OPERATING LEASE.

Criteria .007C and .007D *do not* apply to land leases.

[¶808.2]   Land and Building(s):

.026 A. If the lease meets *either* .007A or .007B:

> *Lessee* — capitalizes land and building separately using present value of minimum lease payments. Building would be amortized over its life. Land is not amortized.

> *Lessor* — treats as one unit as either a sales-type or a direct-financing lease if .008 is also *met in full*

> If .008 is not met, treat as an operating lease.

.026 B. If the lease *does not meet* .007A or .007B, the rules for determination (for both lessor and lessee) are more complex, hinging on fair value, lease term and present value. Recourse should be made to .026 of the full lease standards.

[¶808.3]   Equipment as well as Real Estate:

.027 Estimate (by the most appropriate method) the portion of the lease payments applicable to the equipment and apply the criteria of .007 and .008 separately to the equipment (for both lessee and lessor respectively).

[¶808.4]   Part of A Building:

.028 A. If both the cost and the fair value can be objectively determined for that part of the larger whole, both lessor and lessee are guided by the rules for .026A and .026B above — (Land and Buildings)

.028 B. If both cost and fair value *can not* be objectively determined:

> *Lessee* — treats lease per .007C *only*, using the estimated life of the entire building, and if the criteria is met, capitalizes and amortizes over the term of the lease

> *Lessor* — treats as an operating lease.

When the economic life of the facility is indeterminate (such as airport facilities or terminal space) or when fair value is inapplicable as in governmental properties, such leases should be treated as *operating leases*.

[¶808.5]   Leases Between Related Parties:

.029 Except for below, these leases follow the same criteria of .007 and .008, with the nature and extent being disclosed.

Exceptions:

.030 In consolidating or using the equity method, profits or losses between related parties should be accounted for under the rules used for those methods

.031 When a subsidiary's *principal* business is leasing to the parent (or affiliates), consolidation *must* be used. The equity method cannot be used.

[¶808.6]   Sales and Leasebacks:

This transaction involves the sale of property by the owner and the lease of that same property back to the same seller.

.033 SELLER-LESSEE:

When the lease meets *one* of the criteria in .007, the seller-lessee is to treat it as a capital lease. When the lease *does not* meet any of the criteria under .007, it is treated as an operating lease, and profit or loss is prorated over the expected use-time of the asset in proportion to the rental payments. Profit or loss on the *sale* is deferred and amortized in proportion to the amortization of the leased *asset*.

.034 PURCHASER-LESSOR:

A lease meeting the criteria of .007 *and* .008 is recorded as a *purchase* and a *direct-financing lease*.

A lease not meeting the criteria is treated as a *purchase* and an *operating lease*.

[¶808.7]   Leveraged Leases:

.042 Definition:

A leveraged lease is one having *all* the following characteristics:

A. It involves at least three parties: A lessee, a long-term creditor and a lessor (called the "equity participant"); *and*

B. The amount of financing provided by the long-term creditor is sufficient to provide the lessor with substantial "leverage" and it is *nonrecourse* as to the general credit of the lessor (even if there is recourse to the specific property and its unremitted balance of rentals); and

C. The lessor's net investment declines during the early years and rises in later years of the lease-life; and

D. Even though *excluded* from provision .006B ("Direct-Financing Leases"), the lease meets the definition therein. Leases meeting the definition of a "sales-type lease" under .006B are accounted for as described in .017.

Note that *all* of the above are needed to meet the definition of a "leveraged lease."

.041 *Lessee* — treats leveraged leases the same as non-leveraged leases.

Lessor — more intricate. Consult the full standards — .043 through .047.

[¶808.8]   Other Lease Data:

Participation by Third Parties — see .020 through .022 of the full standards.

Changes in provisions, renewals or extensions — see .014 of the full standards.

Definitions:
> Related parties — see .005a of full standards. Implicit interest rate — see .005k of full standards.

Subleases and substituted leases — (under either original or new agreements), see .035 through .040 of full standards.

[¶809]   EFFECTIVE DATE AND TRANSITION

For all lease transactions and agreement revisions entered into on or after January 1, 1977:

[¶809.1]   Mandatory Date

Retroactive application and restatement of leases entered into *prior* to Jan. 1, 1977, is *not* mandatory now, but *will be mandatory* after *Dec. 31, 1980*. However, the Statement encourages retroactive application and restatement (for all periods presented), but does not mandate it until 1981. (See next)

[¶809.2]   Interim Provisions

If retroactive application was *not* made for those lease commitments at Dec. 31, 1976, the following provisions *apply until retroactive restatement is made:*

A. For leases which are treated as OPERATING LEASES under the *prior* standards, but which *would* meet the new standard for *"Capital Leases,"* disclose for the years ending Dec. 31, 1977 and after: (until Dec. 31, 1980)

1. The balance sheet amounts which would be determinable under the new standards, *and*

2. The effect on net income had the new standards been applied.

B. For those leases treated as OPERATING LEASES under the prior standards, but which *would* meet the new standard for *"Direct-Financing"* or *"Sales-Type Leases,"* disclose for the years ending Dec. 31, 1977 and after (until Dec. 31, 1980) the effect which the new standards would (upon application) have on:

1. The change in net worth, *and*

2. The effect on net income.

C. For leveraged leases, treated in a manner other than prescribed in the new standards, disclose for years ending Dec. 31, 1977 and after (until Dec. 31, 1980) the effect which the new standard on application would have on:

   1. Net changes in total assets and in total liabilities, *and*

   2. Net income.

[¶809.3]   Rules for Restatement:

1. Include the effects of leases in existence during periods covered by the financial statements

2. Balance sheets as of Dec. 31, 1976, and income statements for periods beginning *after* Dec. 31, 1976, financial summaries and other data should be restated to conform with the new standards

3. All prior periods presented for comparative purposes should be restated where practicable per the new standards

4. For the earliest period *restated* (not *presented),* the cumulative effect on the beginning retained earnings should be determined and shown in the determination of net income for that entire earliest period restated. Disclose the amount and explain, if applicable, why it was impractical to restate any prior periods presented.

[¶810]   LEASEHOLD IMPROVEMENTS

Lease agreements frequently provide that the lessee is to pay the costs of any alternations or improvements of the leased premises. At the end of the lease period, these alterations or improvements become the property of the lessor. The only economic benefit to the lessee is the right to use these improvements during the lease period. Therefore, such improvements should be amortized over the life of the lease or the useful life of the improvements, whichever is shorter (regardless of whether the lease itself is treated as an asset acquisition or as a lease).

[¶811]   INTANGIBLE ASSETS

Intangible assets are categorized into two classes: (AC 5141.01)

1. Identifiable intangible assets — those having specific identity and usually a known limited life. The limitation may be a legal regulation, a contractual agreement or the nature of the intangible itself; for example, a patent, copyright, franchise, trademark and the like.

2. Unidentifiable intangible assets — those having no specific identity and an unknown life. Goodwill is the most notable example.

Identifiable intangible assets should be recorded at their cost. If the asset is acquired in a transaction other than a purchase for cash, it is to be valued at its fair value or the fair value of the consideration given, whichever is more definitely determinable. If several identifiable intangible assets are acquired as a group, a separate cost should be established for each intangible asset. The cost or assigned basis should be amortized by systematic charges to income over the expected period of economic benefit usually set by law or by contract. If it becomes apparent that the period of economic benefit will be shorter or longer than that originally used, there should be an appropriate decrease or increase in annual amortization charges.

The costs of *unidentifiable* intangible assets such as goodwill are normally amortized on a straight-line basis over a period not exceeding forty years. (AC 5151.29). Arbitrary shorter periods are not to be used unless specific factors pinpoint a shorter life.

Unidentifiable intangible assets are usually measured as the excess paid over the identifiable assets.

The cost of an intangible asset, including goodwill acquired in a business combination should not be written off to income in the period of acquisition nor charged as a lump sum to capital surplus or to retained earnings, nor be reduced to a nominal amount at or immediately after acquisition. (AC 5141.21 & .28)

The question of whether other costs of internally developed identifiable intangible assets are to be capitalized or expensed is not delineated by the Standards Board. Questions have arisen regarding the capitalization of the cost of a large initial advertising campaign for a new product or capitalizing the cost of training new employees. The interpretation is that there is no encouragement to capitalize these costs under existing standards. (AC U 5141.002)

[¶812]   RESEARCH AND DEVELOPMENT COSTS (AND PATENTS)

Under the latest standards of financial accounting and reporting for research and development costs adopted in October, 1974, (AC 4211.01—.63) and the subsequent extensions of that section to cover applicability to business combinations accounted for by the "purchase" method (AC 4211.1.01—1.07) and applicability to computer software (AC 4211.3.01—3.10), research and development costs as defined and illustrated in AC 4211 are to be *charged as expense when incurred.* (Note that this is diametrically opposed to the old system of deferral and amortization.)

> *Research* is planned search or critical investigation aimed at discovery of new knowledge with the hope that such knowledge will be useful in developing a new product or service or a new process or technique or in bringing about a significant improvement to an existing product or process. (AC 4211.08a)

> *Development* is the translation of research findings or other knowledge into a plan or design for a new product or process or for a significant

improvement to an existing product or process whether intended for sale or use. It includes the conceptual formulation, design and testing of product alternatives, construction of prototypes, and operation of pilot plants. It does not include routine or periodic alterations to existing products, production lines, manufacturing processes, and other on-going operations even though those alterations may represent improvements and it does not include market research or market testing activities. (AC 4211.08b).

Typical activities which would be included in research and development costs (excluding those done for others under contract) are: (AC 4211.09)

Laboratory research aimed at finding new knowledge

Searching for applications of findings

Concepts-forming and design of new product or processes

Testing of above

Modifications of above

Design, construction and testing of prototypes

Design of new tools, dies, etc, for new technology

Pilot plant posts not useful for commercial production

Engineering activity to the point of manufacture

Certain activities, however, are *excluded* from the definition of research and development and are either expensed or amortized depending upon the apparent periods benefitted: (AC 4211.10)

1. Engineering costs during early commercial production.
2. Quality costs during commercial production.
3. Break-down trouble-shooting costs during production.
4. Routine efforts to improve the product.
5. Adapting to a customer's requirement, if ordinary.
6. Existing product change-costs for seasonal reasons.
7. Routine designing of tools and dies, etc.
8. Costs of start-up facilities other than pilot plant or those specifically designed only for research and development work.
9. Legal work involved in patent applications or litigation, and the sale or licensing of patents.

In the following list, the *italicized* portions represent those elements of research and development costs and expenditures which should be *capitalized* and not expensed immediately. The non-italicized items are those which should be expensed immediately (AC 4211.11)

1. MATERIALS, EQUIPMENT AND FACILITIES: *The costs of materials (whether from the enterprise's normal inventory or acquired specially for research and development activities) and equipment or facilities that are acquired or constructed for research and development activities and that have alternative future uses (in research and development projects or otherwise) shall be capitalized as tangible assets when acquired or constructed.* The cost of such materials consumed in research and development activities and the depreciation of such equipment or facilities used in those activities

are research and development costs. However, the costs of materials, equipment, or facilities that are acquired or constructed for a particular research and development project and that have no alternative future uses (in other research and development projects or otherwise) and therefore no separate economic values are research and development costs at the time the costs are incurred.

2. PERSONNEL: Salaries and wages and other related costs of personnel engaged in research and development activities shall be included in research and development costs.

3. INTANGIBLES PURCHASED FROM OTHERS: *The costs of intangibles that are purchased from others for use in research and development activities and that have alternative future uses (in research and development projects or otherwise) shall be capitalized and amortized as intangible assets in accordance with Section 5141.* The amortization of those intangible assets used in research and development activities is a research and development cost. However, the costs of intangibles that are purchased from others for a particular research and development project and that have no alternative future uses (in other research and development projects or otherwise) and therefore no separate economic values are research and development costs at the time the costs are incurred.

4. CONTRACT SERVICES: The costs of services performed by others in connection with the research and development activities of an enterprise, including research and development conducted by others in behalf of the enterprise, shall be included in research and development costs.

5. INDIRECT COSTS: Research and development costs shall include a reasonable allocation of indirect costs. However, general and administrative costs that are not clearly related to research and development activities shall not be included as research and development costs.

[¶812.1] Writing Off a Patent

A patent has a legal life of 17 years. However, most companies write off patents in much shorter periods since their useful lives are generally shorter than 17 years. Reasons for writing off patents in less than 17 years are as follows:

(1) The patent could have been purchased many years after issuance.

(2) The patent is for a current-fad-type item and sales can be expected to last for only a year or two.

(3) A newer patented item appears on the market which puts an end to the economic usefulness of the patent.

Some companies buy a patent just to protect an older patent they have from becoming outmoded. The cost of the new patent purchase should be written off over the remaining life of the old patent.

[¶812.2] Copyrights

A copyright will now have a legal life of 50 years after author's death, with those prior to December 31, 1977, renewable for 47 years. However, here, as in the case of patents, copyright costs are usually written off in a much shorter period since the economic usefulness of a copyright usually is only a few years. Since the cost of obtaining a copyright usually is nominal (unlike a patent), the amount is usually not amortized but is written off immediately to income. Publisher-held copyrights will now last 75 years, unless reassigned to the author.

[¶812.3]   Franchises

Franchises are identifiable intangibles and, by contract, have a certain number of years to run. They should be written off over that contractual period. Sometimes, a franchise can be terminated by the will of the licensor. In such case, an immediate write-off may be justified.

[¶812.4]   Trademarks

A trademark is an identifiable intangible, usually with an indeterminable life and should, therefore, be written off over forty years unless a shorter life can be determined with reasonable certainty.

In the same category are trade names, brand names, secret formulae and processes, designs, and the right to use certain labels.

[¶813]   GOODWILL

In acquiring a business in an exchange or combination, each individual asset is measured at its fair value. The excess exchange price over those values assigned to individual assets is termed and recorded as 'goodwill.' (AC 1027.07 M-1A3)

Goodwill is an unidentifiable intangible asset. It has no permanent existence (such as land). It has no definite, measurable life. It has neither limited nor unlimited usefulness. Thus, delaying write-off until a loss is certain may cause a dilemma, as would an early write-off. Therefore, the AICPA, in recognition of this problem, has, for conformity, suggested the arbitrary period of write-off at forty years. In addition, the straight-line method of amortization should be used in expensing goodwill.

The amortization of goodwill is generally not deductible for tax purposes. Since the expensing of goodwill creates a lower net income for financial statement purposes than the taxable income for tax purposes, there arises a *permanent* difference as opposed to a timing difference. (AC U-4091.050)

[¶813.1]   Establishing the Goodwill Factor

Goodwill is generally based upon the assumption that earnings will continue, but not forever. The good name and reputation of the sellers will continue to influence the business for a while in the hands of the new owners. It is this lingering influence which is the nature of goodwill. It may be the result of any of, or a combination of, the following:

1. A prized location;
2. Exceptional operating efficiency;
3. Customer and personnel relationships which are unusually satisfactory;
4. Special expertise in business techniques;
5. An unusual product with customer acceptance.

In negotiation to buy or sell a business, one of the problems is always the setting of a mutually satisfactory price on the value of goodwill — over and above the net fair value of the identifiable assets (minus liabilities).

Here are six varied methods of computing goodwill:

Assumed facts for computing the goodwill value; net assets, $1,000,000; profits of last 5 years: $190,000, $195,000, $190,000, $215,000, $210,000; total $1,000,000; average, $200,000

(1) *Years' purchase of past annual profits*
Profits of second preceding year	$ 215,000
Profits of first preceding year	210,000
Total and price to be paid for goodwill	$ 425,000

(2) *Years' purchase of average past profits*
Average profits of last 5 years (as stated above)	$ 200,000
Multiply by number of years of purchase	2
Goodwill	$ 400,000

(3) *Years' purchase of excess profits*

Year Preceding Sale	Profits	12½% of Net Assets	Excess
Third	$190,000	$125,000	$ 65,000
Second	215,000	125,000	90,000
First	210,000	125,000	85,000
Total Payment for Goodwill			$ 240,000

(4) *Years' purchase of average excess profits*
Average profits of past 5 years	$ 200,000
Deduct 12½% of $1,000,000	125,000
Excess	75,000
Multiply by number of years of purchase	3
Goodwill	$ 225,000

(5) *Capitalized profits, minus net assets*
Capitalized value of average net profits, or total value of business:
$200,000 ÷ 12½%	$1,600,000
Deduct agreed value of net assets other than goodwill	1,000,000
Goodwill	$ 600,000

(6) *Excess profits capitalized*
Average profits of past 5 years	$ 200,000

Deduct profits regarded as applicable to net assets acquired — 12½% of $1,000,000	125,000
Remaining profits, regarded as indicative of goodwill	$ 75,000
Goodwill = $75,000 ÷ 25%	$ 300,000

[¶814]   ORGANIZATION EXPENSES

When a corporation is created, there are numerous expenses involved in its creation. Among these are legal fees, stock certificate costs, underwriters' fees, corporation fees, commissions, promotion expenses, etc.

Tax law, which permits organization expenses to be written off over a minimum five-year period, is the factor which causes many corporations to write organization costs off over that period, though the standards permit immediate write-off.

[¶815]   SECRET FORMULAS AND PROCESSES

A formula or process known only to a specific producer may be a valuable asset even though there is no patent involved. Such property usually has economic benefit which continues indefinitely instead of for a limited period.

In those instances in which the life is indeterminate, the forty-year period should be used, amortizing on a straight-line basis, as long as benefit continues and cannot be reasonably pinpointed or rejected.

[¶816]   RETAIL LAND SALES*

For periods ending on and after Dec. 31, 1972, new requirements for financial reporting of retail land sales were promulgated by the Committee on Land Development Companies of the AICPA. Under the guides (which apply to retail lot sales on a volume basis with down payments smaller than those involved in casual sales), payments made on such sales are treated as deposits and not recognized as sales under either the accrual method or the installment method until they equal at least 10% of the contract price, the cancellation period has expired, and promised performance becomes predictable.

[¶816.1]   Accrual Method

The accrual method is required on a project-by-project basis if *all* the following conditions are met:

(1) The properties clearly will be useful for residential or recreational purposes without legal restriction when the payment period is completed.

---

*Reference for this topic: *Accounting for Retail Land Sales* (An AICPA Industry Accounting Guide), AICPA 1973, 41 pages.

(2) The project's planned improvements must have progressed beyond preliminary stages and there is evidence that the work will be completed according to plan.

(3) The receivable cannot be subordinated to new loans on the property, except for construction purposes and collection experience on such contracts is the same as on those not subordinated.

(4) Collection experience of the project indicates that collectibility of receivable balances is reasonably predictable and that 90% of the contracts in force six months after sales are recorded will be collected in full.

All other contracts must be accounted for by the installment method under which revenue is recognized as payments are received, and related selling costs may be deferred.

There are three principal aspects with respect to reporting land sales. They are: (1) timing of revenue, (2) deferral of revenue for future performance obligations, and (3) measurement of revenue. The earlier practice was to count as income the full contract price at the time the contract was executed, even though a buyer made only a small down payment and the completion of the contract was uncertain.

For example, a buyer entered a contract with a land development company for the purchase of a $20,000 homesite. He made a $500 down payment and promised to pay the balance before completion. Under prior rules, the land development company would have counted the entire $20,000 as income, even though a large percentage of such contracts might never have reached completion.

[¶816.2]   Timing of Revenue

Under the present rules, the development company doesn't count the $20,000 as income unless there is a reasonable probability of completion and it collects a down payment of at least 10%.

Each company looks to its own experience to provide a reasonable prediction of the percentage of all the contracts that will be completed.

The number of sales past experience indicates will not be completed should be deducted from the overall gross sales figure and provided for in an allowance for contract cancellations. When a contract is canceled, the receivable from the contract is charged to the allowance account.

The rules also address themselves to determining when a contract cancellation has occurred. According to the guidelines, a contract is considered canceled if less than 25% of the contract price has been paid and the buyer is in default for 90 days or more. If more than 25% but less than 50% of the contract price has been paid, the default period is 120 days; more than 50%, the default period is 150 days.

Where a company's collection experience cannot provide a reasonable prediction of completions, the installment method must be used, not the accrual method. Where refund period policies exist, no portion of the deposit receipts should be reported until the refund period has passed.

[¶816.3] Deferral of Revenue for Future Performance Obligations

Where there are significant future-performance requirements, the earning process is incomplete. Therefore, the portion of the income representing reasonable compensation for the improvement effort and risk must be deferred until the work is performed. The amount deferred is in the ratio of revenue that the unexpended costs bear to the total costs expected to be incurred.

[¶816.4] Measurement of Revenue

Here, we deal with the specific value that should be ascribed to long-term receivables where the interest rate is less than the prevailing rate for an obligation with similar terms, security, and risk.

The credit ratings of retail land purchasers generally approximate those of users of retail consumer installment credit provided by commercial banks and established retail organizations. Accordingly, the effective annual yield on the net investment in land contract receivables should not be less than the minimum annual rate charged to installment borrowers by commercial banks and established retail organizations.

9

Current Liabilities

[¶901]

Current liabilities include the following:

(1) Obligations whose liquidation is reasonably expected to require the use of existing current assets or the creation of other current liabilities. (AC 1027.25 R-9A)

(2) Obligations for items such as payables incurred in the acquisition of material and supplies which are to be used in the production of goods or in providing services which are offered for sale. (AC 2031.07)

(3) Collections received in advance pertaining to the delivery of goods or the performance of services which will be liquidated in the ordinary course of business by delivery of such goods or services. But note that advances received which represent long-term deferments are not to be shown as current liabilites. An example of this would be a long-term warranty or the advance receipt by a lessor of rentals for the final period of a ten-year lease as a condition to the execution of the lease. (AC 2031.07 with footnote 2)

(4) Debts which arise from operations directly relating to the operating cycle. Examples here include accruals for wages, salaries, commissions, rentals, royalties, and income and other taxes; short-term debts which are expected to be liquidated within a relatively short period of time, usually one year; short-term debt arising from acquisition of capital assets; the current portion of a serial note; amounts required to be expended within one year under a sinking fund; loans accompanied by a pledge of a life insurance policy which by its terms is to be repaid within one year. Where the intent in repaying a loan on life insurance is that it will be paid from the proceeds of the policy received upon maturity or cancellation, such an obligation should not be included as a current liability. (AC 2031.07 with footnote 3)

(5) Amounts which are expected to be required to cover expenditures within the year for known obligations, the amount of which can only approximately be determined. An example is a provision for accruing bonus payments.

When an amount is expected to be required to be paid to persons unknown (for example, in connection with a guarantee of products sold), a reasonable amount should be included as a current liability.

It does not include debts to be liquidated by funds accumulated in non-current assets, or long-term obligations incurred to provide working capital for long periods. A contractual obligation falling due within a one-year period which is expected to be refinanced on a long-term basis should also be excluded from current liabilities. (AC 2033.10) Bonds maturing within a one-year period which are to be refinanced by the issuance of new bonds should not therefore be included as current liabilities. Doing so would give a wrong impression of the company's working capital. The bonds should remain among long-term liabilities, with a footnote indicating the maturity date and the contemplated refinancing.

(6) Accounts payable for goods purchased before the end of the accounting period and for which title has passed but which have not been received.

(7) Liabilities for services rendered to your company before the end of the period but not yet billed.

(8) Dividends which have been declared but have not yet been paid.

(9) Liabilities to be liquidated in merchandise arising from the issuance of due bills, merchandise coupon books, and gift certificates.

10

Long-Term Debt

[¶1001]   **BOND PREMIUM OR DISCOUNT**

Liabilities are measured at amounts established in exchanges, usually the amounts to be paid, sometimes discounted. Conceptually, a liability is measured at the amount of cash to be paid discounted to the time the liability is incurred ... Bonds and other long-term liabilities are in effect measured at the discounted amount of the future cash payments for interest and principal. (AC 1027.07 M-1C)

The difference between the face amount of the liability to be paid in the future and the actual net proceeds received in the present for incurring of this debt is amortized over the period to the maturity due-date. When this amount of periodic calculated interest is combined with the nominal face-amount of interest actually paid to debt-holders, the difference is amortized, giving a level, effective rate, and it is called the ''interest'' method of amortization and is an acceptable method to be used. (AC 5361.01 & .02))

Statement presentation: Unamortized discount or premium or debentures or other long-term debt should be shown on the balance sheet as a direct deduction or addition to the face value. It should *not* be shown as a deferred item. The amortized portion of either premium or discount should be shown as interest on the income statement. Issue costs should be treated as deferred charges. (AC 4111.15)

[¶1002]   **EARLY EXTINGUISHMENT OF DEBT**

Bonds and other long-term obligations often contain provisions giving the bond issuer an option to retire the bonds before their maturity date. This option is often exercised in connection with the issuance of new bonds at favorable rates (a refunding).

Usually, the amount paid for early extinguishment will be different from the face amount due and also different from the ''net carrying value'' of the debt.

The "net carrying value" is the sum due at maturity plus or minus the remaining unamortized premium or discount (and cost of issuance). (AC 5362.03b)

On January 1, 1973, standards were adopted for the treatment of this early extinguishment of debt:

1. The difference between the reacquisition price and the *net carrying amount* of the debt (face value plus/minus unamortized items) should be recognized currently *in income* as gain or loss and shown as a separate item, and, if material, shown as an *extraordinary item,* net of related income tax effect. (AC 5362.20 and AC 2013.08)

2. Disclosure of pertinent details should be made.

3. Gains or losses should not be amortized to future periods. (AC 5362.20)

4. The extinguishment of *convertible* debt before maturity should be handled in the same manner. (AC 5362.21)

5. The criteria of "unusual nature" and "infrequency of occurrence" do *not* apply here for the classification of the early extinguishment of debt as extraordinary. (AC 2013.10) The determining factor for classification is *"materiality."*

These existing standards, in effect, prohibit the old practice of applying gains or losses on debt refunded to any new issues of similar obligations.

11

Equity

[¶1101]

"Stockholders' equity" is the most commonly used term to describe the section of the balance sheet encompassing the corporation's capital and retained earnings. Other terms used are "net worth" or "capital and surplus."

Stockholders' equity consists of three broad source classifications:

1. Investments made by owners:
   Capital Stock (Common and/or Preferred) — at par value (legal value) or stated amount (AC 1027.25)
   Additional Paid-In Capital — "In Excess of Par," "Capital Surplus," etc.

2. Income (loss) generated by operations:
   Retained Earnings — the accumulated undistributed annual profits (losses), after taxes and dividends

3. Appraisal Capital — resulting from the revaluation of assets over historical cost (*not* in conformity with GAAP)

Changes in shareholders' equity, primarily in retained earnings, are caused by:

1. Periodic net income (loss) after taxes
2. Dividends declared
3. Prior period adjustments of retained earnings
4. Contingency reserves (appropriations of retained earnings)
5. Recapitalizations:
   A. Stock dividends and split-ups
   B. Changing par or stated value
   C. Reducing capital
   D. Quasi-reorganizations
   E. Stock reclassifications
   F. Substituting debt for stock
6. Treasury stock dealings
7. Business combinations
8. Certain unrealized gains and losses
9. Donations

93

[¶1102]   CAPITAL STOCK

[¶1102.1]   Common Stock

The common stockholders are the residual owners of the corporation; that is, they own whatever is left after all preceding claims are paid off. By definition (AC 2011 D.04), common stock is "a stock which is subordinate to all other stocks of the issuer."

When a corporation has a single class of stock, it is often called "capital stock" instead of "common stock." The three aspects of stock ownership are dividends, claim against assets on liquidation, and share in management. As to these aspects of ownership, common stockholders have the following rights: As to dividends, common stockholders have no fixed rights but, on the other hand, are limited to no maximum payment; their claim against the assets of the corporation on liquidation is last in the order of priority, following all creditors and all other equity interests. The common stockholders, by statute, must have a voice in management. Their voice is often to the exclusion of all other equity interests, but they may also share their management rights with other classes of stock.

Common stock may be classified:

(1) Par and No-Par Stock: Par stock is stock with a stated, legal dollar value, whereas no-par stock lacks such a given value. The distinction today is largely an academic one. However, state laws regarding stock dividends and split-ups and the adjustments of par value may affect the accounting treatment of such dividends.

(2) Classes of Common Stock: Common stock may be divided into separate classes—e.g., class A, class B, etc. Usually, the class distinction deals with the right to vote for separate directors, or one class may have the right to vote and one class may not. The use of class stock is a typical tecnhique used where a minority group wishes to maintain control.

[¶1102.2]   Preferred Stock

The second major type of capital stock is preferred stock, stock which has some preference with regard to dividend payments or distribution of assets on liquidation. In the usual situation, preferred stock will have a preference on liquidation. to the extent of the par value of the stock. In addition, its right to dividends depends on the following classification:

(1) Participating and Nonparticipating Right: If the preferred has a right to a fixed dividend each year but has not the right to share in any additional dividends over and above the stated amount, it is nonparticipating preferred. If it is entitled to a share of any dividends over and above those to which it has priority, it is called participating. For example, a preferred may have the right to a 5% annual dividend and then share equally with the common stock in dividends after a dividend (equal to the preferred per-share dividend) has been paid to the common stockholders.

(2) Convertible Preferred Stock: Convertible preferred is stock which may, at the holder's option, be exchanged for common. The terms of the exchange and the conversion period are set forth on the preferred certificate. Thus one share of $100 par preferred may be convertible beginning one year after issue into two shares of common. If the preferred stockholder converts, he will own two shares of common at a cost to him of $50 per share (this assumes he purchased the preferred at par). A company will issue a convertible security at a time when it needs funds but for one reason or another cannot or does not wish to issue common stock. For example, in a weak stock market, common may be poorly received while a convertible preferred can be privately placed with a large institutional investor. The conversion privilege, from the point of view of the purchaser, is a "sweetener" since it affords the opportunity to take a full equity position in the future if the company prospers. The issuer may be quite satisfied to give the conversion privilege because it means that (assuming earnings rise) the preferred stock, with a prior and fixed dividend claim, will gradually be eliminated in exchange for common shares.

Accounting for a convertible preferred issue follows the usual rules. That is, when the preferred is first issued, a separate capital account will be set up, to which will be credited the par value of the outstanding stock. When conversion takes place, an amount equal to the par of the converted stock is debited to the preferred account. The common stock account will be credited with an amount equal to the par or stated value of the shares issued in exchange for the preferred. Any excess will go to capital surplus.

Both participating (1) and convertible (2) preferred stocks above must be considered in the computation of earnings per share.

(3) Cumulative and Noncumulative: A corporation which lacks earnings or surplus cannot pay dividends on its preferred stock. In that case, the question arises whether the passed dividend must be paid in future years. If passed dividends do accumulate and must be paid off, the stock is cumulative; otherwise, noncumulative.

The preferred may share voting rights equally with the common stock, it may lack voting rights under any circumstances, or it may have the right to vote only if one or more dividends are passed. In the latter case, the preferred may have the exclusive right to vote for a certain number of directors to be sure that its interests as a class are protected.

For cumulative stock, the dividends must be accrued each year (even if unpaid), unless issued with an "only as earned" provision. The effect on earnings per share is the extent of the reduction of net income for this accrual.

[¶1102.3]   Par Value, Stated Capital, and Capital Stock Accounts

The money a corporation receives for its stock is in a unique category. It is variously referred to as "a cushion for creditors," "a trust fund," and by similar expressions. The point is that in a corporation which gives its stockholders limited liability, the only funds to which the creditors of the corporation can look for repayment of their debts in the event the corporation suffers losses is the money received for stock, which constitutes the stated capital account. Consequently, most corporation statutes require a number of steps to be taken before a corporation can reduce its stated capital. These steps include approval by the stockholders and the filing of a certificate with the proper state officer, so that creditors may be put on notice of the reduction in capital.

Stated capital is actually divided into separate accounts, each account for a particular class of stock. Thus, a corporation may have outstanding a class A common, a class B common, a first preferred, a second preferred, etc. Each class would have its own account, which would show the number of shares of the class authorized by the certificate of incorporation, the number actually issued and the consideration received by the corporation.

It is at this point that the distinction between par and no-par stock becomes important. Par stock is rarely sold for less than its par value, although it may be sold for more. In many states, it is illegal to sell stock at a discount from par, and even when not illegal, there may be a residual stockholder liability for that original discount to the creditors. In any case, an amount equal to the par value of the stock must be credited to its capital account, with any excess going into a surplus account, as discussed below. In the case of no-par stock, the corporation, either through its board of directors or at a stockholders' meeting, assigns part of the consideration received as stated capital for the stock and treats the rest as a credit to a capital surplus account. Treating part of the consideration received as stated capital is the equivalent of giving the stock a par value.

[¶1102.4]   Capital Stock Issued for Property

Where capital stock is issued for the acquisition of property in a non-cash transfer, measurement of owners' investment is usually determined by using the fair market value of the assets (and/or the discounted present value of any liabilities transferred). (AC 1027.08 M-2)

When the fair value of the assets transferred cannot be measured, the market value of the stock issued may be used instead for establishing the value of the property received. (AC 1027.08 M-2)

When the acquisition is an entire business, the principle of "fair value" is extended to cover each and every asset acquired (other than goodwill). If the fair value of the *whole* business is considered to be *more* than the individual values, that excess is considered to be goodwill.

The difference between fair value put on the assets received and the *par value* (stated) of the stock issued goes to the Capital-in-Excess of Par Value account (or Additional Paid-in Capital, etc.) as either a positive or negative (discount) amount. Note that this does *not* pertain to any "negative" goodwill which might have been created; said negative goodwill, if any, should be used to reduce, immediately, the non-current assets (except investment securities), proportionately to zero, if necessary, with any remaining excess to be deferred and amortized as favorable goodwill is amortized.

[¶1103]   CAPITAL IN EXCESS OF PAR OR STATED VALUE (CAPITAL SURPLUS)

The term "capital surplus" is still widely used, although the preferred terminology is "capital in excess of par" or "additional paid-in capital."

The capital in exess of par account is credited with capital received by the corporation which is not part of par value or stated capital. It is primarily the excess of consideration received over par value or the amount of consideration received for no-par stock which is not assigned as stated capital.

In addition, donations of capital to the corporation are credited to this account. If stated capital is ever reduced as permitted by law, the transfer is from the capital stock account to this capital surplus account.

This account is also credited for the excess of market value *over* par value for stock dividends (which are not split-ups) and for the granting of certain stock options and rights.

[¶1104]   RETAINED EARNINGS

Accounting Terminology Bulletin No. 1 (August, 1953) recommended the following (terminology bulletins do not have authoritative status, but are issued as useful guides):

1. The abandonment of the term "surplus;"
2. The term "earned surplus" be replaced with such terms that indicated the source such as:
   Retained Earnings
   Retained Income
   Accumulated Earnings
   Earnings Retained for Use in the Business

The 1974 issue of Accounting Trends and Techniques (AICPA) showed that 75% of the companies included in the survey used the title, "Retained Earnings."

Retained earnings are the accumulated undistributed past and current year's earnings, net of taxes and dividends paid and declared.

Portions of retained earnings may be set aside for certain contingencies, appropriated for such purposes as possible future inventory losses, sinking funds, etc.

A Statement of Changes in Retained Earnings is one of the basic financial statements *required* for fair presentation of results of operation and financial condition to conform with GAAP. (AC 1027.17) It shows net income, dividends, prior period adjustments. A Statement of Other Changes in Owners' Equity shows additional investments by owners, retirements of owners' interests and similar events (if these are few and simple, they are put in the notes). (AC 1022.05)

Regardless of how a company displays its undistributed earnings, or the disclosures thereof, for tax purposes, the actual earnings and profits which could have been or are still subject to distribution as "dividends" *under IRS regulations* may, under some circumstances, retain that characteristic for the purpose of ordinary income taxation to the ultimate recipient. (See Tax Section of this book.) The AICPA has no requirement for this disclosure other than normal requirement for the "periods presented," which would usually show the activity in retained earnings for only two years and not prior.

[¶1105]   PRIOR PERIOD ADJUSTMENTS

Prior period adjustments should be limited to those rare items which: (AC 2010.22)

1. Can be specifically related to the operations of particular prior periods, and

2. Are not based on economic events occurring after the end of the prior period, and

3. Depend primarily on persons other than management, and

4. Could not be reasonably estimated at prior time.

Evidence of the uncertainty would have been prior disclosure in the notes to the financial statements of a prior period which described the then-existing condition, probably with a qualified auditor's opinion based on the uncertainty.

Normal changes in accounting estimates are not prior period adjustments. (AC 2010.23)

Litigation settlements and material, non-recurring income tax adjustments are examples of appropriate prior period adjustments. (AC 2010.22)

Retroactive adjustment should be made of all comparative periods presented, reflecting changes to particular items, net income and retained earnings balances. The tax effects should also be reflected and shown. Disclosure of the effects of the restatement should be made. (AC 2010.25)

Goodwill may not be written off as a prior period adjustment.

Former pension contributions under disallowed unqualified plans become prior period adjustments when allowed by the IRS for qualified plans. (TA 5230.02)

[¶1106]   CONTINGENCY RESERVES

A "contingency" is defined as "an existing condition, situation, or set of circumstances involving uncertainty as to possible gain or loss to an enterprise that will ultimately be resolved when one or more events occur or fail to occur." (AC 4311.01)

Loss contingencies fall in three categories: (AC 4311.03)

1. Probable
2. Reasonably possible
3. Remote.

In deciding whether to accrue the estimated loss by charging income or setting aside an appropriation of retained earnings, or merely to make a disclosure of the contingency in the notes to the financial statement, the following standards have been set:

> Accrue a charge to income if *both* of the following conditions are met: (AC 4311.08)
>
> > 1. Information available *before* the issuance of the financial statements indicates that probably the asset will be impaired;
> >
> > and
> >
> > 2. A *reasonable* estimate of the loss *can* be made.

If discovery of the above impairment occurs *after* the date of the statements, disclosure should be made and pro-forma supplementary financial data presented giving effect to the occurrence as of the balance sheet date.

When a contingent loss is only *reasonably possible* or the probable loss cannot be estimated, an estimate of the *range* of loss should be made or a narrative description given to indicate that *no* estimate was possible. Disclosure should be made; but no accrual. (AC 4311.10)

When the contingency is *remote*, disclosure should be made when it is in the nature of a guarantee. (AC 4311.12) Other remote contingencies are not required to be disclosed, but they may be, if desired, for more significant reporting.

General reserves for unspecified business risks are not to be accrued and no disclosure is required. (AC 4311.14)

Appropriations for loss contingencies from retained earnings must be shown within the stockholders' Equity section of the balance sheet and clearly identified as such. (AC 4311.15)

Examples of loss contingencies are: (AC 4311.04)

1. Collectibility of receivables.
2. Obligations related to product warranties and product defects.
3. Risk of loss or damage of enterprise property by fire, explosion, or other hazards.
4. Threat of expropriation of assets.
5. Pending or threatened litigation.
6. Actual or possible claims and assessments.
7. Risk of loss from catastrophes assumed by property and casualty insurance companies including reinsurance companies.
8. Guarantees of indebtedness of others.
9. Obligations of commercial banks under "standby letters of credit."
10. Agreements to repurchase receivables (or to repurchase the related property) that have been sold.

Handling of these loss contingencies depends upon the nature of the loss probability and the reasonableness of estimating the loss — as discussed in the prior paragraphs.

[¶1107]   **RECAPITALIZATIONS**

Essentially, a recapitalization means changing the structure of the capital accounts. It can also mean a reshuffling between equity and debt. A recapitalization may be done voluntarily by the corporation; or it may be part of a reorganization proceeding in a court, pursuant to a bankruptcy or a reorganization petition filed by the corporation or it creditors.

In almost all cases of recapitalizations, stockholder approval is required at some point during the process. This is because a recapitalization may affect the amount of stated capital of the corporation or change the relationships between the stockholders and the corporation or between classes of stockholders. The different categories of recapitalizations are discussed in the following paragraphs.

STOCK SPLIT-UPS, STOCK DIVIDENDS AND SPLIT-UPS IN THE FORM OF STOCK DIVIDENDS

[¶1107.1]   (1) Split-Up

A split-up involves dividing the outstanding shares into a larger number; for example, two for one. In a two-for-one split, each stockholder receives a certificate for additional shares equal to the amount of shares he is presently holding. The split-up is reflected in the corporate books by reducing the par value or the stated value of the outstanding shares. Thus if shares with a par value of $10 are split two for one, the new par becomes $5. No entry is necessary, other than a memo entry. The stockholder adjusts his basis for the unit number of shares.

Reverse Split: The opposite of a split-up is a reverse split, which results in a lesser number of outstanding shares. Stockholders turn in their old certificates and receive a new certificate for one-half their former holdings. The par value or stated value is adjusted to show the higher price per share. A reverse split is sometimes used in order to increase the price of the stock immediately on the open market.

[¶1107.2]   (2) Stock Dividends

As far as the stockholder is concerned, a stock dividend is the same as the stock split; he receives additional shares, merely changing his unit-basis of holding. But the effect is quite different from the point of view of the corporation. A stock dividend requires a transfer from retained earnings of the *market value* of the shares. Capital stock is credited for the par value and capital in excess of par value is credited for the excess of market price over par. (When the shareholder has the option of receiving cash, he must report the dividend as ordinary income.)

Dividends are presumed to be distributions which do not affect the market price because they are *less* than 20% to 25% of the number of previously outstanding shares.

[¶1107.3]   (3) Stock Split-up Effected in the Form of a Dividend

Usually, a stock distribution is either a dividend or a split-up. However, there is another type of distribution, which, because of certain state legal requirements pertaining to the minimum requirements for or the changing of par value, necessitates a different nomenclature.

In those instances where the stock dividend is so great as to materially reduce the market value, it is by nature and AICPA definition a "split-up." However, because certain states require that retained earnings must be capitalized in order to maintain par value, the AICPA standards recommend that those types of transactions be described by the corporation as a "split-up effected in the form of a dividend." The entry would then be a reduction of retained earnings and an increase in capital stock for the *par value* of the distribution. (AC 5561.11)) For income tax purposes, the corporation may be required to show this reduction of retained earnings as a Schedule M adjustment and may technically still have to consider it as available for ordinary-rate ultimate distribution.

[¶1108] CHANGING PAR OR STATED VALUE OF STOCK

This type of recapitalization involves changing from par to no par or vice versa. This is usually done in conjunction with a reduction of stated capital which is discussed in the folllowing paragraph. However, this is not necessarily the case. A corporation, for example, may decide to change its stock from par stock to no-par stock in order to take advantage of lower franchise fees and transfer taxes. Or no-par shares may be changed to shares having par value to solve legal problems existing under particular state statutes. A par value stock which is selling in the market at a price lower than its par must be changed if the corporation intends to issue new stock, because of some state laws which prohibit a corporation from selling its par value stock for less than par value. In such case, the corporation may reduce par value or may change the par to no par, in which case the new stock can be given a stated value equivalent to the price it can bring in the open market.

[¶1109]   QUASI-REORGANIZATIONS

Current or future years' charges should not be made against capital surplus (as distinguished from "earned surplus) however created, instead of the income accounts. (AC 5511.01)

An exception to this rule (called "readjustment") occurs when "a corporation elects to restate its assets, capital stock and surplus and thus avail itself of permission to relieve its future income account or earned surplus account of charges which would otherwise be made there against." In which event, the corporation "should make a clear report to its shareholders of the restatements proposed to be made; and obtain their formal consent. It should present a fair balance sheet as at the date of the re-adjustment, in which the readjustments of the carrying amounts are reasonably complete, in order that there may be no continuation of the circumstances which justify charges to capital surplus." (AC 5581.03)

As an example of how this readjustment might occur, suppose that a company has a deficit in its retained earnings (earned surplus) of $100,000. By revaluing its assets upward, it is possible for this company to create a capital surplus account for the write-up to fair value, then write-off the deficit in retained earnings to that account. From then on, a new earned surplus account should be established and the fact be disclosed for ten years. (AC 5582.02)

[¶1110]   STOCK RECLASSIFICATIONS

Another category of stock recapitalization involves reclassifiying the existing stock. This means that outstanding stock of a particular class is exchanged for stock of another class. For example, several outstanding issues of preferred stock may be consolidated into a single issue. Or, common stock may be exchanged for preferred stock, or vice versa. The object in this type of reclassification is to simplify the capital structure, which in many cases is necessary in order to make a public offering or sometimes to eliminate dividend arrearages on preferred stock by offering a new issue of stock in exchange for canceling such arrearages.

[¶1111]   SUBSTITUTING DEBT FOR STOCK

One form of recapitalization that has become popular in some areas involves substituting bonds for stock.

The advantage to the corporation is the substitution of tax-deductible interest on bonds for nondeductible dividends on preferred stock. Of course, where we are dealing with a closely held corporation, substituting debt for stock in a manner to give the common stockholders a pro rata portion of the debt may be interpreted for tax purposes as "thin" capitalization; and the bonds may be treated as stock anyhow.

Also, to attract new money into the corporation, it is advantageous to consider the issuance of convertible debt securities—bonds to which are attached the rights (warrants) to buy common stock of the company at a specified price. The advantages of this type of security are: (AC 5516.01)

1. An interest rate which is lower than the issuer could establish for nonconvertible debt;

2. An initial conversion price greater than the market value of the common stock;

3. A conversion price which does not decrease.

The portion of proceeds from these securities which can be applied to the warrants should be credited to paid-in capital (based on fair value of both securities) and discounts or premiums should be treated as they would be under conventional bond issuance. (AC 5516.14)

[¶1112]   TREASURY STOCK

Treasury stock is stock which has previously been issued by a corporation but is no longer outstanding. It has been reacquired by the corporation and, as its name implies, held in its treasury. Treasury stock is not canceled stock since cancellation reduces the authorized issue of corporation stock.

In some circumstances, it is permissible to show treasury stock as an asset if adequately disclosed. However, dividends on treasury stock should not be treated as income. (AC 5541)

[¶1112.1]   Treasury Stock Shown at Cost

When a corporation acquires its own stock to be held for future sale or possible use in connection with stock options, or with no plans or uncertainty as to future retirement of that stock, the cost of the acquired stock may be shown separately as a deduction from the total of capital stock, capital surplus and retained earnings. Gains on subsequent sales (over the acquired-cost price) should be credited to capital surplus and losses (to the extent of prior gains) should be charged to that same account, with excess losses going to retained earnings. (AC 5542.13b) State law should be followed if in contravention.

[¶1112.2]   Treasury Stock Shown at Par or Stated Value

When treasury stock is acquired for the purpose of *retirement* (or constructive retirement), until canceled, the stock should be shown at par value or stated value as a reduction in the equity section and the excess of purchase cost over par (stated) value should be charged to capital surplus to the extent of prior gains booked for the same issue, together with pro-rata portions applicable to that stock arising from prior stock dividends, splits, etc. Any remaining excess may be either applied pro-rata to common stock or to retained earnings. (AC 5542.13a)

[¶1112.3]   Treasury Stock as an Asset

If adequately disclosed, it is permissible in some circumstances to show stock of a corporation held in its own treasury as an asset. (This rule was adopted in 1934 upon recommendation of the New York Stock Exchange.) (AC 5541.01)

For example, pursuant to a corporation's bonus arrangement with certain employees, treasury stock may be used to pay the bonus, and, in accordance with the concept of a current asset satisfying a current liability, that applicable treasury stock might be shown as current asset. However, dividends on such stock should not be treated as income while the corporation holds the stock. (AC 5541.01)

[¶1113]   THE GOING CONCERN CONCEPT

There is an underlying presumption in the standards set for financial accounting that a business, once started, will continue functioning and operating as a going concern. For example, the use of historical costs for building and property, which are currently more valuable, presupposes that the *use* of that property will generate more advantages than would present disposition. Deferrals to future periods through systematic allocations also indicate a presumption of longevity.

This presumption of continuance as a going concern is never stated by the independent auditor — never worded in his opinion. On the *contrary*, it is when there appears to be danger of the firm's *not* being able to continue as a going concern that the auditor makes the assertion that "the statements have been prepared on the basis of a going concern," and that he is *unable* to express an opinion because of major uncertainties, which he describes. Therefore, the actual use of the terminology, "going concern," in the auditor's opinion indicates trouble.

Some factors which which may be indicative of *possible* failure to continue as a going concern are (TA 9320.01):

Inability to satisfy obligations on due dates.

Inability to perform contractual obligations.

Inability to meet substantial loan covenants.

A substantial deficit.

A series of continued losses.

The presence of major contingencies which could lead to heavy losses.

Catastrophes which have rendered the business inoperable.

12

Revenue (Income)

[¶1201]

The broad principles upon which net income is determined derive from the pervasive measurement principles, such as realization, and the modifying conventions, such as conservatism. (AC 1022.20)

The entire process of income determination (''matching'') consists of identifying, measuring and relating revenue and expenses for an accounting period. Revenue is usually determined by applying the realization principle, with the changes in net asset value interrelated with the recognition of revenue. (AC 1026.11)

Revenue arises from three general activities (AC 1026.12):

1. Selling products;
2. Rendering services or letting others use owned resources, resulting in interest, rent, etc;
3. Disposing of other resources (not products), such as equipment or investments.

Revenue does not include proceeds from stockholders, lenders, asset purchases or prior period adjustments.

Revenue, in the balance sheet sense, is a gross increase in assets or a gross decrease in liabilities recognized and measured in conformity with GAAP, which results from those profit-directed activities that can change owners' equity. (AC 1026.12)

Revenue is considered *realized* when: (AC 1026.14)

1. The earning process is complete or virtually complete

    and

2. An exchange has taken place

The objectives of accounting determination of income are not always the same as the objectives used for tax purposes.

[¶1201.1] Methods of Determining Income

There are various acceptable ways of determining income, all of which are discussed in other parts of this book:

Revenue (see three general activities above):

1) Accrual method — this is financial accounting and GAAP.
2) Cash method — this is *not* considered financial accounting, and not GAAP, since one of the characteristics of GAAP is the *accrual* of items appropriate.
3. Installment sale method — generally for retail stores.
4. Completion of production method — used for precious metals.
5. For long-term construction contracts:
   A. Completed contract method.
   B. Percentage-of-completion method.
6. For leasing activities:
   A. The direct financing method.
   B. The operating method.
   C. The sales method.
7. The cost recovery method (used for installment sales).
8. Consolidation method — for majority-owned subsidiaries (over 50%)
9. Equity method — for non-consolidated subsidiaries and for controlled non-subsidiaries.

Other types of income requiring special determination:

1. Extraordinary items of income.
2. Unrealized income arising from:
   A. Foreign currency holdings or transactions.
   B. Ownership of marketable securities shown as current assets.

A *shareholder* in a corporation does *not* have income when that corporation earns income (except for a Sub-S corporation). The shareholder has, and reports for tax purposes, income only upon *distribution* of that income in the form of dividends. Generally, distributions of stock — stock dividends and stock splits— are *not* income to the shareholder, but merely an adjustment of the number of shares he holds (for the same original cost plus token costs, if any). However, there are some situations which call for the stockholder to report stock dividends as income. (See Tax Section.)

13

Expenses

Expenses are one of the six basic elements of financial accounting, along with assets, liabilities, owners' equity, revenue and net income. (AC 1022.18)

> Expenses are determined by applying the expense recognition principles on the basis of relationships, between acquisition costs [the term "cost" is commonly used to refer to the amount at which assets are initially recorded, regardless of how determined (AC 1026.28)], and either the independently determined revenue or accounting periods. Since the point in time at which revenue and expenses are recognized is also the time at which changes in amounts of net assets are recorded, income determination is interrelated with asset valuation. (AC 1026.11)

All costs are not expenses. Some costs are related to later periods, will provide benefits for later periods, and are carried forward as assets on the balance sheet. Other costs are incurred and provide no future benefit, having expired in terms of usefulness or applicability — these expired costs are called "expenses." All expenses, therefore, are part of the broader term "cost." These expired costs are not assets and are shown as deductions from revenue to determine net income. (AC 1026.11)

> Expenses are gross decreases in assets or gross increases in liabilities recognized and measured in conformity with GAAP that result from those types of profit-directed activities that can change an owner's equity. (1026.18)

[¶1301.1] Recognizing Expenses

Three pervasive principles form the basis for recognizing expenses to be deducted from revenue to arrive at net income or loss: (AC 1026.20)

1. Associating cause and effect ("matching"):

For example, manufacturing cost of goods sold is measured and matched to the *sale* of the product. Assumptions must be made as to how these costs attach to the product — whether on machine hours, space used, labor expended, etc. Assumptions must also be made as to how the costs flow out (LIFO, FIFO, average costs). (AC 1026.22)

2. Systematic and rational allocation:

When there is no direct way to associate cause and effect and certain costs are known (or presumed) to have provided benefits during the accounting period, these costs are allocated to that period in a systematic and rational manner so as to appear so to an unbiased observer. The methods of allocation should be consistent and systematic, though methods may vary for different types of costs. Examples are: Depreciation of fixed assets, amortization of intangibles, interperiod allocation of rent or interest. (1026.23) The allocation referred to here is not the allocation of expired manufacturing costs within the "cost" area to determine unit or job costs; it is rather the broader area of allocation to the manufacturing area from the unexpired asset account: Depreciation on factory building, rather than overhead-depreciation on Product A, B or C.

3. Immediate recognition (period expenses):

Those costs which are expensed during an accounting period because:

A. They cannot be associated on a cause-and-effect basis with revenue, yet no useful purpose would be achieved by delaying recognition to a future period, or

B. They provide no discernible future benefits, or

C. They were recorded as assets in a prior period and now no longer provide discernible future benefits.

Examples are: Officer salaries, most selling expenses, legal fees, most general and administrative expenses.

[¶1302]   OTHER EXPENSES (AND REVENUE)

Gains and losses: Expenses and revenue from *other* than sales of products, merchandise or services may be separated from (operating) revenue and disclosed net separately. (AC 1027.25 R-9C)

Unusual items: Unusual items of expense or income not meeting the criteria of "extraordinary" should be shown as a separate component of income from continuing operations. (AC 2012.26)

Extraordinary items: Extraordinary items are discussed elsewhere in this book. They should be shown separately — net of applicable taxes — *after* net income from continuing operations. If there are any disposals of business segments, they should be shown immediately prior to extraordinary items — also with tax effect.

14

Cost Accounting

[¶1401]

Cost accounting systems vary with the type of cost (present or future) used. When present costs are used, the cost system is called an *historical* or *actual cost* system. When future costs are used, the cost system is called a *standard cost* system. In practice, combinations of these costs are used even in actual or standard systems. Where there is an intentional use of both types of costs, we sometimes refer to the system as a *hybrid cost* system.

Actual Cost System: Since an actual cost system uses only those costs which have already been incurred, the system determines costs only after manufacturing operations have been performed. Under this system the product is charged with the actual cost of materials, the actual cost of labor, and an *estimated* portion of overhead (overhead costs represent the future cost element in an actual cost system).

Standard Cost System: A standard system is based upon estimated or predetermined costs. There is a distinction between estimated and standard costs, however. Both are "predetermined" costs, but estimated costs are based upon average past experience, and standard costs are based upon scientific facts that consider past experience and controlled experiments. Arriving at standard costs involves careful selection of material, an engineering study of equipment and manufacturing facilities, and time and motion studies.

In either system, adjustment must be made at the financial statement date to the *closing inventory* so that it is shown at actual cost or reasonably approximate actual cost, or at market if lower. (AC 5121.06 footnote) Also, the inventory must bear its share of the burden of overhead. "The exclusion of all overheads from inventory costs does not constitute an accepted accounting procedure." (AC 5121.05)

For interim statements, estimated gross profit rates may be used to determine cost of goods sold during the interim, but this fact must be disclosed. (AC 2071.14a)

It must be emphasized that whatever cost accounting method is chosen by a company, its purpose is primarily an internal management tool directed at controlling costs, setting production goals, measuring efficiencies and variances, providing incentives and establishing realistic relationships between unit costs, selling prices and gross margins. Regardless of costing methods used, generally accepted accounting standards must be followed for the preparation of the financial statements, wherein the valuation must be cost or market, whichever is lower.

Also, either the FIFO or LIFO methods (or the average method) may be used under any cost system. These methods pertain to the assumption of the *flow* of costs, not to the actual costs themselves. Note that *both* methods may be used within one inventory, as long as the method is applied to that portion of the inventory consistently from period to period. Disclosures should be made of any change in method.

[¶1401.1] Integrating Cost System

It is not essential to integrate a cost system with the rest of the accounting system, but it is highly desirable. A cost system is really an extension of the regular system. With an integrated system, entries in the inventory account in the general ledger should represent the sums of figures taken from the cost accounting data. The general ledger inventory accounts (e.g., finished goods, work in process, and raw materials) are the control accounts and they should tie in with the amounts of physical inventories actually on hand. Discrepancies may result from errors, spoilage, or thievery.

Elements of Cost: Production costs consist of three elements: direct materials, direct labor, and manufacturing (overhead) expenses:

Direct Materials: Those materials which can be identified with specific units of the product.

Direct Labor: That labor which can be identified with specific units of the product.

Manufacturing Expenses (Overhead): Those costs (including indirect material or labor) which can not be identified with specific units of the product. These costs represent expenses for the factory and other facilities which permit the labor to be applied to the materials to manufacture a product.

Sometimes, overhead is further subdivided into:

Direct overhead — Those manufacturing costs other than material and direct labor which specifically apply to production and require no allocation from other expense areas;

Indirect overhead — Those expenses which have been allocated into the manufacturing expense area from other more general area.

For financial statement purposes, overhead should not include selling expenses or general or administrative expenses. (AC 5121.05)

[¶1401.2] Cost Terminology (for quick reference)

Here are some brief definitions of various types of costs:

(1) *Historical* — measured by actual cash payments or their equivalent at the time of outlay.

(2) *Future* — expected to be incurred at a later date.

(3) *Standard* — scientifically predetermined.

(4) *Estimated* — predetermined.

(5) *Product* — associated with units of output.

(6) *Period* — associated with the income of a time period.

(7) *Direct* — obviously traceable to a unit of output or a segment of business operations.

(8) *Prime* — labor and material directly traceable to a unit of output.

(9) *Indirect* — not obviously traceable to a unit of output or to a segment of business operations.

(10) *Fixed* — do not change in the total as the rate of output varies.

(11) *Variable* — do change with changes in rate of output.

(12) *Opportunity* — measurable advantage foregone as a result of the rejection of alternative uses of resources whether of materials, labor, or facilities.

(13) *Imputed* — never involve cash outlays nor appear in finanacial records. Involve a foregoing on the part of the person whose costs are being calculated.

(14) *Controllable* — subject to direct control at some level of supervison.

(15) *Noncontrollable* — not subject to control at some level of supervison.

(16) *Joint* — exist when from any one unit source, material, or process come products which have different unit values.

(17) *Sunk* — historical and not recoverable in a given situation.

(18) *Discretionary* — avoidable and unessential to an objective.

(19) *Postponable* — may be shifted to future period without affecting efficiency.

(20) *Out of pocket* — necessitate cash expenditure.

(21) *Differential* — changes in cost that result from variation in operations.

(22) *Incremental* — those added or eliminated if segments were expanded or discontinued.

(23) *Alternative* — estimated for decision areas.

(24) *Replacement* — considered for depreciation significance.*

(25) *Departmental* — production and service, for cost distributions.

---

* The Auditing Standards Executive Committee of the *AICPA* at press-time for this text has issued a draft-proposed statement on opinions concerning unaudited replacement cost information required in certain *SEC* reports.

[¶1402]   JOB ORDER OR PROCESS COST SYSTEMS

There are distinctions between cost systems other than the use of present or future costs.

A *job order system* compiles costs for a specific quantity of a product as it moves through the production process. This means that material, labor, and overhead costs of a specific number or lot of the product (usually identifiable with a customer's order or a specific quantity being produced for stock) are recorded as the lot moves through the production cycle.

A *process system* compiles costs as they relate to specific processes or operations for a period of time. To find the unit cost, these figures are averaged for a specified period and spread over the number of units that go through each process. Process costing is used when large numbers of identical products are manufactured, usually in assembly-line fashion.

Keep in mind that actual or estimated costs can be used with either a job order or process cost system.

[¶1402.1] Benefits and Drawbacks

Whether the job order or process system is used depends on the type of operation. The job order system is rarely used in mass production industries. It is invariably used when products are custom made. Process costing is used where production is in a continuous state of operation as for: Paper, baking, steel making, glass, rubber, sugar, chemicals, etc. Here are some of the relative merits and shortcomings of each method:

Advantages

Job Order	*Process*
(1) Appropriate for custom-made goods.	(1) It is usually only necessary to calculate costs each month
(2) Appropriate for increasing finished goods inventory in desired quantities	(2) Minimum of clerical work required
(3) Adequate for inventory pricing	(3) If there is only one type of product cost computation is relatively simple
(4) Permits estimation of future costs	
(5) Satisfies "cost-plus" contract requisites	

Disadvantages

Job Order	*Process*
(1) Expensive to use — a good deal of clerical work required	(1) Use of average costs ignores any variance in product cost.
(2) Difficult to make sure that all materials and labor are accurately charged to each specific job	(2) Involves calculation of stage of completion of goods in process and the use of equivalent units.
(3) Difficult to determine cost of goods sold when partial shipments are made before completion	

[¶1403]   **HOW TO USE STANDARD COSTS**

Smith Company manufactures only one product, glubs — a household article made out of a certain type of plastic. Glubs are made from D raw material which goes through a single process. Glubs are turned out from D material in a fraction of a day. Smith Company has a process-type cost setup integrated with its other financial records. D material is charged to work in process through requisitions based upon actual cost. Direct labor is charged to work in process based upon payroll. Manufacturing expense is charged to work in process based upon the number of payroll hours. Each day a record of the number of glubs manufactured is kept. This is the responsibility of the production department.

Here's the way the Smith Company process cost system operates: Every month, total figures are worked up for raw material, payroll, factory expenses. Each of these figures is then divided by the total number of glubs produced for that month to arrive at a unit cost per glub. Here is what the unit cost accumulation for the four months shows (this example assumes no work-in-process inventory and no equivalent units):

Unit Cost per Glub Manufactured

	First Month	Second Month	Third Month	Fourth Month	Weighted Average
Material D	$ .94	$ .91	$ .97	$1.10	$ .95
Direct Labor	1.18	1.22	2.00	.70	1.29
Manufacturing Expenses	1.22	1.47	2.11	.82	1.42
	$3.34	$3.60	$5.08	$2.62	$3.66

Right now, glubs are being sold at $4.30, and the present profit appears sufficient. T.O. Smith, the president and major stockholder of the corporation, feels that if glubs were sold at $3.30 each, four times as many could be sold. He also reports that he has learned that Glubco, Inc., Smith's competitor, is going to market glubs for $3.60. Smith thinks that $3.30 is a good sales price since the cost records indicate that glubs were manufactured for as low as $2.62 in the fourth month. Smith Company's accountant says the president is incorrect. He points out that the average cost is somewhere in the area of $3.55 to $3.80 based upon the cost records for six months. Selling glubs for $3.30 would create losses. The factory foreman says that during the third and fourth months there was an error in calculating the number of glubs put into finished goods inventory. From the figures for the fourth month, it appears that the foreman is correct. The unit cost per glub is unusually low. Mr. Smith wants to know the lowest at which he can sell glubs and still make a reasonable profit. The accountant suggests setting up a cost system based upon standard costs. He outlines the following steps:

(1) Purchasing department records indicate that material D should cost no more than 45ᶜ per pound. (According to the chief engineer, it takes approximately

two pounds of D to produce one glub.) The 45ᶜ figure takes future market conditions into account.

(2) A time study of half a dozen workers who produce glubs is made. The average time it takes each of these six men to produce one glub is one-third of an hour. The average hourly wage of these men is $2.10.

(3) Based upon reasonable level of production for the following year, a departmental manufacturing expense or overhead is estimated to be 100% of direct labor.

Based upon the above determinations, the standard cost per glub is $2.30. It is calculated as follows:

Raw Material D: two pounds at 45ᶜ per pound	$ .90
Direct Labor: 1/3 hour at $2.10 per hour	.70
Manufacturing Expense: 100% of direct labor	.70
Total	$2.30

In order to produce glubs at this cost, the following points are agreed upon:

(1) When more than 45ᶜ a pound is paid for raw material D, the excess is to be charged to a special variance account instead of the raw material account. These excesses are to be explained periodically by the purchasing department.

(2) Requisitions for raw material D are to be limited to two pounds of D for each glub to be manufactured. If more than two pounds per glub is issued to meet scheduled production, the excess over two pounds is to be charged to a separate variance account. The reason for any excess will also have to be explained.

(3) The daily number of direct labor hours spent making glubs is to be multiplied by three. This should equal the number of glubs produced that day. Any discrepancy here is probably due to inefficiency. The number of inefficient hours at the standard $2 rate times the 100% manufacturing expense rate is to be charged to a special variance account.

(4) Payroll over $2 an hour is to be charged to a variance account. Only $2 an hour is to be charged to the work-in-progress account. The factory foreman will have to explain hourly labor figures over $2 periodically.

(5) Departmental variations in the 100% of direct labor manufacturing expense burden are to be charged or credited to separate variance accounts. This is to be done each month.

Here's what happened each month after this system was instituted:

Variance Accounts	Fifth Month	Sixth Month	Seventh Month	Eighth Month	Ninth Month
(1) Material D Price	$ 2,100	$ 300	$ 750	$ 0	$ 0
(2) Material usage ...	19,500	13,000	5,000	500	400
(3) Labor efficiency .	8,000	5,050	800	700	300
(4) Labor rate	400	150	(50)	400	100
(5) Mfg. Expense ...	0	5,000	1,000	300	(100)
	$30,000	$23,500	$ 7,500	$ 1,900	$ 700
Units Manufactured ..	48,000	48,000	48,000	48,000	48,000
Variance per Unit	.63	.49	.16	.04	.01
Standard Unit Cost ...	2.30	2.30	2.30	2.30	2.30
Actual Cost	$ 2.93	$ 2.79	$ 2.46	$ 2.34	$ 2.31

Here is what was elicited from discussion with the persons responsible for the different variance accounts:

(1) The purchase price for raw material D exceeded 45ᶜ per pound mainly because of the distance of Smith Company from where D is obtained in the south. The head of purchasing feels that D could be purchased for no more than 45ᶜ if he could have a small office in the south with one assistant who would remain there. It was decided to go ahead and give him the office and the additional employee.

(2) The factory foreman together with the chief engineer has been going over the requisitions of raw material D. More D was needed because some of the glubs had air holes in them and weren't usable. It seems that the pressure used to extrude them wasn't sufficient. The chief engineer says that he can replace the present air die channels with larger ones so that these defects do not recur. The foreman knew that some glubs were scrapped in the past, but it wasn't until this switch to standard costs that he knew how much waste there really was.

(3) The foreman and the industrial engineer who performed the time and motion study discussed the labor efficiency loss. It was their opinion that there were more factory employees than needed to carry out various operations to convert D into finished glubs. It was also learned that some employees could use more training, while others were overskilled for their particular functions. Still others were not producing enough for some reason or other. Both men felt that a training program instructing employees in the efficient use of available tools would increase efficiency. Further time and motion studies on every phase of the production process were intitiated.

(4) There was not much variance in labor rate, but it was hoped that the training program would release more technically skilled and higher paid employees for use in the more complicated production steps.

At the end of the seventh month, it was obvious that the steps taken were beginning to pay off. The additional costs incurred in carrying out these steps (for example, the additional employee in purchasing and the southern office) created a manufacturing overhead variance where none had existed before; but the success in other areas outweighed this.

At the end of the ninth month, everyone agreed that the switch to standard costs had exceeded expectations. The new lower production cost would help expand the market for glubs. Smith Company was also in a good competitive position compared with Glubco since it probably could now undersell it.

This illustration shows the advantages of standard costs:

(1) Control and reduction of costs;

(2) Promotion and measurement of efficiencies;

(3) Calculation and setting of selling prices;

(4) Evaluation of inventories;

(5) Simplification of cost procedures.

[¶1404]   **DIRECT COSTING**

Another type of cost accounting which is used for internal purposes but not for financial or tax reporting purposes is "direct costing." This is a method in which only those costs which are a consequence of production of the product are assigned to the product — direct material cost, direct labor cost, and only variable manufacturing overhead. All fixed manufacturing costs are treated as expenses of the period.

The methods of recording costs for direct material and direct labor are similar under direct costing and conventional costing. It is in the method of reflecting manufacturing overhead that the systems differ. In a direct costing system, overhead costs are classified as fixed or variable. In conventional costing, only one overhead control account is used. In direct costing, two control accounts are used — a direct overhead account and an indirect overhead account. The direct overhead account is for variable expenses — those that vary with the volume of production. The indirect overhead account is for fixed expenses — those that do not vary with production. These are charged as expenses of the period rather than as costs of the finished product. Research costs, some advertising costs, and costs incurred to keep manufacturing and nonmanufacturing facilities ready for use are considered expenses of the period. Under direct costing, direct labor, direct material, and overhead costs that vary with production find their way into the inventory. The other manufacturing overhead expenses are charged off currently against income. The important reason behind direct costing is not to value inventories, but to segregate expenses.

[¶1404.1] **Effect of Direct Costing on Financial Statements**

Direct costing if used on the financial statements (for internal use) would produce the following results:

(1) Where the inventory of manufactured goods does not fluctuate from one accounting period to the next, there should be no difference between net income using direct costing or net income using conventional costing.

(2) Where the inventory does fluctuate and is increased, net income under direct costing will be lower. *Reason:* Fixed overhead costs under direct costing will have been charged to the current period instead of deferred by increasing the value of inventory. Under conventional costing, the value of the ending inventory will have been increased by these fixed overhead costs.

(3) Where inventory decreases, net income under direct costing will be higher than conventional costing. *Reason:* Fixed overhead costs included in the value of the inventory under conventional costing will now increase the cost of goods sold, thereby reducing income.

15

Employee Benefits

[¶1501]

Over the years, the types of fringe benefits offered employees have evolved as methods of helping employees avoid or delay the impact of individual income taxes. At the same time, government has effectively paid half of the costs, because for every corporate deductible expense-dollar, there is the corresponding maximum federal tax saving of 48%, plus state tax savings.

The competition to provide higher benefits represents an increasing awareness of the value of human resources (labor) and the costs of training and keeping good personnel. Both monetarily and psychologically, the employer tries to satisfy by providing favorable motivation for extended, continued employment.

The inducements are many: Modern equipment, comfortable working conditions, medical facilities, lounges and restaurants, employee discount stores, year-round temperature control, use of the telephone, and, more lately, staggered hours or optional choice of working-time.

Among the dollar inducements are the following:

Annual (or short-term) benefits:

1. Bonuses — with timed-deferral of cash payment to be most beneficial to the employee (shifting income);
2. Transfers of property, rather than cash;
3. Wage continuation plans (sick-pay);
4. Expense reimbursement or allowances;
5. Meals and lodging away from home;
6. Moving and relocation expenses, including guarantee of non-loss on home sale;
7. Courtesy discounts on products handled;
8. Hospitalization and health insurance;
9. Medical reimbursement plans;
10. Group life term-insurance coverage.

Long-term benefits:

    1. Deferred compensation arrangements:
       A.   Stock option compensatory plans
       B.   Pension and Profit-Sharing plans
       C.   Other deferred compensation contracts;
    2. Key-man (non-term) life insurance.

The discussion following centers on these long-term benefits.

[¶1502]   DEFERRED COMPENSATION PLANS

STOCK OPTION PLANS

[¶1502.1]   Non-compensatory Plans

A plan is considered to be non-compensatory when it possesses all four of the following characteristics: (AC 4062.07)

    1. Almost all full-time employees may participate; and
    2. Stock is offered to employees equally based on a uniform percent of wages; and
    3. The time for exercise is limited to a reasonable period; and
    4. The discount from the market price of the stock is not greater than would be reasonable in an offer to stockholders or others.

An example of a non-compensatory plan is one that qualifies under Section 423 of the IRS Code. (See Taxes)

[¶1502.2]   Compensatory Plans

Stock issued to an employee under any plan *except* a non-compensatory plan (above) *is considered to be a* compensatory plan and calls for the recognition of *compensation expense* by the employer.

The time of earliest measurement (issuance, date of grant) is the determinant factor as to when to book the compensation. The fact that the employee may not be able to receive or sell the stock for some years does *not* affect the compensation. (AC U 2011.274)

At the time of issuance (the date of the agreement), if the facts of the option price and a market price are known, the difference between a *higher* market price and the option price (the price at which the employee may buy the stock from the company) is considered to be compensation — at that time, not later. However, if the granting of the options is predicated upon the rendering of *future services,* the compensation calculated may be deferred to the period of future benefit (to be derived from those services). The excess (or bargain) is the theoretical benefit availed to the employee for his services, past, present or future.

For example, assume the employee's services would extend over two years (current and next-year), the entry would be:

Current Year

Employees Compensation (current expense)	50.	
Unearned Compensation (holdover)	50.	
Capital Surplus		100.

Market Price at issuance	$ 10.	
Option price	9.	
Excess per share	$ 1.	
100 shares @ $ 1.	$100.	

Next Year

Employees Compensation (expense)	50.	
Unearned Compensation		50.

Any "unearned compensation" should be shown as a separate reduction of stockholders' equity. (AC 4062.14)

No compensation is recognized if the option price equals or exceeds the market price at option issuance date.

Note again that the *exercise* date is not pertinent — yet.

For *tax* purposes, the amount deductible by the corporation is not applicable or determinable until the time the employee must pick up ordinary income, a factor which varies according to the plan as specified under IRS regulations. Thus, both the period and amount of expensing will probably differ for tax purposes, thus creating timing differences. Also, the difference between the compensation originally booked and the tax-deductible amount goes to Capital Surplus. (AC 4062.15 to .17)

[¶1502.3] Earnings Per Share

All shares which could be issued under the arrangement are considered "as if" issued and considered to be common stock equivalents and outstanding for earnings per share computations. If applicable, the treasury stock method is used to determine the incremental shares. (AC U 2011.274)

Compensatory stock options may thus affect *both* factors in the EPS formula: The numerator, for the compensation expense; and the denominator, by the addition of the equivalent shares.

Both primary and fully diluted computations are affected, if 3% or more.

[¶1502.4] Tandem (alternate) Stock, Elective Plans, Phantom Stock

Sometimes, stock plans for employees contain provisions for an election of alternative rights or options. These plans which combine rights are called "tandem stock'' or ''alternate stock'' plans. If the election to acquire stock under either right decreases the other right, it is called a ''phantom stock'' plan. (AC 4062 A.14)

[¶1503] PENSION (AND PROFIT SHARING) PLANS

This text *does not* concern itself with the accounting requirements for maintaining and reporting the position and activities of and within the fund itself.

This discussion deals with the *expense* portion which a company may or may not claim for financial accounting and reporting purposes — the accounting for the *cost* of the plans, which may or may not coincide with the allowable tax deduction permitted the corporation, or with the amount required for funding.

(Non-corporate entities, as well as self-employed individuals, should examine the latest ERISA provisions — the Employees Retirement Income Security Act of 1974, P.L. 93-406, with updates — for a comprehensive detailing of the extended deferment privileges now available.)

[¶1503.1]   Timing of Payments into Funds

One extremely important tax factor which must be considered by the employer and the statement-preparer is the timing of actual payments into the pension or profit sharing fund.

All claimed expenses must have been actually disbursed (not merely accrued) by the legally required tax-return filing date, *including* all permissible extensions. Thus, a late filing of an 1120, without extension, would bring about disallowance of the claimed expense contribution to a pension plan, if the payment had not actually been made by March 15 (calendar year taxpayer).

Preparers of financial statements should be aware of the possibility of a ''subsequent event'' disclosure, or a timing difference note-requirement for known late payments.

[¶1503.2]   The Expensing Standards

In the absence of convincing evidence that the company will reduce or discontinue the benefits called for in a pension plan, the cost of the plan should be accounted for on the assumption that the company will continue to provide such benefits. This assumption implies a long-term undertaking, the cost of which should be recognized annually whether or not funded. Therefore, accounting for pension costs should not be discretionary. (AC 4063.16)

The cost of *all* benefit payments made to the fund should be charged to income, none to retained earnings. The annual provision for pension cost should be based on an accounting method which uses:

1. *An acceptable actuarial cost method,* which is rational and systematic and consistently applied, resulting in reasonable measure of pension costs from year to year (assigning separate portions to past or prior service cost). (AC

4063.23) These methods may be based on the accrued benefit cost method or several projected benefit cost methods. (AC 4063.20)

> *and*

2. The actuarial cost determined above should fall *between* the following *minimum* and *maximum* computations: (AC 4063.17)

MINIMUM

Should *not* be *less* than the total of:

A. Normal cost, and
B. Interest on unfunded prior service cost, and
C. A provision for vested benefits, but *only* if the actuarially computed value of the vested benefits *exceeds* the total of:
>   1. The pension fund, and
>   2. Balance sheet pension accruals
>   *(less)*
>   3. Balance sheet pension prepayments or deferrals
>   But only if this excess is not at least 5% less than the same year's beginning excess.

This provision for vested benefits should be the *lessor* of:
>   1. The amount, if any, by which 5% of the beginning excess is greater than the amount of the *reduction* in excess for the year, or
>   2. The amount needed to aggregate:
>   A) Normal cost, and
>   B) Equivalent 40-year amortization (cost per year) of past service costs — unless fully amortized — *plus* consideration for amortizing applicable amendments thereto, and
>   C) Interest equivalents based on what would have been earned had prior year provisions been funded.

MAXIMUM

Should *not* be *greater* than the *total* of:

A. Normal cost, and
B. 10% of past service costs until fully amortized, and 10% of applicable amendments, and
C. Interest equivalents on the difference between provisions and amounts funded.

The complicated formula presented above will not usually pertain to those professionally administered plans engaging the services of professional actuaries. For an independent auditor, confirmation by the actuary is usually enough to substantiate the required corporate contribution. The guidelines should be more carefully observed by those companies which self-administer their own plans.

The difference between the amount expensed and that actually paid into the fund should be shown on the balance sheet as accrued or prepaid pension costs. (AC 4063.18)

If the company has a legal obligation in *excess* of the amounts paid or accrued, the excess should be shown as both a deferred charge and a liability. (AC 4063.18)

Except to the extent above, unfunded *prior* service cost is *not* a liability for the balance sheet. (AC 4063.18)

All employees who would reasonably be expected to receive benefits under a pension plan should be considered in the cost calculations, considering turnover also. (AC 4063.36)

[¶1504]   **PROFIT SHARING PLANS**

Contributions are based upon independent action taken by the corporate Board of Directors, tied to the profit of the year, under a profit sharing agreement approved by both management and employees. The authority for the contribution is reflected in the minutes of the corporation. The IRS also approves the plan.

The IRS imposes a combined maximum tax-deductible limit for companies having *both* plans.

[¶1505]   **ACTUARIAL GAINS AND LOSSES**

Reported gains or losses within the plans should be considered, generally on the average method, and only to the extent that they might necessitate a change in the contribution requirement. These gains or losses are usually reflected in the computations made by the fund administrator in the determination of the amount needed to be contributed by the corporation to keep the plan properly funded, subject to the minimum and maximum considerations.

[¶1506]   **DEFINED CONTRIBUTION PLANS**

These plans specify either:

1. Benefits will be based on defined *contributions,* or
2. Contributions will result in defined *benefits.*

In circumstance (1), the contribution is the pension cost for the year. Circumstance (2) requires the determination of pension cost in the same detailed manner described above. (AC 4063.38 to .39)

[¶1507]   **INSURED PLANS**

Usually the amount of net premium payment determined by the insurance company is the proper pension cost for the employer, provided dividends, termination costs and other factors are handled properly by the insurance company. (AC 4063.41)

[¶1508] COMPANIES WITH MORE THAN ONE PLAN

Actuarial methods may differ, but accounting for each plan should follow the stated standards. (AC 4063.37)

[¶1509] SOCIAL SECURITY BENEFITS AND PENSION PLANS

Some pension plans provide for reduced benefits to the extent of Social Security benefits. In estimating future benefits for present value purposes under the plan, estimate must also be then made for the Social Security benefits applicable. (AC 4063 A.07g)

[¶1510] ERISA REQUIREMENTS

No change in accounting standards is necessitated by the new participation, vesting or funding requirements of the 1974 Act, because the determination of proper cost still falls under the minimum-maximum rules. (AC 4063-1.03) However, significant increase in the dollar amount of the pension cost contribution caused by the requirements should be disclosed when the plan first becomes subject to the Act. (AC 4063-1.04)

[¶1511] OTHER DEFERRED COMPENSATION CONTRACTS

Other contracts should be accounted for individually on an accrual basis with the estimated amounts to be ultimately paid systematically and rationally allocated over the period of active employment from the time the contract is effective until services are expected to end or the contract expire. However, deferring expenses is permissible to match future services. (AC 4064.01)

For annuity or lump-sum type settlements in these plans, the annual accrual should still be accrued over the time of active employment, so that the total expenses booked to the end of employment should equal the estimated present value of the money to be paid the employee (or his survivors). (AC 4064.02 and footnote)

[¶1512] KEY-MAN LIFE INSURANCE

The acceptable method of accounting for premium costs incurred in buying key-man (non-term) life insurance is to first charge an asset account for the period's increase in the cash surrender value of the policy and then expense the difference between that increase and the premium paid. The ratable charge method is not acceptable. (AC U 4064.001 to .004) This procedure applies only to those policies under which the corporation is the ultimate beneficiary. But the procedure also applies to those policies which may be taken on "debtor-corporation" officers.

A loan on a life insurance policy of an officer can be shown in either of two ways:

1. As a current liability if the company intends to repay it within the current year; or

2. As a deduction from the amount shown as cash surrender value if the company does *not* intend to repay it within a year. If it runs to the death of the insured, it is deducted from the proceeds, if the corporation transmits them to the survivors. (Footnote to AC 2031.07)

Although the corporation is the beneficiary of these funds on a pay-out of the policy, the proceeds are usually used to pay benefits to the employee's family, to redeem stock, or for some other like purpose beneficial to the employee.

[¶1513]   MISCELLANEOUS CONSIDERATIONS

In a business combination, the rule for assigning an amount for the assumption of pension cost accruals (AC 1091.88 Footnote 14) should be the greater of:

1. The accrued pension cost computed in conformity with the accounting policies of the acquiring company, or
2. The excess, if any, of the actuarially computed value of the vested benefits over the amount of the fund.

In the disposal of a business segment, costs and expenses directly associated with the decision to dispose should include such items as: (AC 2012.17)

1. Severance pay;
2. Additional pension costs;
3. Employee relocation expenses.

In pooling of interest, employee compensation and stock option plans, if reasonable, may carry over to the acquiring company without violating the precepts of pooling. (AC U 1091.126 to .132)

16

Imputed Interest on Notes Receivable or Payable

[¶1601]

The AICPA sets forth the appropriate accounting when the face amount of certain receivables or payables ("notes") does not reasonably represent the present value of the consideration given or received in certain exchanges. The objective of these rules is to prevent the form of the transaction from prevailing over its economic substance. (AC 4111.01)

(*Present value* is the sum of future payments, discounted to the present date at an appropriate rate of interest.)

The Opinion states that:

(1) When a note is received or issued solely for cash, the note is presumed to have a present value equal to the cash received. If it is issued for cash equal to its face amount, it is presumed to earn the stated rate of interest. (AC 4111.10)

(2) When a note is received for cash and some other rights or privileges, the value of the rights or privileges should be given accounting recognition by establishing a note discount or premium account, with the offsetting amount treated as appropriate. An example is a five-year noninterest-bearing loan made to a supplier in partial consideration for a purchase of products at lower than prevailing market prices. Under such circumstances, the difference between the present value of the receivable and the cash lent to the supplier is regarded as (a) an additional cost of the purchased goods and (b) interest income, amortized over the life of the note. (AC 4111.06)

(3) When a note is exchanged for property, goods, or services and (a) interest is not stated, or (b) it is stated but is unreasonable, or (c) the stated face amount of the note is materially different from the current cash sale price of goods (or services), the note, the sales price, and the cost of the property (goods or services) should be recorded at their fair value or at an amount that reasonably

125

approximates the market value of the note, whichever is more clearly determinable.

Any resulting discount or premium should be regarded as interest expense or income and be amortized over the life of the note in such a way as to result in a constant rate of interest when applied to the amount outstanding at the beginning of any given period.

The Opinion also provides some general guides for determining an "appropriate" interest rate (AC 4111.12-.13) and the manner of amortization for financial reporting purposes. (AC 4111.14-.15)

17

Extraordinary Items

[¶1701]

Income statement presentation requires that the results of *ordinary operations* be reported first and applicable provision for income taxes provided for that ordinary operating income then be deducted therefrom. Then, in order, the following should be shown:

1. Results of discontinued operations (AC 2012.08):

   A. Income or loss from the operations discontinued for the portion of the period until discontinuance — shown net of tax, with the tax shown parenthetically;

   B. Loss (or gain) on disposal of the business segments, including provision for phase-out operating losses — also shown net of tax parenthetically.

2. Extraordinary items.

   Should be segregated and shown as the last factor used in arriving at net income for the period. Here also, the caption is shown net of applicable income taxes, which are shown parenthetically. (AC 2012.11)

   Note that extraordinary items do *not* include disposal of business segments as such, because they are segregated and shown separately prior thereto (as above).

An example of the reporting of the above:

	1976	1975
Income from continuing operations before income taxes	$ xxx	$ xxx
Provision for income taxes	xx	xx
Income from continuing operations	$ xxx	xxx
Discontinued operations (Note): Income from operations of discontinued Division B (less applicable taxes of $xx)	$ xx	

	1976	1975
Loss on disposal of Division B, including provision for phase-out operating losses of \$ xx (less applicable income taxes of \$ xx)	xx	xx
Income before extraordinary items		xxx
Extraordinary items (less applicable income taxes of \$xx) (Note)		xx —
Net Income	\$ xxx	\$ xxx
Earnings per share:		
Income from continuing operations	\$ x.00	\$ x.00
Discontinued operations	x.00	x.00
Extraordinary items	x.00	x.00
Net Income	\$ x.00	\$ x.00

Note that earnings per share should be broken out separately for the factors of discontinued operations and extraordinary items, as well as for income from (continuing) operations. (AC 2012.08 — .09; AC 2012.11 and AC 2011C.03 Exhibit B)

The criteria for classifying a transaction or event as an ''extraordinary item'' are as follows (AC 2012.20):

Extraordinary items are events and transactions that are distinguished by their unusual nature *and* by the infrequency of their occurrence. Thus *both* of the following criteria should be met to classify an event or transaction as an extraordinary item:

1. *Unusual nature* — the underlying event or transaction should possess a high degree of abnormality and be of a type clearly unrelated to, or only incidentally related to, the ordinary and typical activities of the entity, taking into account the environment in which the entity operates.

2. *Infrequency of occurrence* — ''the underlying event or transaction should be of a type that would not reasonably be expected to recur in the foreseeable future, taking into account the environment in which the entity operates.''

Items which are *not* to be reported as extraordinary because they may recur or are not unusual are: (AC 2012.23)

1. Write-downs of receivables, inventories, intangibles, or leased equipment.
2. Effects of strikes.
3. Gains or losses on foreign currency translations.
4. Adjustment of accruals on long-term contracts.
5. Gains or losses on disposal of business segments.
6. Gains or losses from abandonment or sale of property, plant or equipment used in the business.

Note that some highly unusual occurrence might cause one of the above types of gains or losses and should be considered extraordinary, such as those resulting from: major casualties (earthquake), expropriations, legal restrictions. Disposals of business segments, though not extraordinary in classification, should be shown separately on the income statement, just prior to extraordinary items, but after operations from continuing business.

Miscellaneous data pertaining to extraordinary items:

Bargain sales of stock to stockholders are *not* extraordinary items, but they should be shown separately. (TA 4110.04)

A gain or a loss on sale of coin collections by a bank is *not* an extraordinary item. (TA 6100.06)

18

Earnings Per Share

[¶1801]

It is mandatory that earnings per share (EPS) data be shown in conjunction with the presentation of financial statements, annual or interim, and that such data be shown on the face of the income statement. (AC 2011.12)

Such amounts should be presented for:

1. Income before extraordinary items, and

2. Net income.

It is customary to show the earnings per share for the extraordinary items also.

There are basically two types of capital structure involved in the calculation of EPS:

1. A simple capital structure, or

2. A complex capital structure.

Corporations with complex corporate structures should present two types of earnings per share data:

1. Primary earnings per share, based on outstanding common shares and those securities that are in substance equivalent to common shares, and

2. Fully diluted earnings per share which reflect the dilution of earnings per share that would have occurred if all contingent issuances of stock had taken place. (Reduction of less than 3% is not deemed sufficient to cause dilution.)

Earnings per share should be presented for all periods covered by the income statement. If a prior period has been restated, the earnings per share should also be restated for that period.

The underlying simple basic formula for calculating EPS is:

Net income (earnings) *divided by* number of shares outstanding (common only)

or:

$$\frac{\text{Earnings (net income)}}{\text{Number of common shares outstanding}} = \text{EPS}$$

The *dollars* are always the numerator; the *number* of shares the denominator.

130

The complexity of determining either factor in the formula increases as the corporate's capital structure expands into more exotic types of equity security and potential types of equity security.

Refer now to the *Fact Sheet* presented next and to the illustrations which follow based on that fact sheet:

[¶1802]   FACT SHEET FOR EARNINGS PER SHARE ILLUSTRATIONS

		(in thousands of dollars)	
INCOME STATEMENT	1976	1975	1974
Income before extraordinary item	$ 12,900	$ 9,150	$ 7,650
Extraordinary item — net of tax	900	900	—
Net Income	$ 13,800	$ 10,050	$ 7,650

SHARE INFORMATION

	(in thousands of shares)		
Common stock outstanding:			
Beginning of year	3,300	3,000	3,000 *
Issued during year	—	300(3)	—
Conversion of preferred stock (1)	500	—	—
Conversion of debentures (2)	200	—	—
End of year	4,000	3,300	3,000
Common stock reserved under employee stock options granted	7	7	—

Weighted average number of shares (see calculations):

1974 — 3,000,000 shares weighted average
1975 — 3,150,000 shares weighted average
1976 — 4,183,333 shares weighted average

* issued at 1/1/74
(3) issued at 7/1/75

(1) *Convertible preferred stock:* 600,000 shares issued at the beginning of the second quarter of 1975. Dividend rate is 20ᶜ per share. Market value was $53 at time of issue with a cash yield of 0.4% as opposed to bank prime rate of 5.5%. Warrants to buy 500,000 shares of common stock at $60 per share for a period of five years were, in addition, issued along with this convertible preferred. Each share of the convertible stock was convertible into one common share (exclusive of the warrants).

During 1976, 500,000 shares of the preferred stock were converted because the common dividend exceeded the preferred. But, *no warrants were exercised* during the year.

(2) *Convertible debentures:* 4% with a principal amount of $10,000,000 (due 1994) were sold at 100 in the last quarter of 1974. Each $100 debenture was convertible into *two* shares of common stock. The entire issue was converted at the beginning of the *third* quarter of 1976, when called by the company. (None were converted in 1974 or 1975.)

The prime rate at issue in 1974 was 6%. The coupon face rate of the bonds was 4%. The bonds had a market value of $100 when issued.

Additional information:

Market price of the common stock: (average prices)

	1976	1975	1974
1st quarter	50	45	40
2nd quarter	60	52	41
3rd quarter	70	50	40
4th quarter	70	50	45
Dec 31 closing price	72	51	44

Cash dividends on common stock:

Declared and paid *each* quarter	$1.25	$ .25	$ .25

[¶1803]   **ILLUSTRATIONS**
                        (Based on the Fact Sheet)

1974 — SIMPLE CAPITAL STRUCTURE

The simplest computation involves those companies with:

1. Only common stock issued, and
2. No change in outstanding number during the year, and
3. Net income arising without any extraordinary items.

For 1974, the first year of the company's operation on the fact sheet, the EPS would be:

$$\frac{\text{Income}}{\text{\# shares outstanding}} \quad \text{or} \quad \frac{\$7,650,000}{3,000,000} \quad \text{or} \quad \$2.55 \text{ per share.}$$

1975 — EXPANDED SIMPLE CAPITAL STRUCTURE

The significant changes in 1975 affecting EPS:

1. The extraordinary item of income of $900M, requiring separate disclosure; and
2. The 300,000 shares issued during the year, requiring the computation of a weighted average.

Computing the weighted average — determine the number of shares outstanding at the end of each quarter and divide by four:

1st quarter	3,000,000
2nd quarter	3,000,000
3rd quarter	3,300,000
4th quarter	3,300,000
	12,600,000 divided by 4
	or 3,150,000 shares

The employee stock options are *under* 3% of the aggregate outstanding, so they are not considered dilutive and are ignored in the EPS calculation. (AC 2011.15 footnote)

Proper *disclosure* for the 1975 EPS would be:

Earnings per common share:	1975	1974
Income before extraordinary items	$2.90(4)	$2.55
Extraordinary item	.29(5)	—
Net Income	$3.19	$2.55

(4) $9,150,000 divided by 3,150,000
(5)   900,000 divided by 3,150,000

(In the above example, the dilution factors used *below* are not applicable, appearing on the fact sheet merely for use in the complex structure example next.)

1976 — COMPLEX CAPITAL STRUCTURE

The significant changes in 1976 affecting EPS:

1. The number of common shares (equivalents) represented by the warrants; and
2. The number of common share equivalents represented by the 600,000 shares of convertible preferred stock, issued in 1975; and
3. The additional EPS computation required for the full dilution assumption.

1. The number of common shares (equivalents) represented by the warrants:

$60 exercise price X 500,000 warrants or $30,000,000

$30,000,000 divided by $70 share market price	428,572 (shares)
500,000 shares minus 428,572	71,428 (shares)

Weighted average of the warrant shares: Not applicable for any quarter prior to the third quarter of 1976 because the market price did not exceed the exercise price:

First quarter 1976	—
Second quarter 1976	—
Third quarter 1976	71,428
Fourth quarter 1976	71,428
	142,856 divided by 4

Warrant share equivalents — or 35,714 shares

2. The number of common share equivalents represented by the convertible preferred stock:

	1976	1975
Number of shares of preferred stock issued in 1975	600,000	450,000*
Less the number of shares of common stock issued on conversion in 1976 (500,000). But, these shares were issued at various times during the year. Based on even issuance, the weighted average is ½ or	(250,000)	—
The equivalent shares with potential issue factor	350,000	450,000

*Based on weighted average from start of second quarter

	1976	1975
The weighted average number of common shares and equivalents is therefore:		
Shares outstanding at beginning (incl. 7/1/75 issue)	3,300,000	3,150,000
Shares issued on conversion of preferred stock (as above)	250,000	—
Shares issued on conversion of the debentures — 200,000 at 7/1/76; weighted average is 100,000	100,000	
Equivalents for the warrants (as prior)	35,714	
Equivalents for the convertible preferred stock above	350,000	450,000
Total weighted average (primary)	4,035,714	3,600,000

3. Additional share calculation to determine full dilution:

	1976	1975
Remaining shares applicable to convertible debentures	100,000	200,000
Shares applicable to warrants	(35,714)	—
Shares applicable to warrants based on yearend price of $72 — $60 X 500,000 divided by $72, with result subtracted from 500,000	83,333	
Add primary weighted shares above	4,035,714	3,600,000
Shares for full-dilution EPS	4,183,333	3,800,000

Proper disclosure of EPS for 1976 would then be:

	1976	1975
Primary earnings per common share and common equivalent shares (Note __):		
Income before extraordinary item	$ 3.20(1)	$ 2.54(1A)
Extraordinary item	.22(2)	.25(2A)
Net Income	$ 3.42(3)	$ 2.79(3A)
Fully diluted earnings per common share (Note __)		
Income before extraordinary item	$ 3.11(4)	$ 2.46(7)
Extraordinary item	.21(5)	.24(8)
Net Income	$ 3.32(6)	$ 2.70(9)

(1) $12,900,000 divided by 4,035,714 or $ 3.20
(2)   900,000 divided by 4,035,714 or   .22
(3)   13,800,000 divided by 4,035,714 or $ 3.42

(1A)   9,150,000 divided by 3,600,000 or $ 2.54
(2A)   900,000 divided by 3,600,000 or   .25
(3A) 10,050,000 divided by 3,600,000 or $ 2.79

(4)   13,004,000 divided by 4,183,333 or $ 3.11
        (above includes $104,000 addback for debenture interest)
(5)   900,000 divided by 4,183,333 or ___.21
(6)   13,904,000 divided by 4,183,333 or $ 3.32

(7)   9,358,000 divided by 3,800,000 or $ 2.46
        (includes $208,000 for interest on debentures)
(8)   900,000 divided by 3,800,000 or ___.24
(9) $10,258,000 divided by 3,800,000 or $ 2.70

The illustrations here do *not* cover the following topics:

1. Disclosure requirements for financial notes (AC 2011C.04)

2. Handling of dividends paid or unpaid on convertible stocks (AC 2011A.06)

3. Subsequent events which require supplemental calculations (AC 2011.23)

4. Anti-dilution (AC 2011.30)

5. The test for common stock equivalent status (including the treasury stock method) (AC 2011.31 — .38)

6. Details of calculating dilution under the treasury stock method (AC 2011.38)

7. Effect of stock splits or stock dividends on number of shares (AC 2011A.03)

8. EPS in business combinations (AC 2011A.04)

9. Discussion of the ''if converted'' method of computation (AC 2011A.06)

10. Discussion of the ''cash-yield'' test for the consideration of equivalents (AC 2011.33)

11. Effect of contingencies involved in share issuance (AC 2011A.16)

12. Securities of subsidiaries (AC 2011A.20).

Some of the above topics may be illustrated best in financial statements issued by prominent public corporations. They may also be researched further in the sections indicated in the AICPA's ''Accounting Standards'' volumes (3 and 4).

19

Statement of Changes in Financial Position (Funds Statement)

[¶1901]

One of the *required* basic financial statements (along with the balance sheet, statement of income, statement of changes in retained earnings and related notes and disclosures) is the "Statement of Changes in Financial Position" (formerly, and sometimes now, called the "Funds Statement"). (AC 1027.17 R-1) The requirement applies to all profit-oriented businesses, regardless of whether they use "current assets/current liabilities" classifications or not. (AC 2021.07)

As with the other statements, information should be presented for two comparative periods (at least). However, for interim reports, this statement is not required.

The complete statement of changes in financial position of a period "should include and properly describe all important aspects of the company's financing and investing activities." (AC 1027.18 R-4) This concept extends the elements of inclusion beyond those merely encompassing the factors in "working capital."

Earlier concept: The concept of *funds* in funds statements (Statement of Source and Application of Funds) was varied somewhat in practice, with resulting variations in the nature of statements. For example, *funds* were sometimes interpreted to mean *cash* or its equivalent, and the resulting funds statement was a summary of cash provided and used. Another interpretation of *funds* was that of *working capital* (current assets less current liabilities), and the resulting funds statement was a summary of working capital provided and used. The funds statement, therefore, excluded certain financing and investing activities because they did not directly affect cash or working capital.

Present concept: The standards now provide for the inclusion of the following elements in the Statement of Changes in Financial Position (AC 2021.14):

1. Working capital (or cash provided from or used in operations for the period):

A. If the format shows the *flow of cash,* other components of working capital (inventory, receivables, payables) are then directed to the sources and uses of *cash* and should be so disclosed in detail. (AC 2021.12a)

B. If the format shows the *flow of working capital,* the components of net change in working capital for the current period (and the comparative period presented) should be analyzed and shown in detail. (AC 2021.12b)

2. All other sources and applications of funds which affect (net) working capital.

Funds statements are required for each year income statements are presented, though detail is required only for the current year. (AC U2021.001)

[¶1901.1] WORKING CAPITAL

The *components* of "working capital" are current assets and current liabilities. The term working capital in the professional parlance indicates the *excess* of current assets over current liabilities, and the more appropriate description is "net working capital." (AC 1027.24 R-9A)

Current assets include cash and other assets that can be expected to be turned into cash or consumed during the normal operating cycle — usually one year.

Current liabilities are basically those which will probably be satisfied within the same cycle (one year).

The flow of working capital: (This is the factor "Funds Provided by Operations" in the SOURCES OF FUNDS below.)

Working capital provided from operations for period:

1. Income (loss) before extraordinary items.

2. Add (or deduct) expenses not requiring outlay of working capital in the current period (such as depreciation).

3. Caption the total of above as "Working Capital provided from Operations exclusive of extraordinary items."

4. Add (or deduct) working capital provided by extraordinary items.

5. Add (or deduct), adjusting income for extraordinary items included which did *not* affect working capital.

6. (Total) Funds Provided by Operations (Working Capital)

[¶1901.2]

After the above has been determined, the other factors in the display are then calculated and displayed (overall) as follows:

SOURCES OF FUNDS:

Funds provided by operations (as above)	xx	
Other sources of funds	<u>xx</u>	xx

APPLICATION OF FUNDS   (xx)

Increase (or decrease) in funds
(Net change in working capital)   xx

The remaining information comes from the required disclosure of the following additional elements needed to arrive at and explain the net increase or decrease in (net) working capital for the period. Each factor should be classified as a "source" or an "application" as appropriate: (AC 2021.14)

1. Outlays for purchases of long-term assets, detailed as to class;
2. Proceeds from sale of long-term assets (detailed as to class);
3. Reduction of long-term debt or preferred stock by conversion to common stock;
4. Issuance, assumption, redemption or repayment of long-term debt;
5. Issuance, redemption or purchase of capital stock for cash or for assets other than cash;
6. Dividends (except stock dividends and split-ups).

Working capital is a significant factor from several points of view. To creditors and credit grantors, it is an indication of the debtor's ability to repay. Management, stockholders and creditors want to know how it changes from year to year. Therefore, it is important to classify current assets and current liabilities properly.

[¶1901.3]   Information from Statement

The Statement provides management and stockholders with the following type of information:

(1) Where the profits were applied.

(2) The reason that dividends were not larger or why the company was able to distribute dividends in excess of current earnings or where there was a net loss for the period.

(3) The reason for the decrease in net current assets although the net income is up or vice versa.

(4) The reason money may have to be borrowed to finance purchases of new plant and equipment when the required amount is exceeded by the "cash flow"; i.e., the sum of the net income and depreciation.

(5) How increases in plant and equipment were financed.

(6) Where the proceeds of the sale of plant and equipment resulting from a contraction of operations were applied.

(7) Where the proceeds for the retirement of debt came from.

(8) What was done with the proceeds derived from an increase in outstanding capital stock or from the bond issue.

Hilton Hotels Corporation
and Subsidiaries

*Consolidated Statement
of Changes in Financial Position*

	Year Ended December 31,	1975	1974
Source of Funds	Net income	$ 42,381,000	17,279,000
	Depreciation	19,166,000	22,104,000
	Gain on sales of properties and write-down of investments (net of tax provision of $12,174,000 and tax benefit of $359,000)	(22,239,000)	(206,000)
	Deferred income taxes	719,000	1,721,000
	Equity in earnings of 17% to 50% owned companies	(5,904,000)	(2,446,000)
	Working capital provided by operations, exclusive of sales of properties and write-down of investments	34,123,000	38,452,000
	Sales of properties and write-down of investments		
	Proceeds	84,981,000	6,332,000
	Long-term portion of debt transferred	(18,808,000)	—
	Tax provision and benefit	(12,174,000)	359,000
	Long-term debt financing	—	8,000,000
	New Yorker property mortgage debt	—	6,847,000
	Reduction of investments	7,086,000	2,868,000
	Other — net	2,054,000	1,631,000
		97,262,000	64,489,000
Use of Funds	Property and equipment additions	15,254,000	35,705,000
	Reacquisition of New Yorker property	—	7,766,000
	Reduction of long-term debt	24,075,000	20,291,000
	Payment of cash dividends	7,450,000	7,757,000
	Purchase of treasury stock	25,463,000	5,208,000
	Additional investments	3,339,000	4,784,000
	Deferred taxes on casino receivables	971,000	928,000
	Settlements of prior income taxes	1,486,000	1,483,000
	Other changes in deferred tax liabilities	—	2,098,000
		78,038,000	86,020,000
Net Increase (Decrease) in Working Capital		$ 19,224,000	(21,531,000)

*Summary of Changes in
Components of Working Capital*

		1975	1974
Increase (Decrease) in Current Assets	Cash and temporary investments	$ 22,013,000	(25,271,000)
	Accounts and notes receivable	104,000	7,704,000
	Inventories	1,657,000	1,039,000
	Prepaid expenses and other	71,000	532,000
		23,845,000	(15,996,000)
Increase (Decrease) in Current Liabilities	Accounts and notes payable	(7,002,000)	5,587,000
	Accrued expenses and other	(3,085,000)	2,413,000
	Current maturities of long-term debt	(6,904,000)	580,000
	Federal and state income taxes	21,612,000	(3,045,000)
		4,621,000	5,535,000
Net Increase (Decrease) in Working Capital		$ 19,224,000	(21,531,000)

20

Foreign Currency Translations

[¶2001]

The principle of conservatism *generally* requires the use of historical cost, and increases or decreases in assets or liabilities brought about by market conditions are not recorded until actual transfer or exchange occurs. (AC 1027.09 S-4 & S-5)

However, there are two exceptions, now accepted as standard procedure, which require the consideration of the *market price*, matching it to historical cost, and recording the *unrealized* loss or gain for the period, to reflect the market price of the asset (or liability), generally at balance sheet date.

This chapter is concerned with one of those exceptions — *foreign currency translations*. The other exception is in the handling of marketable securities, covered separately in this Accounting Section.

Foreign currency transactions involve changes in the amount of U.S. Dollars required to satisfy obligations (either receivables or payables) and also conversion of foreign holdings, generally stated in the currency of the foreign country.

In dealing with foreign currency translations, there are primarily two broad areas of distinction, involving translations for:

1. Domestic statements which include receivables or payables that are *invoiced* in foreign currency, and payable in that foreign currency, requiring calculation of effective U.S. Dollar obligations at statement date. (The AICPA calls this "Foreign Currency *Transactions*" — AC 1083.003)

2. Domestic parent companies which have foreign subsidiaries or branches, with financial statements prepared in terms of foreign currency, involving assets, liabilities, equity and income — and which involve consolidation, combination or the equity method. (Called "Foreign Currency *Operations*" — AC 1083.003)

[¶2001.1]   1. Foreign Currency Transactions

The following procedure should be followed for those dealings which *do not* involve the branch or subsidiary structures: (AC 1083.007)

A. *At date of transaction* — record the transaction using the exchange rate of the date of the transaction;

B. *At first balance sheet date next* — convert the stated values above to the rate at balance sheet date for balance sheet items (amounts owed by and to the company). The net difference becomes the unrealized gain/loss for the income statement;

C. Running records should be maintained to distinguish then the *realized* gains and losses which are effectuated upon *actual* settlement date of the obligations. Two points to observe:

    1. Income tax is based on the realized gain or loss on date of settlement of obligation; and

    2. The rate of exchange at the *date of settlement* will undoubtedly be different from the prior year-end rate reflected, and due distinction must be made between the unrealized portion of gain/loss *already*, booked and the *difference* in matching it to the culminating *realized* amount. There will be only a *partial* gain or loss to pick up now on the income statement.

D. At each *subsequent* balance sheet date, obligations must again be restated to reflect the new year-end exchange rate, creating additional unrealized gain or loss for the income statement (and involving the partial effects mentioned directly above).

Reasonable averages (usually monthly) may be used for numerous transactions, such as sales or purchases.

Due diligence should be exercised in pricing the *inventories* resulting from purchases. The cost or market rule should be applied with consideration given to a possible *lower* year-end conversion rate than the rate on the date of purchase. Here too, reasonable averages may be used lacking detailed costing records. (See ¶ 2001.3 below.)

[¶2001.2]   2. Foreign Curency Operations

The following procedures should be followed for consolidation, combination or use of the equity method: (AC 1083.010-.012)

A. *Prior* to translation, the foreign statement should be prepared to conform to generally accepted U.S. accounting principles; and

B. Balances representing cash and amounts receivable and payable shall be adjusted to reflect the *current* rate of exchange (balance sheet date); and

C. All other items should be translated in a manner which *retains* their measurement basis:

    1) Accounts which are carried at *past* prices should be translated at the historical rate (the exchange rate in effect at the time of the transaction — such as property purchase date), and

    2) Accounts which are carried at current sale or purchase exchange rates should be translated at the current rate.

Revenue and expenses should be translated as if they had been translated on the date of occurence. (Averages may be used) *Exception:* Expenses such as depreciation and amortization, which are based on the historical cost, should be translated at the historical cost rate. (AC 1083.013)

The net balancing factor required for the balance sheet, combined with the net revenue/expense conversion amount — for the *first* year of translation — would give the net unrealized gain or loss for the income statement. The second year and the years thereafter would involve the consideration of the opening balance of unrealized amount forwarded (but unmarked) in the opening figure of retained earnings.

Forward contracts involving currency hedging commitments or speculations require special handling. (AC 1083.022 to .028)

[¶2001.3]   Inventories — Applying the Rule of Cost or Market, (whichever is lower)

To apply the rule of *cost or market, whichever is lower* (Section AC 5121.09), *translated historical cost* shall be compared with *translated market*. Application of the rule *in dollars* may require write-downs to market in the translated statements even though no write-down in the foreign statements is required by the rule. It may also require a write-down in the foreign statements to be reversed before translation if the translated market amount exceeds translated historical cost; the foreign currency cost shall then be translated at the historical rate. Once inventory has been written down to market in the translated statements, that dollar amount shall continue to be the carrying amount in the dollar financial statements until the inventory is sold or a further write-down is necessary. (AC 1083.046)

To the extent losses are recovered in the same year, gains on market translation (based on *prior* write-downs) may be recognized. (Footnote to AC 1083.046)

21

Business Combinations* and Investments in Subsidiaries

[¶2101]

This chapter deals with the *accounting* treatment of dealings involved with the following types of business combinations and acquisitions:

1. Those *combinations* occurring when a corporation and one or more *incorporated* or *unincorporated* business *are united into one* accounting entity, with that single entity then carrying on the activities of the prior separate entities. Two methods of accounting are applicable here:

    A. The Purchase Method, or

    B. The Pooling of Interests Method

2. Those *stock acquisitions* (or stock investments) wherein one corporation *buys the voting common stock* of another corporation — sometimes acquiring voting control, sometimes not — with both entities continuing as separate, individual, distinct operating corporations.

Three methods of accounting are applicable here:

    A. The Consolidation Method (or the alternate Combining Method)

    B. The Equity Method

    C. The Cost Method

In each of these methods, the investment in the subsidiary's stock appears on the books of the owning company as an investment asset.

---

* On August 19, 1976, the FASB issued for comment a discussion memorandum on "Accounting for Business Combinations and Purchased Intangibles."

In order to clarify the distinctions involved — as a quick reference — these major points should be considered:

1. Consolidation, the Equity Method and the Cost Method all pertain to the acquisition of *voting stock* by the buying company.

   Pooling and Purchase pertain to the acquisition of *assets* and usually liabilities (inventory, plant, equipment, etc.)

2. How to distinguish between pooling and purchase:

   A. With *pooling,* the *acquiring* company uses its *own capital stock* to exchange for the capital stock of the acquired company. For example, a stockholder of Company B (the *acquired* company) will, after pooling, hold stock in Company A, the acquiring company. Company B's stock will have been canceled. Or, a third Company C might be formed with both A & B companies folding into Company C. Pooling is usually a tax-free combination, provided all requirements are met.

   B. With *purchase,* the acquiring company buys the assets (usually net of liabilities), and the acquired company (the one selling the assets) must usually account for gain or loss on the sale of the individual assets, involving the recapture provisions of the tax law.

   C. Pooling involves the exchange of stock.

   Purchase can involve either stock, cash or property. (AC 1091.15)

   D. In *purchase,* the assets are valued at *fair value,* usually creating goodwill.

   In *pooling,* there is no change in asset value, since they are picked up at net *book* value.

   E. Under both pooling and purchase, the acquired company is subsequently liquidated.

   F. A combination of *both* methods is unacceptable. (AC 1091.43)

3. With *stock acquisitions,* all companies continue separate operations even though under new ownership or managerial control. Accounting records are maintained for each distinct company, and each company prepares financial statements independent of the other company. However, public release of those statements is guided by the rules of consolidation or the equity method.

4. With stock acquisitions:

   A. Use the *cost method* when owning less than 20% of the stock *and* exercising *no* effective managerial control.

   B. Use the *equity method when owning 20% or more* (influence is presumed) — or when owning less than 20% *but with substantial managerial* influence. Also, use the equity method when owning *over 50%* and *not using the consolidation method.*

   C. *Use the consolidation method* when ownership is *over 50%* (majority interest), *unless* conditions exist (described later) which constitute exception to the rules of consolidation and permit the use of the equity method.

Note that financial accounting (and the SEC) require consolidation for over 50% holdings, with exceptions noted, but the IRS requires a minimum 80% voting control for consolidated tax returns.

Consolidation must also be used for subsidiaries whose principal activity is leasing property or facilities to the parent or other affiliates. (AC 5131.15)

When *not* using consolidation, and the holdings are over 50%, the equity method must be used for all unconsolidated subsidiaries (foreign as well as domestic).

When holdings are 50% or under, down to 20%, you must use the equity method, since significant managerial voice is presumed (unless you prove the contrary).

Further details of each of these methods are now presented.

(See Journal Entries in the Appendix.)

[¶2102] THE COST METHOD — STOCK ACQUISITIONS

The cost method: An investor records an investment in the stock of an investee at cost, and recognizes as income dividends received that are distributed from net accumulated earnings of the investee since the date of acquisition by the investor. (AC 5131.06a)

Dividends from the investee's earnings are entered as income;

Dividends in *excess* of investee's earnings after date of investment reduce the cost of the investment;

Losses of the investee (after acquisition) should be recognized under the "marketable security" standards.

For the investor, under the *cost method,* dividends only are to be picked up as income (with cash being debited).

[¶2103] THE EQUITY METHOD — STOCK ACQUISITIONS

The equity method: An investor initially records an investment in the stock of an investee at cost and adjusts the carrying amount of the investment to recognize the investor's share of the earnings or losses of the investee after the date of the acquisition. The amount of the adjustment is included in the determination of net income by the investor, and such amount reflects adjustments similar to those made in preparing consolidated statements including adjustments to eliminate intercompany gains and losses, and to amortize, if appropriate, any difference between investor cost and underlying equity in net assets of the investee at the date of the investment. (AC 5131.06b)

Proportionate share of earnings, whether distributed or not, increase the carrying amount of the investment and are recorded as income;

Dividends reduce the carrying amount of the investment and are *not* recorded as income;

After investment, a series of losses by the investee may necessitate additional reduction in the carrying amount.

Under the equity method, the proportionate share of earnings (losses) of the investee (subsidiary) is picked up as income (loss), with the investment asset account being debited (or credited for a loss). Dividends, when received, are thus merely a conversion of part of that increased investment value to cash.

Both the investment and the share of earnings are recorded as single amounts. Market devaluation is *not* applicable. (AC 5132.06)

[¶2103.1] The equity method should be used (for foreign or domestic subsidiaries):

1. When owning *20% or more* of the voting stock of the investee (significant control is presumed); or

2. When owning *less than 20%* and the investor can demonstrate the exercise of significant control; or

3. When not consolidating those investees in which more than 50% is owned; but the equity method should not be used if consolidation is justified; or

4. For participant's share of joint ventures.

The equity method *should not* be used:

1. When consolidation is proper for over 50% control; or

2. When ownership is below 20% and there is *no* demonstrable control (use the cost method); or

3. When the principal business activity of the subsidiary is leasing property or facilities to the parent or other affiliates (consolidate instead).

"Voting stock interest" is based on the *outstanding* shares without recognition of common stock equivalents. (AC 5131.18)

[¶2103.2] Applying the Equity Method (AC 5131.19)

1. Follow the rules of intercompany profit and loss eliminations as for consolidations;

2. At purchase of stock, adjust investment to reflect underlying equity and amortize goodwill, if any;

3. Show investment as a single amount, and show income as a single amount, except for (4) below;

4. Show share of extraordinary items separately, net of tax;

5. Any capital structure change of the investee should be accounted for as in consolidations;

6. When stock is sold, account for gain or loss based on the carrying amount then in the investment account;

7. Use the investee's latest financial statement;

8. Recognize non-temporary declines in the value of the investee's stock by adjusting the investment account;

9. Do not write investment account below zero; hold over any losses until future gains offset them;

10. Before picking up share of investee's income, deduct any cumulative preferred dividends (paid or unpaid) not already deducted by the investee;

11. If the level of ownership falls to the point which ordinarily calls for the cost method, stop accruing earnings undistributed, but apply dividends received to the investment account;

12. If changing from the cost method to the equity method for any one investment (because of change in ownership), make the necessary retroactive adjustments;

13. If goodwill is created in (12) above, it should be amortized.

[¶2103.3] Income Taxes

1. Set up a deferred tax based on the investor's proportion of the subsidiary's net income (after tax), based on the investor's rate of tax, *unless:*

   If it appears that the *undistributed earnings* of the investee meet the *indefinite reversal criteria* (see elsewhere in this text), do *not* accrue taxes, but make disclosure.

2. For dividends received, pull applicable tax out of deferred taxes and put in tax payable account;

3. Disclose applicable timing differences.

(See also Journal Entries in Appendix, Timing Differences and Disclosures in this text.)

[¶2104] THE CONSOLIDATION METHOD — STOCK ACQUISITIONS

There is a presumption that consolidated statements are more meaningful than separate statements and that they are usually necessary for a fair presentation when one of the companies in the group directly or indirectly has a controlling financial interest in the other companies. (AC 2051.02)

Assets, liabilities, revenues and expenses of the subsidiaries are combined with those of the parent company. Intercompany items are eliminated. (AC 5131.04)

Earned surplus of a subsidiary company from *prior* to acquisition does *not* form part of the parent's consolidated earned surplus, and dividends therefrom do not constitute income. (AC 2051.01)

The purpose of consolidated statements is to present the financial data as if it were one single unit.

[¶2104.1] Rule for Consolidation

The usual condition for a controlling financial interest is ownership of a majority voting interest, and, therefore, as a general rule ownership by one company, directly or indirectly, of over 50% of the outstanding voting shares of another company is a condition pointing toward consolidation. (AC 2051.03)

Do *not* consolidate:

1. When control is likely to be temporary; (AC 2051.03) or
2. Where control does *not* rest with the *majority* holder (example: subsidiary is in reorganization or bankruptcy); (AC 2051.03) or
3. Usually, for foreign subsidiaries (See later in this chapter); or
4. Where subsidiary is in a dissimilar business (manufacturer vs. financing); or
5. When the equity method or the cost method is more appropriate for the four conditions named above.

Note that the equity method should *usually* be used for all majority-held subsidiaries which are not consolidated, unless the cost method is necessitated by lack of influential control.

Foreign subsidiaries come under special standards and cost (with proper disclosure) may sometimes be used. (AC 2051.18 to .20) (See later in this chapter.)

[¶2104.2]   Other Considerations

A difference in fiscal period is no excuse for *not* consolidating. When the difference is no more than 3 months, use the subsidiary's fiscal-period report. Where greater than 3 months, corresponding period statements should be prepared for the subsidiary.

Intercompany items should be eliminated. (See later in this chapter.)

For partial years:

1. The year of acquisition: Consolidate for the year and, on income statement, deduct pre-acquisition earnings not applicable to the parent. (AC 2051.10)
2. The year of disposition: do not consolidate income; show only equity of parent in the subsidiary's earnings prior to disposal as a separate line item. (AC 2051.11)

Shares held by the parent should *not* be treated as outstanding stock in the consolidation. (AC 2051.12)

When a subsidiary capitalizes retained earnings for stock dividends or split-ups effected as dividends, such transfer is not required for the consolidated balance sheet which reflects the accumulated earnings and capitalization of the group (not the subsidiary). (AC 2051.17)

[¶2104.3]   Combined Statements

This is the showing of the individual company statements *plus* the combined consolidation, which combination reflects all intercompany eliminations.

Examples of when to use combined statements: (AC 2051.21)

1. Where one individual owns controlling interest in several related corporations; or
2. Where several companies are under common management; or

3. To present the information of a group of unconsolidated subsidiaries; or

4. When it is necessary to show the individual operations of parent as well as subsidiaries, as well as the consolidated results — for creditors usually. This type is also called a ''Parent-Company'' statement. (AC 2051.23)

[¶2104.4]   Limitations of Consolidated Statements

Along with their advantages, consolidated statements have certain limitations:

(1) The separate financial position of each company is not disclosed.

(2) The dividend policy of each company cannot be ascertained.

(3) Any financial ratios derived from the consolidated statements are only averages and do not represent any particular company.

(4) A consolidated income statement does not show which companies have been operating at a profit and which have been losing money.

(5) Creditors who are concerned with the financial resources of individual companies would not get the information they desire.

(6) Disclosing liens or other particulars of individual companies may require extensive footnotes.

(See Journal Entries for example of Consolidating Entries.)

[¶2105]   THE PURCHASE METHOD — BUSINESS COMBINATIONS

The Purchase Method accounts for a business combination as the acquisition of one company by another. The acquiring company records at its cost the acquired assets less liabilities assumed. A difference between the cost of an acquired company and the sum of the fair values of tangible and intangible assets less liabilities is recorded as goodwill. The reported income of an acquiring corporation includes the operations of the acquired company after acquisition, based on the cost to the acquiring corporation. (AC 1091.11)

The financial statements should be supplemented after purchase with proforma statements showing: (AC 1091.96)

1. Results of operations for the current period as if the combination had occurred at the beginning of the period; and

2. Results for the immediately preceding period also presented as if they had combined.

The AICPA has listed some general guides for the assigning of values to certain individual items, as follows: (AC 1091.88)

Receivables at present values of amounts to be received, less allowances for uncollectibles.

Marketable securities at net realizable values.

Inventories:

 Finished goods at selling prices, less disposal costs and reasonable profit to the acquirer.

 Work in process at selling price, less cost to complete, disposal cost and reasonable profit.

 Raw materials at current replacement prices.

Plant and equipment at current replacement cost if to be used or, if to be disposed of, at net realizable value.

Intangibles (identifiable, excluding goodwill) at appraised values.

All other assets at appraised values (including land).

Accounts and notes payable, long-term debt and other claims payable at *present values,* using current rates.

Accruals at present values also.

Other liabilities and commitments, also at present values, determined by using appropriate current interest rates.

Goodwill should be amortized on a straight-line basis over a period not to exceed 40 years, and only to a shorter period if benefit can be pinpointed.

[¶2106] THE POOLING-OF-INTERESTS METHOD — BUSINESS COMBINATIONS

The pooling-of-interests method accounts for a business combination as the uniting of ownership interests of two or more companies by exchange of equity securities. No acquisition is recognized because the combination is accomplished without disbursing resources of the constituents. Ownership interests continue and the former bases of accounting are retained. The recorded assets and liabilities of the constituents are carried forward to the combined corporation at their recorded amounts. Income of the combined corporation includes income of the constituents for the entire fiscal period for which the combination occurs. The reported income of the constituents for prior periods is combined and restated as income of the combined corporation. (AC 1091.12)

A pooling involves the combination of two or more stockholder interests which were previously *independent* of each other.

The AICPA has said that a business combination which meets *all* of the following conditions should be accounted for as a pooling (AC 1091.46 — .48):

 1. Attributes of the combining companies:

  A. Each is autonomous and not a subsidiary or division for the prior two years; and

  B. Each is independent of the other combining companies.

 2. Manner of combining interests:

  A. Effected within one year in a single transaction per a specified plan; and

B. The corporation issues only common stock identical with its majority outstanding voting stock in exchange for substantially all of the voting common stock of the acquired company at the date of consummation; and

C. None of the combining companies changes the equity interest of the voting common stock in contemplation of the combination within two years *before* the plan or between the dates the combination is initiated and it is consummated; and

D. No company re-acquires more than a normal number of shares and only for purposes other than for business combinations between the dates of initiation and consummation; and

E. The ratio of interest remains the same for each common stockholder, with nothing denied or surrendered, with respect to his proportion before the combination; and

F. Stockholder voting rights are not restricted nor deprived of by the resulting combination; and

G. The plan is resolved at the planned date and no provisions remain pending or carried over after the combination.

3. There is the absence of the following planned transactions:

A. The combined corporation does not intend to retire or re-acquire any of the common stock issued to effect the combination; and

B. The combination does not enter any financial arrangements to benefit former stockholders (such as a guaranty of loans secured by stock issued in the combination); and

C. There is no intent or plan to dispose of any of the assets of the combination within two years after the combination, other than those in the ordinary course of business or to eliminate duplicate facilities or excess capacity.

Financial statements of the current period and of any prior period presented should be presented as though the companies had been combined at the earliest dates presented and for the periods presented. (AC 1091.57)

Disclosure should cover all the relevant details.

[¶2107] FOREIGN SUBSIDIARIES

The following are the possible methods of providing information about foreign subsidiaries: (AC 1081.09)

1. Exclude foreign subsidiaries from consolidation. Include a summary of their assets, liabilities, income and losses for the year and the parent's equity in such foreign subsidiary. The amount of investment in the foreign subsidiary and the basis by which it was arrived should be shown. If the foreign subsidiary is excluded from consolidation, it is not proper to include intercompany profits (losses) which would have been eliminated by consolidating.

2. Consolidate domestic and foreign subsidiaries furnishing information of the foreign subsidiaries' assets, liabilities, income and losses, as stated above.

3. Furnish complete consolidated statements:
   A. Including only domestic companies, *and*
   B. Including the foreign subsidiaries
4. Consolidate domestic and foreign subsidiaries and furnish, in addition, parent company statements showing the investment in and income from foreign subsidiaries separately from those of domestic subsidiaries.

When *not* consolidating, under current standards *the equity method must be used* for unconsolidated foreign subsidiaries (majority-owned), unless those companies are operating under restrictive controls or uncertainties which would affect decisions — in which case, the cost method should be followed. (AC 5131.14 and footnote)

In using the financial data of foreign subsidiaries, the foreign currency translation rules will have to be considered and applied in order to restate that foreign currency in terms of U.S. Dollars, prior to consolidation or the equity method application. (See this text for Foreign Currency Translations.)

Also, deferred taxes will have to be accrued on the undistributed earnings of the subsidiary, *unless* the INDEFINITE REVERSAL CRITERIA apply. (See separate discussion in this text.)

Adjustment is also usually made between foreign taxes accrued and (the rate based on) U.S. income taxes, when the latter is higher, for the subsidiary's financial income.

[¶2108]   DISCs

A Domestic International Sales Corporation (DISC) is typically a 100%-owned domestic subsidiary corporation of a parent manufacturing or sales company, created especially for the purpose of benefiting from special tax provisions under IRS Code Section 991-997, and electing to be taxed thereunder.

The DISC income is derived predominantly (95% by tax law) from export sales and rentals.

The primary accounting aspects are:

1) A DISC is a wholly owned *domestic* subsidiary and should be consolidated with the parent's financial statement, even though the IRS prohibits it for tax purposes;

2) Portions of the DISC's earnings (even though not actually distributed) are considered to be distributed by the IRS and taxable as such to the parent. Therefore, for accounting purposes, clear distinction should be made on the DISC's books setting up a "previously taxed dividend payable." The parent should set up a contra "previously taxed dividends receivable" until such time as the cash transfer is made.

3) For the remaining portion of the DISC's earnings, which are not deemed distributed but which will be picked up as part of the consolidated income, *no entry* should be made for the deferral of applicable income taxes, *unless* there is

indication of impending distribution of those earnings. Since the main purpose of the DISC option is to *defer* taxability of those undistributed earnings, the presumption of non-distribution prevails, and the indefinite reversal criteria applies (see ¶ 2110 below).

[¶2109]   INTERCOMPANY TRANSACTIONS

[¶2109.1]   In Consolidations:

Since consolidated statements reflect the position and results of operations of what is considered a single economic entity, all intercompany balances and transactions must be eliminated. Some of these are obvious. Others are not.

Here are some of the items to be eliminated (done on worksheets which combine the company and its subsidiary figures):

1. The investment account in the subsidiary and its corresponding equity offset (capital stock and applicable retained earnings).

2. Intercompany open account balances, such as loans, receivables, payables arising from intercompany sales and purchases.

3. Intercompany security holdings, such as bonds, including related bond discount or premiums.

4. Intercompany profits where goods or services are exchanged for over cost, such as profits on transfers of inventory or fixed assets. Intercompany profits on fixed asset transfers might also involve adjustments to the accumulated depreciation account. Intercompany profits on inventory may affect both opening and closing inventories of raw materials, work in process and finished goods, as well as cost of sales.

5. Intercompany dividends.

6. Intercompany interest, rents and fees.

7. Intercompany bad debts.

The amount of intercompany profit or loss eliminated is not to be affected by the existence of minority interests. Such items must be eliminated. However, in eliminating them, they may be allocated proportionately between the majority and minority interests. (AC 2051.13)

If "bottom-line" accumulated losses occur to the extent of wiping out the minority interest, any excess losses should then be reflected against the *majority* interest, rather than showing a negative minority interest. However, future earnings should then first be applied to that excessive loss and the positive remaining earnings apportioned between the majority and minority interests. (AC 2051.14)

[¶2109.2]   In the Equity Method

Intercompany gains and losses should be eliminated in the same manner as if the subsidiary were consolidated. However, it is not necessary to eliminate intercompany gain on sales to such subsidiaries if the gain on the sales does *not* exceed the *unrecorded* equity in the *undistributed* earnings of the unconsolidated subsidiary. (AC 2051.19)

[¶2109.3]   In Combined Statements

Intercompany transactions and intercompany profits and losses should be eliminated following the same manner as for consolidated statements. (AC 2051.22)

[¶2110] THE INDEFINITE REVERSAL CRITERIA AND UNDISTRIBUTED EARNINGS OF SUBSIDIARIES

The importance of accruing or not accruing income taxes for undistributed earnings picked up in either consolidating or using the equity method should be checked.

Ordinarily, the parent company must accrue its own rate of tax expense on all income shown on the income statement, including that income required for pickup under consolidating or use of the equity method. Timing differences are thus created until actual distributions (dividends) are received.

However, the AICPA standards recognize certain circumstances under which it is permissible to *omit* this accrual of deferred taxes. The theory is that the timing difference will not be reversed in the immediate future. The concept is known as *"The Indefinite Reversal Criteria,"* and it is based upon the assumption that the subsidiary's earnings will *not* be distributed.

The following reasons are sufficient to justify *non-accrual* of taxes on reflected undistributed earnings of investees (AC 4095.12):

1. The subsidiary has invested or will invest the undistributed earnings indefinitely; or

2. The subsidiary will remit the earnings in a tax-free liquidation; or

3. It is apparent, based on a history of non-dividend payment, that no distribution will be made (as in a DISC company).

However, full disclosure should be made showing: (AC 4095.14)

A. The intention of reinvesting the undistributed earnings, or indefinitely postponing dividend distribution, *and*

B. The amount of the cumulative undistributed earnings and the extent of the tax not yet recognized.

[¶2111] GOODWILL IN BUSINESS COMBINATIONS

No "goodwill" is created in the "pooling-of-interests" method of combining businesses, since assets and liabilities are carried forward to the combined corporation at their recorded amounts.

With respect to the purchase method and stock acquisitions treated under either the consolidation method or the equity method, accounting for goodwill requires its amortization over a period of not in excess of forty years.

Goodwill, as discussed in Chapter 8 of this Accounting Section, is the amount assigned to the excess paid over the fair value of the identifiable net assets acquired.

[¶2112]   NEGATIVE GOODWILL

When the fair value of the net assets acquired *exceeds* the purchase price, "negative" goodwill arises. The standards then call for a reduction in the non-current assets (excluding investment securities) on a proportionate basis to absorb that excess *immediately*. If, in this absorption, the non-current assets are reduced to zero value and an excess still exists, that amount should then, and only then, be shown as a deferred credit, not a part of equity, and amortized to income over an estimated benefit period not to exceed forty years. (AC 1091.91) No part of that excess should be added to equity at time of acquisition. (AC 1091.92)

22

Financial Statements —
Special Requirements

[¶2201]   **DISCLOSURES**

"Financial information that meets the qualitative objectives of financial accounting also meets the reporting standard of adequate disclosure. Adequate disclosure relates particularly to objectives of relevance, neutrality, completeness, and understandability. Information should be presented in a way that facilitates understanding and avoids erroneous implications. The headings, captions, and amounts must be supplemented by enough additional data so that their meaning is clear but not by so much information that important matters are buried in a mass of trivia." (AC 1024.34)

THE REQUIRED PRESENTATION AND DISCLOSURES:

[¶2201.1]   **Required Basic Financial Statements For Comparative Periods:**

Balance Sheet — assets, liabilities, classes of owners' equity, components of working capital disclosed by the format;

Statement of Income — all revenue and expenses of the period per GAAP, gains, and losses distinguished from revenue, extraordinary items net of tax, net income and EPS on face of income statement;

Statement of Retained Earnings

Statement of Changes in Financial Position

Changes in other categories of equity

(Consolidation or equity method for subsidiaries and translation of foreign currencies as applicable).

[¶2201.2]   **Description of Accounting Policies in a "Summary of Significant Accounting Policies"**

With respect to:

Those principles materially affecting determination of financial position, changes in financial position and results of operation;

156

should include the judgments regarding:

A. Recognition of revenue
B. Allocation of asset costs to current and to future periods;
C. Principles and methods involving:
   1). Selection from acceptable alternatives
   2). Those peculiar to that industry
   3). Unusual applications of GAAP.

Examples are disclosure of methods of:

A. Consolidation
B. Depreciation
C. Amortization of intangibles
D. Inventory pricing
E. Recognition of profit on long-term construction contracts
F. Recognition of revenue from franchising
G. Recognition of revenue from leasing operations
H. Policy regarding profit or loss on sale of receivables with recourse (TA 10,010.49).

Should not duplicate dollar information shown in body of statements;
Should cross-refer to financial notes when applicable;
These disclosures also apply to unaudited statements. (TA 9420.04)

[¶2201.3] Related Notes to the Financial Statements:

A. Disclosure of non arm's-length transactions

B. Disclosure of non-monetary transactions

C. Any additional information which might affect the conclusions formed by an informed reader;

   1) Customary or routine disclosures:

     Measurement basis of important assets
     Restrictions on assets
     Restrictions on owners' equity
     Contingent assets
     Important long-term commitments, not
      in the body of the statements
     Terms of owners' equity
     Terms of long-term debt
     Disclosures required by regulatory bodies
      having jurisdiction.

   2) Changes in accounting principles (AC 1051.09) such as:

     Change in method of inventory pricing
     Change in depreciation method
     Change in accounting for long-term
      construction contracts
     Change from recording costs as an expense
      to method of amortizing and deferring them
     Changes in accounting estimates when
      affected by a change in accounting principle
     Change in the reporting entity.
      Consistent switch to straight-line
      method from accelerated method at
      specific life-points is *not* a change.

   3) Subsequent events.

[¶2201.4] **Earning Per Share on the face of the income statement:**

A. For income before extraordinary items (and/or before disposals of business segments)

B. For net income.

Disclosures should cover number of shares outstanding, contingent changes, and possible dilution from potential conversions of convertible debentures, preferred stock, options or warrants.

[¶2202]   DISCLOSURES ITEMIZED

Here is an alphabetic listing of items *requiring disclosure* with short comments thereon, if applicable. The references indicated are from the AICPA volumes, ACCOUNTING STANDARDS (AC references) and TECHNICAL AIDS (TA references).

Accelerated Depreciation Methods (AC 4074.06) — when methods are adopted.

Accounting Policies — see prior "Summary of Significant Accounting Policies.

Allowances (depreciation, depletion, bad debts) (AC 2044.01 - .02) — deduct from asset with disclosure.

Amortization of Intangibles (AC 5141.30-.31) — disclose method and period.

Amounts Available for Distributions (AC 4071.16-.17) — note the needs for any hold-back retention of earnings.

Arrangements with reorganized Debtor (TA 9330.02) — disclose if a subsequent event.

Arrears on Cumulative Preferred Stock (AC 2011A.05 and 5515.02) — the rights of senior securities must be disclosed on the face of balance sheet or in the notes.

Assets (interim changes in) (AC 2071.33) — only significant changes required for interims.

Business Segments*— see footnote below.

Cash-Basis Statements — fact must be disclosed in the opinion with delineation of what would have been had accrual basis been used, if significant variance.

Change in Stockholders' Equity Accounts (AC 2042.02) — in a separate schedule. This is not the changes in retained earnings statement, which is one of the basic required statements.

Change to Declining Balance Method (AC 4074.04) — disclose change in method and effect of it.

---

* FASB: Statement No. 14, issued at press-time for this text, requires reporting on segments contributing 10% or more of the combined amounts.

Changes, Accounting — see prior pages.

Commitments, Long-Term (AC 4311.18-.19) — disclose unused letters of credit, assets pledged as security for loans, pension plans, plant expansion or acquisition; obligations to reduce debt, maintain working capital or restrict dividend.

Commitments to Complete Contracts (AC 4031.16) — only extraordinary ones.

Consolidation Policy — method used.

Construction Type Contracts — method used.

Contingencies (4311.09-.13; 4311.17-.19; 4311.103) — disclose when reasonable possibility of a loss, the nature of, and estimated loss. Threats of expropriation, debtor bankruptcy if actual. Those contingencies which might result in gains, but not misleading as to realization. Disclosure of uninsured risks is advised, but not required.

Contingencies in Business Combinations (AC 1091.78) — disclose escrow items for contingencies in the notes.

Control of Board of Directors (TA 1400.07) — disclose any stock options existing.

Corporate Officer Importance (TA 9390.02) — disclose if a major sales or income factor to the company.

Current Liabilities (AC 2033.15) — disclose why if any omitted (in notes).

Dating (Readjusted) Earned Surplus (AC 5582.01-.02) — no more than 10 years is the term now required.

Deferred Taxes — disclose and also see Timing Differences in this Text.

Depreciation and Depreciable Assets (AC 2043.02) — disclose the following:
Depreciation expense for the period
Balances of major classes of depreciable assets by nature or function
Accumulated depreciation by classes or in total
A general description of the methods used in computing depreciation.

Development Stage Enterprises (AC 2062.10) — are required to use the same basic financial statements as other enterprises, with certain additional disclosures required. Special type statements are not permissible.

Discontinued Operations (AC 2012.08-.19) — disclose separately below continuing-operating income, net of tax, but before extraordinary items. Show separate EPS.

Diversified Company's Foreign Operations (AC 2061.11-.13) — no standards for disclosure yet, being studied by the FASB; however, voluntary disclosure is suggested for revenue by types of activity or customer and separate statements for segments in unrelated activities or dissimilar activities.*

Dividends per Share (TA 4210.02) — desirable, but not required.

---

* FASB: Statement No. 14, issued at press-time for this text, requires reporting on segments contributing 10% or more of the combined amounts.

Earnings per Share — see prior section for presentation, but the following is also required in addition to the data stated there (AC U 2011.353):

1. Restatement for a prior period adjustment
2. Dividend preference
3. Liquidation preference
4. Participation rights
5. Call prices and dates
6. Conversion rates and dates
7. Exercise prices and dates
8. Sinking fund requirements
9. Unusual voting rights
10. Bases upon which primary and fully diluted earnings per share were calculated
11. Issues which are common stock equivalents.
12. Issues which are potentially dilutive securities
13. Assumptions and adjustments made for earnings per share data
14. Shares issued upon conversion, exercise, and conditions met for contingent issuances
15. Recapitalization occurring during the period or before the statements are issued
16. Stock dividends, stock splits or reverse splits occurring after the close of the period before the statements are issued
17. Claims of senior securities entering earnings per share computations
18. Dividends declared by the constituents in a pooling
19. Basis of presentation of dividends in a pooling on other than a historical basis
20. Per share and aggregate amount of cumulative preferred dividends in arrears.

Equity Method (AC 5131.20) — as follows:

1. Financial statements of the investor should disclose in the notes, separate statements or schedules, or parenthetically;
   The name of each investee and % of ownership
   The accounting policies of the investor,
       disclosing if and why any over 20%
       holdings are not under the equity method
   Any difference between the carrying value
       and the underlying equity of the investment
       and the accounting treatment thereof;
2. Disclose any investments which have quoted market prices (common stocks; showing same — do not write down
3. Present summary balance sheet and operating information when equity investments are material;
4. Same as above for any unconsolidated subsidiaries where ownership is majority;
5. Disclose material effects of contingent issuances.

Executory Contracts (AC 5351.08) — disclose rights and obligations under unperformed contracts.

Extinguishment (Early) of Debt (AC 2013.09) — gains or losses should be described, telling source of funds for payoff, income tax effect, per share amount.

Extraordinary Items (AC 2012.10-.12) — describe on face of income statement (or in notes), show effect net of tax after income from continuing operations, also after business disposals if any, show EPS separately for extraordinary item. May aggregate immaterial items.

Fiscal Period Differences (in Consolidating) (AC 2051.05) — disclose intervening material events.

Fiscal Year Change (TA 9210.04) — disclose effect only.

Foreign Items — (AC 1081.06) Assets, must disclose any significant ones included in U.S. statements; (AC 1083.032-.034) gains or losses shown in body of U.S. statement; disclose significant "subsequent event" rate changes; (AC 1081.08) operations, adequate disclosure to be made of all pertinent dollar information, regardless of whether consolidating or not (for foreign subsidiaries).

Headings and Captions (AC 1022.02) — may be necessary to explain.

Income Taxes (and Deferred Taxes) — (see Timing Differences in this Text).

Income Taxes of Sole Proprietor or Partnership — may be necessary to disclose personal taxes to be paid if the money will come from and put a drain on the firm's cash position. (TA 7100.02)

Infrequent Events (AC 2012.26) — show as separate component of income and disclose nature of them.

Interim Statements (AC 2071 and AC 2072) — (see separate chapter in this Text).

Inventories — disclose pricing policies and flow of cost assumption in "Summary of Significant Accounting Policies"; (AC 5121.14) disclose changes in method and effect on income. Dollar effect based upon a change should be shown separately from ordinary cost of sales items.

Investment Tax Credits (AC 4094.18-.21) — disclose method used, with amounts if material. Also, disclose substantial carryback or carryforward credits.

Leases — See Separate Discussion in Chapter 8 (Non-Current Assets).

Legal Restrictions on Dividend Payments (AC 5542.14) — put in notes.

Liability for Tax Penalties (TA 9320.02) — if significant, disclose in notes. May have to take exception in opinion.

Market Value of Investments in Marketable Securities — should be written down to market value and up again, but not to exceed cost for *entire* portfolio per classification — (See Chapter 7).

Non-Cumulative Preferred Stock (TA 5500.07) — should disclose that no provision has been made *because* it is non-cumulative.

Obligations (Short-Term) (AC 2033.20) — disclose in notes reason any short-term obligations *not* displayed as current liabilities

Partnerships, Limited (TA 7200.05) — disclose fact that it's a limited partnership.

Patent Income (TA 5100.20) — disclose if income is ending.

Pension Plans (AC 4063.46) — must disclose the following:
1. Describe and identify employee groups covered by plan
2. The accounting and funding policy
3. The provision for pension cost for the period
4. Excess, if any, of vested benefits over fund-total; any balance sheet deferrals, accruals, prepays;
5. Any significant matters affecting comparability of periods presented.

Pension Reform Act of 1974 (AC 4063.104) — must disclose the effect of future compliance for vesting in the first year *prior* to the date the plan is affected by the law's provisions.

Political Contributions (TA 9310.02) — must disclose if material or not deductible for taxes, or if they are beneficial to an officer.

Pooling of Interests — (See Chapter 21).

Price-Level Restatements — See Chapter 24.

Prior Period Adjustments (AC 2010.15) — must disclose with tax effects. Must disclose in interim reports. (See Chapter 11.)

Purchase Commitment Losses (AC 5121.16-.17) — should be separately disclosed in dollars in income statement.

Purchase Method — (See Chapter 21) (Business Combinations).

Purchase Option Cancellation Costs (TA 2210.04) — yes, disclose.

Real and Personal Property Taxes (AC 4081.16-.19) — disclose if using estimates and if substantial.

Real Estate Appraisal Value (TA 6610.08) — for Development Companies, footnote disclosure might be useful.

Receivables, Affiliated Companies, Officers and Employees (AC 5111.01) — should be segregated and shown separately from trade receivables.

Redemption Call of Preferred Stock (AC 5515.02) — disclose in the equity section.

Renegotiation Possibilities (AC 4042.02-.05) — use dollars if estimable or disclose inability to estimate.

Research and Development Costs (AC 4211.13) — "disclosure shall be made in the financial statements of the total research and development costs charged to expense in each period for which an income statement is presented." Government regulated enterprises should disclose the accounting policy for amortization and the totals expensed and deferred.
(Section AC 4211.106-.107 applies the above provision for disclosure to business combinations.)

Restricted Stock Issued to Employee (TA 4110.05) — disclose circumstance and the restrictions.

Retained Earnings Transferred to Capital Stock (TA 4230.01 — arises usually with "split-ups effected as dividends" and with stock dividends; must disclose and include schedule showing transfers from retained earnings to capital stock. Also, must disclose number of shares, etc., for EPS; must show subsequent event effects.

Sale and Leaseback (AC 5351.19-.22) — (See Chapter 8).

Seasonal Business (Interim Statements) — must disclose, and advisable to include 12-month period, present and past. (AC 2071.18)

Stock Dividends, Split-ups, etc. (AC 2011A.03) — must disclose even if a subsequent event and use as if made for and during all periods presented.

Stock Options (AC 4061.15) — disclose status — (See Chapter 11.) Has effect on EPS.

Stockholders Buy/Sell Stock Agreements (TA 2240.02) — disclose

Subleases — (See Leases in Chapter 8).

Termination Claims (War & Defense Contracts) (AC 4043.20-.23) — shown as current receivable, unless extended delay indicated; usually shown separately and disclosed if material, in income statement.

Treasury Stock (AC 5542.13-.14) — (See Chapter 11). Shown in body of balance sheet (equity section ordinarily); should, in notes, indicate any legal restrictions.

Unconsolidated Subsidiaries (AC 2051.18-.20) — if using cost method, should also give independent summary information about position and operations (also, see Chapter 21).

Undistributed Earnings of Subsidiaries (AC 4095.14) — (see disclosures required when not accruing deferred taxes under Indefinite Reversal Criteria in Chapter 21).

Unearned Compensation — (see Stock Options in Chapter 15).

Unremitted Taxes (TA 9330.01) — disclose only if going concern concept is no longer valid.

(See next section for those disclosures which require *Restatement*.)

(Also, see section next following for *Timing Differences and Taxes,* also *Permanent Differences*.)

[¶2203]   **RESTATEMENTS**

The following alphabetic listing indicates those areas which *require* a restatement (with disclosure) for all prior periods presented in the comparative financial statements: (References, again, are to the AICPA looseleaf volumes, as indicated previously.)

Appropriations of Retained Earnings (AC 4311.20) — any change made to conform with Section 4311 for the reporting of contingencies require retroactive adjustment.

Changes in Accounting Principle Requiring Restatement (AC 1051.27-.30):
1. Change *from* LIFO to another method.
2. Change in long-term construction method.
3. Change to or from "full cost" method in the extractive industries.
Must show effect on both net income and EPS for all periods presented.

Change in Reporting Entity (AC 1051.34-.35) — must restate.

Contingencies (AC 4312.10) — restate for the cumulative effect applying the rules for contingencies.

Earnings Per Share (AC 1051.28) — the effect of all restatements must be shown on EPS, separating as to EPS from continuing operations, EPS from disposals, EPS from extraordinary items and EPS from net income.

Equity Method (AC 5131.21) — restatement required when first applying the method, even though it was not required before.

Extraordinary Items (AC 2012.27) — if a similar one in prior period was not classified as extraordinary, but is now, reclassify now for comparison.

Foreign Currency Translations (AC 1083.035-.037 and 1083.240-.241) — restate to conform with adoption of standards; if indeterminable, use the cumulative method.

Income Taxes (Equity Method) (AC 4096.12) — restate to comply

Interim Financial Statements (AC 2071.25) — restate for changes in accounting principle and for prior period adjustments. If it's a cumulative type change, the first interim period should show the entire effect; if in later period, full effect should be applied to the first period and restated for other periods. (Also AC 2072.10-.13)

Leases — see Chapter 8

Oil and Gas Producing Companies (AC 4097.25-.26) — in conforming with standards, restatement is not required, but it is permissible.

Pooling of Interests (AC 1091.52/.56/.57/.62) — A change in accounting method for pooled unit should be applied retroactively.

In initial pooling, combine year to date, restate prior periods presented, show separate information for independent operations and positions. Purchase method shows pro forma combine (AC 1091.96)

Until pooling is consummated, include the proportion of earnings in ordinary financials; *but* also present statements (retroactively applied) as if pooling had occurred.

Prior Period Adjustments (AC 2010.17/.25) — must restate the details affected for all periods presented, disclose and adjust opening retained earnings. Must also do it for interim reports.

Refinancing Short-Term Obligations (AC 2033.17) — restatement is permitted, but not required.

Research and Development Costs (AC 4211.15/.57/1.06) — In conforming with standards, apply retroactively as a prior period adjustment.

No retroactive recapitalization of costs is permissible. Applies to *purchase* combinations also. Basic rule; expense as incurred.

Statistical Summaries (5 years, 10 years, etc.) (AC 2010.26) — Restate all prior years involved in prior period adjustments.

Revision based on FASB Opinions (AC 510.10) — retroactive restatement is not required *unless* the new standard *specifically* states that it is required.

Note that restatements are *not* required for a change from FIFO TO LIFO; nor for a change in the method of handling investment tax credits.

[¶2204]   TIMING AND PERMANENT DIFFERENCES — INCOME TAXES

Anyone who has prepared the corporation tax return form #1120 knows that Schedule M on the back page of the form calls for an explanation, detailed item by item, of the reasons for the difference between the taxable income shown on the tax return and the net income shown on the filer's financial statement.

This same difference between financial income and taxable income, which has for many years been shown on the tax return, must now also be explained for *financial* statement purposes. These are the "differences" in the terminology "timing difference" and "permanent difference."

The distinction between "timing" and "permanent" goes one step further: "Timing" differences are those which will someday reverse.

"Permanent" differences will never reverse.

A permanent difference, for example, would be an expense taken on the financial statement, which is *never* allowable on the tax return.

A timing difference would be one, for example, which involves an expense taken *now* on the financial statement, but next year or later on the tax return, such as an excess contribution deduction, limited to 5% on the tax return, with carryover permissible.

[¶2205]   PERMANENT DIFFERENCES

Those which will not reverse or "turn around" in other periods: (AC 4091.12/.32)

1. Specific *revenues exempt* from taxability (examples):

   Dividend exclusions

   Interest on tax exempt securities

   Life insurance proceeds

   Negative goodwill amortization

   Unrealized gains on marketable securities*

   Unrealized gains on foreign currency translations*

   Tax benefits arising from stock-option compensatory plans (when booked as income)

---

* These unrealized gains or losses will probably reverse to the extent of the actual at date of finalization of transactions. However, there will always be some portion which will never reverse exactly as booked. This irreversible portion must then be (theoterically) offset in that later period, creating a reverse permanent difference in *that* period.

2. *Expenses* which are *not* tax deductible:

> Depreciation taken on appraisal increases or donated property
>
> Goodwill amortization
>
> Premiums on officer life insurance
>
> Tax penalties and fines
>
> Unrealized losses on securities or currency translations*

3. Those expenses which are predicated upon different bases for financial and tax purposes:

> Depreciation on trade-ins
>
> Statutory depletion vs. cost depletion
>
> Business combinations which treat purchase as ''pooling for tax return or pooling as purchase.

[¶2206]   TIMING DIFFERENCES

Those which *will* turn around or reverse in one or more subsequent periods. Four broad categories: (AC 4091.12/.14 and 4091A)

1. Income — for Accounting NOW — for Taxes LATER
2. Expenses,— for Accounting NOW — for Taxes LATER
3. Income — for Accounting LATER — for Taxes NOW
4. Expenses — for Accounting LATER — for Taxes NOW

1. Items of *income* included for accounting financial statement purposes NOW — not taken on the tax return until a LATER time (examples):

> Gross profit on installment method date of sale/when collected on tax return.
> Percentage of completion method on books/completed contract method for tax return.
> Leasing rentals on books under financing method/actual rent less depreciation for tax return.
> Subsidiary earnings reported now/as received for tax return.

2. Items of *expense* taken on financial statements NOW, not taken on tax returns until LATER (examples):

> Accelerated depreciation used for financials/not for tax return.
> Contributions on financials over 5% limit/carried over for taxes.
> Deferred compensaton accruals/taken when paid on tax return.

---

* These unrealized gains or losses will probably reverse to the extent of the actual at date of finalization of transactions. However, there will always be some portion which will never reverse exactly as booked. This irreversible portion must then be (theoterically) offset in that later period, creating a reverse permanent difference in *that* period.

Estimated costs of various kinds/taken when cost or loss becomes actual and known, such as:guarantees, product warranties, inventory losses, legal settlements, segment disposals, major repairs.

Depreciation based on shorter life for books than for tax return.

Organization costs taken now/amortized for tax return

3. Items of *income* taken into financial books LATER, but reported as income NOW on tax returns:

Rents and royalties deferred until earned/reported when collected for tax return.

Deferred fees, dues, services contracts/reported when collected for tax return.

Intercompany consolidation gains and losses/taxed now if filing separate returns.

Leaseback gains amortized over lease-term/date of sale for tax return.

4. Items of *expense* taken into financial books LATER, but taken NOW on tax return:

Depreciation; shorter lives used for tax purposes accelerated rates on tax return/straight-line on books certain emergency facility amortization taken on tax returns/later on books;

Bond discount, premium, costs taken on tax return/amortized on books

Certain costs which are taken for tax purposes/but deferred for financial purposes, as;

Incidental costs of property acquisitions

Preoperating costs

Certain research and development costs (deferred for financial purposes only those approved exceptions to those which must be expensed) — (see Chapter 8).

[¶2206.1]   Other Considerations Regarding Income Taxes:

Interperiod tax allocation should be followed under the deferred method. (AC 4091.34)

Timing differences may be considered individually or grouped by similarity. (AC 4091.36)

Tax carryback losses (including investment tax credit carrybacks should be recognized in the loss period in which the carryback originated). (AC 4091.43) Carryforwards should not be recognized until realized (then show as *extraordinary* item) unless there is no doubt of realization (then show as part of operating profit or loss). (AC 4091.44-.45)

[¶2206.2]   Balance Sheet Presentation of Income Taxes (AC U 4091.124):

Tax accounts on the balance sheet should be separately classified so as to show:

1. Taxes estimated to be paid currently.

2. *Net* amount of current deferred charges and deferred credits related to timing differences.*

3. *Net* amount of noncurrent deferred taxes related to timing differences.*

4. Receivables for carryback losses.

5. Where realization is beyond doubt, show an asset for the benefit to be derived from a carryforward of losses.

6. Deferred investment credits, when this method is employed.

* Note permissable netting.

[¶2206.3]   Income Statement Presentation of Income Taxes (AC U 4091.122):

All taxes based on income, including foreign, federal, state and local should be reflected in income tax expense in the income statement. (AC U 4091.121)

The following components should be disclosed separately and put on the income statement before extraordinary items and prior period adjustments:

1. Taxes estimated to be payable.

2. Tax effects of timing differences.

3. Tax effects of investment credits (either method)

4. Tax effects of operating losses.

[¶2206.4]   General Disclosures (AC U 4091.127)

In addition, the following general disclosures are required:

1. Amounts of any operating loss carryforwards not recognized in the loss period, with expiration dates and effect on deferred tax accounts;

2. Significant amounts of any other unused tax deductions or credits, with expiration dates;

3. Any reasons for significant differences between taxable income and pre-tax accounting income.

23

Interim Statements (Prepared by Management)

[¶2301]

Guidelines for interim reporting by publicly traded companies have been established by the AICPA (and the SEC).

For those private companies which do not bear the same responsibility for full and adequate disclosure to public shareholders, the guideline for public disclosure should be studied and followed where feasible and relevant for possible self-protection against insurgent parties, since adherence to standards would probably be more defensible than non-adherence.

The following standards for determining information and the guidelines indicated for minimum disclosure now prevail (beginning after Dec. 31, 1973) (AC 2071.30):

1. Results should be based on the same principles and practices used for the latest annual statements (subject to the modifications below) (AC 2071.10)

2. Revenue should be recognized as *earned* for the interim on the same basis as for the full year. Losses should be recognized as incurred or when becoming evident (AC 2071.12);

3. Costs may be classified as (AC 2071.12):

A. Those associated with revenue (cost of goods sold);

B. All other costs — expenses based on;

  1) Those actually incurred, or

  2) Those allocated, based on:

    A) Time expired, or

    B) Benefits received, or

    C) Other period activity.

3. Costs or losses (including extraordinary items) should *not* be deferred or apportioned unless they would at year end. Advertised costs may be apportioned in relation to sales for interims. (AC 2071.15)

4. With respect to inventory (and cost of sales AC 2071.14):

    A. LIFO basis should not be liquidated if expected to be replaced later, but should be based on expected replacement factor;

    B. Do not defer inventory losses because of cost or market rule; and,. conversely, later periods should then reflect gains on market price recoveries;

    C. With standard costs, variances which are expected to be absorbed by year-end should be deferred for the interim, not expensed. *Unplanned* purchase price or volume variance, not expected to turn around, are to be absorbed during the period;

    D. The estimated gross profit method may be used, but must be disclosed.

5. The seasonal nature of activities should be disclosed, preferably including additional 12-month-to-date information with prior comparative figures. (AC 2071.18):

6. Income taxes (AC 2071.19 and .20):

    A. Effective yearly tax rate (including year-end applicable tax-planned advantages) should be applied to interim taxable income;

    B. Extraordinary items applicable to the interim period should be shown separately net of applicable tax and the effect of the tax *not* applied to the tax on ordinary net income.

7. Extraordinary and unusual items including the effects of segment disposals should be disclosed separately, net of tax, for the interim period in which they occur, and they should not be apportioned over the year. (AC 2071.21)

8. Contingencies should be disclosed the same as for the annual report. (AC 2071.22)

9. Changes in accounting practices or principles from those followed in prior periods should be disclosed. (AC 2071.23) and, where possible, those changes should be made in the first period of the year. (AC 2071.28)

10. Retroactive restatement and/or prior period adjustments are required under the same rules applying to annual statements. (AC 2071.25)

11. Changes in estimates are accounted for in the period in which the change is made. (AC 2071.26)

[¶2301.1]   Minimum Data to be Reported on Interim Statements Is as Follows (AC 2071.30):

    1. Sales or gross revenues, provisions for income taxes, extraordinary items (including related tax), cumulative effect of changes in accounting principles or practices, and net income;

    2. Primary and fully diluted earnings per share data for each period presented;

3. Seasonal revenue, costs and expenses;

4. Disposal of business segments and extraordinary items, as well as unusual or infrequent items;

5. Contingencies;

6. Changes in estimates; changes in accounting principles or practices;

7. Significant changes in balance sheet items;

8. Significant changes in tax provisions;

9. Current year-to-date, or the last 12 months, with comparative data for prior periods;

10. In the absence of a separate fourth quarter report, special fourth-quarter adjustments and extraordinary, infrequent or unusual items which occured during that fourth quarter should be disclosed in a note to the annual financial statement. (AC 2071.31)

11. Though not required, condensed balance sheet data and funds flow data are suggested to provide better understanding of the interim report.

Interim reports are usually prepared by management and issued with that clear stipulation.

Accounting firms which issue reports for interim periods are to be guided by auditing standards set for ''Reports on a Limited Review of Interim Financial Information'' in Section 519 of Statements on Auditing Standards, May 1976. (AU 519.01 through .15)

24

General Price-Level Accounting

[¶2401]

One of the most discussed accounting problems today is price-level accounting. Even though the purchasing power of the dollar has been drastically reduced, financial reports treat the dollar as inflexible, presenting historical earlier values.

Considering the consumer price index as indicative of the dollar's purchasing power and applying that index to the net income of a corporation over a long period of time, we would see startling results. We'd find, for example, that the trend of profits might be downward, instead of upward as indicated by historical dollars. We'd also find that the annual depreciation taken on such items as buildings would be wholly inadequate (on a comparative basis) to match the replacement cost today. Yet, to up the value of the property and to raise the annual depreciation charges to conform with the realities is *not* in conformance with GAAP.

In recognition of the wide divergence between the historical dollar and its present worth in terms of purchasing power, the AICPA has agreed that it is useful to present supplementary information in addition to, but not in lieu of, historical statements. Moreover, price-level statements are *not* to be considered as basic statements, *nor* are they required.

[¶2401.1] Guidelines for Preparing General Price-Level Statements

Here are the guidelines suggested for preparation of these supplementary statements (AC 1071.27 —.49):

1. Follow the same accounting principles as for historical statements except for changes in purchasing power.
2. Use an index of the general price level.
3. Present in terms of general purchasing power at the latest balance sheet date.
4. Distinguish between monetary and non-monetary items.

5. Items having both characteristics should be classified based on the purpose for which they are held, usually evidenced by their treatment in historical accounting.

6. *Non-monetary* items should be restated to current general purchasing power at the end of the period. No price level gains or losses are recognized on the income statement for non-monetary items *until* the item is disposed of. All opening balances are converted with the new closing rate and retained earnings are adjusted directly.

7. *Monetary* items are already stated in dollars of current general purchasing power, so they should appear at the same amount.

8. Income statement items should be restated to current general purchasing power at period-end using averages.

9. Income tax is stated at the historical statement figure converted.

10. Gains or losses on monetary items should be recalculated using the end-of-period purchasing power. They are not related to subsequent events.

11. General price-level gains or losses themselves should be shown as separate items.

12. Comparative information should be updated to the current purchasing power level.

13. Foreign statements, branches or subsidiaries should be converted first to U.S. dollars, then to general purchasing power.

14. Partially restated financial statements should not be presented.

15. The notes should explain the basis of preparation of the information and what it purports to show.

16. Disclosures should be made for:

   A. Retained earnings and the roll-forward effects for;
      Beginning of the year balance:
      Opening balance restated to general purchasing power at beginning of year
         plus (or minus)
      Amount required to update *opening* balance to *end* of year general purchasing power;

   B. Income taxes stated are based on historical costs (actual) before the restatement and are then restated.

An index of the general price level, not an index of the price of specific goods or services, should be used.

The Gross National Product Implicit Price Deflator (GNP) is the one most commonly used. It is issued quarterly by the Department of Commerce. A few companies use the Consumer Price Index, which is issued monthly by the Department of Labor. The two do not deviate significantly over a long period.

Index numbers are expressed as percentages of a base year. 1958 is the base year for the GNP Deflator. In using the index number, it must be correlated to the varied years (and usually quarters) of acquisition of the non-monetary assets.

For a detailed listing of balance sheet items classified as to monetary and/or non-monetary status, it is suggested that reference be made to the AICPA Section 1071, Appendix B, in the looseleaf standards. (AC 1071B.01 through B.04)

Important theory is: Only monetary items affect the GPL gain or loss; non-monetary items affect it only upon disposition, and then, only to the extent based on the "adjusted" (GPL) cost matched to actual disposition price.

25

Financial Forecasts and Social Reporting

FINANCIAL FORECASTS

There is an increasing interest in the preparation of financial forecasts and projections. Though few companies render forecasting specifics to the general public, many prepare financial projections for banks and lenders, underwriters and prospective investors, especially for such financing as bond issues for public facilities and real estate ventures.

The SEC, after having historically prohibited the inclusion of forecasts in reports filed with it, has recently (Securities Act Release 5581, April 28, 1975) agreed to permit the inclusion of certain statements regarding future operations.

The AICPA in a Statement of Position (75-4, August 1975) (TA 10,080.01—.36) offers some recommendations on presentation and disclosure of financial forecasts. The recommendations do *not* apply to cash flow or tax basis forecasts. Moreover, the position statement is for guidance only and *not* to be interpreted to mean that the publishing of financial forecasts is recommended or that a financial forecast is deemed to be part of the basic financial statements. (TA 10,080.10) Briefly, these recommendations are:

1. The format should be the format for the historical statements.

2. The financial forecast should include (if applicable):

   A. Sales or gross revenues.

   B. Gross Profit.

   C. Provision for income taxes.

   D. Net income.

   E. Disposal of business segments and extraordinary, unusual or infrequent items.

   F. Primary and fully diluted earnings per share data for each period presented.

   G. Significant anticipated changes in financial position.

175

3. They should be prepared on a basis consistent with GAAP and should include a "summary of significant accounting policies."

4. Changes in accounting principles from historical statements should be disclosed.

5. They should be expressed in the single, most probable forecasted result.

6. Ranges of variation should be presented only as supplements to the single most probable forecasted result.

7. Significant management assumptions concerning future events and circumstances should be disclosed.

8. Updated forecasts should be issued to reflect significant changes in assumptions or circumstances.

[¶2502]   **SOCIAL REPORTING**

The subject of "Social Reporting" was researched by a study group on Objectives of Financial Statements of the AICPA (Robert M. Trueblood, Chairman). They sought to treat with the topic of auditing social reports.

Conventional accounting standards and techniques measure a company's financial performance and may be inadequate to measure the company's social contribution to the community at large.

More and more companies are becoming interested in social responsibility accounting. At the very least, they are interested in determining the real costs of their social programs and their overall benefit to the community. They are also interested in providing stockholders with information which shows how well they are meeting their social responsibilities.

One of the difficulties with social responsibility accounting is the difficulty of explaining social benefits in dollar terms. Some management consultant firms have managed to do it. Abt Associates, Inc., for example, has developed an elaborate social cost benefit report, publishing annually a "Social Income Statement" and a "Social Balance Sheet." The Income Statements show both net social income to clients and net social income to the community.

Critics are skeptical about the effectiveness of converting social benefits into dollars. They claim that using numbers camouflages the very things the public wants to know. But many of the companies using social responsibility reporting are nevertheless concentrating on the cost side, trying to measure costs. While social cost analysis may be helpful for internal purposes, it does not necessarily indicate that efficient management is either socially responsible or irresponsible and might, in fact, make inefficient management appear to be socially competent.

In the document, *Accounting and Social Reporting,* by Claude S. Colantoni, W.W. Cooper and H.J. Dietzer, which appears in *The Objectives of Financial Statements* — Volume 2/Selected Papers, AICPA, May, 1974, the authors point out three approaches to reporting corporate social responsibility and measurement thereof (Page 287):

1. An inventory (or listing) of representative actions;

2. A traditional financial approach which attempts to associate a dollár cost (of an historical or opportunity cost, perhaps discounted, variety) with such activities in order to identify them as economic events with economic consequences that are congruent with other categories identified in accounting reports; and

3. Still other extensions to social events or events with social consequences which may be either identified with related economic characterizations or else (and better, we think) admit of extensions to other metrics, perhaps of multidimensional variety.

[¶2503] HUMAN RESOURCES (LABOR) ACCOUNTING

Sometimes, in conjunction with Social Reporting, and sometimes separately, consideration is given to a special type of financial reporting which places a monetary present value on the future services of employees. Based on expected labor turnover rates, accumulated costs and expenses of recruitment, training and development of employees, values are capitalized and amortized as assets.

In either or both the capitalizing of future labor values or the costs of employee development, separation is made in the equity section for the retained earnings resulting from the computation of and pertaining to those human resources.

The comparative conventional report is usually presented in conjunction therewith.

The most widely publicized and disseminated report of this type is the "Total Concept" annual report prepared by R.G. Barry Corporation and Subsidiaries.

SECTION TWO

TAXES

26

Taxes — Methods and Changes

[¶2601]

Most everyone knows *something* about taxes. No one knows *everything* about taxes. Accountants are presumed to know taxes. Generally speaking, they probably are familiar with most of the overall, basic, more prominent features of the tax law — those sections which have been thoroughly tested in the courts and resolved into the traditional body of the law.

However, because of the intricate provisions and the relief loopholes provided and adjudicated, because of the often ambiguous legal wording and the necessity for interpretive regulations and further testing in the Tax Court, because of the very nature of the taxpayer/IRS adversary relationship, accountants, as well as others, merely serve as perhaps better-informed, but still "opinion-only" experts. The taxpayer himself bears the burden — and the cost — and the responsibility.

The highlights of tax methods, procedures and considerations presented in this section are included merely as timely reminders of certain features of the tax law to be scrutinized. In no way should they be considered all-inclusive or all-instructive.

Further research into the tax law, the regulations, the interpretations and the court decisions is advised. Extensive tax publication services are available, constantly updating the ever-changing features of Federal and State tax laws.

Tax *evasion* is illegal.

Tax *avoidance* is legal. It is statutory.

Tax avoidance is on the books, in the courts — for you to find.

Research all pertinent topics.

[¶2602]   **TAX RETURN PREPARATION**

For many corporations, assembling and analyzing the information needed to prepare the corporate tax returns can be a considerable task. Most, if not all, of the company's accounts have to be analyzed; provision often must be made for various types of allocations for state tax purposes; the activities of many branches, subsidiaries, or affiliates have to be coordinated (and the accounting records may be dispersed over many locations). In addition, the accounting personnel responsible for keeping the corporate books are not likely to be tax men, and the tax department may have to review the accounts with an eye to the tax significance of the various transactions.

How the tax return information will be assembled will depend in large part on the organization of the company. In a small company with few employees, the "tax man" may also be the one in charge of the books and may do all the analysis himself by direct examination of the company's books and records. In larger companies, the task of gathering the tax information may be more or less systematized, depending on the size of the company; the number and geographic location of the divisions, subsidiaries, or affiliates; the location and responsibilities for the accounting records; and the existence of a separate tax department.

In any event, however the information is put together — whether by direct examination of the books and records by the "tax man," direct interviews of various accounting personnel by the tax department representatives, use of questionnaires (completed by the accounting personnel or by the tax department personnel after discussion with accounting personnel) — some system should be devised to make sure all the pertinent information is gathered and analyzed in some systematic and usable form.

The accountant's task in finding tax opportunities or pitfalls may be greatly simplified by the use of a tax-planning checklist which points out some of the planning possibilities. The items on the checklist should be set up in financial audit order and suggest the action to be taken which would bring the desired tax results.

While it may not be necessary to analyze in detail each account for routine items, it probably is necessary to have some formal procedure for analyzing all items that have special tax significance. The checklists enumerate many of the items you may want to check (if they apply) and the reasons for wanting a special analysis of each. With these as starting points, you may readily find other areas of special significance that could be added.

[¶2603]   **INCOME TAXES — ACCOUNTING**

The tax consequences of business transactions are usually determined by their legal status, the accounting treatment of such items, or both. It therefore becomes imperative to plan accounting and legal techniques *before* entering into any transactions.

Once the transaction has occurred and the book entry has been made, it is usually too late to worry about the tax consequences. Even minor issues should be worked out in advance via proper procedures. For example, proper wording of purchase orders will often insure proper description on invoices, so that portions of work done that are deductible as repairs are properly described and billed separately from work done on installations, improvements, etc., that are required to be capitalized.

In order to plan properly, you must know the accounting techniques available to you. Here are the broad choices:

(1) Taxable year.

(2) Cash, accrual, or an approved hybrid accounting method.

(3) Last-in-first-out (LIFO) or first-in-first-out (FIFO) inventory method.

(4) Cost or lower-of-cost-or-market as method of valuation of inventory.

(5) Method of handling time sales.

(6) Method of handling long-term contracts.

[¶2603.1]   **What the Tax Law Requires**

The law specifies only that you compute taxable income in accordance with the method of accounting you regularly employ in keeping your books; however, such method must clearly reflect your income.

Each taxpayer is authorized to adopt such forms and systems of accounting as in his judgment are best suited to his purpose. No uniform method is prescribed for all taxpayers. Nevertheless, the Regulations (Reg. §1.446-1) do provide that:

(1) All items of gross income and deductions must be treated with reasonable consistency;

(2) In all cases in which the production, purchase, or sale of merchandise is an income-producing factor, an accrual method is necessary; and inventories of merchandise on hand (including finished goods, work in process, raw materials and supplies) must be taken at the beginning and end of the accounting period and used in computing taxable income of the period;

(3) Expenditures made during the year should be properly classified as between capital and expense; expenditures for items such as plant and equipment

which have a useful life extending substantially beyond the end of the year must be charged to capital expenditures rather than to expense;

(4) Where capital costs are being recovered through deductions for wear and tear, depletion, or obsolescence, expenditures (other than ordinary repairs) made to restore the property or prolong its useful life should be added to the property account or charged against the appropriate reserve, not to current expense.

Those who neither produce nor sell goods and consequently have no inventories can use either of the two regular methods of accounting, the cash or accrual. This includes artists; authors; artisans, such as carpenters and masons who either use their customers' materials or buy materials for specific jobs only; professionals, such as accountants, architects, attorneys, dentists, physicians and engineers; and brokers and agents rendering services of various kinds;

(5) Special methods of accounting are also prescribed in the Code. Such methods include the crop method, the installment method and the long-term contract method. There are also special methods of accounting for particular items of income and expense;

(6) A combination of methods (hybrid system) of accounting may also be used in connection with a trade or business if consistently used;

(7) The fact that books are kept in accordance with the requirements of a supervisory agency does not mean that income for tax purposes must be computed in the same manner.

[¶2604]   CHOOSING A TAXABLE YEAR

The initial choice of an accounting period is generally within the control of the taxpayer. However, many taxpayers forfeit this right by giving the matter haphazard, last-minute consideration. The result is that they adopt an annual accounting period ill-suited to their business needs.

[¶2604.1]   Four Possible Choices

Under the Code, only four types of taxable year are recognized. They are (Reg. §1.441-1):

(1) *Calendar Year:* A 12-month period ending on December 31;

(2) *Fiscal Year:* A 12-month period ending on the last day of any month other than December;

(3) *52-53 Week Year:* This is a fiscal year, varying from 52 to 53 weeks in duration, which ends always on the same day of the wek, which (a) occurs for the last time in a calendar month, or (b) falls nearest the end of a calendar month;

(4) *Short Period:* A period of less than 12 months (allowed only in certain special situations such as initial return, final return, change in accounting period, and termination of taxable year by reason of jeopardy assessment).

The conditions for each type of annual accounting period may be summarized as follows:

Taxable Year	*Conditions*
(1) Calendar year *must* be used by a taxpayer if he	(a) keeps no books, (b) has no annual accounting period, or (c) has an accounting period (other than a calendar year) which does not qualify as a fiscal year.
(2) Fiscal year *may* be used by a taxpayer if	(a) he keeps books, (b) he has definitely established such fiscal year as his accounting period and (c) his books are kept in accordance with such fiscal year.
(3) 52-53 Week taxable year *may* be used by a taxpayer if	(a) he keeps books, (b) he regularly computes his income on a 52-53 week basis, and (c) his books are kept on such 52-53 week basis.

[¶2604.2]   Checklist in Picking a Year

Consider	*Here's Why*
Get a natural business year	Your heavy income may come in the fall. But your expenses are not incurred until the following spring. You would not use a calendar year. Income would always be ahead of the expenses connected with it.
Close your year at a convenient time	Inventories can be taken and financial statements prepared most conveniently when business activities are low. If the plant shuts down during vacation period, consider year-end at that time.
Professional service	Legal and auditing talent may also be less harried during the slack period. Better service and care will be given to your audit and tax return.
Several business interests — tax saving by the use of various fiscal years for different income sources	Gives rise to a postponing of a tax on income until subsequent years when the income might be lower. Postpones paying the tax to years where you might have losses to offset it.
Renewal of contracts	Leases, labor contracts, and other renewals can be negotiated in the slack period when the pressure of business will not cause hasty decisions.

[¶2604.3] 52-53 Week Tax Year

When this type of taxable year is used, the taxable period must always end on the same day of the week; this will be either Friday or Saturday, whichever is the last working day. It must always end, too, on either: (1) the date such last day of the week last occurs in the same calendar month; or (2) the date such last day of the week falls which is nearest the last date of the same calendar month. (This could be as late as the third day of the following month.)

A change to or from a 52-53 week year involves special rules with respect to the tax year and the tax return. Here they are:

(1) If the change results in a short period of less than seven days, no short period return is required; the short period is added to the following tax year.

(2) If the change results in a tax year of more than six months or less than 359 days, a short-period return is required and income must be annualized; this must be done on a daily basis, using a 365-day year.

Approval to change to a 52-53 week year isn't required if the change is made to a 52-53 week year ending on a particular day with reference to the end of the same month on the last day of which the prior tax year ended. For a change with reference to any other month, the regular rules (described below) apply.

[¶2604.4] Shift of Tax Year With Permission

If a taxpayer does receive permission to change his accounting period, a return should be made for the short period beginning on the day after the close of the old taxable year and ending at the end of the day before the day designated as the first day of the new taxable year (§443). Generally, if a return is made for a short period, it is necessary that the income for the period be annualized and then divided by the number of months in the short period. The tax is then computed on that amount.

Example: Assume a taxpayer is filing a return for a three-month period and his net income for that period (April 1 to June 30) is $90,000:

$$\$90,000 \times 12 = \$1,080,000$$
$$\$\ 1,080,000 \div 3 \ (\text{months in short period}) = \$360,000$$

Tax on $360,000	$159,300*
Tax for short period is ¼ or	$39,825

*1976 rates (20% on 1st $25,000; 22% on next $25,000; 48% on bal.)

To prevent inequities, §443 provides that on the taxpayer's establishing the amount of his taxable income for the 12-month period, computed as if the period were a taxable year, the tax for the short period shall be reduced to the greater of the following:

(1) An amount which bears the same ratio to the tax computed on the taxable income for the 12-month period as the taxable income computed on the basis of the short period bears to the taxable income for the 12-month period; or

(2) The tax computed on the taxable income for the short period without placing the taxable income on an annual basis.

Let us assume further that the taxpayer's net income from July 1 to March 31 was only $180,000 — that the nine months after the short period showed a decrease in net profit.

Here's how the inequity is eliminated —

Tax on $270,000 = $116,100
(three-months) $\dfrac{\$\ 90,000}{\$270,000} \times \$116,100 = \$\ 38,700$

Tax on $90,000 = $29,700
Since $38,700 is greater than $29,700, it will be used as the tax for the short period. The taxpayer would then apply for a refund of $1,125 ($39,825 — $38,700).

How to get permission: Application for permission to change must be made on Form 1128 by the 15th day of the second month following the short period needed to effect the change. The motive for the change must be a business reason and not one of tax avoidance.

[¶2605]   CHANGE OF ACCOUNTING METHOD

Income for tax purposes must be computed under the same method of accounting regularly used by you in keeping your books. If you have not used a method regularly or if the method regularly used does not clearly reflect income, the Commissioner can compute your income under a method which he considers clearly reflects your income.

Except for some special situations, you may not change your method of accounting without the prior consent of the Commissioner. If you make a change in your accounting method without prior consent, you will be required to make adjustments for pre-1954 Code years as well as post-1954 Code years. Pre-1954 Code year adjustments are not required if the change was initiated by the Commissioner.

It becomes important, therefore, to know whether a change constitutes a change in accounting method or merely a correction of an error (not requiring consent).

Consent is *required* for the following changes:

(1) From the cash to the accrual basis;

(2) Method of valuing inventory;

(3) From/to completed contract method from/to percentage-of-completion method or a change from/to any other method to the contract method:

(4) Those involving special methods, such as the installment method or crop method;

(5) Those specifically enumerated in the Code.

Consent is *not* required for the following changes:

(1) Correction of mathematical, posting or timing errors;

(2) Correction of bad debt reserves;

(3) Changes in estimated useful lives of depreciable assets.

Normally, a corporation is likely to use the accrual method of accounting. But some service companies will use the cash method. And in special types of businesses, specialized methods may be desirable. Appendix D summarizes the workings of the various accounting methods available for tax purposes and the advantages and disadvantages of each.

[¶2605.1] Adjustments Required When a Change In Accounting Methods Is Made

A change in accounting method may be made either by the Commissioner or the taxpaper. If involuntary, the adjustments are based strictly on the 1954 Code years. If initiated by the taxpaper, all adjustments are necessary for the pre-1954 Code years. But the Code prescribes reliefs for the extent of the tax attributable to the increased income reportable for the year of change.

Also, the effect of some changes are prorated over a 10-year period (from the changeover year), such as:

(1) A change from cash to accrual method;

(2) A change in depreciation method;

(3) A change to the reserve method for bad debts;

(4) Changes necessitated by the regulations.

[¶2605.2] When Changes Are Considered To Be Initiated by Taypayer

Although the Regs are pretty explicit in the way in which you should go about requesting a change of accounting method you may inadvertently cause a change. For example, it has been held that just changing the method on your return or changing at the *suggestion* of a revenue agent adds up to a change of method initiated by you. This is to be distinguished from the case where the agent *instructs* you to change.

Under the present procedure (effective for applications mailed after December 17, 1970), application for permission to change an accounting method or practice is filed on Form 3115 within the first 180 days of the year to which the change is to apply.

Adjustments resulting from the change are taken ratably "over an appropriate period, prescribed by the Commissioner, generally ten years," beginning with the year of change. Applications generally receive favorable consideration if the taxpayer agrees to the ten-year spread or any other approach suggested by IRS.

27

Assets

CASH

Where the corporation has accumulated large amounts of cash, the possibility of the imposition of the accumulated earnings penalty should be checked. The penalty may be avoided if this situation can be corrected in time.

The penalty is not imposed if the accumulation is reasonable for purposes of carrying out the financial needs of the business. Also, the penalty may be avoided by a timely distribution of dividends or by a timely Subchapter S election.

Note that the accumulation problem can not be avoided by the investment of excess cash in tax-exempt bonds. Although the tax-exempt interest is not subject to the penalty, its accumulation may cause the imposition of the penalty.

Where the corporation's cash position is meager, the company might consider the use of a sale-leaseback of its plant or other real estate. This may produce additional funds from two sources: one from the sales proceeds and the second from the tax benefits that may be derived from rental payments. There would be a tax benefit to the extent that the rental payments exceed the depreciation that the company was taking on the fixed assets.

Note that for cash basis taxpayers, certain types of income are considered to be constructively received for tax purposes, such as: interest credited on bank accounts and matured interest coupons.

[¶2702] **ACCOUNTS RECEIVABLE**

Here tax savings may be realized by switching to a more advantageous method of reporting income. A change to the installment method of reporting sales may defer taxes for a company that sells its products on an installment basis, which option is available under either cash or accrual method.

Another possible tax-saving switch is to change from the strict write-off method for bad debts to the reserve method. Where the strict write-off method is preferred, tax savings may result by writing off part of the worthless debts.

There is also the election to switch from the long-term contract to the completed contract method of reporting income.

[¶2703]   **INVENTORIES**

In an inflationary market, a company will want to consider changing the method of valuation of inventories from FIFO to LIFO. The change, however, would affect the company's earnings for financial purposes because, if the company chooses to use LIFO for tax purposes, it *must* use the same method for financial reporting.

Where there is damaged, outmoded, or shopworn merchandise, tax savings may be realized by writing down the value of this merchandise.

A taxpayer who uses inventories must use the accrual method of accounting.

Supplies, are not, in themselves, inventoriable. They become so only when acquired for sale or to be physically a part of merchandise intended for sale.

If you use the lower of cost or market for valuing inventory, the tax rule is that each item must be taken into consideration separately — i.e., the cost and market of each item must be compared. The Treasury does not recognize the right to value aggregates of similar inventory items on a total cost or market, whichever is lower, basis.

Taxpayer can elect in the first return the method of valuing inventory which conforms to the best accounting practice in the trade or business and which clearly reflects the income. The usual methods are (1) cost and (2) cost or market, whichever is less.

Taxpayer can elect in the first return the method of measuring cost [by specific identification, first-in-first-out (FIFO), LIFO, etc.] Elections can be changed only with Commissioner's permission.

The Treasury does *not* for manufacturers, allow the use of "Prime Costing" (no overhead in inventory) or "Direct Costing" (the inclusion of only variable overhead).

Retailers can elect to use the retail inventory method. Other options are available in certain specialized fields (farming, security dealers).

The last-in-first-out method (LIFO) can be elected by making application on Form 970, filed with the return for the first year the method is to be used.

[¶2703.1]   **Change of Inventory Method**

Except for LIFO, which the taxpayer adopts by election, change in inventory method for tax purposes is treated as a change of accounting method, and the Commissioner's consent must be obtained. Since tax saving isn't sufficient to warrant a change, state in your request the business objective you seek to accomplish.

Recomputation of the opening inventory according to your new method will ordinarily be required; the resulting adjustment should be included in determining the income for the year of change, but you may be able to spread the adjustment over the current and the preceding two years.

Statement of an inventory valuation basis in the first return is a binding election, even if there is no difference at that time between this method and some other method you try to use later. If permission to change is granted but you fail to make the change for the year approved, you must request permission again if you want to make the change in a later year. However, the Commissioner can't take advantage of an oversight to force the use of an inconsistent method.

[¶2703.2]   LIFO

For tax purposes, when LIFO is used, only cost — not the lower of cost or market — may be used.

The following LIFO rules pertain to the tax-law requirements. Since LIFO may be used for tax purposes only if also used in financial reports, the tax rules for LIFO influence the use of LIFO for financial reporting purposes, too.

How goods on LIFO are to be valued: Goods comprising the beginning inventory of the first year on LIFO must be valued at average cost. The average cost of units in each inventory class is obtained by dividing the aggregate cost of this inventory class, computed according to the inventory method previously employed by the taxpayer, by the number of units on hand. In effect, each unit is considered to have been acquired at the same time.

Goods of a specified type on hand at the close of a taxable year are treated as being, first, those included in the opening inventory of the taxable year in the order of acquisition and, secondly, those acquired in the taxable year. The taxpayer is given permission to value any physical increment of goods of a specified type at costs determined in one of the following ways:

(a) By reference to the actual cost of the goods most recently purchased or produced;

(b) By reference to the actual cost of the goods purchased or produced during the taxable year in the order of acquisition;

(c) By application of an average unit cost equal to the aggregate cost of all of the goods purchased or produced throughout the taxable year divided by the total number of units so purchased or produced, the goods reflected in such inventory increase being considered for the purposes of the LIFO rules as having all been acquired at the same time.

Instead of applying costs as above, the taxpayer may use the "dollar-value" method which is the computation and application of an index computed by comparing the total base year LIFO inventories (opening and closing inventories) and converting the increase to current prices by using an index (Reg. § 1472-8).

[¶2703.3]   Retail LIFO for Department Stores

The Regulations permit department stores to use LIFO in connection with the retail method of inventory, on the basis of the semiannual price indices prepared by the Department of Labor.

The retail method of inventory valuation is suitable for retail establishments and businesses where selling prices are very closely related to cost. It isn't suitable to a manufacturing concern. It has found favor because it is relatively easy to use in the control of merchandise inventories, especially those that involve numerous items.

Where records of cost and selling prices are kept, this method permits a sound valuation for inventories. Compared with other methods, it is simple and inexpensive. Valuation is made by converting the current indicated retail value of an inventory into its related costs. Advantages are: (1) inventory for statement purposes can be obtained without a physical count; (2) the cost of each item of purchase is avoided; (3) ratios for merchandise turnover are more dependable because more inventory figures are available for ascertainment of average inventory methods.

[¶2703.4]   LIFO for Sub Using FIFO

IRS says that an affiliated group may use the FIFO method of valuing the inventory of one of its members in preparing *consolidated financial statements* for credit purposes and for the purpose of reporting to stockholders even though the member corporation uses the LIFO method for tax purposes. While §472(c) requires the sub to use the LIFO method *in its financial statements* used for purposes of credit or stockholders, it does not require that the *consolidated statements* of the affiliated group be restricted in this same manner. The requirements of the statute are satisfied as long as the subsidiary uses a consistent method for valuing its inventory.

[¶2704]   SECURITIES AND OTHER INTANGIBLES

Account for all on hand at beginning of year. Analyze acquisitions and dispositions during the year for gain or loss, long-term or short-term (depending on holding period). Determine whether any securities were written off as worthless during the year.

Income from investments may be increased by switching from taxable bonds paying ordinary interest to tax-exempt bonds. Also, switching from interest-bearing securities to dividend-paying stocks may boost income because of the special 85% dividends-received deduction. When the switch produces a capital loss, the loss may be carried back for a quick carryback refund, (not, however, to increase a net operating loss of a carryback year).

Owning less than 80% of another company may provide tax savings through dividend deductions. But owning at least 80% of a company provides the special privilege of filing consolidated returns. Affiliated corporations which do not file consolidated returns are allowed a 100% deduction for "qualifying" dividends (as defined in the Regulations) received from affiliates.

[¶2705] **PROPERTY, PLANT AND EQUIPMENT**

Buying new qualified investment property with a useful life of seven years or more gives the company the full 10% investment credit. Lesser credits are allowed for shorter-life property and for used property. There is a carryback/forward provision as well as a recapture charge-back for early dispositions.

When selling property, the objective is to have *gains* taxed at favorable capital gain rates and losses treated as ordinary losses.

Before selling equipment, a company should consider a trade-in. Also, for equipment which has low resale value but high book value, abandonment rather than sale should be considered. With this approach, the loss is ordinary rather than capital.

Depreciation provisions which may offer tax advantages (see Appendix):

> Accelerated depreciation
>
> Additional first-year depreciation (maximum $2,000 expense)
>
> Shorter useful lives, possibly, than those used for financial statement purposes
>
> Capitalizing certain costs incurred in acquisition or building of plant or equipment
>
> For assets placed in service after 1970, the use of the Class Life Asset Depreciation Range System (ADR) may be advantageous

[¶2705.1] **Acquisitions and Dispositions of Property**

Acquistion of Fixed Assets: Determine if the investment credit is available. Take into account nature of acquired asset, cost, whether new or second-hand, useful life, whether acquired by trade-in of old equipment.

Disposition of Fixed Assets: Consider whether there is gain or loss, type of gain (long-term or short-term), whether any depreciation will be *recaptured* as ordinary income under §1245 (personal property) or §1250 (real property), whether there will be recapture of all or part of investment credit, whether any dispositions at a loss will arise in the same year the company has capital gains.

Installment Sales: Gain on the dispositions of fixed assets may often be reported as an installment sale. Payment received in year of sale cannot exceed 30% of sales price. Gather details of transaction to see if it qualifies. Also keep in mind the imputed interest rule where the sales contract does not call for interest payments or the interest is stated at less than 6%. The IRS will now impute interest to equal 7%. (Rates are subject to change by the IRS.) Losses cannot be reported on the installment basis.

Capital Loss Carryovers: If any transactions result in a capital gain, are there capital loss carryovers from prior years to offset these gains? And if net result from this year's capital transactions is a loss, it may be carried back three years and forward five, but the carryback may not increase a net operating loss.

The financial side of the acquisition, maintenance, and disposition of plant and equipment is the concern of the corporate accounting officer. And a good deal of that concern will involve the tax benefits involved in the acquisition of plant and equipment and the pitfalls in their disposition.

On the acquisition side, we are concerned with the cost of the equipment — both initial cash outlay and overall cost — and also with the cash flow that may be generated by depreciation deductions, the investment credit, as well as other tax savings that may be generated by equipment acquisitions.

A basic question that must be answered in relation to equipment acquisition is whether to buy outright (via financing, in most cases) or lease. To be taken into account in determining the relative immediate and future costs of buying and leasing is the availability of depreciation deductions, especially accelerated depreciation methods and shorter period writeoffs available under the ADR System which allow for a quicker recovery of costs of equipment.

On the disposition side, tax consequences also play a considerable part. Previously deducted depreciation or taken investment credits may create taxable income on dispositions. Also, there was a time when the entire profit on a sale in excess of book value was treated as capital gain. As you know, to the extent the profit is generated by post-1961 depreciation deductions this is no longer the case; the gain, to that extent, gets ordinary income treatment under § 1245.

In addition to the factors mentioned above, other tax considerations enter the picture when we are dealing with the acquisition, maintenance, or disposition of plant and equipment:

— Which accelerated depreciation method will charge off the costs fastest via the largest possible depreciation deductions? Which ones are you eligible to use? When might you switch from one method to another?

— Should a shorter or longer useful life be elected for equipment purchased this year? Should depreciation deductions be stepped up or lowered?

— When might it be better to slow down your rate of writeoff?

— How and when can you support a faster charge-off rate via a shorter useful life because of technological or economic obsolescence or intensive use?

— What happens if you acquire used rather than brand-new equipment?

— Should you trade in old equipment when you acquire new equipment? Or should you sell your old equipment to an outsider? Or, perhaps, abandon it?

— How about improvements to leased property — how quickly can you charge them off?

— What about your repair and maintenance policy? How's that going to affect your ability to recover your costs via tax deductions?

[¶2705.2]   Investment Tax Credit

An investment tax credit (Form 3468) of up to 10% (extended through 1980) is allowed for qualified investments in Section 38 property acquired, constructed or placed in service beginning January 22, 1975. The extent of the credit varies depending upon the useful life of the property and whether it is new or used.

Since this relief provision in the law is subject to perennial scrutiny and amendment by Congress and is used in varying degrees as an economic stimulus, taxpayers should familiarize themselves each year with the specific credits allowable, the limitations thereon, the carryback and carryforward features and the recapture chargeback provisos.

It is also important to note that the investment tax credit is *not* limited to corporations. Self-employed persons can also benefit from this allowance.

[¶2705.3]   Special First-Year Depreciation Allowance

You can write off as much as $2,000 in addition to regular depreciation in the year you buy machinery, equipment, or other nonreal property items. A corporation can get a 20% deduction in the year of purchase on property investment of up to $10,000.

Because of the $10,000 limitation on investment outlays, the best tax break comes where a company embarks on a program of systematic replacement or increase in its equipment over a period of years. By limiting investment to $10,000 each year, it can get the maximum advantage of this provision. For example, a business buying $30,000 of machinery in one year gets a $2,000 deduction (20% of $10,000); while another, buying $10,000 of machinery in each of three years, would get a $2,000 deduction in each of the three years.

The effect of the 20% first-year writeoff when used with the 200%-declining-balance is to step up the recovery of equipment investment by about 10% over the first half of the life of the property. Under the 200%-declining-balance method about 65% of cost is recovered in the first half of the life of the asset. When the 20% first-year writeoff is added, the recovery over the first half of the life of the property is boosted to about 72%; with sum-of-the-digits, from about 73% to about 79%.

The immediate 20% writeoff is available on the purchase of both new and second-hand equipment. And you still get your ordinary depreciation deduction on the balance of the cost.

There are some *technical rules* you have to follow to be eligible for the special 20% first-year writeoff:

(1) The property has to have a useful life of at least six years.

(2) You cannot buy property from related interests between whom losses are disallowed (Sec. 267).

(3) The property can't be purchased from a corporation with which the purchaser files a consolidated return. And the entire group filing a consolidated return is entitled to only one 20% deduction.

(4) Property received by gift or inheritance is not eligible.

(5) If you trade in property as part of your purchase, as much of the basis of the new property as is a carryover of the basis of the traded-in property does not count in applying the 20% writeoff.

[¶2705.4]   Disposition of Equipment or Plant

A major factor arising in the disposition of depreciable property used in a trade or business is the income tax effect. Basically, there is an advantage in that gains on dispositions are treated as capital gains,* and losses, as ordinary losses (§1231). However, with depreciation recapture, part or all of the gain may be treated as ordinary income.

[¶2705.5]   How to Figure the § 1231 Gain or Loss

(1) Add together all your §1231 gains and losses. You include here gains and losses on involuntary conversions — which would include net casualty gains for both businesses and individuals — of property held more than the short period. But note, a net casualty loss to business on investment property is not included in the §1231 calculation, but is treated as an ordinary loss.

(2) If the net result is a gain, you report all the transactions going into the calculation as capital gains and losses — with the net result that you have a net long-term gain. If the net result is a loss, you report all the items going into the calculations as non-capital transactions, giving ordinary income and deduction — with the net result that the net loss is treated as an ordinary loss.

The proper use of Form 4797 and possibly Schedule D, if applicable, will provide the necessary net effective figures.

[¶2705.6]   Recapture of Prior Depreciation Deductions

Since 1962, Congress has passed laws that have cut down a good deal on the capital gain opportunities on the sale of depreciable property. This was accomplished by "recapturing" depreciation. In other words, to the extent the gain reflects previously deductible depreciation, the gain is taxable as ordinary income. For personal property, all post-1961 depreciation can be "recaptured" (§1245). For real estate, the recapture rule applies to post-1963 depreciation and, for the most part, applies only to the extent that accelerated depreciation claimed exceeds straight-line depreciation. Recapture of pre-1970 depreciation is reduced 1% for each month that property is held after 20 months. Post-1969 excess depreciation is for residential property and rehabilitation expenditures 100% recaptured, unless the property is held for over 100 months, in which case the percentage decreases by 1% per month (there would be no recapture if held for 16 years and 8 months) (Section 1250).

---

* The 1976 Tax Reform Act changes the holding period from the old six months to *nine* months for 1977 and to twelve months for years after 1977.

[¶2705.7]   Recapture of Investment Credit

The investment credit, or part of it, is recaptured if the qualifying property is disposed of before the end of the estimated useful life. For example, if the full credit was taken on the basis of a ten-year life but the asset was disposed of after only six years, credit would have to be recaptured for the difference between the credit taken based on the ten-year life and what it would have been, based on a six-year life.

[¶2705.8]   Other Considerations

If There's a Loss: Suppose your tax basis for the old equipment is higher than its present value. That means you'd really have a loss on the trade-in. Since a trade-in is a tax-free exchange, you would not get any immediate tax benefit from that loss; the old basis would carry over and become part of the basis of the new property (that plus what you pay for the new property in addition to the depreciated basis of the old property becomes the basis of the new property). On the other hand, if you *sold* the old equipment to a third party, you'd have an immediately deductible tax loss. You could then use the cash received on the sale plus the tax benefit from the loss to help pay for the new equipment.

Caution: Sell to a third party; if you sell it to the seller of the new equipment in a separate transaction, chances are IRS would treat it as a trade-in anyhow. Where you can't find an outside customer for the property, you can still get a tax deduction for your basis by abandoning the old equipment.

If There's a Profit: If you'd have a taxable profit were you to *sell* your old equipment, examine the advantages of a trade-in, where no gain is recognized, because it is carried over, in effect, as a reduction of the basis of the newly acquired property.

If the property were sold at a gain, the gain would be treated as a capital gain, but it would also be subject to both the depreciation and the investment tax credit recapture provisions.

Intangible Assets: Intangible assets can provide valuable deductions. Amortization is allowed for such intangible assets as research and development expenses, organization expenses, patents, copyrights and franchises.

[¶2706]   CONTAINERS

Many companies sell merchandise in returnable containers, the customer being charged for the container at the time of sale and receiving a refund or credit upon the return of the container. Typical are bottles, cases, kegs, barrels, and reels in which beverage companies, brewers, and manufacturers of wire and cable sell and ship their products. The question arises: When is the charge for the container reportable as income?

If title to the container *passes* to the customer, the transaction is treated as a sale and the amount billed for the container is taken into income by the seller. When the container is returned, the seller treats the refund or credit made to the customer as a repurchase of the container. If title *does not pass,* then the amount charged for the container is treated as a "deposit liability." Refund of the container deposit merely cancels the liability.

However, unclaimed deposits may be converted into taxable income if they build up to an excessive amount or if the seller, by a bookkeeping entry, transfers any part of the "deposit liability" account to his surplus account.

[¶2707] PREPAID EXPENSES AND REAL ESTATE TAXES

Prepaid Expenses: For both the accountant and the tax collector, an accrual-basis taxpayer must generally deduct prepaid expenses ratably over the years to which they relate (unlike the accrual of prepaid income). One exception is prepaid advertising expenses. These expenses are deductible in the year they accrue, although the benefits from such expense may extend over a period of years. Advertising catalogs may, however, be amortized over the expected life.

The Treasury requires cash-basis taxpayers to defer specific types of prepaid expenses. For example, a cash-basis taxpayer must ratably deduct prepaid rent. The Treasury usually justifies deferral on the grounds that the prepayment constitutes a capital asset which should be amortized ("useful life" test) or is merely a "deposit."

If interest is prepaid for a period extending more than thirteen months beyond the end of the current taxable year, it will consider the deduction of such interest in the year of payment as materially distorting income. Prepayments for shorter periods may also be questioned. Another area is the prepayment of insurance premiums, where the IRS has questioned pro rata apportionments beyond one year.

Real Estate Taxes: Accrual-basis taxpayers can deduct real estate taxes on the date they accrue, i.e., the lien date. Thus, for example, if the taxpayer was on a calendar-year basis and the taxes for the year accrued on December 1, the taxpayer would be entitled to deduct the entire amount although the taxes might relate to the next calendar year. However, a taxpayer who wishes may elect under a special provision (§461(c)) to prorate the taxes over the period to which they relate.

On sales of real estate, proration of the real estate tax is required between the buyer and seller, regardless of the cash or accrual basis used by other party, though the timing of the deduction may differ.

An accrual-basis taxpayer can elect to accrue property taxes ratably over the period to which the taxes relate. The election can be made without consent in the first year provided it is made no later than the due date of the return. The Commissioner must approve adoption after the first year. The election is made by a statement attached to the return for the first taxable year, stating the method of accounting used and the period of time to which the taxes are related.

Organizational Expenditures: Section 248 permits you to treat organizational expenditures as deferred expenses (formerly they were generally deductible only in the year of dissolution). With the election made, the expenses are written off ratably over a period of 60 months or more, beginning with the month the corporation began business.

Election is made by a statement attached to the return; it must be filed not later than the date prescribed by law for filing the return for the year in which the election is made. The statement should show: (1) a description of the expenditures; (2) amount of expenditures; (3) the number of months over which the expenditures are to be deducted.

Organizational Expenditures include: Legal costs in preparing the charter, by-laws, minutes; accounting costs incidental to the organization procedure; state fees; expenses of preliminary meetings.

[¶2708]   LEASEHOLD IMPROVEMENTS

The costs of leasehold improvements are capital expenditures which are not currently deductible. For tax purposes, they are depreciated over their useful lives or amortized over the remaining period of the lease, whichever is shorter. In some cases, however, improvements made by a tenant may be deducted, if they are made in lieu of rent.

If you are a lessee with an option to renew, the question arises as to whether the renewal period should be included in the remaining life.

For tax purposes, to avoid controversies as to probability of renewal, specific rules have been set down. Renewal periods are to be taken into account in determining the period over which amortization is to take place if the initial term of the lease remaining upon the completion of the improvements is less than 60% of the useful life of the improvements. Even if you do not meet the 60% rule, you can still amortize over the initial term if you can estabish that, as of the taxable year of the improvements, it is more probable that the lease will not be renewed than that it will be renewed.

Example (1): You put up a building on property you lease. The building has a 35-year life. The lease has 21 years to run, with a renewal option of 10 years. Since the 21-year original term is 60% of the 35-year life of the building, you can write off your building cost over 21 years, unless there is a reasonable certainty you'll renew.

Example (2): You put up an improvement with a 30-year life on a leasehold having a remaining term of 15 years with 20-year renewal period. The 15-year remaining term is only 50% of the life of the improvement. So you have to use the combined terms of the lease (35 years) in your computation, since the building's life of 30 years is less than the combined term you depreciate over the 30-year period. However, you can still use the 15-year period if you can prove it is more probable that you will not renew the lease than that you will.

[¶2709]   THE COST OF ACQUIRING A LEASE

The cost of acquiring a lease is amortized over the life of the lease. If less than 75% of the cost is attributable to the remaining term of the lease, you must take into account the renewal period as well as the remaining initial period for the purposes of amortization.

28

Liabilities

[¶2801]

Liabilities to Stockholders: Interest, rent and salary owed to related parties (stockholders) should be given special attention; they have to be paid within two and one-half months after the close of the taxable year.

Deferred Income: Where income is received in advance of a sale or services to be rendered, the special election to defer sales should be considered.

Notes and Bonds Payable: Tax incentives favoring debt over stock capitalization should be considered.

Accued Liabilities: A company on the accrual basis should consider the advantages of accruing employee bonuses in the current year and paying them in the next year. The same company may consider employee trusts which usually allow accrual before payment.

[¶2801.1]   Reserves for Estimated Costs and Expenses

The general rule is that an expense is deductible by a cash-basis taxpayer when he pays it and by an accrual-basis taxpayer when his liability is fixed.

Where a taxpayer receives income for services he is to perform in the future, the question arises as to when he may deduct the expenses attributable to such income.

If a liability is certain and all events to fix the fact have occurred, it may be accrued. Where uncertainty, or contingency exists, no liability may be accrued until the debt is certain. When a liability is fixed, with the amount uncertain, reasonable estimates may be used and the difference to actual accounted for in the year of exact determination.

[¶2801.2]   Contested Liabilities

How should you treat an expense which you pay in full but continue to contest because you believe you have no obligation to make payment?

The Supreme Court in *Consolidated Edison,* 366 U.S. 380, held that a contested property tax was not deductible until the contest was finally terminated, despite the fact that payment of the tax was made in a prior year. The Court stated that the tax could not be accrued because the payment was in the nature of a "deposit."

The Revenue Act of 1964 revised this rule by *requiring* the taxpayer to deduct the contested liability in the year it is paid, even though the contest is resolved finally in a later year.

As an example of how this provision works, assume the following situation: An accrual-basis taxpayer has a $100 liability asserted against it. It pays the $100, but later contests the liability in a court action. The court action is settled for $80. The law requires the taxpayer to deduct $100 initially, then pick up $20 in income in the later year of court decision.

When law doesn't apply: Where payment is not made until after the contest is settled, an accrual-basis taxpayer may accrue the deduction in the year in which the contest is settled, although the actual payment is made in a later year.

Example: An accrual-basis corporation has a $100 liability asserted against it. The corporation contests it. The contest is settle for $80. In the succeeding year it pays the $80. The company has to accrue the $80 in the year of settlement and deduct it then. If any portion of the contested amount is refunded, such refund must be included in income unless it comes within the "tax benefit" rule (§111). Under the tax benefit rule, to the extent a prior deduction did not result in a tax benefit, the recovery of that deduction item is not taxable.

Liabilities are included: Generally, the rule applies to contested local or state taxes. But it is equally applicable to any other contested liability.

Transfer of Funds Requirement: One of the requirements necessary for the deduction is that taxpayer transfer money or "other property" to satisfy the liability. When money is transferred to a bona fide escrow agent, you can usually take the deduction as long as the funds are no longer within your control.

Contingent Items: Reserves for contingent expenses, though used for financial reporting, are not usually deductible for tax purposes (except for bad debt reserve additions). Some may be deductible if the liability is fixed. An analysis must therefore be made concerning such items. Estimates of *amounts* may be used and deducted, so long as the fact of liability is fixed.

29

Equity

[¶2901]

Capital: The dividend payments should be timed to suit the *stockholders'* tax situation whenever possible. Tax savings may be realized by having the corporation defer payment or split payment over two or more years.

Using appreciated property for dividends should be considered. A corporation realizes a taxable gain when it distributes appreciated property to redeem its stock. But this is not true when it distributes certain appreciated property as a dividend, without the surrender of stock (Regulations should be checked).

[¶2902]   TAX BENEFITS IN CAPITALIZATION

In financing business operations we have these broad objectives, each of which has tax prospects, as follows:

(1) *Minimize the Risk:* This means cushioning against loss by getting the maximum charge-off against fully taxable income.

(2) *Maximize the Gain:* This means setting the stage for the best possible conversion of income into capital gain and for getting as much of the money back tax free as possible by way of a recovery of the investment.

(3) *Minimize the Cost of Capital:* This means making the carrying charges tax deductible: fully deductible interest or rent rather than nondeductible dividends.

[¶2902.1]   Tax Guidelines in Capitalization

Tax factors have vastly increased the costs and the risks of financing. In shaping the form and the capital structure of a business, we must consider:

(1) Dividends are paid out of after-tax earnings.

(2) Interest paid on debt is tax deductible.

(3) From the investor's viewpoint (and this become important in close corporations), losses on stock are subject to capital loss restrictions and can be used to offset ordinary income to only a limited extent. However, there is a special exception for small business stock (§1244) which allows ordinary losses on the worthlessness of the stock (see discussion below).

(4) Individual losses on debt are usually subject to the same restriction. Bad debts from nonbusiness operations will be short-term losses and thus will first offset short-term gains. (And losses on advances to a closely held business generally are treated as nonbusiness bad debts.)

(5) Worthless securities (stock, bonds, debentures, or notes with coupons or in registered form) owned by a domestic corporation in an affiliated corporation may be fully deductible as ordinary losses [Section 165(G)].

(6) When a corporation starts to earn income, an investor will have to pay tax on the return he receives on his investment in stock. Even if part of the stock is redeemed, he is likely to be charged with having received a taxable dividend to the extent of the corporation's accumulated earnings.

On the other hand, corporate funds may be used to repay debt without tax to the investor. Thus an investor stands to recover the money he advances for bonds or notes without having taxes eat into his capital.

(7) A corporation can borrow money at a much lower net cost than it can take money for stock. The cost of servicing debt is tax deductible, while the cost of servicing equity money must come out of net after-tax money. Thus, at a 48% tax rate, 3% borrowing costs only 25% as much as issuing a 6% preferred.

[¶2902.2]   "Thin Corporation" Risk

Because of the tax advantages of debt over equity, an attempt is frequently made to disguise equity as debt. Where the debt far exceeds the equity investment, the Treasury will contend that the corporation is "thinly capitalized." In that case, it argues that the debt is really equity and treats it as such.

Debt-Equity Ratio: We will usually want to set up the highest ratio of debt to equity that is reasonably sure to be accepted by the Treasury and the courts. Rejection of the ratio means that at least some of the debt capitalization will be called equity, with a resulting loss of some of the tax benefits.

"Business Purpose" and "Intent" Tests: Although some Tax Court decisions have relied on the ratio test rather than the intent (finding whether a real debtor-creditor relationship was intended) or business purpose test (disregarding form where the transaction is sham) in determining the status of the corporate debt, there has been a definite trend to find the "true intent" of the parties. Where the ratio is way out of line, IRS may well push that contention rather than "business purpose" if it is felt that the ratio issue would be easier to sustain.

The Tax Court shows a trend away from the ratio test, but a lack of consistency is apparent. Tests emphasized as determinative in preceding cases are ignored in later ones. The only consistency to be found is the search for business purpose or nontax motivation.

Here are some of the things the Tax Court looks for:

(1) Permanent capital structure, (2) risk of the business, (3) acquisition of permanent assets, (4) commencement of new business, (5) expectation of repayment regardless of earnings or success, (6) normal creditor safeguards, (7) presence or absence of security, (8) outside investor standard, (9) use of formal debt instruments, (10) intention to assert rights of creditor, (11) intention of action to enforce, (12) pro rata advances, (13) practical subordination, (14) ratio, (15) substantial economic reality, (16) business purposes, (17) real or true intent, (18) substance vs form, and (19) sham.

How to protect capitalization: Taking into account the various theories cited by the courts, here is a guide which should prove helpful in protecting your capitalization against IRS attack:

(1) The amount of capital invested should compare favorably with other businesses in the same industry. If possible, there should be enough of an investment to acquire all the assets essential to carrying on the business. It may be wise to explore the possibility of operating on a limited scale to show that the invested capital is at least adequate for that purpose. Consider entering into leasing deals.

(2) Try to create a reasonable amount of debt (an amount that can be paid off through normal operations). Debt which earns interest should be kept within the limits of projected earnings.

(3) Make sure the debt instruments are clear and unambiguous. They should show an unconditional obligation at a reasonable interest rate at some certain future time. Avoid subordination or predicating debt payments on earnings.

(4) Give some form of collateral whenever possible.

(5) Keep records to show the debtor-creditor relationship. Listing the transactions in the minutes and all financial accounts is helpful.

(6) On transferring assets to the corporation in exchange for both stocks and debt, allocate the consideration clearly on the books. Separate transactions are preferred where possible. The assets should be valued at their true appraisal value.

(7) Avoid loans in proportion to shareholdings.

(8) Have the financial records (including correspondence, minutes, and other documents) indicate good business reasons for the debts. Nontax considerations for the debt have been frequently cited as all important by the courts.

(9) Weigh the debt against the risk of repayment. If it appears too risky, chances are such loans will be considered to be capital.

(10) When payments of interest and principal are not discharged on time, creditors should take some sort of realistic approach to enforcing the obligation. Written demands for payment should be made.

(11) Do not disregard the debt-equity ratio even though current decisions soft-pedal it. Ratios in the 1:1 to 3:1 range cannot harm the stockholders, but a higher ratio (over 4:1) is an always present hazard.

(12) Maintain characteristics of a loan. Not only is it necessary to maintain the substance of a valid debtor-creditor relationship — interest at the going rate, maturity date, etc.—but the securities should also have the formal characteristics of debt.

Attributes of indebtedness: As indicated above, when a court examines a "thin" corporation situation, one of the criteria it applies is the validity of the debt. In other words, does the instrument which purports to be an evidence of indebtedness rather than of equity have all the attributes of an instrument of indebtedness?

The best the courts have been able to do is to make a list of appropriate tests and decide each case on the basis of how it comes out on the tests as a whole. Here are the tests.

(1) *Name:* What you call the security on its face, on your books and tax returns, and in representations to prospective purchasers can't be ignored. But the terms and legal effect are more significant.

(2) *Intent:* This may appear from the actions of the parties. For example, although the certificate has been drawn in the form of stock, evidence that the investors had insisted on a fixed rate of interest and certainty of payment may indicate that a loan was intended. The use of a stock form might be explained away by the necessity of compliance with state statute.

(3) *Certainty of Payment at a Fixed Rate:* This is, of course, strong indication of a debt. The fact that the holders are given the right to sue or to have a receiver appointed indicates a debt. Absence of these rights may negate the idea of certainty of payment. But a limitation on the amount of debt the corporation can incur or how much of its property it can encumber is not significant; many common stocks have such provisions.

(4) *Maturity Date:* A fixed maturity date is characteristic of a debt.

(5) *Payment Only Out of Net Earnings:* This indicates the corporation controls the payments and, therefore, might be a stockholder relationship. But it's not conclusive any more than a provision that distribution must be made, regardless of profits, is conclusive of a debtor-creditor relationship.

(6) *Right to Share in Profits:* This is the opposite of certainty of fixed payments and indicates a stockholder relationship.

(7) *Subordination to Claims of Creditors:* This is some indication of a stockholder relationship but is not given much weight.

(8) *Voting Rights:* This is usually a characteristic of stockholdings. But absence of such rights is not considered material, since neither preferred stock nor bonds, as a rule, can vote.

(9) *Risks and Hazards of the Business:* It is the stockholder, rather than the creditor, who is the adventurer. The degree of risk is a factor.

[¶2902.3] Special Treatment for Small Business Stock ("1244 stock")

As indicated above, one problem with stock is that, should there be a decline in value and the investors realize a loss, normally the loss will be a capital loss. This form of loss, of course, has a limited tax value. However, it is possible to issue stock (within certain limits) so that it qualifies under §1244 of the Internal Revenue Code. When this is done, losses realized may be deducted by the investor as ordinary losses.

The ordinary-loss rule of §1244 applies whether the loss was incurred on sale of the stock or on its becoming worthless. It can be used only by the original purchaser of the stock. In order to qualify for this special treatment, the following requisites have to be met:

(1) Such stock cannot be issued in a total amount of more than $500,000; and the entire equity capital of the corporation, including the §1244 stock, cannot exceed $1,000,000, meeting the statutory definition of a "small business corporation."

(2) A formal plan for the issuance of the small business stock must be adopted, and the stock must be issued during the next two years. When such plan is adopted, any offering to issue unissued stock of a previous plan offering "1244 stock" must first be canceled. The total of all the stock issued under all the plans offering "§1244 stock" cannot exceed $500,000.

(3) The stock must be issued for money or property and not for stock or securities.

(4) The corporation issuing the stock must be an operating company.

(5) If §1244 stock was issued for property in a tax-free exchange and the basis for the property was higher than its fair market value, the deductible loss on the §1244 stock is limited to that fair market value.

(6) Ordinary losses on small business stock are limited to the basis originally acquired on its issuance. Such losses cannot be increased by increasing basis as a result of subsequent capital contributions. Any such increase must be applied to other stock.

The loss that an investor can take in any one year under §1244 is limited to $25,000. (Where a joint return is filed, the maximum is $50,000.)

[¶2903]   SUB-CHAPTER S CORPORATIONS

Under Code Sections 1371-1379, a closely held corporation may, under unanimous election by the shareholders, choose to be taxed as a Sub-Chapter S ("tax-option") Corporation, provided it meets with the specific provision of the statute.

The election is made on Form 2553 and may be filed any time during the month preceding or initiating the taxable year. The rules for meeting the qualifications are quite specific. Because of the many ramifications involved in comparing advantages and disadvantages of choosing this status, stockholders should seek competent advice before making this election. Changing corporate and individual tax rates and provisions from year to year sometimes increases, sometimes decreases the tax advantage of this provision.

Under this election, shareholders choose *not* to pay corporate tax on the corporation's income, but, instead, pay their respective individual rates on their share of the entire taxable income, *whether distributed or not*. Unlike a partnership which is usually a conduit of income and deduction, the tax-option corporation's taxable income is computed basically the same as other corporations with that income then taxed directly to the shareholders — reasonable officer-stockholder salaries, for example, are allowable deductions for the Sub-S Corporation to arrive at net taxable income, while partnerships would treat them as withdrawals, with the pre-salary income passing through for tax purposes.

The Sub-S election may offer overall tax advantages, and closely held corporations should carefully examine the benefits (risks) involved. Domestic corporations (not members of affiliated groups) may, under the 1976 Tax Reform Act, have more than 10 stockholders during the first five years under Sub-S, but never more than 15, if the extra shareholders acquired their stock by inheritance. Also, if a corporation has already been operating under Sub-S for five years (prior to the Tax Reform Act), it may have 15 shareholders.

[¶2904]   PROFESSIONAL CORPORATIONS

Organizations of doctors, lawyers, accountants and other professionals duly organized under state laws as professional associations or corporations are now generally recognized by the IRS as corporate entities.

So, they inherently now have the choice of being taxed as:

1. Corporations, or
2. Sub-Chapter S Corporations.

In the past, combinations of professional persons were considered to be partnerships for tax purposes with all income earned, whether distributed or not, flowing through to the individual returns. In addition, deferment of income for retirement purposes and later taxation was extremely limited in comparison with what could be deferred for corporate officials.

Now, with the IRS recognizing professional associations as corporations, the tax benefits available are much wider.

For example, if the structure chooses to be taxed as a *corporation* (by *not* choosing the Sub-S option):

1. The owners can achieve the maximum favorable tax correlation by regulating salaries and dividends (but incurring the additional tax on *corporate* net income).

2. They can defer approximately 25% of their compensation (higher than under any other structure) by a combination of both pension and profit-sharing plans.

3. They can get the benefit of corporate deduction for such items as: health insurance, medical reimbursement, group term-life insurance, sick pay, meals and lodging away from home for corporate purposes and other forms of deferred compensation.

If they exercise the *Sub-S option*, professional corporations will:

1. Eliminate the corporate form of double taxation (on dividends) by being taxed on all earnings, whether distributed or not, effectively (with exceptions) being taxed as if it were a partnership, yet having some of the corporation-type benefits;

2. *Not significantly benefit* by retirement provisions, because Sub-S shareholder-owners must *include* in their personal *gross* income any retirement contributions made (for them) *over* 15% of their earned income — or over $7,500 — (per taxable year) whichever is *less*. This is the same restriction applying to partners and sole proprietors. Also, they cannot benefit from forfeitures of employee-participants (as they can in the corporate structure). But the allowable deduction does reduce gross income, leaving the option for use of the standard deduction, if beneficial to the individual.

In other-than-tax considerations, and excluding the factor of personal liability for professional malpractice, the corporate structure for the professional group offers the same advantages and disadvantages of a regular corporation.

[¶2905]   **RECAPITALIZATIONS**

A recapitalization may be tax free or taxable, depending on how it is accomplished. An exchange of stock for stock—i.e., common for common or preferred for preferred—is tax free regardless of whether or not a reorganization or recapitalization is involved (§1036). In other cases, to get freedom from taxes, you need to meet the reorganization rules.

[¶2905.1]   Tax-Free Recapitalizations

Tax-free recapitalization should have a proper plan of reorganization and a good business purpose. In determining whether an exchange is tax free, you'll have to rely on your interpretation of the law and regulations; there is no complete listing of exchanges that are tax free or not tax free. Here is a brief summary of the types of exchanges and their tax results.

Stock for Stock: The following exchanges have been held to be tax free:

(1) A surrender to the corporation for cancellation of a portion of its preferred stock in exchange for no-par value common stock.

(2) A surrender of common stock for preferred stock previously authorized but unissued. However, see §306 stock.

(3) An exchange of outstanding preferred stock having priorities with reference to the amount and time of payment of dividends and the distribution of the corporate assets upon liquidation for a new issue of common stock having no such rights.

(4) An exchange of common for common or preferred for preferred could also qualify as a recapitalization with no gain or loss resulting.

(5) An exchange of outstanding preferred stock with dividend arrearages for a similar amount of preferred stock plus an amount of stock (preferred or common) applicable to the arrearages. But this exchange cannot be made solely for the purpose of effecting the payment of dividends for current and immediately preceding taxable years on the preferred stock exchanged. If it is, an amount equal to the value of stock issued in lieu of such dividends can become taxable.

Bonds for Bonds: An exchange of bonds for bonds in equal principal amounts is tax free. However, the fair market value of the excess of principal amount of bonds received over those surrendered is taxable as "boot," and if the securities are capital assets to the holder, this excess is taxed as capital gain.

Bonds for Stock: A discharge of outstanding bonds for preferred stock instead of cash is tax free (The same result could probably be achieved with any type of security). The entire exchange is tax free with no allocation as to the interest on the arrearages. Further, stock worth less than the principal amount of bonds surrendered may be distributed to creditors with no taxable result.

Stock for Bonds: A distribution of bonds or other securities in exchange for the surrender of stock is taxable. In addition, if the corporation has substantial earnings on hand, a distribution of bonds to the common stockholders (whether or not pro rata) is likely to be taxed as a dividend. But where the distribution of bonds is to preferred stockholders (rather than pro rata to common stockholders) on a non-pro rata basis, capital gain or loss may result.

[¶2905.2]   Recapitalization Exchanges Taxed as Dividends

There are four reasons why a recapitalization exchange may be taxed as a dividend. It is important to avoid having your exchange fall into any one of these danger zones. The four possibilities are:

(1) *Distribution of "boot" where there are corporate earnings available for distribution.* Distribution of "boot" automatically means a tax of some sort; and if the corporation has undistributed earnings, the Treasury will be tempted to charge that distribution of the "boot" was a distribution of the earnings.

(2) *Redemption of stock treated as a dividend.* To avoid this, the redemption must be one of the following: (a) not essentially equivalent to a dividend; (b) substantially disproportionate; (c) a complete termination of stockholder's interest.

(3) *Failure to meet "net effect" test.* Regardless of technical compliance with the law, a recapitalization can be taxed if it fails to meet the "business purpose" test. The "net effect" test is a refinement of the "business purpose" test. It means that the recapitalization will be taxed if its net effect is to accomplish a distribution of earnings.

(4) *Preferred stock bailout.* A preferred stock dividend followed by sale or redemption of the preferred stock is taxable as a dividend to the extent the corporation had earnings and profits.

[¶2905.3]   Elimination of Arrearages in Dividends or Interest

A recapitalization is often used as a means of eliminating back dividends on preferred stock or back interest on bonds. Generally, the investor will be given a new security to replace the defaulted one plus something to take the place of the arrearage. Only some exchanges for this purpose will be tax free.

Dividend or interest arrearages could be eliminated tax free only by replacing them with new stock. In the case of dividend arrearages on preferred stock, the arrearage might be eliminated by issuance of new preferred in exchange for the old preferred, the amount issued being sufficient to cover both the old preferred and the back dividends. In the case of bond interest, the back interest might be eliminated by issuance of new bonds in the same amount as the old bonds, plus preferred stock to cover the back interest. However, there are exceptions if the arrearage pertains to the current or preceding taxable years.

[¶2905.4]   When to Use a Taxable Recapitalization

In most discussions of the tax effects of recapitalizations, the stress is placed upon avoiding taxability. This doesn't always produce the best result. For example, in the usual bonds for preferred stock recapitalization, there is no spread between the basis of the old securities and the value of the new ones. In this case, since there is no gain, it makes no particular difference whether the recapitalization is taxed. And where basis exceeds value, it will be desirable to have the exchange taxed in order to realize a loss.

Even where there is a tax, it will be at the capital gain rate unless the corporation has earnings and the recapitalization is equivalent to the payment of a dividend. Depending upon the circumstances, it may be advantageous to effect a taxable recapitalization, rather than a nontaxable one.

[¶2906]   **DIVIDENDS**

Cash Dividends, Stock Dividends, Rights and Split-ups: In making distributions to shareholders, corporations should be aware of the possible tax effect to the distributee (shareholder).

Cash dividends are taxable at ordinary rates to the recipient in the year of receipt, if the distribution is out of current profits or accumulated retained earnings. Portions of the dividend may be capital gain distributions; portions may be non-taxable distributions. Distinctions must be indicated on the 1099-DIV sent to the recipient ($10 or more).

Stock dividends are ordinarily non-taxable to the recipient at the time of distribution, merely adjusting his basis by changing the number of shares owned at the same prior cost. Stock rights usually increase the cost-basis and the number of shares. However, there are some circumstances under which stock dividends/rights *may* be taxable in the year of issue, such as distributions when the recipient has an alternative option of receiving cash or property from the corporation, or in disproportionate distributions, or distributions involving preferred or convertible stocks — these instances may involve a pickup of income at the *market price* at the time of distribution.

"Stock Split-ups" and "Stock Splits Effected in the Form of a Dividend" (to conform with State laws) change the holding basis of the stock to the recipient. The corporation may have to make Schedule M adjustments on its Form 1120, if the stock distribution entailed an adjustment of retained earnings, because such earnings, if *not* taxable upon distribution, may still be considered available for cash dividend distribution by the IRS and, therefore, at some future day, taxable at regular individual rates when and if distributed in cash [Section 312 (d)].

[¶2907]   **OTHER EQUITY CONSIDERATIONS**

Net Operating Loss Carryover: Determine the availability of carryover losses from prior years for possible reduction of current year's taxes.

Retained Earnings: Federal and many state returns require an analysis of the retained-earnings account.

"Schedule M" Adjustments: Gather the data needed to prepare Schedule M—the schedule that reconciles the company's income per its books with the income according to the tax return. Items involved may include losses (e.g., net capital losses) not allowed as tax deduction; income items picked up in prior years for book purposes but for the current year for tax purposes, or vice versa; or deductions picked up currently for tax purposes but not for book purposes, or vice versa.

30

Income

CONFLICTS BETWEEN TAX AND BUSINESS ACCOUNTING

The conflicts between tax accounting and generally accepted business accounting center around the questions: (1) *when* is it income? and (2) *when* is it deductible? To illustrate the differences that have existed in these two areas, we include the following list which was submitted by the American Insitute of Accountants to the House Committee on Ways and Means in connection with the Hearings on the 1954 Code. (See the *Expense Section* following for listing of "Divergencies involving the time of allowance of deductions.")

Divergences Involving the Time of Recognition of Revenues

(A) Revenues, deferred for generally accounting purposes until earned, but reportable for tax purposes when received:
    (1) Revenues susceptible of proration on a fixed-time basis or on a service-rendered basis:
      Rentals.
      Commissions.
      Revenues from maintenance and similar service contracts covering a specified period.
      Warehousing and trucking fees.
      Advertising revenues.
      Advance royalties on patents or copyrights.
      Transportation ticket and token sales.
      Sales of coupon books entitling purchaser to services.
      Theatre ticket sales.
      Membership fees.
      Tuition fees.
      Laboratory fees.
    (2) Revenues susceptible of proration over average duration of demand:
      Life memberships
      Revenues from service contracts extending over life of article serviced or period of ownership by original owner.
(B) Revenues deferred for general accounting purposes until right to retain them is substantially assured, but reportable for tax purposes when received:
    (1) Receipts under claim of right.

(C) Revenues accrued for general accounting purposes, but not reportable for tax purposes until collected:

    (1) Dividends declared.

    (2) Increase in withdrawal value of savings and loan shares.

[¶3001.1]   Income Received in Advance

Frequently, a taxpayer receives payment for services he has not yet performed (e.g., club membership dues, magazine subscriptions). The question then is, in what year does the taxpayer have to report these payments as income?

Accounting Rule: The accountant says that you have no income until it is actually *earned;* that the mere receipt of cash or property does not result in a realization of income. The accountant treats the prepayment as a liability which obligates the recipient to perform services before he can be said to have *earned* the payment. (This problem applies to accrual-basis taxpayers; cash-basis taxpayers are considered to have *earned* a prepayment when it is received.)

Tax Rule: You have income when you have the *right to receive* it, even though it is not earned. Thus, cash payments received in advance, negotiable notes received as advance payments, and contract installments due and payable are taxable to the recipient as advance income, even though these payments are for services to be provided by the taxpayer in a subsequent tax year (*American Automobile Association,* 367 US 687; *Schlude,* 372 US 128). Here is a composite tax picture:

Type of Income	Basis	Extent Taxable	Authority
Cash receipts	Cash or accrual	Full amount	*American Automobile Association,* 367 US 687; *Schlude,* 372 US 128.
Negotiable notes	Cash	Fair market value	*Pinellas Ice Co.,* 287 US 462; Reg. §1.61—2(d) (4).
	Accrual	Face Value	*Schlude,* 372 US 128; *Schlude,* TC Memo 1963-307; *Spring City Foundry Co.,* 292 US 182.
Unpaid contractual payments due and payable under terms of the contract	Cash	None—no fair market value	Est. of *Ennis,* 23 TC 799; *nonacq.,* 1956-2 CB 10; *Ennis,* 17 TC 465.
	Accrual	Face Value	*Schlude,* 32 TC 1271.
Unpaid contractual installments not due under the contract nor evidenced by notes	Cash	None	*Schlude,* 372 US 128.
	Accrual	None	*Schlude,* 372 US 128.

The tendency of the courts seems to be to require reporting prepaid receipts. A furrier was required to include in income advance payments for fur coat orders and was not allowed to estimate the cost of goods sold for the year receipts were included in income *(Hagen Advertising Displays, Inc.,* 47 TC 139; *Boyce,* Ct. Cls., 405 F.2d 526. But see *Artnell Co.,* 7th Cir., 400 F.2d 981, where a baseball team deferred preseason sales receipts).

Special Relief Provisions: Sections 455 and 456 of IRC were enacted to provide special relief from the results of *Schlude.*

(1) *Accrual-basis taxpayers* may defer prepaid income from service contracts or from the sale of goods. See *Rev. Proc. 71-21* and Regs. §1.451-5.

(2) *Publishers* may elect to spread prepaid subscription income, §455.

(3) *Membership organizations* organized without capital stock which do not distribute earnings to any members and do not report income by the cash receipts and disbursements method may spread their prepaid dues income ratably over the period (not to exceed 36 months) during which they are under a liability to render services.

[¶3001.2]   Repayment of Income Received Under Claim of Right

Since the tax law requires the accrual-basis taxpayer to include payments received (although not yet earned) in taxable income when received, it obviously disagrees with good accounting practice on how to treat such payments if they must be repaid.

If you are required to repay money received under a claim of right, the tax law says you can deduct it in the year of repayment.

The inclusion of disputed income in year of receipt and the allowance of a deduction in the year of repayment result in a distortion of the taxpayer's income in two years. It can also result in higher tax liability (for example, where the taxpayer is in a higher tax bracket in the year of receipt than in the year of repayment or the tax rates are higher in the year of receipt than in the year of repayment).

Relief Provisions: Section 1341 eliminates the inequity if the amount of repayment exceeds $3,000; the taxpayer may reduce his tax for the year of repayment by the amount of tax he would have saved in the year of receipt had he been permitted to exclude the subsequent repayment from the original amount received. Alternatively, he may deduct the amount repaid in the year of repayment if that will result in a smaller tax to him.

The relief provision does not apply to refunds, allowances, bad debts, etc., applicable to sales of inventory or stock in trade.

Section 1341 also provides relief to a *recipient* of income who is required to repay all or part of such income in a later year.

Prepaid interest is not income received under ''claim of right.''

[¶3002]   INCOME TAXES — TIMING INCOME AND EXPENSES

Once a corporation is past the 48% rate break in earnings, it has nothing to gain taxwise in shifting income from one year to another in terms of rates, unless there are future rate changes. (The 1975 rates of 20% on the first $25,000, 22% on the next $25,000 and 48% on the balance have been extended through 1977 by the 1976 Tax Reform Act).

But there can still be reasons for shifting income and expenses. One year may have so many deductions already that additional income can be picked up tax free. True, if the income were not picked up, the current year's loss could be carried back three years and forward seven. But, perhaps the prior years were also loss years and no immediate benefit can be realized from the current year's loss (or if refunds will be available, the years may be subject to tax audit). On the other hand, the current year's deductions may be "light" but the following years' deductions are expected to be "heavy." Shifting income forward can match up the deductions with the income.

Similar results can be achieved by shifting expenses from one year to another. In a year when additional income is desirable, the same effect may be achieved by shifting expenses out of that year.

Where we have installment sales — whether the company is an installment dealer or makes a so-called casual sale of substantial property calling for payment over a number of years — the total tax paid on the income realized from the sale may be the same whether we use installment sale or accrual accounting. We may prefer to use the installment method of reporting the sale for tax purposes so as to match the actual tax payments with the receipt of income.

[¶3003]   HOW TO HANDLE SALES

Gross sales are a decisive factor in determining the income level for a given year. The method of selling and the timing of shipments can control the tax year. In a cash-basis business, it is relatively simple to control the time of payment. Income can be increased for the year by accelerating collections; it can be reduced by either allowing payments to take their normal course or by a delay in billing. For accrual-basis businesses, a sale is taken into income when completed, which is when title has passed under the state law. As a general rule, title passes when delivery has been made, usually determined by reference to the invoice or bill of lading. Thus, an accrual-basis taxpayer can accelerate income by speeding up deliveries. Similarly, income can be reduced by holding off deliveries in the closing weeks of the year.

Long-Term Contracts: Taxpayer has the option of reporting on the percentage-completion method or the completed-contract basis.

Both the percentage-of-completion and the completed-contract methods of accounting are permitted for income tax purposes as long as more than one year elapses from the date of execution to the date of completion and acceptance of the contract (Reg. §1.451-3).

Use of either of these methods is optional; the taxpayer may use the cash or accrual method for other operations although using the percentage-of-completion or completed-contract method for long-term contracts. But once the method of accounting is originally adopted, a change requires IRS approval.

[¶3004] INSTALLMENT SALES

A company may be making installment sales and not using the installment method of reporting the income. Under the accrual method it is picking up the entire income in the year of sale. Tax rules permit installment reporting of income on either cash or accrual basis, thus spreading the tax effect over the period payments are received.

In addition to installment dealers, who can elect to use the installment method for their installment sales, casual installment sales of more than $1,000 and installment sales of real estate can be reported under the installment method for tax purposes on a sale-by-sale basis if certain rules are met. Payments in the year of sale, including demand bonds or notes or readily tradeable paper, cannot exceed 30% of the selling price. (Reg. § 1.453-1) Unstated interest is also a factor.

[¶3004.1] Installment Sales by Dealers

"Installment dealer" isn't defined in the tax law; no minimum percentage of installment sales is prescribed. Nor is frequency the decisive factor. Regularly engaging in installment selling is the important thing.

On the installment basis, the income arising from an installment sale of real or personal property is reportable for tax purposes *proportionately* when and as the income is actually collected. The theory of the installment method is that each dollar collected includes a *pro rata* recovery of cost (nontaxable) and a *pro rata* receipt of *profit* (which is taxable in the year collected).

For tax purposes, the books of account needn't be kept on the installment basis; they can be kept regularly on the cash or accrual basis. But adequate records must be kept to provide the necessary information for computing the profit portion of the different installments.

The installment method applies only to *gains* from the sale of property. If the installment sale resulted in a *loss*, the loss must be deducted in the year of sale.

Expenses: A *dealer* must deduct the expenses in the year when paid (on the cash basis) or when incurred (on the accrual basis). He cannot apportion or spread the expenses over the years when the income from the installment sale is reported as collected.

[¶3004.2]   Choice of Installment Method by a Dealer

For tax purposes, a dealer can switch to installment reporting without prior approval. All he needs to do is reflect the proper figures, with appropriate supporting schedules, in his return. A dealer can use the installment method for reporting installment sales and the accrual method for reporting sales on open account.

Change of Method: Once the taxpayer begins installment reporting, he needs the Commissioner's approval to switch to accrual reporting. (If changed within the first three years, the taxpayer can revoke his election automatically by filing amended returns for those years.) A dealer switching from accrual to installment reporting must report, when collected, the unrealized profit on receivables outstanding at the time of the switch. The fact that the entire profit was accrued and reported in the period the receivable arose doesn't change this.

Code §453 largely eliminates the double tax that arises from reporting the same income twice. You take the gross profit in the current year attributable to collections of items accrued in a previous year and divide it by the total gross profits of the year of collection. You then apply that fraction to that year's tax to find what percentage of the current tax is attributable to that collection. You then take that same gross profit attributable to the prior year's collection and divide it by the total gross profit of the year of accrual. That tells you what portion of the prior year's tax was attributable to the amount accrued then but collected now. The lesser of the two figures is then applied to reduce the current year's tax. (See Appendix E for example of "Adjustments in tax on change to Installment Method".)

But the relief provisions of §453 do not provide 100% relief in cases where the tax rate for the year of post-change collection is higher than that for the year of prior accrual. When that happens, it may be better to work out the switch from accrual to installment reporting by selling all your accounts receivable prior to switching from accrual to installment method.

[¶3004.3]   Discounting Installment Receivables

There are two types of arrangements a dealer can make with banks or factors to obtain advances on his installment receivables. He can: (1) pledge them; that is, borrow against the receivables as collateral, or (2) discount them; that is, sell them at less than face value.

Under a pledge, the dealer receives a loan of about 85% of the balance due on the installment sales contracts and pays interest on the loan monthly. By discounting, he receives about 85% of the balance due, less a service charge; the remaining 15%, known as a holdback, is placed in a reserve account to secure the dealer's contingent liability as guarantor that the installment balances will be paid.

The installment method of reporting is available to the dealer only if he uses the *pledging* arrangement. If he discounts, he must report all of the income in the year of sale, even though the bank or factor has full recourse against him in the event the purchasers don't pay their installment liabilities.

[¶3004.4]   Installment Sale Treatment for Revolving Credit Sales

Since revolving credit sales sometimes are paid in one payment by the customer, not all such sales are eligible for treatment as installment sales; special rules apply for the determination of apportioning and determining the extent of those sales which may be treated as installment sales [Reg § 1453-2(d) (2) (i)].

[¶3004.5]   Casual Installment Sale of Personalty

The occasional, or casual, sale of a piece of equipment or other personalty can be reported for tax purposes by the installment method if payments in the year of sale do not exceed 30% of the total selling price. Note that unstated interest is *deducted* from the selling price before applying the 30% rule.

Payments in the year of sale include all payments made by the buyer in the year the sale is closed, whether in cash or property. The buyer's note or other evidence of obligation to pay in a later year is merely a promise to pay, not a payment; consequently, it is not applicable until paid.

However, if installment obligations are discounted or otherwise disposed of during the year of sale, they have to be considered as payments in that year. A buyer's note that becomes due and paid during the year is property and must be included as must readily traded bonds or debentures of the purchaser or securities payable on demand.

[¶3004.6]   Installment Sale of Real Property

An installment sale of real property is generally subject to the same rules as a casual installment sale of personal propety. There is the same requirement that the initial payments must not exceed 30% of the total selling price and the same rules for determining what must be included in payment in year of sale. However, there is no minimum selling price required.

Also keep in mind that while a mortgage on the property isn't payment even if assumed by the buyer, a mortgage which the buyer assumes or takes subject to is treated as payment received in the year of sale where such mortgage exceeds the seller's basis for the property sold (Reg. §1.453-4(c)).

[¶3004.7]   Installment Computation for Sale of Realty

Total profit is divided by contract price; the resulting percentage is the percent of each payment received that must be reported by the seller as income. Contract price is the entire amount the seller will receive (excluding payments on existing mortgages except to the extent they exceed the seller's basis).

Suppose we have a selling price of $25,000 and a cost basis of $15,000. The buyer assumes an existing $5,000 mortgage and gives his own mortgage for the balance due, payable over a 20-year period. Down payment is $5,000, and payments in the first year total $1,000, of which $600 represents interest. Thirty percent of the selling price of $25,000 would be $7,500; and since a total of only $6,000 was received in the year of sale (less than 30%), the sale qualifies for installment reporting.

Here is the computation for the first year.

Selling price	$25,000	
Cost basis	15,000	
Gain	$10,000	
Payments received		$6,000
Less interest (reported as ordinary income)		600
Principal amount received		$5,400
Selling price	$25,000	
Less mortgage assumed	5,000	
Contract price	$20,000	
Profit percentage ($10,000÷$20,000)	50%	
Reportable gain (50% X 5,400)		$2,700

On the accrual method, the reportable gain would be $10,000 instead of only $2,700.

[¶3004.8]   Disposition of Installment Obligation

If an installment obligation is sold or otherwise disposed of, there is gain or loss in the amount of the difference between the basis of the obligation and the proceeds in the case of a sale, and the fair market value of the obligation in the case of any other disposition. For example, if unrecovered cost is $75, unrealized profit is $50, and the dealer sells for $100, he has a $25 gain. If he gives the obligation away and it is worth $90, he has a $15 gain. In either case, the gain is capital gain if the original transaction gave rise to capital gain and ordinary income if the original transaction gave rise to ordinary income.

[¶3005]   CONSIGNMENT SALES

Selling on consignment will defer income until sale by the consignee. Thus, delivery to distributors on consignment postpones income. Instead of taking sales into account upon delivery, as where sales are made on open account, income on consignment sales is deferred while the goods are held on the distributor's floor.

Thus, a manufacturer can defer income by placing his sales on a consignment basis. And, conversely, he can accelerate income by shifting to an open-account basis. He might do this, for example, in order to use up an operating loss which is about to expire. Consigned goods (out) remain part of the manufacturer's inventory until sold.

Approval and Return Sales: Sales on approval aren't reflected in income until the buyer decides to take the goods. The parties agree the buyer is to take possession of the goods temporarily, with the understanding that if the goods aren't satisfactory, he owes nothing to the seller except their return. New and perishable products are frequently sold this way. Title does not pass until buyer approves.

Substantially the same business result, but with different tax consequences, can be achieved by a transaction known as "a sale or return." Seller and buyer agree that the goods will pass to the buyer on delivery but that he may return them if they prove unsatisfactory. The income must be taken up immediately, even though the buyer may subsequently return the goods. Here, title passes on delivery. The form of the contract determines whether the transaction is a sale on approval or a sale with return privileges.

If you have been using a contract which provides for sale with the privilege of return, you can defer a large slice of income simply by changing the contract to one for sale on approval. Or, if you have been selling on approval, you can bring a lot of additional sales into a given year by changing your contract to one providing for sale on delivery with the privilege of return.

Consignment and Approval Sales under the Uniform Commercial Code: Where the term *consignment sale* or its equivalent is used but nothing else is said, the UCC says the transaction is treated as a sale or return. Thus, if the parties want the income postponed until the buyer resells the goods, merely using the *consignment sale* designation is probably not enough; the contract should spell out the details of when the title is to pass. Whether this is desirable in view of other consequences under the UCC — e.g., rights in the goods of the buyer's creditors — is something to be decided by the parties.

[¶3006] OTHER FACTORS AFFECTING SALES

Here are some other areas involving sales where timing techniques may be employed for tax purposes.

Conditional Sales: In a conditional sale, the seller delivers merchandise to a buyer who contracts to pay for it over a period of time. The seller stipulates that title is not to pass until the price has been fully paid.

The sale is not legally complete until final payment is made and title has passed to the buyer. Nevertheless, for tax purposes, the sale price must be taken into income when the property has been transferred to the buyer. Unless we set up very substantial conditions precedent to the passing of title, over and above mere payment of the purchase price, we haven't deferred the realization of income.

Sales of specific goods on which work must be done: When a contract for the sale of specific goods calls for the seller to do something to the goods to put them into a deliverable state, the property does not pass to the purchaser until such things are done unless the parties agree otherwise. Thus, the accrual seller will realize no taxable income until he places the goods in a deliverable state or title passes to the buyer, and to this extent he can control his receipt of taxable income.

Sales on Open Account: Where such goods, in a deliverable state, are "unconditionally appropriated" (i.e., "identified to," under the UCC) to the contract by either the buyer or seller with the consent of the other, the title in the goods passes to the buyer. Delivery of the goods to a *carrier* for shipment to the purchaser, even if such shipment is made C.O.D., constitutes an "unconditional appropriation." If the seller wants a larger taxable income in a particular year, he can realize it by simply increasing the rate of shipments. If, on the other hand, he wants to postpone taxable income, he can slow up on the shipments or other acts of "unconditional appropriation."

Sales Returns and Allowances: Where credits or refunds are made for damaged or unsatisfactory merchandise, the deduction becomes available when the liability is admitted. This usually occurs when a credit memo is issued by the seller to the buyer. The deferment of credit memos can throw deductions into the following year. Quick approval of credits for returned merchandise can reduce the current year's income.

Contingent Income: Are there some sales booked to which the company does not have an enforceable right at year-end? Perhaps the income should not be picked up for tax purposes.

[¶3007]   OTHER ORDINARY INCOME

Dividend Income: Breakdown between foreign and domestic payors of dividends is necessary for federal tax purposes — e.g., domestic dividends are generally subject to 85% dividend deduction; foreign dividends may be subject to credit for foreign taxes paid. Intercorporate dividends of affiliated corporations should be earmarked for elimination on consolidated returns. 100% deduction is now allowed for qualifying dividends received by affiliated corproations from other affiliates in the group, as long as consolidated returns are *not* filed.

No dividend deduction is ordinarily allowed for DISC dividends. (See discussion of DISC Corporations later in this text.)

Royalty and License Income: Allocation between foreign and domestic royalty or license income may be required for federal tax purposes (including foreign tax credit). It is important to have details about possible withholding of tax at the source. State allocations may also depend on source of the income.

Rental Income: It is very important to keep location information of properties throwing off the rental income for state allocation purposes. In addition, rent paid by related taxpayers (e.g., subsidiaries) may be subject to reallocation by IRS on audit unless they have good substantiation for amounts paid.

Interest Income: Source of payments is necessary for possible exemption of some of the income from either or both federal and state taxes.

Foreign Income, Blocked: In regard to income received or accrued in foreign currency which is not convertible into United States currency, a taxpayer has the election of deferring reporting the income until the restrictions are lifted or including it in his present year's income.

[¶3008]   **IMPUTED INTEREST**

Suppose you are about to sell a piece of property for $100,000; $30,000 down and the balance in 10 equal installments. If you receive 6% interest on the unpaid installments, that would come to about $25,000 over the 10-year period. Instead of charging interest, you might have set the price at $125,000 and taken payments of $12,500 per year.

At one time, that $25,000 would have come to you as capital gain. Since the 1964 tax law, it comes in as ordinary income. Each payment you receive is discounted back to the date of the sale to find the interest portion of that payment, and that portion is taxable as ordinary income.

For a sale or exchange to be covered by these rules, there must be a contract for the sale or exchange of property under which some or all of the payments are due more than one year after the date of the sale or exchange. Once this requirement is met, the rules can apply to all payments which are due more than six months after the date of the sale or exchange.

The imputed interest rules apply to the seller only if some part of the gain from the sale or exchange of the property would be considered as gain from a capital asset or from depreciable property. If the property is sold at a loss or if no gain is recognized, the rules will nevertheless apply if, had there been a taxable gain, some part of it would have been considered as gain from a capital asset or from depreciable property. And the fact that gain is ordinary income because of the application of the depreciation recapture provisions (§1245, 1250) makes no difference.

How to Determine Unstated Interest: Basically, the law provides that the IRS is to set a proper interest rate at which interest is to be imputed. In its Regulations, the IRS has set this rate at 7% compounded semiannually. IRS has also retained the 6% simple interest test. If the rate of interest specified in the contract is below this 6% rate, or, if no interest is specified at all, then there is a "total unstated interest" at 7% compounded semiannually. (Reg. 1.483-1(g)). Since there is a difference of over 1% between the 6% simple interest rate and the 7% compounded semiannually imputed interest rate, this means that by stating a minimum of 6% in your contract you can pick up an additional more-than-1% as capital gain instead of ordinary income.

Once we determine the total imputed interest, we then apportion it equally to the installments under the contract as follows:

(1) Determine the present value of each installment payment using the specified interest rate. This is done by discounting each payment from its due date back to the date of the sale or exchange. Thus the present value of a payment is the amount which, if left at interest at the prescribed rate from the date of the sale to the due date of payment, would have increased to an amount equal to the amount of the payment.

(2) Deduct the sum of all the present values from the sum of all the payments under the contract. The resulting figure is the total unstated interest under the contract.

(3) This amount is then spread pro rata over the total payments involved so that the same percentage of each payment is deemed to be imputed interest.

Where some or all of the payments are indefinite in amount as of the time of sale, the unstated interest for each indefinite payment will be determined separately as received, based on elapsed time between sale and receipt.

Imputed Interest Rule can endanger installment sale reporting: In addition to its stated effect, the imputed interest rule can also have far-reaching side effects. For example, in a typical casual or real estate installment sale, if any part of the installments due in future years is held to be interest, this could reduce the selling price to a point where the down payment exceeds 30% and the sale would not quality for the favorable tax treatment.

31

Expenses and Costs of Sales

CONFLICTS BETWEEN TAX AND BUSINESS ACCOUNTING FOR EXPENSES

As there are conflicts in the timing of entering and recognizing income, as indicated in the prior chapter, so too are there divergencies in the recognition of deductions. The following list of expense-timing differences was also included in the submission by the AICPA to the House Committee on Ways and Means in connection with 1954 Code Hearings:

Divergencies Involving the Time of Allowance of Deductions:

(A) Costs and expenses, recognized for general accounting purposes, on basis of reasonable estimates, in period of related revenues; but not deductible for tax purposes until established with certainty by specific transactions:
   (1) Sales returns and allowances.
   (2) Freight allowances.
   (3) Quantity discounts.
   (4) Cash discounts allowable to customers.
   (5) Allowances for customers' advertising.
   (6) Provision for return of commissions resulting from cancellations of related contracts.
   (7) Costs of product guarantees.
   (8) Deferred management compensation and incentive bonuses.
   (9) Vacation pay.
   (10) Pending injury and damage claims.
   (11) Rentals on percentage lease with minimum.
   (12) Provisons for major repairs and maintenance regularly done at intervals of more than a year.
   (13) Professional services rendered but unbilled.
   (14) Social Security taxes on unpaid wages.
   (15) Retailers' occupation taxes on credit sales.
   (16) Costs of restoration of property by lessee at termination of lease.
   (17) Contractors' provisions for restoration of property damaged during construction.
   (18) Costs of handling, packing, shipping, installing, etc., of merchandise already sold.

(19) Provisions for future costs to be incurred in collection of accounts receivable arising from installment sales, where profit is reported in the year of sale.
(20) Provisions for losses on foreign exchange.
(21) Allowances for perpetual care of cemetery (where not actually segregated from receipts).
(B) Expenses, deferred for generally accounting purposes to period of related benefit, but deducted for tax purposes in year of payment or incurrence of liability:
(1) Advertising expenses from which benefit has not yet been obtained, including costs of preparation of catalogues not yet put into use.
(C) Property taxes recognized for general accounting purposes ratably over the year for which they are levied, but deductible in toto for tax purposes on a certain critical date.

The foregoing differences do not include conflicts which result from Congressional policy decisions. These include, on the *income side,* tax-exempt interest, tax-free exchanges, exemption of life insurance proceeds, capital gains, etc., and, on the *deduction side,* percentage depletion, amortization of emergency facilities, loss carryovers and the disallowance of excess charitable contribution, losses on wash sales, losses on sales between certain relatives or related business interests, capital losses, etc.

The special treatment accorded these items originates from social, economic, and revenue considerations which, in the main, are unrelated to accounting principles.

[¶3102]　　　INCOME TAXES—ELECTIONS

The taxpayer has an accounting election for tax purposes as to a variety of things. Following is a check list of the more important elections:

[¶3103]　　　BAD DEBT METHODS

Accrual-basis taxpayer can elect either to deduct specific bad debts or make additions to reserve for bad debts. Election is made on first return on which a bad debt is claimed; it's binding for subsequent years. If he wants to change from one bad debt method to the other, the taxpayer must obtain permission from the Commissioner. (Usually, the change is from charge-off to reserve to get the charge-off deductions *plus* the deduction for setting up the reserve.) However, you can get "automatic consent" if you're willing to spread the benefits. To apply for the automatic switch from specific writeoff to the bad debt reserve method, you must file Form 3115 (Application for Change in Accounting Method) within 180 days of the beginning of the tax year for which you want to change with the District Director. You should attach a copy of Form 3115 to your return for the taxable year of change.

Then, unless you receive a letter from the District Director denying you permission because your application on Form 3115 wasn't timely filed, you may assume that the change has been granted.

Initial Reserve Limitation: The amount of reserve that you set up initially at the end of the year of change is to be determined by dividing total net losses on bad debts for the five years before the change year by the sum of the amounts of outstanding trade receivables at the end of each of these five years, and then multiplying the amount of outstanding trade receivables at the end of the year of change by this percentage. Receivables sold or to be sold shortly after the end of the change year are not be be included in computations.

Maximum Tax Benefit: The addition to your reserve for bad debts can only be deducted ratably over a ten-year period. So, the maximum added yearly tax benefit you get is 10% of the addition to the bad debts reserve account. For the year of change, your bad debt deduction will consist of your specific writeoffs plus 10% of the addition of your initial addition to the reserve. In the next nine years, your deduction will consist of your addition to the reserve for that year plus 10% of the initial addition of the year of change. The amount of reserve for the year of change must be considered in determining subsequent additions.

Partial worthlessness can either be charged off as it occurs, or the deduction can be postponed until the year in which the debt becomes entirely worthless. A mere decline in market value isn't sufficient to warrant a charge-off.

Analysis of ratios of reserves to sales for current year and average of previous five years is needed to substantiate current deduction if there is an examination by IRS.

[¶3104]   DEPRECIATION METHODS

Depreciation methods permitted by the tax law include: (1) straight-line method (equal annual installments), (2) declining-balance method (up to double the straight-line rate), (3) sum-of-the-years-digits method (rate is a fraction, the numerator being the property's remaining useful life at the start of the tax year and the denominator being the sum of all the years' digits corresponding to the estimated useful life at acquisition), and (4) any other consistent method which during the first two-thirds of the property's useful life does not give greater depreciation than under the declining-balance method (§167 (b)).

Method number (4) embraces use of a sinking fund, writeoffs on the basis of periodic appraisal, unit of production, etc. However, most taxpayers who do not use the classic straight-line method employ instead one of the acceleration methods, either the 200%-declining-balance method or the sum-of-the-years-digits method.

Another possibility that should be mentioned is a combination of the straight-line method and the 200%-declining-balance method. With this method, you use the 200%-declining-balance method, which gives you extra large deduction in the early years. At the point where this starts to peter out, you switch to straight-line which can be accomplished without consent of the Commissioner (Reg. §1.167 (e)-1)

A good deal of what you do here will depend on prior years' actions. But you will want to analyze the existing situation to see if special, quick writeoffs are justified as to special assets; whether it's time to switch from double-declining-balance to straight-line on certain assets. Where new assets were acquired during the year, whether accelerated depreciation should be used as to them even though you use straight-line as to your other assets; whether you are using adequate salvage provisions; and whether you are taking advantage of the right to disregard salvage where permissible.

The 1969 Tax Reform Act restricted the use of accelerated depreciation for real property to 150% and also tightened the recapture rules. It also provided quicker writeoffs for certain types of properties and improvements. Low-income housing rehabilitation may be depreciated over a 60-month period. Pollution control facilities which are certified by governmental authorities may also be amortized over a 60-month period (§169) and so may railroad rolling stock, child-care facility and on-the-job training facility expenditures.

The applicable allowable depreciation (or amortization in lieu of depreciation) methods and rates may be summarized as follows:

Declining-balance method, 200% rate is allowed for new tangible personal property with a useful life of three years or more; all types of newly constructed real estate structures acquired before July 25, 1969; only on new residential rental property where 80% or more of gross rentals are from dwelling units.

Declining-balance method, 150% rate is allowed for new tangible personal property; newly constructed rental property acquired after July 24, 1969.

Declining-balance method, 125% rate is allowed only for used residential rental property acquired after July 24, 1969, and having a useful life of 20 years or more, or if the Commissioner permits it on application for other types.

Sum-of-the-years-digits method is allowed only for new tangible personal property and new residential rental property.

Straight-line (useful life) method is allowed for all depreciable property, new or used, personal or real.

Straight-line method (no salvage value), 60 months applies to low-income rental housing rehabilitation expenditures; certified pollution control facilities; certain railroad rolling stock.

Additional first-year 20% depreciation write-off is also permitted (regardless of which method above is used) to the maximum extent of $2,000 depreciation (the same maximum applies to an *entire* affiliated group.)

The taxpayer has a further election:

For assets placed in service after 1970, depreciation rates used may be based on either:

1) Estimated Useful Life, generally based on guidelines in Rev. Proc. 62-21 or prior IRS Bulletin F;

2) The Class Life Asset Depreciation Range System (ADR).

Regulations regarding the use of ADR are quite extensive and detailed. Taxpayers should study this election further. It offers many taxable advantages.

[¶3105]   OTHER ELECTIONS

Leasehold Amortization: Need information about cost of improvement, useful life, remaining term of the lease, renewal options available. For example, if remaining life of lease is less than 60% of useful life of improvement, amortization must be over remaining lease life *plus* renewal periods, but not longer than useful life of improvement. Or, if lessor is an affiliate, shortest available life over which amortization may be taken is useful life of improvement. Location of leased property is also useful information for state allocation purposes.

Trademark and Trade Name Amortization: Examine costs of trademarks or trade names incurred during the year (including cost of acquisition other than purchase), protection, expansion, registration (federal, state, or foreign), or defense of trademark or trade name; cost can be written off over at least a 60-month period rather than capitalized.

Patent Amortization: Examine patent data to determine whether there is any basis to increase deduction—e.g., patent has become worthless.

Bond Premiums: Bondholder can elect to amortize bond premium on wholly taxable obligations to maturity or to date on which the bond is first callable if the deduction is smaller. The bond premium, which is deductible, reduces the basis of the bond. Taxpayer makes the election by claiming the deduction in the first taxable year for which he wishes it to apply. It applies to all bonds and can be revoked only with Commissioner's permission.

Every taxpayer must amortize premium on wholly tax-exempt bonds, even though no tax deduction results, thus reducing the basis annually.

Carrying Charges: There is an election to deduct or capitalize taxes, interest and other carrying charges in connection with the following kinds of property:

(1) Unimproved and unproductive real property. The election is to deduct or capitalize taxes, interest and other carrying charges.

(2) Real property being developed or improved. The election is to deduct or capitalize costs up to the time construction or development has been completed; for instance, interest on construction loans, Social Security taxes on own employees, sale or use taxes on materials used in development or improvement of property, and other necessary expenditures paid or incurred in connection with this work.

(3) Personal property. The election is to deduct or capitalize interest on loans to purchase the property or to pay for transporting or installing, sales and use taxes paid on the property, Social Security taxes on own employees used in transporting

and installing the property, paid or incurred up to the date installed or first put into use, whichever date is later.

Election to capitalize any item is made by filing a statement with the return, stating the items being charged to capital (Reg. §1.266-1(c) (3)). Commissioner's consent is not required.

Circulation Expenditures: Publisher can elect to capitalize rather than deduct expenditures made to establish or increase circulation. Year-to-year expenditures to maintain circulation cannot be capitalized but must be deducted currently.

The election, if made, must be applied to all expenditures to increase circulation in the present or later years, except where the Commissioner permits change on written application.

The election is made by a statement attached to the first tax return to which it is applicable.

Depletion: Bear in mind that a taxpayer has no election, in the true sense of that word, in selecting a depletion method. What actually happens is that he must make a computation for depletion based on both the cost and percentage methods and then select the method which results in the greatest deduction, regardless of whether it will be a disadvantage to the taxpayer (Code Section 612 and 613). This computation is to be made each year.

Cost depletion formula:

$$\frac{\text{Original Cost} + \text{Development Expense}}{\text{Estimated Units of Recovery}} = \text{Unit Depletion}$$

Unit Depletion × Units Extracted and Sold = Cost Depletion Allowed

Percentage depletion is the lesser of the statutory percentage of gross income (varies from 22% on down, depending upon the statutory classification and definition under Sections 613 and 613A, with gas and oil also having additional limitations) from the property or 50% of the net computed without the depletion deduction.

Foreign Taxes: With respect to income, war profits and excess profits taxes paid or accrued to a foreign country, a taxpayer has the option to take credit against income taxes or a reduction from gross income. (Code Sections 901-905).

Involuntary Conversion: Taxpayer can use recovery to either replace or restore property and avoid tax or pay the tax and step up the basis of newly acquired property.

To avoid the tax, the taxpayer must replace or restore the property within the time beginning with first date of known imminence of condemnation or the actual date of destruction and ending two years after the end of the first taxable year, or a later approved IRS date (three years for real property).

Mining—Development Expenses (Excluding oil or gas well): Taxpayer can either deduct these in the year they were incurred or capitalize them and deduct them ratably over units of ore as produced or minerals as benefited. These expenses do not include exploration expenses or expenditures for depreciable property (§616). For a mine in the development stage, the election applies only to the excess of expenditures over the net receipts from ores or minerals produced during the year. Election, if made, applies to all development expenditures. It is made by a written statement filed with the Director of Internal Revenue with whom the return is filed or by a rider attached to the return. A new election is made each year.

Mining—Exploration Expenses: All such expenditures paid or incurred after 1969 are deductible (§617). Such expenditures made for the discovery of a new mine are subject to recapture when the mine begins producing, with some exceptions as under Section 1245.

Research and Experimental Expenses: Expenses for research and experiment can be treated as current expense, or the taxpayer can elect to treat them as deferred expense. If deducted currently, all research and experimental expenses must be included; this method must be followed consistently unless permission to change is obtained from the Commissioner. If the election is to defer expenses, it also must apply to all expenses and be consistently followed, and they are amortized over 60 months or more.

Election is made no later than the time for filing the return for the year in which the expenses were paid or incurred; it is made by a statement attached to the return for the first taxable year and should show: (1) amount of each type of expenditure; (2) description of the nature of the expenditure; (3) the period over which the expenditure is to be deducted.

The right to amortize stops when a patent is issued, from which time the costs are depreciated over the life of the patent.

Rent Expenses: Examine rent agreements in first year of agreement to see if there are any purchase options that might warrant IRS treating the rental as a purchase. In this connection, compare the rent called for where there is an option with what the rent would have been without an option. Rents paid may also be needed for state allocation formulas.

Compensation: Details of officers' compensation are required for tax returns—names, Social Security number, address, title, time devoted to business, percentage of stock owned (common and preferred), amount of compensation and expense account allowances. As to other compensation, it's a good idea to reconcile the total compensation claimed on the tax return with the amounts shown on the payroll tax reports. Note that the compensation shown on the payroll tax reports is on a cash basis, so a reconciliation to the amounts of compensation claimed as deductions on the tax return which is on the accrual basis is necessary. This reconciliation will help justify your deduction if your tax return is audited.

Information on interest, rents and other payments to officers and stockholders may also be required for state tax returns.

Note the statutory definition of what must be included as "expense account allowance."

[¶3106]   EMPLOYEE BENEFITS

[¶3106.1] "Reasonable" Compensation

All payments to compensate an employee for services which are ordinary and necessary to the operation of the business are deductible *provided* they are "reasonable."

What Is Reasonable? Determining reasonable compensation is not an easy task. The courts themselves have a hard time determining what is reasonable under certain facts. Nevertheless, here is a list of the several factors usually considered by the courts in dealing with this problem: (1) The employee's special qualifications; (2) the nature, extent and scope of his work; (3) the size and complexities of the business; (4) the prevailing general economic conditions; (5) comparison of salaries to dividends; (6) rates of compensation for comparable positions in comparable concerns; (7) the "arm's length" element in the compensation deal; (8) consideration for past services and compensation in prior years; (9) comparison of salaries paid with employee's stock ownership.

As a general rule of thumb you can say that reasonable compensation is the amount that would ordinarily be paid for like services by like enterprises under like circumstances.

For new corporations, it is generally a good idea to establish a high salary base for officer/stockholders and place this information (with reasons) in the minutes of the corporation. If economic circumstances change, take exception in the minutes for lesser salaries.

[¶3106.2]   Cash and Stock Bonuses

The cash bonus is used to assure the employee of an immediate share of the company's profits over and above his regular compensation. In a noncontractual plan, the amount of the bonus, who is to get it, and, in what proportions, are usually determined on a year-by-year basis—depending on the amount of profits.

Under a formal contractual basis, the employee knows before-hand exactly what to expect. If a certain profit is reached, he gets a definite amount as his share.

The stock bonus plan is exactly like the cash bonus except, of course, that the payment is made in company stock. The big advantage of paying employee's bonuses in stock rather than cash is that the company can retain the cash to be used in the business. Furthermore, the corporation gets a compensation deduction for the market value of the stock.

[¶3106.3]   Stock Options

Stock options give the employee the opportunity to purchase the company's stock at a profit if the market price of the stock rises above the option price. The employee, in effect, gets a "free ride" on the appreciation of his company's stock.

"Qualified stock options" (those which qualify under the Internal Revenue Code) have special tax advantages. No income tax is imposed on the employee either at the time the option is granted or exercised. The option price, however, must not be less than the market value of the stock at the time the option is granted. When the employee eventually sells the stock, he has capital gain on the entire gain provided the stock was held for three years from the date of exercise.

There are three other types of stock option plans, each with distinctive tax treatments and definitions: "Employee Stock Purchase Plan," "Restricted Stock Option Plan," and "Nonstatutory Stock Option Plan." The degree of capital gains tax or ordinary tax, and the timing thereof (to the recipient) varies under each method.

Ordinarily, the employer claims an expense (compensation) *for financial statement purposes* for the difference between the option price and a higher market price at the first date all facts become known. *For tax purposes,* the date of exercise of the option is usually the determinant factor in calculating the allowable deduction for the employer. Until exercise, therefore, a timing difference for the tax exists for financial statement purposes (See Accounting Section in this text for further discussion.)

[¶3106.4] Deferred Compensation Arrangements

With the fantastic growth of business over the years, the arrival of high corporate and individual tax rates, and the increased public interest in retirement planning, there has evolved a mass of intricate and involved deferred compensation plans to attract new employees or retain old employees.

Under a deferred compensation plan, payment of compensation presently earned is postponed to a future period. If the plan qualifies as an exempt trust under §401 IRC, the employer gets an immediate deduction for a contribution — even though the employee does not receive the sum until a later time. However, under a non-qualified deferred compensation contract, the employer gets a deduction only when he actually pays the deferred compensation to the employee (who is taxed at that time).

Under a nonqualified plan, the employer can pick and choose who will benefit; he is not commited to a class of employees or any other rigid requirement as provided for qualified deferred compensation plans. Generally, this arrangement is less ambitious than qualified plans and therefore more attractive to smaller organizations.

Most often, the nonqualified deferred compensation plan is used for a key executive. The ordinary plan is to have the company accumulate funds for the benefit of the executive and pay them out to him in post-retirement years when he is in a lower tax bracket.

[¶3106.5]   Popular Stock Plans

Before the 1969 Tax Reform Act, the "Restricted Stock Plan" was one of the hottest stock plans. The 1969 Tax Reform Act tightened the restricted stock option rules. A restricted stock option is now taxable at the time of disposition of the stock, *provided* that, at the time of *granting* of the option the price was within 85% of the then-market price of the stock. In addition, if the market price at *exercise* date is less than *grant* date, the employee may use the *lesser* amount. The increment over option price is treated as both compensation and added-cost basis. Also, the option can not be transferrable, except by death.

[¶3106.6]   Tandem Stock Plans

The 1969 Act also tightened the benefits of qualified stock options, making nonqualified stock options more attractive. Thus, many companies turned to the use of nonqualified stock options, either issuing them alone or in tandem with qualified stock options.

Under tandem plans, an executive was granted a qualified stock option and a nonqualified stock option for the same number of shares. The options were given simultaneously or at different times. In some cases, the options were exercisable at the same time, with the qualified options expiring in five years and the nonqualified option expiring in ten years.

Effective January 3, 1973, stock options issued in tandem do not meet the requirements of a "qualified stock option" (§422).

[¶3106.7]   Insurance Plans

Insurance is a significant vehicle for funding or providing employee benefits. Here are some of the most popular plans.

Key-man Insurance: This is insurance on a key-man's life. It is deductible only if the *employer* is not directly or indirectly the beneficiary and if the premiums are in the nature of compensation and not unreasonable.

Split-Dollar Insurance: The employee pays a portion of the premium to the employer under this plan (life insurance), and that portion reduces the amount included in his income (the includable amount would be, in effect, the employer's share of the premium). Any policy dividends received by the employee are also included in his income.

Group Term Life Insurance: This arrangement offers an employee an opportunity to acquire low-cost life insurance because it's purchased for a "group." Under a "group term" plan the employee can get up to $50,000 of insurance protection from his employer tax free; that is, all premiums paid on over that amount of insurance must be included in income. But the plan has to be a group *term* plan. Permanent insurance (whole life policies) does not qualify under this provision.

Group Health: This plan provides for the reimbursement of medical and hospitalization expenses incurred by an employee. Premiums are tax deductible by the employer and not taxable to the employee — even though the plan provides for the protection of the employee's family. This plan is widely used by many employers to provide their employees with at least the basic health and accident protection. Of course, individual health plans for particular employees are also used.

[¶3106.8] Qualified Pension and Profit-Sharing Plans

TAX ADVANTAGES OF QUALIFIED PLANS

(1) *Employer:* The employer gets a current deduction for amounts contributed to the plan, within specified limits, although no benefits may have been actually distributed to the participating employees that year. This permits an employer to accumulate a trust fund for his employees with 100-cent, before-tax dollars which, in effect, represent 52-cent after-tax dollars to the employer. The employer expense for the contribution to a qualified plan may be accrued at year-end, but it must be paid no later than the legal time of filing the return (including extensions).

(2) *Employees:* The tax to the employee is deferred until the benefits under the plan are actually distributed or made available to him. If the employee receives a lump-sum distribution, a portion of it may be capital gains (based on years of participation prior to 1974) and the remaining taxable portion is subject to ordinary income rates, but there is a special 10-year averaging option available.

(3) *Trust Fund:* The income and gains on the sale of trust property of the trust fund are exempt from tax, in effect, being postponed until distribution. Funds, which are compounded tax free under a qualified plan, increase at a much greater rate than if such funds were currently distributed to employees and personally invested by them. In the latter case, the amount received by the employees is subject to two tax bites — when he receives the benefits and again on the investment income earned on what is left.

CHOOSING BETWEEN PENSION AND PROFIT SHARING

Profit Sharing	*Pension*
(1) Generally favors younger employees.	(1) Generally favors older employees.
(2) Need not provide retirement benefits.	(2) Must provide retirement benefits.
(3) Contribution can be made only if profits exist	(3) Contributions must be made for profitable as well as for loss years.
(4) Even in profitable years the amount of contributions, if any, can be left to discretion of management.	(4) Amount of contribution is not discretionary; it must be actuarially justifiable and tied to definitely determinable benefits.
(5) Contributed amounts generally cannot exceed 15% of year's payroll for participants.	(5) No maximum limit on contributions as long as they are actuarially justifiable and total compensation is within IRC §162's limitations.
(6) Forfeitures may be allocated in favor of remaining participants.	(6) Forfeitures must be used to decrease future cost to employer.

Profit Sharing	*Pension*
(7) No more than 50% of participant's account may be invested in life insurance.	(7) May be completely funded by investment in life insurance.
(8) Broad fringe benefits can be included (incidental accident and health insurance).	(8) Limited fringe benefits can be included (disability pension).
(9) Employer may never recover any part of contribution or income therefrom.	9) Employer on termination of plan may recover excess funds which arose as a result of actuarial error.

ERISA

The Employee Retirement Income Security Act of 1974, commonly called ERISA, substantially changed the rules and set new minimum standards for employees' trusts, most notably in the following areas:

1) Participation rules

2) Vesting rights

3) Funding requirements.

In addition, the tax and information forms which are required to be filed with the IRS (and in some cases with the Department of Labor) were changed and are constantly being revamped.

Arguments both for and against the new law are being debated, and much confusion still surrounds its administration, regulation, interpretation and effect. Professional advice should be sought for updating old plans and for instituting new plans, as well as for assuring conformance with the required new regulations and reporting.

Non-corporate entities and individuals should also pursue the tax deferral opportunities now expanded for them under the new law

[¶3107]   HOW TO SHIFT BUSINESS EXPENSES

Here is how to shift expenses, depending on whether you want to boost the current year's or the following year's deductions:

(1) *A cash-basis taxpayer can pay all bills by December 31,* including prepayment of such items as taxes and interest. If it wants to defer expenses, it will hold off payment until January. You can't get a deduction for certain prepayments — even if you are on the cash basis (e.g., insurance premiums, rents) — especially if they cover more than one year's period.

(2) *Rush through repairs,* buy office supplies, pay research and experimental costs if you want the deduction this year. Hold off if you want it next year.

(3) *Accrual-basis taxpayers can pick up sales returns and allowances* by December 31 to get a deduction this year — after December 31 for a deduction next year.

(4) *Have your lawyer and accountant bill you* before year-end if you want to accrue or pay the bill for the taxable year.

(5) *Junk or abandon equipment,* etc., before the year's end for deduction this year — next year for a deduction next year.

(6) *Research and development costs* can be swung over to future years or deducted now. If you spent money on a research program this year for the first time since 1953, you can deduct it all this year. Or if you've been deducting these expenses currently in previous years, you can continue to do so. Or, if you want to push the expenses forward, you can write them off over a period of 60 months or more. Once you switch to amortizing your costs, you have to do so in the future unless you get permission from IRS to switch .

(7) *Switching from bad debt writeoffs to reserve method* brings more deduction into this year. Theoretically, this switch can double up your bad debt deduction; but, as a practical matter, since you need IRS' permission to switch, IRS will make you spread the additional deduction over a ten-year period. So you can only increase your deduction by 10% this year.

(8) *Corporate contribution deductions can be accrued* this year if paid within 2½ months after the end of the tax year. So, where the corporation is short of cash now but wants the deduction this year, make sure you pass the appropriate corporate resolution making the contribution and calling for payment no later than 2-1/2 months after the end of your tax year.

(9) *Items in dispute — contested taxes or other liabilites —* must be deducted when they are paid, even though a contest which finally determines the liability is resolved in a later year. This applies to accrual as well as cash-basis taxpayers. So, if you are anxious to get the deduction this year, pay the liability by year-end.

(10) *Losses on worthless assets* have to be shown by an identifiable event in the year the loss is taken. Where worthlessness may be difficult to prove, dispose of the asset in the year you want the loss.

Here are some other considerations that you should have at the end of the year:

[¶3107.1]   Business gifts at year-end

Since year-end is often the season of making business gifts, it's important to check your lists carefully to be aware whether or not you are making total gifts to one person of more than $25 — the deductible ceiling on a business gift. In addition, you ought to be aware of the definition of business gifts and where you can avoid falling within the definitions.

Maybe your "Gift" can qualify as Entertainment: There's no ceiling on entertainment costs; but you have to have full substantiation.

Generally, says IRS, where an item might be either entertainment, on the one hand, or a gift or travel cost, on the other, it will be considered entertainment. But packaged food and beverages given to a customer, for example, for use at some other time are gifts.

As for theatre and similar tickets of admission, if you go along, it's entertainment, even if you give the tickets to your guest. If you don't go along, you can treat the expense either as entertainment or a business gift.

[¶3107.2]   Audit your pay setup at year-end

Wages and salaries are by far the most compelling income and expense factor in many a business. The final months of the year provide the last opportunity to arrange compensation policies for minimum tax cost — both for employer and for employees.

Here are some of the important points you will want to watch:

Are office-stockholders getting the best "tax" salary? That's the amount at which any increase will cost the employee-stockholder more in taxes than the corporation will save by the increase and at which any decrease would cost the corporation more than the employee saves.

Bonus Declarations: Year-end bonus declarations and payments boost this year's compensation deductions. But you always have to be concerned with the problem of reasonableness. Suppose part of the compensation is disallowed as being unreasonable. The corporation loses the deduction and the employee still has income for what he received — so we have a double tax. If the corporation can use more deductions now but doesn't have the cash, it can accrue them (assuming, of course, the corporation uses the accrual method of accounting). It gets the deduction now, and the employee has income when he receives it.

But keep in mind the special rules; if the employee is a more-than-50% stockholder, the corporation has to pay the accrued salaries or bonuses within 2-1/2 months after the end of the year. Otherwise, it loses its deduction altogether.

Unusual Transactions: Check all transactions during the year of an unusual nature — outside the scope of what the corporation normally does — to determine whether any special tax problems exist as to any of these transactions.

[¶3108]   OTHER TAX-EXPENSE CONSIDERATION

Charitable Contributions: Examine charitable contributions in the form of donations of the company's own product. Deduction is based on market value less the amount which would have been treated as ordinary income had it been sold, since it is considered ordinary income property. In effect cost is used.*Where deduction is based on accrual to be paid within two and a half months after close of taxable year, make sure the proper corporate resulution was passed before year-end. Also, compare total contributions with 5% limit and

---

*The 1976 Act changed this to basis plus ½ of appreciated value — not to exceed twice basis.

determine whether there is a carryover to subsequent years. In computing total, also take into account carryover from prior years.

. **Payroll Taxes:** As in the case of compensation, the payroll taxes paid by the employer and deductible as expenses should be reconciled with the payroll taxes shown on the payroll tax returns, since the taxes on the payroll returns were computed on a cash basis and your deduction for income tax purposes may be deducted on the accrual basis.

Interest Expense: Analysis may be necessary to determine whether some interest paid may not be deductible for state tax purposes (in some states) where paid to affiliates or officer-stockholders.

Inventory Write-Downs: Examine basis for write-downs and keep sufficient backup information to support the write-down (or merchandise destruction) in the event of an examination.

Repairs: An analysis of the amounts expensed as repairs during the year should be made to see if all pass as repairs and are not likely to be held to be improvements. Where the items are very numerous, it is likely that a revenue agent will test the account. An analysis of the larger items — e.g., those costing $1,000 or more — made in advance, with sufficient data to back up the deduction of each of these items as a repair, may be very helpful if the return is audited.

Reimbursed Travel and Entertainment Expenses: Make sure there is adequate substantiation by the employees who are reimbursed and that the accounting system used by you has sufficient internal control The employee accounting to you may also have to substantiate his deductions on his own tax return. The absence of proper backup in the form of vouchers, invoices, mileage reports, etc. on the corporation's part can jeopardize its deductions, since a prerequisite is adequate substantiation. Many companies use credit cards specifically to pinpoint these expenses by employees.

State Income and Franchise Taxes: These should be accrued on the federal tax return for the current year although not yet paid. Also check to see whether taxes that have been prepaid and therefore deferred on the books are nevertheless deductible for federal income taxes (as is allowed in many situations — e.g., property taxes may be deducted in the year they accrue even if the period of the tax extends beyond the taxable year). However, a few state franchise taxes specifically pertain to ensuing years and are not deductible until then (California).

Sales and Use Taxes: Where a company has a number of locations, it may be advantageous to review the policies at each location and make sure that only those sales and use taxes to which a particular location is subject are being paid or allocated.

Also, be informed as to the possibility of being liable for the sales tax in situations where ''location'' may not be a factor, such as direct mail sales or shipments.

[¶3109] INFORMATION FOR STATE ALLOCATIONS

Types of Locations: Determine whether the sales in any particular state are subject to any tax at all by that state. For example, where no offices are maintained within the state and orders are subject to acceptance outside the state and goods are shipped from outside the state, it may be that no franchise/income tax is due on sales made in that state. If you are subject to tax, however, consider the following data for the purpose of allocation under each state's own allocation formula:

Sales Data: For each state, you will want to know how much sales were billed to customers within that state, totals of sales reflected by shipments to all customers (wherever located) from points within the state, total sales reflected by shipments from within the state to customers within the state, total sales credited to a sales office within that state (a salesman who lives within the state and works out of his home, there being no "formal" office within the state, does not usually count as a sales office within the state).

Average Fixed Assets: For each physical location of the company, determine the balances at the beginning and end of the year (and the average by adding and dividing by two) of the net book values of the fixed assest — e.g., land, buildings, furniture and fixtures, equipment. Some states require the use of cost (California).

Inventories: For each physical location get the values of all inventories at beginning and end of year and average.

Payroll: For each state, determine the total payroll actually paid out during the year to employees in that state.

Officer/Stockholders: Determine if information is needed for separate disclosure of sums paid or accrued to officer/stockholders — salaries, rent, interest — and the extent of loans to or from officers.

Taxes: Some states require separate itemization of all taxes by type paid everywhere and specifically within the state.

(See also Chapter 33.)

32

Special Areas

[¶3201] TAXATION OF FOREIGN OPERATIONS

The availability of foreign tax shelters has been under heavy congressional attack in recent years. Building up corporate profits from foreign operations in a holding company in a country which does not subject such companies to any severe tax has been hard hit by provisions which tax "unrepatriated" foreign profits to the American investors.

In the following paragraphs you will find a brief review of the tax rules applying to the various ways in which foreign operations may be conducted.

[¶3202] Foreign Branches

For U.S. tax purposes, the branch operation represents only one part of a single entity and its results emerge in a single income tax return. Profits made from foreign sources are taxable immediately whether they are retained in the foreign country or returned to the U.S. In combining the income from the foreign country and the U.S., losses sustained abroad can be used to reduce U.S. income taxes if domestic profits have been earned.

Although segregation of branch profits is not necessary for computation of U.S. income taxes, it is necessary for foreign tax credit computation purposes since the credit is limited by the percentage of income from foreign sources.

[¶3202.1] Domestic Corporations

Resident foreign operations conducted through a domestic subsidiary corporation are handled by the subsidiary just as the parent handles its branch operation. Current profits brought to the parent via the dividend route are eligible for the 85% (in some cases 100%) dividend-received deduction, and, on liquidation, profits can be brought to the parent tax free under Section 332.

Western Hemisphere Trade Corporations: A domestic corporation which derives 95% of its gross income from sources outside the United States can qualify for the special deduction, which is determined by reducing its taxable income by the fraction of 14/48 of that income.*

The corporation's total business must be conducted, except for incidental purchases, within the Western Hemisphee, and 90% of its gross income must be derived from the active conduct of a trade or business. IRS agrees that the corporation need not set up an office, factory or permanent establishment in a western hemisphere country and that the corporation can arrange for title of goods sold to pass outside the U.S.

Possessions Corporations: Domestic corporations deriving a large portion of their income from sources within U.S. possessions may under certain circumstances avoid U.S. income taxes with respect to all income derived from sources without the U.S.: 80% of the corporation's gross income must have been derived from sources within U.S. possessions and 50% must have been derived from the active conduct of a trade or business within that possession.

[¶3202.2]   Foreign Corporations

Foreign corporations fall into one of two basic categories. They are either controlled foreign corporations or they are not. If they are not controlled foreign corporations, they are eligible for the advantages which have long been associated with foreign business operations; i.e., no current U.S. tax on foreign-source income, no problem under U.S. tax law in accumulating earnings, freedom to transfer funds from one foreign operating form to others, and capital gain on liquidation. On the other hand, if they are controlled foreign corporations, they are still not subject to U.S. tax on current foreign source earnings; but all or part of their current earnings can be currently includable in the gross income of their parent company or stockholders.

Foreign corporations are themselves taxable only on U.S.-source income even though the worldwide operations of the company are entirely managed in the U.S. Resident foreign corporations — those engaged in a trade or business within the U.S. — are taxed on their entire gross income from U.S. sources less allowable deductions and credits. Nonresident foreign corporations — those not engaged in business in the U.S. — are taxed at a fixed flat rate of 30% on fixed or determinable, annual or periodical gains, profits and income from U.S. sources, such as interest, dividends, rents, salaries, wages, royalties. etc.

[¶3202.3]   Controlled Foreign Corporations

A controlled foreign corporation is one in which, after giving effect to various attribution-of-stock-ownership rules, more than 50% of the voting stock

---

*The Tax Reform Act of 1976 starts phasing out this deduction in 1976 and eliminates it entirely after 1979.

is owned on any one day in the taxable year by U.S. citizens, residents, corporations, partnerships, trusts and estates. A "U.S. shareholder," by definition, would be any U.S. citizen resident, domestic partnership, corporation, estate or trust which owns 10% or more of the voting interest (as part of 50% controlling interest).

The "U.S. shareholder" must include in its (his) gross income his share of the statutory defined: (1) Subpart F income, (2) previously excluded Subpart F income withdrawn from less developed countries, and (3) increases in earnings invested in U.S. property by the controlled foreign corporation.

[¶3203] DOMESTIC INTERNATIONAL SALES CORPORATIONS

A DISC (Domestic International Sales Corporation) is a corporation which is given special tax benefits under the Code (§991-997). It's not subject to corporation income tax. The tax on *up to* 50% of its income is deferred until actual distribution to the shareholders. Typically a DISC is a subsidiary of a U.S. parent manufacturing or sales corporation.

When the profits of a DISC are distributed to a corporate shareholder, the latter is treated as if it received the profits in the first instance. Thus, in lieu of an intercorporate dividends-received deduction, (there is *no* 85% or 100% deduction), the profits are treated as if they had been received directly from a foreign source.

The advantage of a DISC is the shifting of foreign sales and its related income from a manufacturer or producer to the DISC where, in effect, up to half the income remains untaxed forever, until and unless distributed.

[¶3203.1] How to Qualify as a DISC

A corporation must meet the following tests to qualify as a DISC for a taxable year:

(1) Gross Receipts Test: At least 95% of a corporation's gross receipts for the taxable year must comprise qualified export receipts.

(2) Assets Test: At least 95% of the corporation's assets at the close of its taxable year must be qualified export assets.

(3) Capitalization Requirement: A corporation must have at least $2,500 of only one class of capital stock each day of the year to qualify as a DISC.

(4) Election Requirement: A corporation must have elected to be treated as a DISC during the 90-day period immediately prior to the beginning of the taxable year. Once made, an election continues in effect until revoked or is terminated by reason of a continued failure to qualify as a DISC over a five-year period (*Rev. Proc. 72-12*).

(5) Incorporation Requirement: A DISC must be incorporated under the laws of any state or the District of Columbia; associations otherwise qualifying under the tax law as corporations will not qualify.

[¶3204]   **BUSINESS ACQUISITIONS —
                    SALES AND PURCHASES**

TAX CONSIDERATIONS

Much of the planning of the purchase or sale of a business is influenced by the tax consequences. What follows is a summary of the major tax considerations and the alternatives available to bring about the desired results.

[¶3204.1]   **How to Maximize Tax Benefits**

If business assets are sold as a unit for a lump-sum consideration, the sales proceeds must be allocated among the individual assets of the business, and the gain or loss computed accordingly. The owner is not permitted to treat the sale of his business as the sale of a single capital asset. Moreover, the burden of proving that any portion of the sale proceeds is attributable to the goodwill and other capital assets of the business is on the vendor. The problem may be eased by drafting the contract or bill of sale to provide for specific prices for each individual asset in the business. The buyer will want to allocate as much of the purchase price as possible to depreciable assets. He may prefer to rely on an appraisal if he can't get a favorable allocation agreed to in the contract.

No gain is recognized to the corporation if it sells its assets and liquidates under IRC §337 (except for §1245 and 1250 property).

The following chart illustrates the tax effects and the conflicting desires of buyer and seller involved in allocating the purchase price of the business:

Asset	*Price Benefiting Buyer*	*Price Benefiting Seller*
(1) *Capital* (Goodwill, trade name, covenant not to compete ancillary to sale of goodwill)	Low (not depreciable)	High (Capital gain)
(2) *Property used in the trade or business:*		
(a) Machinery, fixtures, etc.	Medium (recoup cost via depreciation)	Medium (ordinary loss under §1231)*
(b) Land	Low (not depreciable)	High (capital gain or ordinary loss under §1231)
(c) Copyrights (purchased for use in the business)	Medium (recoup cost via amortization)	High (capital gain or ordinary loss under §1231)
(d) Patents	Medium (recoup cost via amortization)	High (capital gain under §1235)

Asset	Price Benefiting Buyer	Price Benefiting Seller
(3) *Noncapital:*		
(a) Inventory and stock in trade	High (recoup via cost of goods sold)	Low (ordinary income)
(b) Accounts receivable	High (recoverable as collected)	Low (ordinary income)
(c) Copyrights and intellectual property sold by the creator	Medium (recoup cost via amortization)	Low (ordinary income)
(d) Covenant not to compete	Medium (usually recoup cost via amortization)	Low (ordinary income)
(e) Interest on deferred payment of purchase price	Medium (deduct as ordinary business expense)	Low (ordinary income)

*May realize income if depreciation recapture is involved (§1245).

[¶3204.2]   Sale of Stock vs. Sale of Assets

Here are the opposing considerations of the seller and buyer on the sale of a corporate business.

The seller wants to sell stock, because:

(1) He has a *clean* deal, realizing capital gains (unless he has a collapsible corporation).

(2) There is no problem of depreciation recapture at ordinary income rates under §1245 and 1250.

(3) There is no problem of recapture of any investment credit.

(4) It is easier to set up an installment sale; if the corporation makes the sale of assets, it can't then distribute the installment obligations to the stockholders without tax consequences.

The buyer wants to buy assets, because:

(1) He need not worry about any *hidden* or contingent corporate liabilities.

(2) He gets a basis for the assets acquired equal to their market values — i.e., what he paid for them. If he acquires stock, the corporation's basis for the assets does not change even if the assets have appreciated considerably. He can, however, acquire the stock of the corporation and liquidate the acquired corporation tax free within two years. The price paid for the stock will be the price assigned the assets (§334(B)(2)). The liquidating company in this case will be stuck with recapture of depreciation (income) under §1245 or 1250.

[¶3204.3]   Goodwill vs. Covenant not to Compete

The buyer writes off the noncompete agreement over the period of its restriction. He gets no tax writeoff for goodwill. The seller, on the other hand, gets capital gain on the sale of his goodwill but ordinary income for the covenant. The agreement should be as explicit as possible regarding the intent of the parties respecting either or both goodwill and a covenant not to compete. Courts will not usually set aside executed agreements.

[¶3204.4]   Bird's-Eye View of Tax Rules

The following table sets forth the various ways in which a corporate business can be sold and the tax consequences to the buyer and seller in each case.

Type of Transaction	Tax Consequence to Seller	Tax Consequence to Buyer
Sale of assets by the corporation.	Corporation realizes gain or loss in same manner as proprietorship. If proceeds are then distributed to the stockholders in liquidation, a second tax (capital gain) is paid by them. *But the tax at the corporate level can be avoided by a statutory liquidation.*	Purchase price is allocated in same manner as in purchase of sole proprietorship.
Sale by corporation after adopting a liquidation resolution and distribution within 12 months (§337).	Corporation pays no tax on its gain — stockholders pay a tax on liquidation. (But corporation can have income if depreciation or investment credit recapture is involved.) This method is not available if corporation is collapsible.	Same as above.
Liquidation under §336 and distribution of assets to stockholders and subsequent sale of the assets by them.	Stockholders pay a capital gains tax on liquidation (unless corporation is collapsible). Corporation has no taxable income on liquidation unless there's depreciation or investment credit recapture. They get a stepped-up basis for assets received; so they have no gain or loss on the resale. But must make sure corporation didn't enter into sales negotiations before liquidations; otherwise the double tax will not be avoided.	Buyer's basis is what he pays for the assets — allocated in same manner as on purchase of sole proprietorship.

Type of Transaction	*Tax Consequence to Seller*	*Tax Consequence to Buyer*
Liquidation by corporation within one month (§333).	No gain or loss recognized on liquidation, but corporation can have income if depreciation or investment credit recapture is involved. Basis for assets received is basis for stock. Gain is then recognized on subsequent resale — with nature of the gain on each item depending on the nature of the asset in the hands of the selling stockholder. *Warning:* if corporation has earnings and profits, there is a dividend on liquidation. Cash and securities distributed are immediately taxable, too.	Same as above.
Sale of stock in the corporation.	Seller generally gets capital gain — unless the corporation is collapsible.	Buyer has a basis for his stock equal to what he paid for it; the corporation retains the same basis for its assets as before the sale. But if the assets have appreciated in value and 80% or more of the stock was purchased by a corporation within a 12-month period, the purchased corporation can be liquidated within two years and the basis stepped up to the purchase price of the stock (§334(b) (2)). Depreciation or investment credit recapture can result in the liquidation.

Type of Transaction	Tax Consequence to Seller	Tax Consequence to Buyer
Tax-free acquisitions via one of several types of reorganizations.	Seller usually acquires stock in the buying corporation; there is no gain or loss on the transaction recognized for tax purposes. In some types of reorganization transactions, *boot* (cash or other property other than the permitted stock) is received. Then, to extent the boot does not exceed the gain, it is taxable (usually as capital gain; where shown to be such, it may be a dividend). Seller's basis for his new stock is same as his basis for his old, increased by any recognized gain and decreased by boot received.	The buyer's basis for the property acquired is generally the same as the basis of the property to the transferor prior to the transfer. But if there was any recognized gain to the transferor on the exchange, then the buyer's basis is increased by that gain (§362(b)).

[¶3205] ACQUIRING COMPANIES WITH TAX LOSSES

At one time there was a considerable traffic in loss companies — a profitable operation would acquire a loss company in order to use the acquired company's carryover loss to offset its own income. A number of restrictions in the Code, plus IRS' strict interpretations in its regulations, make the acquisition of loss companies today very difficult.

[¶3205.1]   Available Routes for Acquiring Loss Companies*

Here is a rundown of the various routes that may be used, what you have to do, and the pitfalls you have to overcome:

(1) Acquisition of Stock of a Loss Company: Here, the general idea is to acquire control of the loss company, put profitable operations into it, and have the loss carryovers available to offset the profits of the new profitable operations. Two obstacles must be overcome — IRC §382(a), and 269. Assuming the acquisition of the stock creates at least a 50-percentage-point change of ownership of the stock, the loss carryover is disallowed unless the company continues

---

*After December 31, 1977, new provisions will substantially change the carryover provisions. The 1976 Act should be examined.

to carry on a trade or business substantially as it did before the 50-percentage-point change. The requirement for carrying on the same business applies for the two-year period beginning in the year of the change of ownership. The obvious strategy is to continue the old business for two years and add a new business at the same time.

(2) Acquiring a Loss Company via a Reorganization or Liquidation: Under §381 (a), where a loss company is acquired in a reorganization (other than stock-for-stock — i.e., a so-called "B" reorganization), the loss becomes available to the acquiring company. Here, too, however, there are a number of limitations.

In the first place, the stockholders of the loss company must end up with at least 20% of the value of the stock in the acquiring corporation. For each percent less than 20% with which they end up, 5% of the loss carryover is disallowed *(IRC §382 (b))*. Here, too, we have to consider §269.

Another limitation involves acquisitions of companies via liquidation. A tax-free liquidation of a subsidiary under §332 qualifies. But a liquidation to which §334(b)(2) applies does not qualify. What that means is that if a corporation buys 80% of the stock of another corporation (i.e., the loss company), it cannot liquidate the acquired company within two years and thereby acquire the loss. If the liquidation takes place during the two-year period, §334 (b)(2) automatically applies and the loss cannot pass over to the acquiring corporation. So, you have to wait two years. And during that two-year period, you have to meet the rules of §382(a) since there is a 50-percentage-point change of ownership; so you must continue the old business of the acquired corporation during that two-year period.

[¶3205.2]   How §269 Affects Loss Company Acquisitions

Even if you get over the hurdles of §382, you may be stopped by §269. This section disallows the carryover loss if the principal purpose of acquiring the loss corporation is the avoidance or evasion of tax. And §269 applies even though the acquired corporation (the one that had the loss) is the one that wants to use the carryover where there was no good business purpose in the acquisition.

[¶3206]   OTHER CARRYOVER ITEMS FOR TAX PURPOSES

Although the net operating loss carryover is the most important one, it isn't the only one allowed. Twenty other permitted carryovers are listed in §381 (where there is a reorganization or tax-free liquidation) as follows:

(1) Predecessor's earnings and profits carried over to successor; deficit carried over to extent of successor's earnings accumulated after the transfer, earnings for year of transfer to be prorated for this purpose.

(2) Capital loss carryover, prorated similar to operating loss proration.

(3) Accounting method of distributor or transferor to be used by successor.

(4) Same with inventory method if inventories are taken over, unless several predecessors or predecessor and successor used different methods.

(5) If declining-balance, sum-of-the-digits, or similar method of depreciation other than straight-line was used by the transferor or distributor, the successor will be treated as the transferor or distributor for purposes of the depreciation deduction on assets taken over, to the extent that the transferor's or distributor's basis is carried over.

(6) Gain from installment sales of the distributor or transferor must continue to be reported on the installment basis by the successor if the latter receives installment obligations on the transfer.

(7) Amortization of bond discount or premium must continue to be reported or deducted where the transferor or distributor left off if the bonds are assumed by the successor.

(8) Deferred exploration and development expenditures of transferor or distributor must be deducted by the successor as if it were the transferor or distributor.

(9) Deductions for contributions to employees' trust or annuity plan and compensation under deferred payment plan continued by the successor as if it were the transferor or distributor.

(10) If the successor recovers bad debts, taxes, or delinquency amounts previously deducted by the transferor or distributor, it is taxable to the extent it would be taxable if it were the transferor or distributor.

(11) For the purpose of applying the nonrecognition rules in involuntary conversions, the acquiring corporation is to be treated as the distributor or transferor corporation after the date of the distribution or transfer.

(12) The dividend carryover allowed personal holding companies.

(13) Amounts used or set aside for pre-1934 indebtedness of personal holding companies deductible if paid or irrevocably set aside by the successor.

(14) If the amount of stock, securities, and property of the acquiring corporation was determined by including the assumed obligations of the transferor or distributor, subsequent payment of the obligation won't give rise to a deduction; otherwise, the payment can be deducted if it would have been deductible by the distributor or transferor if paid or accrued by it and the assumption gives rise to a liability after the date of the distribution or transfer. This applies to amounts paid or accrued in taxable years beginning after December 31, 1953, even though the distribution or transfer occurred before the effective date of the 1954 Code provisions relative to liquidations or reorganizations.

(15) Deficiency dividend of a personal holding company allowable to the transferor or distributor if paid by the transferee.

(16) Percentage depletion on waste or residue of prior mining by the transferor or distributor allowed to the successor as if it were owner or operator of the mine.

(17) Charitable contributions paid by the transferor or distributor in the year ending on the date of the transfer and in the preceding year in excess of the amount deductible are allowable to the acquiring corporation in its first two taxable years which began after the date of transfer or distribution, subject to the 5% limitation and other limitations in §170 (b)(2).

(18) Excess contributions which the wholly owned subsidiary had made to a qualified pension plan, in the same way as if the acquiring corporation were the subsidiary; this carryover privilege is limited (see §381(c)).

(19) Pre-1954 adjustments resulting from a change in method of accounting.

(20) Credit for investment in certain depreciable property.

[¶3207]   CONSOLIDATED TAX RETURNS

Consolidated returns can be filed by affiliated groups of corporations. Basically, an affiliated group is one where there is a common parent and 80% control at each level of the chain of corporations. Thus losses of one company can be set off against the income of another. In effect, all the corporations are being taxed as a single economic unit. Tax accounting with reference to *intercompany transactions* conforms closely to general consolidation accounting principles for financial statements.

Certain corporations are excluded from the affiliated group for this purpose and are thus ineligible to participate in the filing of a consolidated return. These corporations are: (1) corporations exempt under §501; (2) insurance companies; (3) foreign corporations; (4) possessions corporations;* (5) China Trade Act corporations;* (6) regulated investment companies and real estate investment trusts; (7) unincorporated businesses which have elected to be taxed as corporations under §1361; and (8) DISC or former DISC corporations.

One hundred-percent-owned Canadian or Mexican corporations can be treated as domestic corporations and thus be eligible to participate in the filing of a consolidated return, at the election of the domestic parent, if the corporations were organized and maintained solely for the purpose of complying with the laws of such country as to the title and operation of property.

Where consolidated returns are filed, the affiliated group is deemed by law to have consented to all the consolidated return regulations prescribed by the Internal Revenue Service. These regulations are extremely complex and in some case have been deemed a sufficient reason by affiliated groups for not filing consolidated returns.

Once consolidated returns are filed, they must be continued to be filed in succeeding years, unless IRS gives its permission to change. Note that some states (like New Jersey) do not permit the filing of consolidated returns for franchise/income taxes.

---

*The 1976 Act makes ineligible those electing the Section 936 possessions tax credit.

[¶3208]   **MULTIPLE CORPORATIONS/**
                          CONTROLLED GROUPS

For tax purposes, "controlled" groups are of two kinds:

(1) Parent-subsidiary type

(2) Brother-sister type.

Each type is defined in Code Section 1563. In the latter type, the rules of attribution pertain and should be thoroughly examined for pertinence and applicability.

All individual members of controlled groups are, for the purposes of certain statutory tax advantage provisions, considered to be one aggregate unit, entitled to only *one* benefit in the following areas:

(1) *Surtax Exemption* — for 1975 and later, only one exemption ($50,000 through 1977) is permitted the entire group. The exemption may be divided in any fashion by consent (attached to the returns).

(2) *20% Additional First-Year Depreciation* — is limited to one maximum for the entire affiliated group.

(3) *Accumulated Earnings Credit* — for 1975 and later, only one $150,000 accumulated earnings credit is permitted to a controlled group, with the single credit divided *equally* unless approval is obtained from the Commissioner for unequal allocation.

(4) *Investment Tax Credit* — the maximum credit of $25,000 must be apportioned among all members of the group.

Each member of the controlled group is still allowed separate and individual 100%-dividends-received deductions for dividends from affiliates.

33

State Taxes

[¶3301]

Virtually all states impose some form of franchise and/or income tax on corporations. The basis for either or both taxes varies from state to state, as does the definition of the terminology. For the corporation involved in interstate commerce, these state taxes can present some onerous burdens. You need detailed records in order to work out the various allocation or apportionment formulas called for by the states involved (so as to avoid imposing a tax on more than what is applicable to that state). Sometimes with proper planning, taking into account the needs of the business, it is possible to avoid altogether the taxes of some of the states with which your company has contact.

In addition to an income or franchise tax, some states impose a capital values tax, and a large number have a sales and use tax. This can become a burden when the states insist that you collect the use tax from customers to whom you sell in that state, even though you have no office or other permanent contact within that state. In the paragraphs that follow, we consider these taxes, when they apply, and what you can do about them in some situations.

[¶3302] CORPORATE INCOME TAXES

There are three basic types of state corporate income taxes:

(1) A state may impose a tax on all income arising out of or derived from property located within the state. Often these taxes will be imposed without regard to whether business is conducted within the geographical confines of the state. Where a company has a manufacturing plant or real property located in a state which imposes taxes upon income from property located within the geographical confines of the state, it will be subject to the tax on the income which can be traced to that property. A more difficult situation arises where a corporation's income is derived from intangible property and rights like patents, copyrights, royalties, and licenses. Where the situs of this property can be traced to a state which imposes a tax on income from property located within the geographical confines of the state, this type of property will be subject to the tax.

(2) Some states which impose a corporation income tax base it on income from business conducted in the state. If the state basis was restricted to business conducted within the state, it might be that investment-type income derived from property in the state would not be reached. However, using the example in the prior paragraph, the tax imposed upon income from a business conducted within the geographical confines of a state would reach a manufacturing plant located within the state. The applicability of a tax imposed upon income from a business conducted within a state to income from real estate or other tangible property located within the state would generally depend upon the use to which the property is put, the language of the particular statute, and its administration.

(3) Some states impose a tax upon income attributable to or derived from sources within the state. This probably affords the widest possible tax base for a state attempting to tax foreign corporations.

Note that some states, like New Jersey, do not permit the filing of consolidated returns.

[¶3302.1]   Apportionment of Tax

Most of the states have some form of apportionment formula. For the most part, states imposing a corporate income tax on businesses involved in interstate commerce use a multifactor apportionment formula in an effort to insure that the formula is a proper one — one which would meet the test laid down by the Supreme Court. However, a single-factor apportionment formula is not necessarily invalid. A large number of the states imposing a corporate income tax use a formula based on the following factors:

(a) Receipts attributable to the taxing state;

(b) Payroll attributed to or located in the taxing state;

(c) Tangible property attributable to or located within the taxing state.

Often the formula will provide for a separate allocation of items like capital gains income, rents, royalties, and dividends. Income of this type may be allocated to the situs of the property, the place of its use, the domicile of the owner, or the source of the income.

Unitary and Separate Businesses: Some states which impose an apportioned corporate income tax on foreign corporations apply the apportionment formulas only to unitary businesses. A unitary business is one which has basically one income-producing activity and its separate divisions are connected with and directed towards this activity. Thus a company which both manufactured and sold its products, even though it operated through separate departments or divisions, would be a unitary business. Where two or more businesses of different types are conducted independently of each other, they are sometimes entitled to use their own separate accounting for purposes of apportioning income under state apportionment formulas.

[¶3302.2]   What Is a Sufficient "Nexus"?

A foreign corporation will have sufficient nexus or connection with the taxing state where it has assets or property within the borders of the taxing state. Similarly, where a foreign corporation qualifies to do business within a particular state by complying with the provisions of the state "qualification" statute, the corporation will be deemed to have established a domicile or residence within the state, giving that state a sufficient "nexus" for taxing that corporation.

Merely deriving income from within a state may be a sufficient nexus, unless:

(1) The corporation is engaged in truly minimal operations within the taxing state.

(2) The state's tax statute is not sufficiently broad to reach, in whole or in part, the particular type of activity which the foreign corporation is engaged in. (Some states have not revised their corporate income tax structure since the decision of the Supreme Court in the *Northwestern-Stockham* decisions.)

(3) The tax, although described as a corporate income tax, is not really a corporate income tax but essentially a privilege tax, so it may not be imposed upon a corporation which is engaged solely in interstate commerce as to the taxing state.

[¶3303]   HOW TO AVOID A STATE'S INCOME TAX

There are situations when a corporation can plan its operations so as to avoid all or part of the taxes imposed in one or more states from which it derives income.

[¶3303.1]   Planning Activities Within a State

Where a state taxes only companies doing business within the geographical confines of a state, the state's taxing authority may be avoided if you avoid activities which will bring your corporation within the definitions of the state tax law. Often this will mean that you cannot maintain an office in the state, maintain servicemen in the state, sell on consignment to in-state agents, and execute or perform contracts.

[¶3303.2]   Withdrawing from a State

Where your contacts with a state are reduced to the point that qualification is no longer required under the state's corporate statutes, you should consider withdrawing from the state. Most state corporate statutes have provisions whereby companies which have qualified under the laws of the state can subsequently withdraw.

[¶3303.3]   Taking Advantage of Apportionment Formulas

Often by carefully planning your activities and locating property, payroll, or other factors which enter into apportionment formulas in states which do not consider those factors in apportioning income or minimize those factors in their allocation formulas, you can reduce the over-all tax bite.

[¶3304]   CAPITAL VALUES TAX

Many states impose a tax upon the capital value of corporations. A capital values tax imposed on domestic corporations will generally tax the entire capital value of the corporation. However, apportionment is required when a capital values tax is imposed upon the property of a foreign corporation doing business in the state. The capital values taxes are generally based on the following factors: (a) actual value, (b) debt capital, and (c) capital stock.

Actual Value: A foreign corporation may be taxed on the entire property which it employs in a particular state — this would include physical property located in the state even though it is used primarily in interstate commerce. However, a state's authority to tax the intangible property of a foreign corporation is restricted. A state may tax the entire property — tangible and intangible — of a domestic corporation.

In some states credits are given in calculating the actual value on which the capital values tax is imposed for property which is reached by the state's property tax.

Debt Capital: In some states the amount of debt can be a factor in determining the basis for the capital values tax. Where a state seeks to use "debt capital" as a basis for a tax imposed upon foreign corporations, it must apportion the debt capital — a foreign corporation's tax liability will be limited to the proportion of the debt capital which may be apportioned to the state.

Capital Stock: A capital values tax can be based upon the capital stock of the corporation. Most states levy a tax of this form on domestic corporations (in the form of a franchise tax) and on foreign corporations which are qualified to do business within the state. Where a tax or fee based on the capital stock of the corporation is levied upon the capital stock of a foreign corporation, there is generally either a reasonable floor or minimum or provision whereby it is apportioned — i.e., a foreign corporation is required to pay the tax on only that portion of its authorized capital stock which would be apportioned to the activities or capital employed within the geographic confines of the state.

[¶3304.1]   Apportioning Intangible Property for Capital Values Tax

Intangible property presents a special problem for a capital values tax. Where a capital values tax on foreign corporations must be apportioned, it is necessary to establish a situs of the intangible property owned by a foreign corporation. Several basic theories have arisen as to the situs of intangible property:

Domicile: The traditional theory is that corporate intangible property has a situs in the state wherein the corporation is incorporated. This is known as the domicile theory of situs. A few states have provided by statute that intangible property has a situs in the state wherein the principal office of the corporation is located rather than the state in which the corporation is incorporated. Tangible property would have a situs where it is physically located.

Business Situs: In some states a doctrine of "business situs" for intangible property has developed. Under the business situs theory, intangible property may be taxed in the state where it has its situs or the intangible property came into existence. For example, an account receivable — a typical example of business intangible property — would have a situs in the state wherein the account arose. Other forms of business intangible property would have a situs where the business out of which they arose was conducted.

[¶3305]   SALES AND USE TAXES

Where a corporation makes sales to consumers within a state (i.e., not for resale) from goods located within the state or it otherwise retains places of business within the state from which the sales are made, it is required to collect sales taxes in those states which impose this tax.

The big problem arises for companies engaged in interstate commerce which make interstate sales to customers in states imposing a sales tax. Usually, there is no basis for the state to impose a sales tax. But to "protect" the sales tax, the state imposes a "compensating use" tax. The tax is imposed on the buyer located in the state on goods acquired from without the state and not subject to the sales tax but which would have been subject to the sales tax had it been purchased within the state. Although the tax is imposed on the user within the state, the state in most cases would have difficulty enforcing the tax. So, it attempts to find some basis for having the *seller* (who is located outside the state) collect the use tax from the buyer and remit it to the buyer's state.

SECTION THREE

MANAGEMENT

34

Capital Structure

[¶3401]

By capital structure, we mean the division of the corporation's capital between debt and equity and the various classes within those categories.

Essentially, the capital structure is a means of allocating risk of loss, participation in profit, and control of management. The final decision on the capital structure is usually governed by the kind of money which is available and the terms on which it can be obtained. Nevertheless, in organizing a new corporation or in raising additional financing for an existing company, management should make a serious effort to formulate the financial structure which will be most desirable for the business in the long run.

[¶3401.1]   Basic Principles to Follow

It is easier to obtain money from both equity and debt sources if the financial plan reflects basic economic principles. Generally, bonds are issued when future earnings of a corporation promise to be large and reasonably certain; preferred stock is issued when earnings are irregular but show promise of exceeding preferred stock dividend requirements; common stock is issued when earnings are uncertain and unpredictable. These principles are not automatic. Tax considerations may alter them. Debt financing has tax advantages.

[¶3401.2]   Highest Return on Capital

The highest potential return on capital investment and the largest potential for capital appreciation are produced by the combination of the smallest possible proportion of equity investment — common stock — and the highest proportion of fixed amount debt. This is called trading on the equity. A business borrows money in the hope that the borrowed funds will produce more earnings than the interest rate payable on the money. The danger is that failure to earn a rate of return higher than the interest payable on the borrowed money will consume basic capital and possibly result in creditors taking the business assets.

As an illustration, a business with $100,000 in capital stock can make 10% on capital. If it borrows another $100,000 and keeps its 10% earnings rate on the capital it uses, common stockholders will get a 14% return after paying 6% on the borrowed money. If the earnings rate can be increased to 15%, common stockholders will get a 24% return. But if the earnings rate on the capital employed declines to 5%, common stockholders will receive only 4%. It the corporation earns only 2% on its $200,000, 6% will still be payable on the $100,000 of borrowed money and the common stockholders' capital will be dissipated by 2% a year.

Increased earning power, inflation, or any other factor which operates to increase the dollar value of assets benefits common stockholders exclusively — not the holders of fixed-value notes or bonds or of preferred stock. So the owners of the business will profit to a greater degree from appreciation in value and sustain any loss at a faster rate when there is a low proportion of common stock and a high proportion of fixed value obligations.

[¶3401.3]   Taking Minimum Risks

Maximum safety calls for all common stock and no fixed obligations to pay interest and redeem loans. But debt may be advantageous to raise capital and to maximize income and capital gain posibilities. So a business may have to make a judgment on how far it can go into debt. Caution and prudence of lenders may, to a considerable extent, determine this factor. In general, a lender will want the borrower to have as much money at risk as the lender has; so this may restrict borrowing to somewhere between 40 and 60% of invested capital. Often the owners will want to advance money to their business on a temporary basis, and this could increase the proportion of debt.

Wise limits on the proportion of capital to debt vary in each situation, depending on the earnings prospects, stability of the business, and the financial position and skill of its management. The presence of one or more of the following factors, where a loan is required, would suggest caution before lending funds:

(1) Instability of prices and volume.

(2) Abnormally high percentage of fixed cost.

(3) High rate of turnover.

(4) Low ratio of profits to sales.

For example, a retail store should borrow proportionately less than an apartment house venture or a printing plant with a large fixed investment in heavy machines.

When expansion seems necessary or advantageous, good financing requires a high ratio of stocks to debt to provide borrowing power for future needs. However, if the owners are sure of their future earnings prospects and earning power and feel that a relatively short operating period will prove their judgment, they may borrow as much capital as they need — or can get — and hold off issuing stock until they can get a higher price for it. And, also, because the capital requirements of a successful business can be expected to increase sharply, it may be wise to hold back enough stock so that additional stock is available for expansion needs without heavy dilution of the owner's interest and control.

[¶3401.4]   Maintaining Control of Company

A financing plan that will bring in enough outside funds and also maximize control is often accomplished by giving sole voting power to a small common stock issue. The danger always exists that the owners' control will be lost and their interest diluted if they do not foresee and prepare for the rising financial requirements that successful operation brings. When further capital is needed, the owners may have to release too large a portion of their stock holdings to keep full control.

A preferred stock issue is usually used to secure the investor's money when some of the investing group contribute intangibles such as services, special skills, patent rights, etc., and so are entitled to a share of the profits over and above the normal return for cash investment. Again the owner of the underlying equity must anticipate and make sure that the financial requirements of a successful business can be obtained without loss of his control and dilution of his interest. The use of preferred stock allows the owner to retain a larger proportion of the common. When the business becomes larger, issuance of additional voting stock may reinforce the owner's control by making it more difficult for another to purchase a controlling stock interest.

35

Leases and Leasebacks

Leases today loom large in financing the acquisition of plant and equipment. The lease may be part of a sale-leaseback package or it may be the alternative to an outright purchase. A lease is preferred by some lessees because it does not usually require a large outlay of cash.

[¶3501]   **LEASE OR BUY?**

This is a decision that many taxpayers are often faced with. And it cannot necessarily be made on the basis of lowest net-after-tax cost alone — although, of course, the net-after-tax cost is a big consideration. Often the scales may be tipped in favor of rental because (1) the burden of maintenance is usually on the lessor and (2), via a lease of comparative short duration plus renewal options, the lessee is in a position to switch more easily to a newer type of machine that makes his previous machine obsolete than he'd be if he owned the original machine outright.

But the cost is undoubtedly a big factor. And in arriving at the net-after-tax cost, we have to take into account the impact of the various tax factors on each type of acquisition.

Before making the comparison, however, let's get straight just what we are comparing. On the one hand, we have a rental of a machine we do not own. On the other hand, we acquire ownership. What's more, we can acquire ownership by financing our purchase — a very large initial cash outlay may not be necessary. Most acquisitions today are made via the financing route. So, in a sense, in comparing rentals with purchases, we are comparing two different costs of money — the interest factor that's built into the rental structure and the interest that's paid for the equipment loan. And the tax factors have a considerable effect on determining the net cost.

Making the Comparison: Insofar as the rent paid is concerned, that's generally fully deductible for tax purposes. In addition, the lessor can pass through to the lessee the investment tax credit. Thus, the net cost is the gross rent

263

less the tax benefit derived from both the deduction for rent and the investment credit.

On the purchase side, the buyer is paying both purchase price plus interest. The interest is tax deductible. In addition, he gets an investment credit and depreciation deductions. The depreciation deductions are made up of both a special first-year writeoff (limited to 20% of a maximum cost of $10,000) plus his annual depreciation on a straight-line basis or some accelerated basis (if he's eligible for it). Thus, his net cost is the total of purchase price plus interest reduced by the tax benefits derived from the investment credit, the interest deductions and the depreciation deductions.

[¶3501.1]   How to Set Up the Figures to Make the Comparison

There are a vast variety of rental arrangements available, and there are numerous financing arrangements available, as well. Rather than attempt to deal with a specific illustration that may or may not apply to the type of equipment you are likely to rent or buy, we have set forth below two worksheets. One is for determining the first-year, after-tax cash cost of renting and the other for determining the first-year, after-tax cash cost of buying. Thus, you can insert your own figures on the worksheets and come up with a comparison that has meaning for you.

Worksheet for Determining First-Year, After-Tax Cost of Renting

1. Gross rent .... $ _____
2. Applicable tax rate .... _____
3. Tax saved via rent deduction (Line 1 x Line 2) .... $ _____
4. Net after-tax cost for first year (Line 1 minus Line 3) .... $ _____

Worksheet for Determining First-Year, After-Tax Cost of Buying

1. Total cost of acquired assets[1] .... $ _____
2. Cash down payment in first year .... $ _____
3. Other first-year installments paid .... _____
4. Interest paid on unpaid balance .... _____
5. Total cash outlay in first year (total of Lines 2, 3, and 4) .... $ _____
6. First year writeoff (20% of Line 1, or $10,000 whichever is smaller)[2 & 3] .... _____
7. Regular depreciation (figure depreciation on basis in Line 6 using the particular method applicable and taking into account portion of year the asset is held) .... $ _____
8. First-year depreciation (same as Line 6)[3] .... _____
9. Interest paid (same as Line 4) .... _____
10. Total deductible items (total of Lines 7,8, and 9) .... $ _____

Worksheet for Determining First-Year, After-Tax Cost of Buying

11. Total tax saved by deductions (Line 10 x
tax rate) .... $ _____
12. Net after-tax, first-year cost (Line 5 minus
Line 11) .... $ _____

[1]Normally the total cost will be the contract price for the acquired assets. But if there is a
trade-in, use adjusted basis — i.e., basis of the assets traded in plus balance paid or payable.

[2]If a trade-in is involved, substitute for the amount on Line 1 (for the purposes of this computation) the amount paid or payable for the equipment over and above the amount allowed by the seller
for the trade-in.

[3]Use this first-year write-off *only* if cannot use it on other purchases.

[¶3502] PLANT FINANCING VIA LEASEBACKS

Here is a hypothetical example of a typical sale-leaseback deal. By working
through it, we can see how the figures affect both buyer and seller.

A corporation uses a plant in its business which it has owned for 15 years.
Original cost was $1,000,000, of which $700,000 was allocated to the building
and $300,000 to the land. It has taken $450,000 of depreciation, so its basis for
the whole property is now $550,000. In the 16th year it decides to sell the
property to an investor corporation if it can get a 15-year leaseback. The sale
price is $750,000, with a net rental under the lease equivalent to a 15-year
amortization of the $750,000 at a 6% return — or a rental of $77,225. Assume
that the investor corporation can allocate $500,000 of its purchase price to the
building for depreciation purposes.

The Seller: The seller corporation has a $200,000 gain on the sale and so pays a
capital gains tax of $50,000. If it had borrowed $700,000 (the new amount it gets
after the capital gains tax) at 5% interest payable over 15 years, on a constant
payment basis the yearly payment would have been $67,450. So over the 15-year
period the seller would have paid a total of some $1,012,000 instead of some
$1,158,000 (15 times $77,225) which it pays on the sale-leaseback. But in the case
of the mortgage, the seller only gets a tax deduction for the $312,000 interest that
it pays. This together with the $250,000 depreciation that the seller had left on
the property would have meant a total tax deduction of $562,000 or, at 48%
corporate rates, a saving of $270,000. So the mortgage would have cost the seller
$742,000 ($1,012,000 minus the tax saving). But under the leaseback the seller
gets a tax deduction for the entire rental paid, so there it would get a saving of
$556,000 (52% of the entire 15-year rental), which would mean a cost to the
seller for the leaseback of $602,000 ($1,158,000 minus $556,000). So the sale-
leaseback costs the seller $140,000 less than what the mortgage would have cost.

The Buyer: The buyer under the sale-leaseback gets a deduction over the
15-year period of the lease, assuming that is the remaining life of the building, of

$500,000, the amount that it allocated to the building. This means that $500,000 of the rent income is protected from tax. The tax on the remainder is $316,000, so the net to the buyer on the sale-leaseback over the 15-year period is $842,000. If the buyer had taken a mortgage position in this or similar property for $750,000 at 5% interest, it would have received $1,084,000 with $334,000, the interest, taxable to it (the remainder would have been mortgage amortization). This would have meant a total tax of about $160,500 or a net after taxes to the buyer of $923,500. This is almost $100,000 more than the buyer's net in the case of the leaseback.

What the figures mean to both parties: Figures don't always tell the whole story. Here are some additional factors which can mean a great deal to one or both parties.

To the Seller: The seller pays $140,000 less (net after tax deduction) than it would in the case of a mortgage. But to get this the seller has given up its ownership of the property at the end of the lease. At present, the land is valued at $250,000. So the seller appears actually to lose some $110,000. But this is deceptive. Seller's building wears out at the end of the lease and because of the favorable aspects of the deal to the buyer, the buyer would be able, at the time of the sale-leaseback, to give the seller an option to renew for, say, another 10 or 15 years at a very low rental. And any improvements constructed by the seller during the renewal term would be depreciated by the seller. Also the sale-leaseback provides the seller with the maximum amount of financing; since with property worth $750,000 it would be hard, due to legal limitations on the amount of the mortgage in relation to market value in most states and to the desire by mortgagees for protection, to get a mortgage for the full market value.

To the Buyer: In effect, the buyer has $100,000 of his investment left in the property at the end of the original lease term. But the buyer has gotten out his 5% yield plus the rest of his "principal" and will own property worth at least $250,000 if land values do not change. So the buyer can afford to give the seller a renewal lease at a rental of only $8,000 a year and still get an 8% before-tax return on its $100,000. By this method, during the renewal term, the seller will have the land on a tax-deductible basis. And if the renewal lease is set up properly, any improvements, such as a new building erected by the seller, will not be income to the buyer. At the end of the renewal term or the original lease if the seller does not renew, the buyer still owns the land.

[¶3502.1]   Special Forms of Sale-Leasebacks

Besides the conventional sale-leaseback between two unrelated parties, there are some specialized forms of setting up this type of a transaction.

New Construction: Here a builder may arrange for the financing for a new plant which he is constructing for a business corporation by getting that corporation to agree to lease the property and by interesting an investor in the purchase of the property upon completion. In the meantime, the builder will obtain construction financing unless the investor is an insurance company or pension trust which can handle the financing from commencement of construction.

Exempt Organizations: Educational and charitable organizations and other tax exempts have been heavy buyers in these deals. They enjoy a favorable tax status and so can afford to offer the seller a good deal — the seller deducts the rent, but the charity is not ordinarily taxed on it as income unless it is unrelated to its exempt functions. Consequently, the charity will be able to charge less rent than an ordinary investor. Also a charity or educational institution is exempt from local realty taxes, usually.

When you sell to a tax-exempt organization, it will pay you to hold on to the furniture and equipment and any other depreciable property which the buyer doesn't want. The buyer gets no benefit from the depreciation deduction since he pays no tax. You might as well keep these deductions for yourself.

36

Business Acquisitions

The accounting and financial officers of the company will be intimately involved in any arrangements to buy a business or sell the existing business. Questions of value, technique (purchase or sale of assets or stock), accounting treatment (will the acquisition qualify as a "pooling of interest"?), tax consequences, desirability of the acquisition or sale may all be within the province of the chief financial officer and his staff.

[¶3601]   **FORCES BEHIND BUSINESS SALES AND ACQUISITIONS**

Many businesses diversify and build up sales volume by acquiring other businesses. Capital values can be built by acquiring additional product lines, moving into new territory, etc. Financial statements may be improved. Taxes may be saved by acquiring companies with operating losses. This is done through tax-free exchanges. The seller avoids tax and gets money locked up in his company at favorable capital gain tax rates or tax free.

We see increasing use of a combination of methods that include leases, mortgage financing, and percentage and deferred purchase arrangements. They give maximum retention of capital for regular business operations.

[¶3601.1]   **Benefits of Merging**

Here's a list that will orient your own thinking and help you in any trades or negotiations with other firms:

(1) *Many young companies just don't have the cash* to realize their potentials. This is particularly true in areas which require nationwide merchandising, heavy development work, and expensive productive equipment.

(2) *Diversification* is a major reason for acquisitions. The reasons for seeking diversification are numerous. For example, a company may be seeking

to get into the so-called areas of tomorrow; e.g., electronics, chemicals, atomic energy. By picking up a company already in one of these fields, it may get into the desired area much more economically than otherwise. Diversification may also be sought where a company needs considerable funds to expand into a particular new field. By first diversifying, it hopes to broaden its profit base and increase its growth; then, the new funds generated by growth can be used to get into the areas the company originally sought to enter. Diversification may also be sought by companies in cyclical business by acquiring companies not subject to severe ups and downs. In this way, the acquiring company hopes to make its financial problems less burdensome in the periods when it needs substantial financing and to overcome periods of low revenue when business is contracted.

(3) *Some firms merge with others to get into a new line because investors do not value the industry or its earnings very highly.* Unless such companies can substantially convert into another industry, they cannot realize a large mark-up in capital values.

(4) *Many companies realize that they must have more volume to carry the research and overhead staff necessary to stay competitive today.* The volume required to carry necessary research will vary industry by industry. For example, one company doing about $12 million a year acquired enough additional lines of business to bring its volume up to $20 million. Anything less would have made the firm hard pressed to carry on the research and staff services needed to compete with others in its industry.

(5) *Plants become idle* as a result of a company's product lines becoming obsolete or volume drops off for some other reason. The company finds itself with excess plant capacity. Where this plant capacity — e.g., machinery, equipment, etc.— is in good shape and is not itself obsolete, acquiring a new business may be the best way of making use of this excess plant capacity. This may be a far better solution than a gradual shutdown and a contraction of the existing business.

(6) *Companies are sometimes acquired to get their special attributes.* For example, it may be desirable to get the key personnel of a particular company, and the only way is to get the company as well. In other cases, an acquired company may have special machinery already available which might cost a considerable amount in dollars and time to reproduce. Sometimes the acquired company may have a sales organization which would be just what the acquiring company needs. It may be more economical to acquire the company than to try to build up a similar sales organization.

(7) *Some new, successful companies are taxed so high that there's very little left for investors and expansion.* These make ideal buys for other firms with loss carryovers, which might be used to protect subsequent profits earned by the combined operation.

(8) *Some companies have found that it doesn't pay to fool with a product line which doesn't yield a specified volume.* One company decided to dispose of

all subsidiaries and divisions which did less than $10 million a year. Many companies are trying to earn the premium which investors pay for stability of earnings. They seek diversification which will allow one line to hold up and balance off other lines which run through recessions.

(9) *Many companies go on the block because their owners are faced by a personal estate tax squeeze* and aren't able to get money out of a profitable business to make their personal portfolio liquid. The only solution is to sell part or all the business at capital gains rates or merge with a publicly traded company.

(10) *Many businesses don't want to distribute dividends* but would prefer to use accumulated earnings to acquire other products and expand into new territory or product lines.

(11) *Closely held companies or companies with cash and mortgagable assets locked up in the corporation offer a good buying opportunity* — (a) to companies with fairly marketable stock, which can acquire the locked-up assets by an exchange of stock, or (b) to companies with a cash surplus which permits them to buy stock or assets at a discount (likely because the original owner has to pay a heavy tax rate if he taps the assets by taking a dividend distribution).

(12) *Some companies with strong earnings position can reap big advantages by picking up a smaller company.* Suppose the market values a firm 15 times earnings. If the firm can then pick up a smaller company for 5 or 6 times earnings (frequently possible), it will realize an automatic profit for its stockholders and still be able to plough some earnings into building up the new acquisition.

(13) *When two companies in the same business merge, they can often bring about a number of operating economies.* Bulk purchasing for both companies may cut the unit cost of purchases. In some cases, duplicating facilities may be eliminated — e.g., one warehouse may serve the purposes of both businesses and one warehouse may therefore be eliminated.

37

Financing — Short Term

[¶3701]

Banks, finance companies and factors are the usual sources of short-term funds, although some bank and finance company loans may run for a fairly long term or provide for a continuing line of credit.

Short-term credit may be available on the strength of the overall financial soundness of the borrower or for specific collateral — often, accounts receivable.

[¶3702]   ARRANGING FOR CREDIT LINES WITH BANKS

The most readily available and frequently used source of money for a business is a bank loan. But, for most businesses, banks are only a source of temporary money. To qualify for an unsecured bank loan, a company has to be substantially established and adequately supplied with equity money. The exceptions are those cases in which the bank is lending on the strength of the personal credit of the proprietor or principal stockholder or somebody else who underwrites the loan for the borrowing business.

In dealing with banks, it is important to understand the nature of a commercial banking operation. The money it lends is that placed with it by depositors plus its own capital. A portion of the deposited money is set aside in reserves, another portion is held to meet the depositors' regular demands for cash, and the remainder is available for loans. Neither banking laws nor banking practice permits investment in a business or making capital loans in lieu of equity capital.

[¶3702.1]   Selecting a Bank

The choice of a bank is important in the development of proper credit facilities, and a good banking connection once made is a valuable asset. As a general rule, it is not necessary to shop around for a banking connection — a local bank can usually meet the company's banking needs in a thoroughly satisfactory manner. Some companies deliberately patronize more than one bank with the idea that if one bank turns down a request for a loan, the other will grant the loan. But this may backfire. One bank may want quick repayment for fear that the other will get repayment first. Where the local bank has restrictions which make it unable to meet the company's requirements, it is wise to go to another bank. But ordinarily it pays to give one bank all your business, in the expectation that the bank will take care of a good customer in time of financial stress. Banks prefer the exclusive arrangement. In times of financial need the bank whose officials have a good working knowledge of a company's operations and financial background can take care of its credit needs more quickly and effectively.

[¶3702.2]   How the Banker Judges a Borrower

The banker will study the financial statements of the borrower, using many of the ratios described in this book.

In addition, he will want further information which he will get partially from discussion with the prospective borrower, partially from checking his credit files, and partially from checking with other creditors. The customer's or prospect's credit file, the accumulated information about a particular business and its owner, is of tremendous importance in every loan decision. It is a marked trail which leads the experienced lending officer back through the history of the organization and its officers and enables him to uncover and evaluate information that might not otherwise be made available to him.

The banker will want to know these things about the prospective borrower:

(1) Its character, ability, and capacity.

(2) What kind of capital resources does it have?

(3) What kind of business organization is it? How good are its executives? What has been its sales trend?

(4) Will the loan be a sound one? Are any of the following conditions present to an extent which would throw doubt on the financial soundness of the business:
(a) Heavy inventories in relation to sales.
(b) Excessive dividends and salary withdrawals.
(c) Heavy loans to officers of subsidiary organizations.
(d) Large past-due receivables.
(e) Top-heavy debt.
(f) Too much invested in fixed assets.
(g) An overextended position — i.e., scrambling to apply income and funds to pay the most insistent creditors.

[¶3702.3]   Types of Bank Accommodations

A company should familiarize itself with the various kinds of loan accommodations a bank is willing to extend, the interest rates, terms, and security requirements of each.

A Line of Credit: A line of credit is merely a declaration by a bank that until further notice it is prepared to lend up to a stated maximum amount on certain terms and conditions to the prospective borrower. Since the line of credit is only a declaration of intent, it can be canceled at any time. The availability of a line of credit is very valuable because, instead of fixed credits which call for continuing interest, only amounts of money actually used, plus a small commitment fee on any portion of the original commitment not actually consumed, are charged, which add up to inexpensive financing.

The application for a line of credit is not an application for a loan but simply an arrangement under which the bank agrees to make loans if funds are needed. But even so, a bank conducts an intensive investigation before granting the line of credit.

Term Loans: A business loan which runs for a term of more than one year with provisions for amortization or retirement over the life of the loan is a term loan. Such a loan, even if secured, will depend upon the bank's appraisal of the long-range prospects of the company, its earning power and the quality of its management. The term is usually a maximum of ten years.

Short-Term Loans: Short-term bank loans are obtained either by individual borrowing or by obtaining a *line of credit* against which advances may be obtained. Short-term borrowing is available to companies that have sufficient credit to minimize the bank's risk. The loan is granted on the basis of a study and analysis of the financial position of the company. The security for these loans is a series of promissory notes which evidence the cash advance. These notes have maturity dates calling for repayment within one year, at which time they are reviewed, repaid, reduced or extended. Short-term loans are particularly effective for seasonal financing and the building up of inventories or to keep things running smoothly during spurts of seasonal activity. Before granting a short-term loan, the bank may require that between 10% and 20% of the loan actually made be kept on deposit, or that the loan be cleaned up at least once a year to assure the bank that the business is remaining liquid and to prevent the use of bank credit as permanent funds.

Character Loans: These are short-term, unsecured loans, generally restricted to companies or individuals with excellent credit reputations.

Installment Loans: Large banks generally grant this type of loan. Installment loans are made for almost any productive purpose and may be granted for any period that the bank allows. Payments are usually made on a monthly basis; and as the obligation is reduced, it often may be refinanced at more advantageous rates. The installment loan can be tailored to the seasonal requirements of the company.

Equipment Loans: An increasingly popular method of raising funds is to borrow money against machinery and equipment. There are two main ways of handling equipment loans. The first is to pledge equipment to which the company has an unencumbered title as security for the loan. The second method is via an installment financing plan.

Time Purchase Loans: Many special types of time purchase loans are available to finance both retailer and consumer purchase of automobiles, household equipment, boats, mobile homes, industrial and farm equipment, etc., and are made for varying periods of time, depending on the product. This category also includes accounts receivable financing, indirect collections and factoring.

Inventory Loans: These loans are available if the merchandise or inventory can qualify as collateral. The requirements are stiff and the loans are limited to certain classes of inventory.

Accounts Receivable Loans: Small banks are not usually equipped to offer this type of loan, and the majority of their business customers are too small to take advantage of it. Under this loan, the bank takes over the company's accounts and notes receivable as collateral for the loan.

Warehouse Receipt Loans: Under this plan, goods are stored in warehouses and the warehouse receipts are used as security for a loan to pay off the supplier. As fast as the company is able to sell the merchandise, it pays off the bank loan. This loan permits the company to get along without a large amount of working capital.

Collateral Loans: A company may be able to obtain bank loans on the basis of such collateral as chattel mortgages, stock and bonds, real estate mortgages, and life insurance (up to the cash surrender value of the policy). Even with collateral, the bank will still give great weight to the company's ability to repay. The bank may turn down the application for a loan, no matter how good the collateral, if there is not a clear showing of ability to repay.

[¶3703]   SHORT-TERM BORROWING FROM COMMERCIAL FINANCE COMPANIES

A commercial finance company will frequently step in where a commercial bank will not. Commercial finance companies charge a higher rate and will sometimes take more risk and almost always take on more clerical work to protect their money. Because many companies in the commercial finance field are also engaged in factoring, there is a tendency to confuse the two. Factoring is the service rendered through the assumption of the credit risk on sales purchased from the factored company and the acceptance of the bookkeeping and collection responsibilities for the resulting receivables. In contrast to factoring, the commercial finance company does not guarantee against credit losses on sales to customers.

Finance companies do not "lend" money — they provide revolving working capital. Perhaps this is a subtle distinction; but if a company requires borrowed money it should, if qualified, resort to the many commercial banks throughout the country to satisfy that need. Banks and commercial finance companies are not in competition with one another. Finance companies are among the largest borrowers of money from commercial banks, and commercial banks very frequently refer their customers to finance companies when the capital position of the prospective borrower is insufficient for the bank to grant the credit lines needed.

Funds advanced by commercial finance companies are secured by collateral — mainly accounts receivable — and the finance company has recourse to the borrowing firm. The decision to advance the necessary funds is based, among other things, upon the character and ability of the company's management, its diversification and performance, the quality of the assets pledged, and the ability of the company to operate at a profit if the funds are made available to it.

Commercial financing of accounts receivable and other collateral provides a flexible borrowing arrangement whereby a borrower will receive the funds needed, in the amounts needed, and at the time needed. The accounts receivable outstanding are self-liquidating through their collection. To keep interest charges at a minimum, the financed company may borrow only the funds it needs as and when needed. This method can be contrasted with the fixed-dollar loan, which carries a constant interest cost that must be met.

[¶3703.1]   Accounts Receivable Financing

Accounts receivable are accepted by some banks and most commercial credit companies as collateral for a line of credit. Individual banking practices vary, however, and the borrower should become familiar with local banking requirements. The financing of accounts receivable involves the assignment by the borrower to the lender of the borrower's accounts receivable. These accounts receivable are security for advances which the lender makes to the borrower simultaneously with each assignment. As the proceeds of the assigned accounts are collected, they are turned over to the lender and applied to reduction of the indebtedness, the excess being returned by the lender to the borrower. The borrower remains responsible for the payment of the debt, even though the primary source of payment are the proceeds of the assigned accounts receivable. If the proceeds of the assigned accounts receivable are insufficient to repay the amount advanced, the borrower is liable for the deficiency. This is one important difference between accounts receivable financing and factoring. The factor purchases the accounts receivable from the borrower and assumes the risk of loss from any bad accounts.

Accounts receivable may be financed on a notification or a non-notification basis. Under a notification plan, the receivables are pledged and payment is made directly to the lender, but the borrower remains responsible for the payment. The lender notifies the borrower's customers that their accounts have been assigned and directs them to make payments directly to him. Under the more satisfactory and more commonly used non-notification plan, the borrower collects as agent for the lender. This method is preferable because the relationship between the borrower and his customers is not disturbed and the financing arrangement remains confidential.

[¶3703.2]   Functions of Accounts Receivable Financing

The primary function of accounts receivable financing is to release funds tied up in these accounts, thereby giving a company working capital. Financing of receivables may put a borrowing company in a stronger position for sales expansion and may improve its credit standing by providing funds to discount its own payables.

Accounts receivable financing should be employed in conjunction with a cash forecast and financial plan. The financing will be used according to the plan's estimate of how much cash will be required before the expended cash comes back from customers. Whenever there is a shortage of working capital but available accounts receivable that are not yet due, the borrower is in a position to raise cash to meet his current needs. Of course, this financing aid is not the final answer to the problem of inadequate working capital; but it is a means of temporary relief, especially in seasonal industries where receivables are concentrated in a short period of the year and so are not acceptable collateral for long-term financing.

[¶3703.3]   Mechanics of Accounts Receivable Financing

Before accepting accounts receivable as collateral, the lending agency will evaluate the risks and investigate the facts involved. Through analysis and investigation of the borrower's financial history and related factors, the lending agency can decide if it wants to assume the risk and how the risk can be minimized. At the outset it should be emphasized that certain types of businesses do not lend themselves to receivable financing. Most service enterprises fall into this category. This is because a serviceman may damage the customers' goods and offset any receivable that may be due. The same risk appears in businesses that furnish special orders. And generally factors do not look with favor on unstable industries.

Other considerations involve the accounts themselves. The lender will look to see if the accounts are acceptable for financing. Usually any account that represents a bona fide obligation owed to the borrower from a creditworthy customer without the probability of setoff or the like is available for financing. Under certain conditions, partial billings against unfinished contracts may be financed. The lender will have to be assured that these invoices are payable on regular terms and won't be unduly delayed. Under most circumstances, long-term dating will not disqualify the receivables unless there is undue hazard in their collection.

After the lender has satisfactorily completed his investigation, a basic contract between the lender and the borrower will be executed defining the rights and obligations of the parties. The contract is generally needed because accounts receivable financing contemplates a series of transactions rather than a single isolated loan. Many lenders require yearly contracts. While the agreements vary with the situations, a typical agreement might provide that the borrower assign all accounts receivable, or a selected group of them, to the lender as security. In return the lender agrees to advance funds up to 80% of the face value of the accounts receivable pledged, usually specifying a dollar maximum which can be borrowed. Periodically, schedules of customers' invoices are submitted to the lender to replenish borrowing power. Under this type of arrangement, the borrower, when cash is needed, simply lists the invoices which he wants to finance on the lender's standardized form and the lender advances the cash upon presentation of the form. The borrower should avoid arrangements where it is necessary to get clearance on each individual invoice. Blanket deals are much easier to administer, since invoice schedules are simply submitted periodically on accounts that have blanket approval and the lender worries about individual account limits.

[¶3703.4]   Equity Adjustments

Upon the collection of the accounts, the financing company generally receives a larger amount than the percentage advanced. However, the full difference between the gross amount of the invoice and the percentage advanced is seldom realized upon payment because of returns, allowances, and discounts. The excess, known as "equity," is credited to the client's accounts. There are several possible dispositions of the equity. It may be:

(1) Applied on account to reduce the amount of funds advanced to the client, especially if the advances to the client exceed the percentage called for by the agreement;

(2) Immediately transmitted to the client by check;

(3) Accumulated and transmitted periodically;

(4) Applied on account to reduce the advance until the client no longer requires financing.

[¶3703.5]   Cost of Accounts Receivable Financing

There are various methods of computing charges on open accounts receivable. The most common are:

(1) Straight interest on the amount of funds advanced expressed either as a rate per annum, per month or per diem. The rate of interest is applied to the average daily balances;

(2) A commission on the accounts assigned plus, in some cases, interest on the funds advanced. The logic behind the commission is that regardless of the amount of funds advanced against the assigned accounts, a major expense is incurred in handling the bookkeeping involved. The commission more accurately reflects the cost of maintaining the account;

(3) Charges may be expressed as a percentage of the average balance of the collateral assigned;

(4) A minimum charge may be required as assurance that the financing company will meet its expense in initiating and servicing the account;

(5) Graduated rates may be applied in any of the above methods, reflecting the decreasing operating costs per dollar advanced as the account grows larger.

Rates on the accounts receivable loan vary widely. Commercial bank rates may range from 8 to 9% or higher per annum on the balance in the loan account. Some banks add a small service charge to cover the sizable amount of clerical work involved, such as one-half of one percent based on total receivables pledged or a flat amount for originally setting up the loan. As has already been pointed out, banks do not often go into accounts receivable financing, so that the borrower will probably have to turn to a commercial finance company for the loan. The cost of financing accounts receivable through a finance company is high. They may charge from 1/30 to 1/40% of the face value of the accounts pledged for each day they are outstanding. This may cost the borrower 15% per annum on a loan where the advance is 75% of the face value of the receivables. The rates may range from 14% to 18%, or higher, depending on the overall interest cost of money.

[¶3703.6]   Split Loans

There may occasionally be a situation where a company's credit standing may no longer entitle it to unsecured borrowing, but its financial position may still be far better than that of the usual finance company client, and therefore the company may not be willing to pay the high finance company charge. In this case the finance company may be able to work a *split loan* with a bank at a reduced rate for the borrower. The finance company will approach the bank and do all the preliminary work of setting up the loan. The split loan is a three-way arrangement among the borrower, the finance company and the bank. Under this arrangement, the finance company advances half the needed funds and takes full charge of administering the accounts receivable, which are the security for the entire arrangement. The bank does no work except to lend the other half of the needed funds without guarantee by the finance company. The bank relies on the judgment of the finance company and is able to employ its funds at a good rate with no more expense than any unsecured loan would entail and with greater safety because both lenders are protected by the lien on the accounts receivable. The benefit to the borrower can be seen from the following figures:

Assume the finance company rate is 16%, the prime bank interest rate is 8% and the rate for a split loan is 12%. If the borrower had used the finance company exclusively, he would have paid 16%. Here, he pays 16% on half the loan and 8% on the other half, or a net rate of 12%.

[¶3704]   FINANCING THROUGH A FACTOR

Factoring is primarily a credit business in which the factor checks credits and makes collections for his client. He also purchases his client's accounts receivable without recourse, thereby guaranteeing the client against credit losses. This is the basic service of a factor; and for this service he receives a fee.

Normally the account debtor is notified that the account was purchased by the factor and that payment thereof is to be made directly to the factor.

In this operation the factor checks the credits, makes the collections and assumes the loss in the event the accounts are not paid. Up to this point, however, the factor has passed no funds to his client. He has purchased the accounts and has agreed to pay for them on their net due dates.

Under the standard factoring contract, the factor buys the client's receivables outright, without recourse, as soon as the clients creates them by shipping merchandise to customers whose credit the factor has investigated and approved. Cash is made available to the client immediately on shipment; and, thus, in effect, he sells for cash and can turn his receivables into cash as fast as he creates them. The arrangement is flexible, however, to the extent that the client may withdraw the full proceeds of the sale or leave the proceeds with the factor until their due date. He is charged interest only for money withdrawn prior to the due date. Thus he has a 100% demand privilege on the funds available to him but pays interest only on funds actually used.

However, the factor will make cash advances to the client on the receivables prior to their maturity. For example, let us suppose that the factor purchases accounts receivable amounting to $40,000 from his client, without recourse, due in 60 days. In this case, the factor owes the client $40,000 which must be paid in 60 days. The factor, however, will advance, say, $35,000 to the client immediately, to make operating cash available. The other $5,000 will be paid when due. The factor will charge interest on the funds advanced to the client, and at current rates. If these advances are not enough to meet the needs of the client — and this occurs frequently in seasonal business — the factor will also make short-term, supplementary loans secured by inventory, fixed assets or other acceptable collateral.

[¶3704.1]   Non-notification Factoring

Non-notification factoring is now available to clients in many fields who sell directly to customers in the retail trade. In this type of factoring, the factor purchases the receivables outright without recourse but does not assume the collection function without specific request. The client makes collections himself, and the customer is not notified of the factoring arrangements. The fee for non-notification factoring may be less than that charged for notification factoring.

[¶3704.2]   Bank and Factor in Combination

Frequently, a commercial bank can not provide all the loan funds a growing company needs. Its balance sheet is not liquid enough or it can't clear off the bank debt every six or twelve months. A factor can provide funds to clear off bank loans periodically or make additional bank credit possible by guaranteeing accounts or replacing accounts receivable with cash.

[¶3704.3]   When Should You Factor?

First, can you factor? Yes if:

(1) You sell on normal credit terms;

(2) Eighty to 90% of your customers are rated;

(3) Your annual volume is about $300,000;

(4) Your rate of return and customer complaints are not excessive.

What will factoring do for you? It converts your sales into cash sales. It can give you additional working funds to expand, modernize or whatever will improve your business.

Now, what will it cost you? You pay a service charge and interest. Interest will be 11% or 12% or more per annum on money actually used on a daily basis. The service charge, depending on the risk in your accounts and the amount of handling required, will be from three quarters of one percent to one and one-half percent of the receivables purchased. But against this, you can credit;

(1) Salaries of credit and collection people;

(2) Elimination of bad debt writeoff;

(3) Interest on money borrowed to carry sales and accounts receivable.

[¶3704.4]   What the Factor Wants to Know

The first points a factor considers are the type of sales and the selling terms of the borrower. The sales should be on open account, so as to create accounts receivable that can be sold. The terms of the sale determine the value of the account to the factor. The shorter the terms of payment, the faster the factor can expect to turn over his investment and the lower his rates. If payment terms are extended, the factor will have a long wait to realize his investment and will charge a higher rate, one that might be prohibitive.

Credit information on the accounts should be available. The credit rating determines the risk assumed by the factor when he purchases the accounts without recourse. The factor will expect some credit losses and will include a loss reserve in his charges. A factor will not enter into a factoring agreement unless almost all of the borrower's regular customers seem to be good credit risks.

The arrangement should continue over an extended period of time — something more than a few months. Factors do not like to get involved in short-term deals.

The volume of accounts is important. The annual volume should be about $300,000 — individual receivables should be over $100. Just as in any business, the larger the earnings prospect, the more attractive the deal is. It does not pay a factor to handle a small volume. The size of the individual accounts controls the factor's costs. The greater the balance of the accounts, the smaller the percentage of fixed cost in its collection.

The factor will examine the records to determine if there is an abnormal percentage of returns and complaints. If the percentage of returns as compared with sales is too high, the factor may take this as a warning signal and back out of the transaction.

[¶3704.5]   Provisions of Factoring Contract

The business of the present-day factor is to purchase accounts receivable upon much the same basis that tangible assets are bought and sold. The typical contract first provides that the client agrees to sell to the factor as absolute owner, and the factor agrees to purchase from the client without recourse to the client (with certain exceptions) all accounts receivable created by the client in the ordinary course of his business. The factor usually has recourse to the borrower for returns or allowance for bad debts or errors in pricing.

[¶3705]   INVENTORY LOANS

Inventories are not as liquid as accounts receivable, and a bank or finance company will generally want to secure its advances by accounts receivable and go to inventories only after the business has exhausted its ability to borrow on receivables. Receivables convert into cash automatically, they present fewer legal problems, they don't go out of style or become technologically obsolete or suffer drastic price declines. But inventory financing is important, particularly to businesses that must build up a stock to meet a seasonal demand.

Inventories can be borrowed on, usually if these conditions are met:

(1) The inventory is readily salable — that is, no great sales effort would be required to turn it into cash to satisfy the loan if that should become necessary;

(2) The inventories consist of basic commodities which will not deteriorate or become obsolete within the period of the loan;

(3) The legal technicalities necessary to protect the lender's position in the event of bankruptcy can be met.

You will be able to borrow, if at all, only on your stock of raw materials or finished merchandise. Work in process has little value for borrowing purposes. No lender wants the responsibility for finishing up and selling work in process.

Here's what a lender will want to know about your inventory before he decides whether and how much he can lend on it:

(1) Is the price fairly stable or does it fluctuate sharply?

(2) How broad a market is there for the commodity?

(3) Are there any governmental restrictions on its sale?

(4) Under what conditions may the commodity be stored and for how long?

(5) Is the item closely graded by the trade?

(6) How does the condition of the commodity affect its value?

(7) Is the commodity usually sold in certain standard sizes, and does the commodity under consideration comply with those standards?

(8) Is there any danger of obsolescence in the near future due to technological changes?

(9) What should the costs of liquidation be, such as sales commissions, parking and transportation charges?

(10) Can the commodity be hedged by the purchase of futures?

[¶3705.1]   The Problem of Protecting the Lender

The Uniform Commercial Code which has been adopted in most jurisdictions, including all the leading commercial and industrial states, has eliminated a lot of the legal problems that formerly existed in connection with inventory financing.

The Code rules relating to after-acquired property, future advances, dominion and control of the collateral by the debtor, commingling of goods, and transferring the lien on the collateral to the proceeds make possible so-called "floating liens." The concept of a floating lien is that of a lien on a shifting stock of goods or inventory; that is, a lien on collateral in more or less constant flux and undergoing quantitative and qualitative changes. It is a concept that responds to a long-felt need of businessmen for an effective device giving a lender a security interest on goods and materials which the debtor is permitted to retain, process, manufacture or otherwise change and sell, and also covering the proceeds of the sale and the new goods and materials bought by the debtor with the proceeds in a continuing cycle of business activity. The chattel mortgage has been unable to satisfy this need because of problems in connection with description of the property covered, after-acquired property, and the power of the debtor to sell the collateral and to use the proceeds.

The fact that the Code makes legally possible a floating lien does not mean that the secured creditor's interest in collateral covered by the lien will necessarily be entitled to priority over all liens subsequently attaching or perfected in the same collateral. It may be subordinate to subsequent purchase money interests, and there will be problems of priority as against federal tax liens.

Also, of course, a purchaser from the debtor in the ordinary course of business will get good title. However, the lender's lien may attach to the proceeds of the sale or the resulting account receivable.

In jurisdictions that haven't adopted the Code, the lender will be looking to protect his lien either under a Factors' Lien Act or the Uniform Trust Receipt Act or by taking actual or constructive possession of the inventory. The lender's actual possession of the goods is rarely feasible, and it won't be often that he can be given constructive possession by having the goods placed in a regular public warehouse and having him hold warehouse receipts. This can be cumbersome and expensive because it necessitates transferring the goods to and from the borrower's premises, plus storage charges. Field warehousing may be a more feasible alternative. Both these continue to be used in Code jurisdictions, although the underlying legal requirements may vary somewhat from pre-Code law.

[¶3705.2] Field Warehouse Financing

A field warehouse is created by a warehouse company leasing, at a nominal rent, a portion of the buyer's premises where the pledged inventory is to be stored. This space is segregated from the rest of the buyer's premises by a partition, wire fence or other appropriate means. Separate locks are installed to prevent any person from entering the storage space without the consent of the warehouse company. Signs are probably posted all about the leased premises indicating that the space is under the control of the warehouse company and not the borrower. The purpose of this is to assure that the borrower's creditors will not be misled into thinking that they can lay claim to this inventory or that they are secured by the fact that this inventory is on the borrower's premises.

The warehouse company hires a custodian, usually putting on its payroll a stockman who has been looking after the inventory for the borrower. Warehouse receipts are issued to the lender.

Commercial finance companies have worked up a method of handling the whole chain of transactions from the acquisition of raw material to finished inventory for accounts receivable. Withdrawals from the warehouse are replaced by a steady stream of new raw materials and finished goods going into the warehouse. The sales invoice goes into the hands of the commercial finance company to replace finished goods shipped out of the warehouse. The net effect is to add a substantial increment of working funds to the business. As the finance company furnishes funds to buy raw materials, it is repaid out of advances on the finished product and then gets repaid for these advances out of cash paid upon the collection of the accounts receivable created when the finished product is sold.

[¶3705.3] The Factor's Lien

The use of a field or other warehouse is usually not practical where the borrower must retain possession of the inventory for further processing. Field warehousing is unnecessary in states where there are factor's lien laws, because the procedure where a factor's lien is available can be much less cumbersome and less expensive than field warehousing.

The lien agreement between the borrower and the lender must be placed on public record and usually provides that the borrower will report to the lender at frequent intervals the nature and value of the inventory in the hands of the borrower at that time. The borrower agrees that it will, upon a reduction in its inventory, make payments to the lender on its loans equal to or greater than the amount of the inventory reduction. The law usually requires that a notice, in a specified form, of the existence of the factor's lien be posted in a conspicuous place at the principal entrance to the place of business of the borrower. For obvious reasons, the lending agency usually requires a liberal margin of inventory values against its advances, inspects the inventories at frequent intervals and follows loans of this kind with exceptional care.

This procedure gives the lender a good lien on practically every piece of inventory located on the premises. A factor's lien is not operative against bona fide purchases for value of the merchandise, who purchase it from the borrower in the ordinary course of business without actual notice of the lien. These purchasers get good title to the merchandise free and clear of the lien, but the lien of the lender attaches to the account receivable created by the sale. It is very important that the lender adhere strictly to the notice, posting and filing requirements of the statute which makes the factor's lien available.

The usual transaction involving the financing of inventory on a factor's lien contemplates a combined inventory and accounts receivable financing operation. The lender expects the inventory advances to be repaid out of the proceeds of the accounts receivable created by the sale of the inventory after it has been processed. The borrower expects to finance part of his cost of production by receiving additional advances on accounts receivable as they are created and assigned to the lender.

[¶3705.4]   Trust Receipts

A trust receipt is a financing instrument in the form of an agreement between a bank (the lender), called the entruster, and a person, firm, or corporation (the borrower), called the trustee. It shows that certain goods or property, or evidence of title to these goods or property, having been acquired for financing purposes by the lender are released by it under specified conditions to the borrower. While the goods are in the borrower's possession, the lender retains ownership until the goods or property, or the evidence of title to goods or property, are properly accounted for by the trustee to the entruster. This accounting is through payment or otherwise, as set out in the instrument.

The trust receipt is used for interim financing of staple commodities when it is necessary to release pledged goods from a warehouse in order to sell or process them. Another wide use is in financing, under a "floor-planning" arrangement.

Floor Planning: This term refers to the use of the trust receipt to finance the purchase by dealers or distributors of motor vehicles, household appliances and other products that may be readily identifiable as to specific units and that have other than a nominal unit value. Under such a financing arrangement, the products are actually paid for by a bank or other lending agency, which obtains title through the payment of a draft with bill of lading attached, for the purchase price, or through a bill of sale or otherwise. Then, in effect, the products are released by the lender to the borrower for inventory and sales purposes against the borrower's note and trust receipt. The trust receipt provides, in effect, that the borrower will hold the products in trust for the lender for the purpose of sale at not less than a specified minimum sale price per unit and will, pending sale, return the products to the lender upon demand. Or, upon sale, the borrower will keep the proceeds of sale segregated and deliver such proceeds to the lender immediately.

Floor Plan Terms: Frequently, the lender will advance for the original purchase no more that 90% or less of the invoice cost of the products to be financed. It will usually require the monthly curtailment of any advances outstanding at the end of three months, with complete liquidation required within six months after the date of purchase. Interest on daily loans outstanding is usually billed to the borrower at regular monthly intervals.

Floor Plan Procedures: During the period of outstanding advances, the lender will have a valid security interest (except against an innocent purchaser for value) in the products held by the borrower under trust receipt, provided they are clearly identifiable and the lender has observed all requirements of law surrounding trust receipt financing. These requirements may vary to some extent with the laws of each state but usually they include the necessity of placing on public record a "Statement of Trust Receipt Financing" which, in effect, is merely a notice that the borrower is engaged in trust receipt financing with a specified lender. At frequent but irregular intervals, the lender will make a detailed physical check of the products held by the borrower under trust receipt to establish their continued availability and to inspect their condition.

Observing Floor Plan Terms and Procedures: The business using this method of inventory financing must take exceptional care to see that, when floor-planned products are sold, the proceeds of sale are delivered promptly to the lender to apply on outstanding advances. As the name implies, a trust receipt arrangement requires the trust of the lender in the integrity of the borrower. The latter must avoid any appearance of irregularities that might lead to the destruction of the confidence.

38

Financing — Long-Term

[¶3801]

The basic distinction within a corporation's capital structure is that between equity and long-term debt. Short-term debt, even though it is anticipated that it will be renewed, is normally considered a current liability.

Long-term debt is generally shown as a separate category of liabilities and is distinguished from a stock issue in the following ways: (1) the corporation makes an absolute promise to pay the full amount at maturity; (2) the corporation promises to pay a fixed interest at periodic intervals; (3) the debt is frequently, but not necessarily, secured by specific assets of the corporation or by its assets generally; (4) the debt is frequently, but not necessarily, issued under an indenture under which a trustee is appointed to act as the creditors' representative in dealing with the corporation. Long-term debt is ordinarily in the form of bonds, although there is today a greater use of notes because Federal tax stamps need not be purchased in connection with a note issue.

Actually, the line between debt and equity is often very difficult to draw despite the clear-cut distinctions that are indicated above. The most typical of the "hybrid" forms is the income bond, on which interest is paid only during such years as the corporation's income is sufficient for that purpose. If such a bond has a very long maturity, it is very similar to a stock issue. The problem is particularly acute in the case of smaller corporation (so-called "close" corporations) where the stockholders seek to provide equity capital to the corporation in the guise of debt so that interest payments will be deductible by the corporation.

[¶3802]   **LONG-TERM BONDS**

Long-term bonds are normally issued either in registered or coupon form. A coupon bond contains a coupon for each interest date during the life of the bond. When the interest date is reached, the bondholder clips the coupon and sends it to

286

the corporation and subsequently receives his interest payment. Coupon bonds are transferable merely by delivery and, hence, create a problem of safekeeping for the bondholder. A registered bond, on the other hand, is registered with the corporation, and interest payments will be made directly to the registered owner until such time as the corporation is notified of a transfer. Registered bonds can only be transferred by negotiation (i.e., endorsement by the present owner) and are therefore less risky to hold.

[¶3802.1]   Principal, Interest, and Maturity of Long-Term Bonds

A bond issue will normally be made up of a large number of bonds identical in all respect (except sometimes as to maturity). The usual denomination for a bond is $1,000, although in some cases "baby bonds" of $100 denominations have been issued to appeal to the smaller investor. The bond's interest rate is selected on the basis of two considerations: (1) the current scale of money rates; (2) the quality of the company issuing the bonds. If the interest rate is set too low, the bond issue will be salable only at a substantial discount from par or may not be salable at all. If the interest rate is too high, the corporation will be paying more than necessary for the money it obtains. Once the bonds have been issued, their price will fluctuate depending on changes in money rates and in the condition of the company. It is unusual for a publicly traded bond to have the same market rate as nominal rate — that is, it is unusual for the bond to be traded at exactly par value.

The current range of money rates plays a role in determining whether a long-term bond issue should be considered at all. Current interest rates are plotted on a graph according to the maturity of the various issues. This is called a "yield curve." An upsweeping yield curve means that the longer maturities yield the highest interest rates (the normal situation, since there must be some inducement for lenders to tie up their money for the longer periods). However, there are occasions when the yield curve will be downsweeping; i.e., interest rates for the shorter maturities will be higher than those for the longer maturities. Obviously, the best time for a long-term bond issue is when the yield curve is downsweeping, since long-term money is then cheaper than short-term money. On the other hand, if the yield curve is sharply upwards, short-term money may be so much cheaper that it would be wise to arrange the necessary financing through short-term loans (assuming they are available) with the intention of refinancing with long-term debt at some later date when the yield curve is more favorable.

The maturity of long-term debt may range anywhere from five years to 100 years. A bond issue may have a single maturity date for all the bonds or may be a serial issue, with a certain proportion of the bonds maturing at different dates. With a single maturity, the company must be prepared to pay off the entire issue at one time or refinance. A serial issue spreads the corporation's obligation over a period of years and, thus, is somewhat similar to a sinking fund.

[¶3802.2]   Secured Bonds

For blue-chip corporations of the very highest quality, specific security for a bond issue is probably of very little importance to the market because of the high credit standing of the company. But for other companies, the security underlying a bond may be an important factor in determining its marketability. Secured bonds can be divided into four classes:

(1) Real Property Mortgage Bonds: These are bonds secured by real estate owned by the corporation. The face amount of the bonds will normally not exceed two-thirds of the appraised value of the real estate in the case of first mortgage bonds. In addition, second or third mortgage bonds can be issued.

(2) Equipment Obligation Bonds: These are bonds secured by chattel mortgages on personal property owned by the corporation. A special form of such bond is the equipment-trust certificate under which title to the property remains with the lender who leases it to the corporation until such time as the debt is paid. Equipment-trust certificates are most often used in the railroad industry.

(3) Collateral Trust Bonds: These are bonds secured by investment securities in companies other than the borrower. The borrower is entitled to the interest or dividends from the securities, but they may be sold by the lender in case of the borrower's default.

(4) General or Blanket Mortgage Bonds: These are bonds secured by all the assets of the corporation. These bonds normally preclude any further issues of secured debt by the corporation unless they specifically provide that they may be subordinated to future bond issues secured by specified assets.

One major problem that frequently occurs in secured bonds is the inclusion of an after-acquired property clause. This clause provides that the mortgage securing the bond issue will automatically be expanded to include all property or specified property subsequently acquired by the corporation. Sometimes this is limited to new property which is acquired to replace property originally included under the mortgage, but on other occasions the clause covers all new property acquired by the corporation and thus increases the security of the bondholders. If a corporation has such a bond indenture in existence and wishes to avoid subjecting new property to the outstanding mortgage, it may be able to proceed in one of the following ways:

(1) Acquire the new property subject to a purchase money mortgage, which ordinarily has priority over the after-acquired property clause;

(2) Organize a subsidiary company to hold the new property;

(3) Lease instead of buy the new property;

(4) Acquire the new property in connection with a merger or consolidation, which frequently renders the after-acquired clause inoperative;

(5) As a last alternative, the outstanding bonds can be redeemed.

[¶3802.3]   Guaranteed Bonds

The guarantee is a less common form of creating security for a bond issue, but nevertheless it is met with on a fair number of occasions. A guarantee differs from a mortgage in that the creditor is entitled to look to another person rather than to specified property as additional protection for his loan. The three most common types of guarantee bonds are as follows:

(1) Individual Guarantees: These are most often used in close corporations where all or some of the stockholders may sign the bonds or notes individually and thus assume personal liability in addition to the corporate liability.

(2) Guarantees by Corporate Parents: A corporation may decide to carry out some of its operations via subsidiary corporations. In that case, if the subsidiary sells a bond issue, the parent corporation by guaranteeing the bonds can sometimes make the bonds salable at a lower interest rate. Although corporations cannot, as a general rule, guarantee the obligations of others, most states make an exception for subsidiary corporations or for guarantees made within the scope of the corporation's business operations.

(3) Joint Guarantees: These are most common in the railroad industry where two or more railroad corporations may guarantee the bonds of a facility which is jointly used by them, such as a terminal building.

[¶3802.4]   Debenture Bonds

These are unsecured bonds backed only by the general credit of the corporation. In the case of small and many medium-sized companies, debenture bonds are considerably riskier than either secured or guaranteed bonds. There are two primary categories of debentures:

(1) Nonsubordinated Debentures: These, on their face, make no provision for subordination to any future bond issues. However, if the bond indenture says nothing further, these bonds will automatically be junior in lien to any future bond issues which are secured by specific corporate assets. To prevent this from happening, the lender may insist that the indenture contains a provision limiting the total amount of future debt which the corporation may issue or a provision that the debenture bonds will have an equal status with any future mortgage bonds or secured bonds issued by the corporation.

(2) Subordinated Debentures: Of all types of debt, these most resemble a stock issue. The subordination clause places the lender last among all the creditors of the company, past or future. The advantage to the corporation is that it preserves its future borrowing power, while at the same time creating deductible interest rather than nondeductible dividends. This type of bond issue will appeal to persons who are prepared to assume greater risk than the usual bondholder but who also want a priority position as against the common stockholders. Debenture bonds are very similar, therefore, to preferred stock. In fact, the debentures will frequently carry a conversion privilege as a "sweetener," thus giving the bond-holder the option to change his interest to stock in the event the company is successful.

[¶3802.5]   Discount Bonds

Sometimes bonds may be issued at a discount instead of calling for interest. For example, a bond with a face of $1,000 may be issued at $750. At maturity, the bond will be redeemed for $1,000.

This type of bond is not usually used except by closely held companies. But tax problems may be created by a discount bond.

To the extent there is an "original issue discount" — and this can arise with a discount bond or with any bond which is issued at a discount — and the bondholders realize this discount, either on redemption or through sale to other holders, the gain realized is treated as ordinary gain. Gain not attributable to the original issue discount — i.e., gain that might arise from purchasing a bond as between bondholders at a further discount — is treated as capital gain. Thus, from the bondholder's point of view, original issue discount when realized will be the same as interest income.

From the corporation's point of view, discount should be amortized over the life of the bond, thereby increasing proportionately each year's interest expense. Where a premium is received, it too is amortized over the life of the bonds, thereby decreasing each year's interest expense.

[¶3802.6]   Special Features of Bond Issues

Any or all of the following special types of provision may be found in a bond issue:

(1) Sinking Funds: A sinking fund requires the corporation to set aside a certain amount of cash each year so that at the maturity of the bond issue there will be sufficient funds to pay off the bondholders. The annual contribution may be set up in one of several different ways. For example, an increasing amount may be required each year on the theory that the underlying asset becomes more productive. Or, higher amounts may be required in the earlier years because increasing maintenance charges are anticipated as the asset grows older. If the sinking fund reserve is retained by the corporation until the maturity of the bond issue, the corporation may invest the funds in some form of investment which is both safe and liquid, such as Treasury obligations. On the other hand, the indenture may provide that the sinking fund cash is to be used to purchase bonds on the open market or from individual bondholders drawn by lot. Whatever the specific use of the sinking fund, it acts to increase the security of the remaining bondholders.

(2) Restrictions on Cash Payments: A bond indenture frequently prohibits the corporation from paying out cash dividends or using cash to reduce capital unless a minimum amount of surplus is retained. Stock dividends, however, are normally not prohibited since they do not involve the outflow of cash.

(3) Convertibility to Stock: This has already been mentioned in connection with debentures. In setting conversion terms (the price of conversion), the corporation determines whether or not it wishes to force conversion. If it is issuing the bonds only as a temporary measure, it will give relatively easy conversion terms so that the bondholders are encouraged to take stock as soon as possible. On the other hand, if the corporation prefers the bonds (for example, because the interest is deductible), it may set the conversion terms to be attractive only after a period of years.

(4) Callability of Bonds: This is a provision frequently inserted in a bond indenture for the protection or benefit of the corporation issuing the bonds. It permits the corporation to redeem the entire bond issue by paying the call price, which usually is set somewhat above par. For example, if the bonds have a face value of $1,000, the corporation may be permitted to call them at $1,050. The time at which the bonds may be called may begin either immediately or after a certain number of years. A callability provision has a disadvantage from the borrower's point of view since it puts a limit on the price potential of the bond. If interest rates decline, the bond price will rise as a consequence and, apart from the call price, may reach a level substantially above par. However, if the corporation has the call privilege, it will probably exercise it when bond prices begin to rise, because this means the corporation can refinance by issuing a new bond issue at lower interest rates.

[¶3803]   **TERM LOANS BY BANKS AND INSURANCE COMPANIES**

Term loans are a common way of providing intermediate financing, i.e., from one to five years and sometimes up to ten years. The parties frequently proceed on the assumption that a term loan will be renewed each time it becomes due, provided of course that the financial condition of the business warrants such renewals. While such debt may therefore remain on the company's books for very long periods of time, it is nevertheless classified as intermediate because the lender has the option at relatively frequent intervals to terminate the loan.

There are numerous purposes for intermediate borrowing. One of the most common is to provide adequate working capital. A company may be under-capitalized from the start or it may find that in times of prosperity more capital than anticipated is tied up in inventory and accounts receivables. In such case, a term loan can supplement the firm's own equity investment. Another common use of the term loan is to acquire equipment with relatively short lives. Depreciation of the equipment affords tax-free cash which is available to pay off the loans; when new equipment is again required, the loan can be renewed. Finally, a term loan is often used when the company is actually seeking long-term funds but decides that the time is not propitious for floating long-term debt or for a public issue of stock. Typically, companies are reluctant to issue long-term debt when interest rates are very high or to issue common stock when the market is quite weak.

Interest rates on term loans will, as befits their intermediate status, fall somewhere between the extremes of the maturity yield curve. They will tend to rise during periods of business expansion as the commercial banks are called upon to increase their business loans, and conversely term loans will be in less demand during times of economic recession. Commonly, the interest is in the form of a discount, whereby the bank deducts annual interest at the inception of the loan. This will of course make the actual interest rate higher than the nominal rate.

As regards repayment of principal, a term loan may be a standing loan, a fully amortized loan or a partially amortized loan. In the last case, the loan is called a balloon loan since a portion of the principal will remain due at maturity despite regular payments of principal. Generally, unsecured term loans will require some amortization, particularly if they run for more than one year. On the other hand, if the loan is secured by stocks or bonds or by other assets of the borrower, no or very little amortization may be required even though the loan is for a longer term.

[¶3803.1]   Restriction in Term Loan Agreements

A term lender will be particularly interested in the borrower's cash flow rather than net income after taxes. The reason for this is that over a relatively short period, a company may be fully capable of paying off a term loan out of its cash flow, even though it may go through a temporary period of declining or nonexistent earnings. Or under opposite circumstances, a company may anticipate a large net income but may have a very small cash flow due to the need to purchase new equipment, pay off other loans, etc. Important provisions in the term loan agreement which act to restrict the borrower include the following:

Additional Debt: The lender may impose restrictions on the borrower's right to incur additional debt. This is more likely where the term debt is unsecured and new debt, by virtue of security provisions, may place the term loan in a subordinated position.

Restriction on Dividends: A common provision is one forbidding dividends unless net profits and/or cash flow reach designated amounts.

Restrictions of Cash Payments: In addition to limiting dividend payments, the loan agreement may limit other cash payments not out of income. For example, surplus may not be used to retire existing stock or for investment in foreign subsidiaries.

Restrictions on Salaries: In the case of smaller companies, a lender may insist that salaries, bonuses and other compensation be restricted to stated amounts.

Minimum Working Capital: The effect of the preceding restrictions is to insure that the company has sufficient working capital for its needs. In addition, the loan agreement may specifically provide for a minimum working capital position.

Barring Merger or Consolidation: Finally, the lender may insist that no merger or consolidation take place while the term loan is outstanding. The reason for this is that such a combination may deprive the borrower of necessary cash or may place the term loan in a very subordinated position.

39

Investing Working Capital
for Short-Term Periods

[¶3901]

The amount of current assets which must be maintained by the business to sustain its working capital needs will vary, depending on such matters as the rapidity of inventory turnover, the length of the collection period, and the extent to which current assets are reduced by capital replacement, dividends and similar needs of the business.

Regardless of the absolute amounts needed by a particular business, it is a general principle of business finance that cash should be conserved whenever possible. In other words, the amount of inventory should be no higher than that needed to sustain the normal sales volume of the business and every effort should be made to collect receivables as soon as possible.

Until quite recently, this principle of conserving cash led most financial officers to favor large cash balances in corporate checking accounts, since this represented 100% liquidity. The view was taken that any type of investment represented an unnecessary business risk. But this is now regarded as too conservative and, since it denies the business any return on its cash, too costly a practice to follow.

[¶3901.1] The Minimum Need for Cash

There are at least five reasons why a minimum cash balance must be maintained:

(1) Immediate Liabilities: The company must have cash for its payroll and for other liabilities, such as tax payments or trade accounts which must be paid in the next few weeks.

(2) Emergencies: It is possible that the business will need a sum of cash for

294

some emergency purpose or perhaps even to make a highly advantageous purchase which must be consummated at once.

(3) Purchase Discount: Companies like to have sufficient cash on hand to be able to take advantage of all purchase discounts. While, today, many companies look upon the cost of merchandise or other items purchased as the net cost after discount, nevertheless failure to pay a bill within a discount period can be quite expensive. For example, merchandise purchased on a 2%/ten; net/30-basis will, in effect, pay 2% interest for the use of the money for 20 days if the bill is not paid within the 10-day period. This is the equivalent of a 36% interest rate. Hence it becomes important to pay all bills within the discount period, and so it is important to have sufficient cash on hand to take advantage of the discounts.

(4) Compensating Bank Balances: Most commercial banks require that borrowers maintain a compensating deposit with them. For example, a company borrowing $100,000 may be required to maintain a continuing deposit of $20,000. This, of course, increases the actual interest cost to the business and is one of the reasons why the stated interest rate normally does not represent the true cost of money.

(5) "Window-Dressing": This is a purely psychological factor but one which should not be overlooked. Even though a company has excellent reasons for maintaining an extremely low cash balance, such a figure on its balance sheet may prove disconcerting to stockholders and creditors, who may feel that the business is short of working capital, one of the most common reasons for business failure.

[¶3901.2]   Nature of Risks in Investing Cash

In theory, conversion of cash into any other form of investment creates three possible kinds of risks: credit, money, and liquidity.

(1) Credit Risk: This is the risk that the organization which issues the investment obligation will fail or will otherwise be unable to honor its obligation. Where the organization is the U.S. Government, this risk is almost nonexistent. The risk is small also for all practical purposes when the organization is a state, municipality or private organization which is insured by an agency of the government. Investors now, however, are more cautious of municipal obligations, after the experience of New York City. On the other hand, investing in common stock of a small enterprise obviously involves a high degree of risk.

(2) Money Risk: This refers to the risk of loss due to changes in interest rates. For example, the price of a U.S. Government bond may fall (even though no credit risk is involved) because interest rates rise, which in turn reflects changes in the supply and demand for money. The existence of money risk precludes any investment of cash in long-term obligations. However, there are forms of short-term investments (Government bills and certificates and time deposits, called "near-money") which involve such a minimum degree of money risk that it can be ignored.

(3) Liquidity Risk: This refers to the absence of a market for the investment. For example, a real estate mortgage may suffer no decline in price due to money risk or credit risk but nevertheless may have no market at the time the holder wishes to sell it. To insure liquidity, corporate cash should be invested in obligations having an extremely active market, the most typical of which are U.S. Government securities.

[¶3901.3]   Types of Investments for Corporate Cash

Having defined the basic type of risk, we may briefly indicate the types of investments which may be appropriate for the investment of corporate cash balances:

(1) Ninety-Day Treasury Bills: Treasury bills are the shortest term obligation issued by the Federal Government and represent an obligation almost equal to actual cash in terms of the various risks outlined above. Treasury bills are issued for 91 or 182 days (there is normally a new issue every two weeks), and their interest rate will vary depending on the degree of monetary ease which prevails. They are completely liquid. They are purchased and sold on a discount basis rather than on the basis of a face value plus accrued interest. They can be purchased only in minimum amounts.

(2) Other Federal Obligations: There are three other classes of Federal obligations: Treasury certificates (maturity of 6 to 12 months), Treasury notes (maturity of 1 to 5 years), and Treasury bonds (maturity of over 5 years). While these involve little credit risk or liquidity risk, they do involve a money risk as their prices will fluctuate in relation to the movement of interest rates.

(3) Certificates of Deposit: The institutions which were hurt most by the transfer of corporate funds from demand deposits to income-bearing investments have been the commercial banks. In an attempt to win back some of the lost funds, commercial banks now offer certificates of deposit. These are issued to a corporation on deposit of a minimum amount of funds (e.g., $15,000-$100,000) for a minimum period of time (e.g., six months) and carry an interest rate which substantially exceeds the current rate on savings accounts. Although the money deposited must remain for the minimum period in order to earn interest, the certificates themselves are negotiable in the money market so that from the point of view of the corporation, there is no problem as to liquidity. Because of the short-term nature of the deposit, there is similarly little risk of loss from changes in interest rates.

(4) Savings and Loan Association Deposits: Until commercial banks began issuing certificates of deposits, much of the corporate funds which were not invested in securities were placed in savings and loan associations. Here, they could earn high interest and normally could be withdrawn upon 30-day notice. While such deposits normally create little money risks or credit risks (since deposits are insured by an agency of the Federal Government), there is some possibility of nonliquidity in the event of a severe economic downturn which could result in a high foreclosure rate, which in turn might mean that some savings and loan associations (which invest primarily in mortgages) might not be in a position to pay their depositors upon demand.

(5) Short-Term Commercial Notes: Finance companies and other monied corporations whose main assets are cash are constantly offering short-term notes to investors for the purpose of raising working capital. These notes, with maturities of from 90 days upwards, are suitable for many corporations since they provide a return slightly higher than that on Treasury obligations and, in the case of the largest finance companies, there is little risk.

(6) Short-Term Corporate Bonds: One type of investment that is used by corporate treasurers is corporate bonds which have only a short time until maturity. In the case of our largest and strongest corporations, their bonds involve small risk. If their bonds are bought at a discount a short time prior to maturity, this also reduces the money risk since even if money rates rise (causing a decline in bond prices generally), the investor knows he must receive at least par at the maturity of the bonds.

(7) Municipal Bonds: This type of investment may yield slightly less than some others, but income is exempt from tax at the corporate level. Such income cannot be distributed as a tax-free dividend.

(8) Commercial Paper: This is a short-term investment that usually pays interest at a rate higher than government obligations. The larger corporations borrow short-term funds in this manner with a 30-day maturity. If they are bought with discretion, the risk factor is moderate.

40

Financially Troubled Businesses

[¶4001]

The corporate accountant's need for handling a company in financial difficulty can arise when it's his own company that's in trouble or when a debtor of his company is the one that has the financial problems. In either case, he might, for example, be concerned with preparing or evaluating a statement of affairs. And he might be concerned with the rules of bankruptcy when his company or the debtor might be thrown into, or voluntarily go into, bankruptcy. More often, rather than outright bankruptcy, he might be involved in working out an arrangement for rehabilitating or reorganizing the company either as debtor or creditor.

[¶4001.1] Statement of Affairs

The purpose of the statement of affairs is to determine how much the unsecured creditors can hope to get from the business if it is liquidated. The statement may be prepared by a trustee in bankruptcy to determine whether the business would be better off being dissolved or continued. It may also be prepared anywhere along the line where a business is in trouble (perhaps in trying to work something out with creditors) to determine the status of the unsecured creditors. (Note that we are referring here to an accounting statement of affairs as distinguished from a statement of affairs prescribed under the Bankruptcy Act, which is a comprehensive debtor's questionnaire.)

Included here is an illustration of a statement of affairs with a statement of the estimated deficiency to unsecured creditors.

X CORPORATION
Statement of Affairs
.............., 19....

Book Value	Assets	Appraised Value	Available to Unsecured Creditors	Estimated Shrinkage
$250,000	Fully Pledged Assets: Land & Building	$180,000		$70,000
	Less: Mortgage Payable (deducted contra)	150,000	$30,000	
30,000	Partly Pledged Assets: Bonds of Y, Inc. (deducted contra)	$32,000		
	Unpledged Assets:			
5,000	Cash	$5,000	5,000	
100,000	Accounts Receivable (less bad debts)	80,000	80,000	20,000
200,000	Inventories	120,000	120,000	80,000
1,000	Goodwill			1,000
$586,000	TOTALS		$235,000	$171,000
	Preferred Creditors (see contra)		55,000	
	Balance Available to Unsecured Creditors		$180,000	

Book Value	Liabilities and Stockholders' Equity	Unsecured Claims
	Preferred Creditors:	
$10,000	Wages Payable	$10,000
40,000	Taxes Payable	40,000
5,000	Estimated Administration Costs	5,000
	Deducted contra	55,000
	Fully Secured Creditors:	
150,000	First Mortgage Bonds and Accrued Interest (deducted contra)	
	Partially Secured Creditors:	
40,000	Notes Payable and Accrued Interest	40,000
	Less: Appraised value of Y, Inc., Bonds	32,000
		$8,000
	Unsecured Creditors:	
300,000	Accounts Payable	300,000
	Stockholders' Equity:	
200,000	Capital Stock	
(159,000)	Deficit	
$586,000	TOTALS	
	Available to Unsecured Creditors Contra	$308,000
	Estimated Deficiency to Unsecured Creditors	180,000
		$128,000

[¶4002]   BANKRUPTCY

You may have contact with the Bankruptcy Act when: (1) You want to obtain for your company the status of a secured creditor in anticipation of the possible bankruptcy of the debtor. (2) You want to protect your company as creditor by putting the debtor in bankruptcy. (3) You want to press a claim against or recover an asset from a bankrupt estate. (4) Your company is the harassed debtor seeking to be discharged of its debt. (5) You want the protection of the court and an appointed trustee to rehabilitate your financially embarrassed business.

The trustee can avoid any transfer which is fraudulent or voidable as to any creditor having a provable claim under the Act and liens obtained by legal or equitable proceedings within four months of bankruptcy while the debtor is insolvent.

[¶4002.1]   Advoidance of Preferences

The trustee has power to avoid preferences. The elements of a preference are: (1) a transfer of the debtor's property (voluntary or involuntary including liens by legal proceedings); (2) while insolvent; (3) for or on account of a prior debt; (4) within four months of the filing of the petition in bankruptcy; (5) enabling the creditor to get a greater percentage of his debt than other creditors of the same class; and (6) the creditor must know or have reasonable cause to believe that the debtor was insolvent at the time of the transfer.

[¶4002.2]   Making Claims Against a Bankrupt

A creditor establishes a claim in bankruptcy by filing what is known as a "proof of claim." You can go into practically any legal stationery store and buy appropriate forms.

All provable claims must be filed within six months of the first meeting of creditors. If a claim is timely filed, it can usually be amended after the six-month period as long as the amendment doesn't amount to an entirely new claim.

Extending credit to a bankrupt after the filing of a petition does not automatically give the supplier an administration expense claim that would be entitled to payment in full. Credit extended after the filing of the petition and before the appointment of a receiver or the adjudication, whichever occurs first, get no better treatment than if it had been extended before the petition was filed.

[¶4002.3]   Putting a Debtor in Involuntary Bankruptcy

Three creditors with claims aggregating over $500 are necessary, except in those cases where the bankrupt has less than twelve creditors, in which event one petitioning creditor will suffice. The creditors will have to show one of the six acts of bankruptcy. The more important ones are a fraudulent transfer, a preferential payment during insolvency, or failure of an insolvent debtor to discharge a judgment within 30 days or 5 days before the sale of property to which the lien attaches. Insolvency here means that the debtor's liabilities exceed his assets taken at fair value.

Why does the creditor want to force involuntary bankruptcy? There are several reasons:

(1) There is a sequestration of assets immediately without the risk of having the bankrupt dissipate or conceal the property available to pay his debts.

(2) There is an orderly administration of the bankrupt's estate as well as a procedure under which claims against it can be expeditiously established.

(3) If the bankrupt has made any substantial preferences— that is to say, if it has favored certain creditors—it can be required to return the property to the estate for ratable distribution among all claims.

(4) There is provision in the Bankruptcy Act for the examination of the bankrupt and witnesses to determine the nature of the acts, conduct and property of the bankrupt whose estate is in the process of administration.

[¶4002.4] Procedure Steps in Bankruptcy Proceedings

The steps in a bankruptcy proceeding are these:

(1) Filing of petition — a voluntary petition constitutes an adjudication; an involuntary petition may be contested.

(2) To contest a petition, an answer has to be filed. Usually, it will deny the act of bankruptcy or deny the insolvency, which is necessary for a preferential payment or permitting a judgment lien to constitute an act of bankruptcy.

(3) The bankrupt must file an inventory of all his property and a list of all his creditors, secured and unsecured, showing the amount owed each. He must also file a "statement of affairs" giving information as to his financial history, the volume of business, his income and other pertinent information. The schedules are prepared in triplicate, filed with the clerk of the court and must be sworn to. The schedule must claim any exemptions the debtor believes he's entitled to; otherwise the exemption may be lost.

(4) When adjudication takes place, the referee fixes a date for the first meeting of creditors not less than 10 days nor more than 30 days after adjudication and gives the creditors written notice of the meeting. The meeting is presided over by the referee, and the bankrupt is required to attend and to submit to a broad examination covering every phase of his operations. If it turns out to be a "no asset" case, the applicant for examination may wind up having to pay the stenographer's fee. This suggests the wisdom of having an agreement with other creditors before assuming the initiative. It's worth noting that the creditors don't have to wait until their first meeting to examine the debtor but can do so even before adjudication.

(5) The trustee in bankruptcy is elected at the first meeting of creditors by a majority of the unsecured creditors both as to number and amount of claims. Claims of secured or priority creditors aren't counted except to the extent they exceed the value of their security or priority. This, of course, can lead to a contest, and the referee will have to decide which claims he'll allow to vote.

(6) The trustee has the key role in bankruptcy proceedings. He must take over and gather together all the bankrupt's assets. To this end, he has the job of uncovering fraud and concealment and recovering preferences and fraudulent transfers. In this job he will be assisted, of course, by the attorney he selects.

[¶4002.5]   How the Assets of the Bankrupt Are Distributed

The Act sets up five classes of claims entitled to priority on distribution. Claimants in a lower order of priority get nothing until everyone in the classes ahead have been paid in full. If there's not enough to pay everyone within the same class, then whatever there is will be split on a pro rata or proportional basis among the members of the class. Here are the five priority classes:

(1) Administrative costs (this takes in almost every expense in connection with the proceeding, including fees for the attorney of the bankrupt, the trustee, the petitioning creditors, and the receiver, and commissions for the trustee and receiver).

(2) Wage claims up to the amount of $600 earned within three months (vacation and severance pay may present problems).

(3) Costs and expenses incurred by *creditors* in successfully opposing a discharge or getting it set aside or in getting evidence resulting in conviction of a bankruptcy offense.

(4) Tax claims — federal, state and local — all stand on an equal footing within the class (taxes accruing during bankruptcy will normally be within the first class). (Officers are by tax law now usually personally liable for certain unpaid corporate taxes.)

(5) Debts having priority under federal law and rent claims entitled to priority under state law. The Federal Government and its sureties seem to be the only ones entitled to priority under federal law; it's still an open question whether federal agencies such as FHA and VA come within the law. Rent claim priority is limited to three months' rent due and owing for actual use and occupancy.

[¶4002.6]   Getting Debts Discharged

From the bankrupt's viewpoint, the discharge of his debts is the most important feature of the entire proceedings. He's entitled to a discharge as a matter of right unless proper objections are made and sustained. For everyone but a corporation, adjudication operates as an automatic application for a discharge. A corporation has to file an application within six months of adjudication, otherwise it will lose its right to a discharge. However, this isn't too important in the case of a corporation, because it usually goes out of business anyway, and in practice corporations rarely apply for discharges.

[¶4002.7]   Grounds for Objecting to or Denying Discharge

There are seven grounds for objecting to and denying a discharge:

(1) Commission of criminal bankruptcy offense at any time in any bankruptcy proceeding.

(2) Failure to keep or preserve books or records showing financial condition and business transactions.

(3) Obtaining money or property on credit by false financial statement (applies only to those in business as sole proprietor, partner or corporate executive).

(4) Fraudulent conveyance or concealment of property in year before filing of petition.

(5) Discharge in bankruptcy or confirmation of an arrangement or wage-earner plan during six-year period before filing petition.

(6) Refusal to obey a lawful order of the court or to answer a material question approved by the court.

(7) Failure to explain satisfactorily any loss or deficiency of assets.

We can sum up these seven grounds by saying that a discharge in bankruptcy is available only to an honest debtor who has kept adequate records, cooperated in the bankruptcy proceedings, and hasn't been through bankruptcy proceedings for more than six years.

[¶4003]   REHABILITATION

The financially embarrassed business can get relief under the Bankruptcy Act or by voluntary agreement with creditors.

[¶4003.1]   Voluntary Agreements

We talk here about composition and extensions outside bankruptcy. In this connection, an arrangement under which the debtor is to pay a percentage of his debts is called a "composition." The main idea of an "extension" is that it gives the debtor more time to pay.

Either a composition or an extension involves two agreements: (1) one among two or more creditors and the debtor and (2) one among the creditors themselves.

Why should the creditors want to approach the matter as a group rather than deal with the debtor on an individual basis? There may be a number of reasons, but certainly one of the more important is that, if a single creditor undertakes to collect the full amount owing him, he may precipitate bankruptcy proceedings either by the debtor or the other creditors. In those proceedings, he may have to return to the bankrupt's trustee any payment made by the debtor as an unlawful preference. And if no payment had been made but he had started legal proceedings which gave him sort of a lien, he would find that his lien was of no value to him, having been dissolved by the bankruptcy proceedings. Hence, a creditor might conclude that it would be better for him to try to work out some arrangement with the debtor and the other creditors rather than to engage in a race to collect his individual debt, especially since he could "win" the race in the first instance only to find himself disqualified in the end.

You can't have an effective composition or extension outside bankruptcy proceedings, however, unless all the creditors go along with it or the great majority of creditors are willing to go along with it and to overlook favored treatment to one or more creditors who won't go along. This is because the dissenting creditors won't be bound by the agreement and can proceed to the recovery of the amount due them by legal process. If you want a composition or extension that will bind the dissenters, the only way to get it is through bankruptcy proceedings or special local proceeding.

Effect of Agreement: A voluntary agreement will generally operate to discharge the debtor only when its terms have been carried out. Thus, a failure to pay notes given under the agreement may operate to revive the original debt even though the agreement doesn't expressly provide for its revival.

Care must be exercised to avoid discharging parties secondarily liable with the debtor. An extension of time of payment may, for example, discharge a surety unless he's agreed in advance to permit the extension.

Preferring Creditors: In a composition there's nothing wrong in "preferring" some types of creditors, where the preference has some rational or legal basis — e.g., the creditors "preferred" hold security or are entitled to some type of priority. Also, all the creditors who are parties to the composition should be told about the preference. A secret promise of a preference or other advantage made to one or more creditors will render the agreement fraudulent and void or voidable.

State Insolvency Laws: Before resorting to a composition outside bankruptcy, be sure to check the insolvency laws of your own state. They may operate as a limiting factor in the use of these agreements.

[¶4003.2]   Assignment for the Benefit of Creditors

The distinction between compositions and assignments for the benefit of creditors isn't always clear. One distinction has been said to be that a composition requires the consent of the creditors while an assignment does not.[1] However, as a practical matter you can't have an effective assignment for the benefit of creditors unless the creditors at least passively acquiesce. If the creditors don't go along with the idea, they may be able to treat the assignment as an act of bankruptcy and throw the debtor into bankruptcy proceedings.

There's another big difference between a composition and an assignment. In a composition, the debtor holds on to his business and works out a readjustment of his debts with his creditors. In an assignment, he turns over his business and

---

(1) In Massachusetts consent of the creditors is required.

all his property to an assignee or trustee to be distributed in payment of his debts. Also, a composition contemplates release of the debtor from further liability; not so in the ordinary assignment, although the creditors can, of course, consent to a release or discharge.

In an assignment, the debtor has what is called "a resulting trust in any assets." This may remain after the creditors have been paid. But the debtor has no equity of redemption; that is, he can't come in at any stage after he's made the assignment and get his property back by paying off his creditors, unless, of course, all of them consent.

Local Variations in Law: Local variations in the law governing assignments must be checked out. Here are the main areas to be watched:

(1) Assignment of part of property. (In some states, a partial assignment is void; in others, it's valid if the part not assigned is open to the remedies of all of the creditors.)

(2) What property passes under a general assignment. [Generally, all property, real or personal, tangible or intangible, including goodwill, trademarks (not personal), patents, interest in insurance policies or assignor's life, and rights under trust; but property held in trust and property fraudulently obtained won't pass.]

(3) Necessity of acknowledging, filing or recording assignment. (Many states have provisions.)

(4) Inventory of property assigned and schedule of creditors who are to participate. (These will usually be included in assignment as a matter of course, but state law requirements should be checked for formal requirements.)

(5) Notice to creditors. (Statutes may prescribe time and form.)

(6) Reservation of control by debtor. (Assignment will be invalid if there is reservation of any degree of control. Debtor can't reserve right to revoke or declare future uses or trusts to which assignment is to be subject.)

(7) Reservation of possession. (Some authorities hold that debtor's reservation of possession will invalidate an assignment.)

(8) Intent to hinder or delay creditors. (Assignment made with a view to debtor's own advantage and to hinder and delay creditors in the just enforcement of their claims is vulnerable to attack as fraudulent.)

(9) Preferential treatment of creditors. (While there's nothing wrong with favoring creditors having recognized priorities, don't include a provision that those creditors will be first paid who will accept their pro rata share on condition that receipt constitutes a full release.)

[¶4003.3]   Rehabilitation under Bankruptcy Act

An embarrassed business can ask a bankruptcy court to protect it from its creditors while a plan of payment is worked out. This is done under Chapter XI of the Bankruptcy Act. Only the financially distressed person or company can initiate a Chapter XI proceeding. Unlike Chapter X which is designated as the corporate reorganization statute, creditors cannot invoke Chapter XI.

The debtor comes into bankruptcy court and says, in effect, that he has been operating a business which is worth saving and that he would like to propose a plan to his creditors. However, he needs the court's help for a period of time in which he can work out such a settlement. The court then, in a sense, places a protective umbrella over this particular business venture and has the power to issue orders preventing the entire world from proceeding against that person's property while the arrangement proceeding is pending. A bankruptcy court has the power to authorize the debtor to operate his business during the time that the proceeding is pending.

In some jurisdictions, a bankruptcy court will insist on the appointment of a receiver to operate the business. In other jurisdictions, in accordance with the express mandate of the statute, the court will permit the debtor itself to operate the business under proper court supervision.

[¶4004]   CORPORATE REORGANIZATION

The trouble with Chapter XI proceedings is that they'll deal with unsecured creditors only. A reorganization plan, on the other hand, can deal not only with unsecured creditors, but with security holders as well. But the plan will be subject to closer control and supervision by the court as well as more stringent statutory requirements than a Chapter XI proceeding. And the chances are good that management will have to yield to a trustee or receiver.

[¶4004.1]   Who Can Start Reorganization Proceedings?

Reorganization proceedings can be instituted by the corporation (voluntary) or against it (involuntary) by three or more creditors whose claims total $5,000 or more, are liquidated as to amount, and are not contingent as to liability or by an indenture trustee acting on behalf of the bondholders. If the corporation is to take the initiative, it can only do so with proper corporate authorization — usually a resolution of the board of directors.

[¶4004.2]   Reclamation Proceedings

Reclamation proceedings are a quick way for a third party to get hold of property which belongs to him which is in possession of the trustee. Of couse, in many situations where it is clear that the third pary is entitled to property in possession of the trustee, he's not going to have to start a reclamation proceeding to get it; but if there's any doubt about the matter, chances are he'll resort to reclamation proceedings. He won't necessarily have to if he's the absolute owner of the property, because he'll win out as against a purchaser from the trustee if it comes to that unless, of course, the property in question is an intangible and negotiable. If the claimant holds a security interest only, the trustee won't hand it over if the property is worth more than the claim it secures. In that case he'll ask

the court either to permit the secured creditor to sell the property outside bankruptcy and pay over the excess or to permit sale by the trustee, free and clear, and
give the creditor an interest in the proceeds. The first course is likely to be
followed only where the property in question is at some distant point and can't be
conveniently sold with the other assets.

[¶4004.3]   Allowance Of Claims

At the first meeting of creditors, a provisional allowance of claims will be
made for voting purposes, but this isn't an allowance for purposes of dividend
participation. However, as a general rule, claims filed at or before the first
meeting will be allowed at that time if no objection is raised. If an objection is
raised by either the trustee or one or more creditors, the referee will fix a date to
hear and determine the points raised. There's no time limit on filing objections,
but the referee may in his discretion refuse to entertain objections filed too late.
Secured and priority claims will be allowed only to the extent they're unsecured.
If a creditor has received a transfer, lien or preference which is voidable, his
claim won't be allowed until he surrenders it to the trustee.

41

Budgeting for Profit Planning

[¶4101]

A budget in its simplest terms is an estimate of future events. This is not a purely random guess, but a forecast which is computed from historical data that has been verified and assumed with some degree of credibility. The volume of sales for the following year, for example, may be estimated by using data from past experience, present-day market conditions, buying power of the consumer and other related factors.

Merely preparing the annual budget, then leaving it unaltered for the remainder of the budget period, is not the purpose. Preparation is only the first step. The second step is for management to control the operations of the firm and to adhere to the budget. Budgetary control is the tool of management for carrying out and controlling business operations. It establishes predetermined objectives and provides bases for measuring performance against these objectives. If variations between performance and objective arise, management alters the situation by either correcting the weakness in performance or modifying the budget. Firms that adopt budgetary control have a better control of operations and are better able to modify them to meet expectations.

[¶4101.1] Types of Budgets

There are two principal types of annual profit budgets: the operating or earnings budget and the financial or cash budget. The earnings budget, as its name implies, is an attempt to forecast the earnings of a company for a future period. To make such forecast, other estimates have to be made. Consequently, we have sales budgets, production budgets (which include labor budgets, materials budgets, purchases budgets, capital expenditure budgets, manufacturing expense budgets), administrative expense budgets, distribution expense budgets and appropriation-type budgets (e.g., advertising, research). The accuracy of each of these budgets determines the accuracy of the earnings forecast.

The cash budget, on the other hand, tries to forecast the utilization of the company's cash resources. It estimates the company's anticipated cash expenditures and resources for a period of operation. Cash budget forecasts, like the earnings forecast, depend heavily on sales forecasts. The amount of sales determines the amount of cash the company has for purposes of its operation.

[¶4102] **THE SALES BUDGET**

The foundation of the entire budget program is the sales budget. If anticipated sales of a praticular product (or project) do not exceed the cost to produce and market it by an amount sufficient to reward the investors and to compensate for the risks involved, the product (project) should not be undertaken. Sales forecasting must be continuous. Conditions change rapidly; and in order to direct one's efforts into the most profitable channels, there must be a continuous review and revision of the methods employed.

[¶4102.1] **Forecasting Sales**

A sales forecast represents the revenue side of the earnings forecast. It is a prediction as to the sales quantity and sales revenue. Sales forecasts are made for both short and long periods.

Forecasting sales with any degree of accuracy is not an easy task. For example, a firm which estimates sales with the expectation that a patent which it holds will not become obsolete may be disappointed.

In general, the business forecaster has two situations: (1) those which he can to some extent control and (2) those which he can only observe, record, interpret, and apply his own situation to conditions created by others. A firm that has a monopoly due to an important patent which it owns is an example of a company which controls the situation. Forecasts made by such a company may be very accurate. In most cases, however, a company has no such control. It must attempt to interpret general conditions, the situation in its own industry, and future sales of its particular company before making forecasts.

Making the forecast is the responsibility of the sales manager, who, with the help of the district managers and the individual salesmen, determines the primary sales objectives for the year. Corrections of the forecasts are made by the heads of the firm so that sales estimates will better reflect expected economic conditions. As conditions change, the forecast is revised.

In forecasting sales, one should not be afraid of being out of step with the crowd. As an example, there have been numerous occasions where a decline in the stock market was accompanied by a rise in business.

Before an estimate of sales is made, you must be reasonably sure that it is attainable. It must be based on the best evidence available.

If a firm desires to sell more than in the past, an analysis of past sales performances must be supplemented by other analyses. Consideration must be given to general business conditions. The effects of political and economic changes throughout the world are quickly reflected on individual business communities. Some of these factors which affect sales are wars, government regulations, and technological developments. This information should be used in appraising the probable effect of these changes on the sales of the firm for the budget period.

Market Analysis: A sales manager needs to know if his firm is getting its full share of potential customer demand as indicated by a market analysis.

The questionnaire is a popular method of reaching consumers, retailers and jobbers. Data collected gives the firm valuable information, essential at arriving at a forecast of sales possibilities.

A market analysis at a given time gives a picture of the present and potential consumption of a product. This picture provides only half the significant information. The other half can be obtained by continuing the survey over a period of time to discover market trends.

Pricing Policy: The sales budget is not complete until the firm decides on a practical policy as to what price can be secured for its product(s). Generally, estimates should be made to conform with the market prices during the budget period.

The next step is to formulate the sales policies of the firm. These policies should be established relative to such considerations as territorial expansion and selection, customer selection, types and quality of products and service, prices, terms of sales and sales organization and responsibility.

Only after a firm has thoroughly analyzed past sales experience, general business conditions, market potentials, the product to be sold and prices and has formulated its sales policies is it ready to develop the sales program.

Measuring Individual Performance: As a basis for measuring individual performance, a rewarding-merit sales standard could be established. A sales standard is an opinion of the best qualified judgment of performance which may reasonably be achieved under ideal conditions. By comparing this standard with the budget estimate (the figure expected) under normal conditions, management has provided the most important tool of sales control.

An example of how a comparison between the standard and budget estimate may serve as a basis for reward is the following: A salesman may be told to produce sales of $150,000 (standard), but the firm may expect him to produce sales of only $125,000 (budget estimate). The salesman does not have to be told what the firm's budget figures are. In his endeavor to reach $150,000, he is trying to better what he believes is the budget figure. Depending on how close he comes to the $150,000, the firm may devise a method of rewarding him. It should be kept in mind, however, that the standard should not be set too high, since it may have a reverse effect if the salesman feels it is unreachable.

[¶4103] THE PRODUCTION BUDGET

After the sales budget has been prepared, the next step is to prepare the production budget which specifies the quantity and timing of production requirements.

While the sales budget is prepared in anticipation of seasonal fluctuations, the production budget endeavors to smooth out the fluctuations and thus make most effective use of productive capacity. This is accomplished by manufacturing for stock over the slow periods and using the stock to cover sales during busy periods.

There are different problems for a firm that sells stock products and one that produces special-order goods. The objective for a stock-order-type firm is to coordinate sales and production to prevent excessive inventories but at the same time to have enough stock to meet sales. A forecast of production in such a firm should enable the executive to arrange to lay out the factory so as to handle the anticipated volume most conveniently. Production in such a firm must be as evenly distributed as possible over the year. It is uneconomical to manufacture the whole period's requirements within a relatively short period at the beginning of the budget period. This involves unduly heavy capital costs of carrying the large inventory. Also, distributing the work over the entire period spreads the labor costs.

With special-order items, the production department has to be prepared at all times to manufacture the goods as soon as possible after receiving the order. Production in this case has to be arranged for the best possible utilization of equipment and labor, so that idle time is reduced to a minimum.

[¶4103.1] Budgeting Production Costs

Production budgets should be rigid as long as conditions remain the same, but they should be capable of prompt adjustment when circumstances change. For example, if a company operates at 70% of capacity in a period and the budget was based on a production volume of 80%, the budget is of little use. The budget will have to be altered to show what production costs will be at the 70% level. It is prudent when planning production at a particular anticipated percentage level to indicate in the budget the estimates of possible production costs at different levels.

[¶4103.2] Preparing the Production Budget

The production budget period may vary in length. However, it is common practice among large corporations to use what is known as a ''product year.'' As an example, the automobile industry will usually start with the introduction of new models. The budget year should include at least one complete cycle of operations so that money tied up in raw materials and work-in process materials may undergo one complete liquidation. Another factor influencing the budget period is the stability of general business condtions. It is more difficult to budget operations during an unstable period, and it is advisable at these times to shorten the budget period.

The production budget should be expressed in terms of physical units. To compute the physical quantities is simple. For example, a simple computation to estimate production required is:

	Units ·
Estimated sales	250,000
Less opening inventory	150,000
Total requirements	100,000
Add: Closing inventory	100,000
Production required	200,000

Before computing the quantity to be produced, it is necessary to decide quantities to be in the inventory at the end of the period. This decision should be based on factors such as:

(a) Adequate inventory to meet sales demands
(b) Evenly distributed production to prevent shortage of material and labor
(c) Danger of obsolescence
(d) High costs of storing large inventories.

Available Facilities: The production program must conform with the plant facilities available and should determine the most economical use of these facilities. The capacity of the plant is measured in two ways: maximum plant capacity and normal plant capacity. All other measurements are in percentages of maximum or normal capacity. Maximum capacity, of course, can never actually be attained. There are many unavoidable interruptions, such as waiting for setup of machines; time to repair machines; lack of help, tools, materials; holidays; inefficiency; etc. However, these interruptions should be looked into to determine how they can be minimized.

Management should also consider whether additional equipment is needed just to meet temporary sales demands. Later, such equipment may be idle. The replacement of old machinery with new high-speed equipment should also be considered. A careful study should help determine which step would be more profitable in the long run.

Records for each product showing the manufacturing operations necessary and a record of each machine showing the operations capable of being performed by the machine together with its capacity should be kept. Estimates must be made of material to be used, number of labor hours and quantities of service (power) required for each product. These estimates are called "standards of production performance." The establishment of these standards is an engineering rather than an accounting task. In this respect, these standards are similar to those used in standard cost accounting.

Cost of Production: The following is an illustration of how cost of production is determined: Assume a concern has a normal capacity of 100 units of product. Current production budget calls for 80 units. Only one product is made; and its production requires two operations, A and B. The standard costs are: variable costs per unit of product, one unit of direct material, $2; operation A (direct labor and overhead), $3; operation B (direct labor and overhead), $5; total $10. Fixed production costs for the budget period are $500, or $5 per unit based on normal capacity. This production cost budget would then be expressed as follows:

Variable costs (80 units @ $10)	$ 800
Fixed costs (80 units @ $5)	400
Costs chargeable to production	1,200
Cost of idle capacity (500 less 400)	100
Total budgeted costs	$1,300

There is a tie-in here between estimated costs, standard costs, and production budgets.

[¶4103.3]   Materials Budget

The purpose of the materials budget is to be sure that there are sufficient materials to meet the requirements of the production budget. This budget deals with the materials for the purchase of raw materials, and finished parts and controls the inventory. How to estimate the material required depends on the nature of the individual company. A company manufacturing standard articles can estimate fairly accurately the amount of raw materials and the purchases required for the production program. Even where the articles are not standard, there is usually a reliable relationship between the volume of business handled and the requirements for the principal raw materials.

Tie-In to Standard Costs: In the preparation of the material budget, there is a tie-in to standard costs. Here is an example of how purchase requirements are computed:

Quantity required for production	300,000 units
Desired inventory at end of budget period	75,000 units
Total requirements	375,000 units
Less: Inventory at beginning of period	80,000 units
Purchase requirements	295,000 units

The next step is to express material requirements in terms of prices. Some firms establish standard prices based on what are considered normal prices. Differences between standard and actual purchase prices are recorded as a price variance.

Factors Affecting Policy: These are

(1) The time it takes the material to be delivered after the purchase order is issued.

(2) The rate of consumption of material as indicated by the production budget.

(3) The amount of stock that should be on hand to cover possible delays in inventory of raw materials.

On the basis of these factors, the purchasing department working with the production department can establish figures of minimum stocks and order quantities of raw materials and parts for each product handled. Purchases in large quantities are advisable if price advantages can be obtained. Bulk purchases are advisable during periods of rising prices but not during periods of declining prices. The unavoidable time lag between order and delivery of the material is also a reason to buy in advance.

Buying in advance does not necessarily involve immediate delivery. The deliveries may be spread over the budget period in order to coordinate purchases with production and to control inventory. To control inventory, it is desirable to establish minimum and maximum quantities for each material to be carried. The lower limit is the smallest amount which can be carried without risk of production delays. If materials can be obtained quickly, the inventory can be held near the lower limit. The advantage of keeping inventory at this lower limit is that it minimizes the cost of storage and possible obsolescence. If materials cannot be obtained quickly, there is the possibility of a rise in prices, and so it is advisable to carry more than minimum inventory.

Goods in Process: The time it takes for material to enter the factory and emerge as a finished product is frequently much longer than necessary for efficient production. Comparisons with other companies may reveal that a firm allows its goods to remain in process much longer than other firms. Investigations should be made to determine the causes of such delays and formulate remedies. These investigations are usually made in connection with the production budget.

Finished Goods: The budget of finished goods inventory is based on the sales budget. For example, if 100 units of an item are expected to be sold during the budget period, the problem is to determine how much must be kept in stock to support such a sales program. Since it is difficult to determine the exact quantity customers will demand each day, the finished goods inventory must maintain a margin of safety so that satisfactory deliveries can be made. Once this margin is established, the production and purchasing programs can be developed to replenish the stock as needed.

[¶4104]   **THE LABOR BUDGET**

The labor budget deals only with direct labor. Indirect labor is included in the manufacturing expense budget. (The manufacturing expense budget include the group of expenses which include, in addition to indirect labor, expenses such as indirect material, repairs and maintenance, depreciation and insurance.)

The purpose of the labor budget is to ascertain the number and kind of workers needed to execute the production program during the budget period. The labor budget should indicate the necessary man-hours and the cost of labor required for the manufacture of the products in the quantities shown by the production budget.

[¶4104.1]   Preparation of the Labor Budget

The preparation of a labor budget begins with an estimate of the number of labor hours required for the anticipated quantity of products. Before this can be done, it is necessary to know the quantity of items that are going to be produced. This information comes from the production budget. If the products are uniform and standard labor time allowances have been established, it is just a matter of multiplying the production called for by the standards to determine the labor hours required. If the products are not uniform but there is uniformity of operations, it is first necessary to translate production into operation requirements. Operation standards then should be established in terms of man- or machine-hours. The quantity of labor required may then be ascertained.

The next step in preparing the labor budget is to estimate the cost of direct labor. These estimates are computed by multiplying the number of units to be produced by the labor costs per unit. The problem then is to predetermine the unit labor costs. Some of the methods of determining these costs are:

(1)   Day rate system;

(2)   Piece rate system;

(3)   Bonus system.

In firms where standard labor costs have been established for the products manufactured, it is necessary only to multiply the units of the product called for in the production budget by the standard labor costs.

A detailed analysis should frequently be made of the differences between actual and estimated labor costs. These should be investigated to determine whether they are justified. An investigation may reveal inefficient workers, wasted time, defective materials, idle time, poor working conditions, high price workers, etc. Responsibility must be definitely placed and immediate action taken to correct those factors which are capable of being controlled.

The budgets for direct labor and manufacturing expenses are not complete until schedules of the final estimates are prepared. The form will vary, depending on the needs of the firm. The following is an example of a schedule of estimated direct labor costs where estimates are shown for each department of the firm:

X CORPORATION

ESTIMATED DIRECT LABOR COSTS
FOR THE PERIOD 1/1/xx to 12/31/xx

Dept.	Quantity to Be Produced	Standard Labor Cost per Unit	Total Estimated Labor Cost
1	127,600	$ .90	$115,000
2	127,600	1.60	204,000
3	127,600	1.12	143,000
		$3.62	$462,000

[¶4105]   CAPITAL EXPENDITURES BUDGET

Since capital expenditures represent a large part of the total investment of a manufacturing concern, the capital expense budget is of great importance. Unwise capital expenditures can seldom be corrected without serious loss to stockholders. The purpose of the capital expenditures budget is to subject such expenditures to careful examination and so avoid mistakes that cannot easily be corrected.

A carefully prepared capital expenditures budget should point out the effect of such expenditures on the cash position of the company and on future earnings. For example, too large a portion of total assets invested in fixed plant and equipment sooner or later may result in an unhealthy financial condition because of the lack of necessary working capital.

[¶4105.1]   Preparation of Capital Expenditures Budget

In preparing the capital expenditures budget, the following information is recorded:

(1) The amount of machinery, equipment, etc., on hand at the beginning of the budget period;

(2) Additions planned for the period;

(3) Withdrawals expected for the period;

(4) The amount of machinery, equipment, etc., expected at the end of the budget period.

Consideration should be given to estimates of additions planned for the period. Additions will be justified if they increase the volume of production and earnings, will reduce unit costs, and the money needed can be spared. Consideration should also be given to the percentage investment for fixed assets as compared with net worth of the firm for a number of years. Various business authorities have realized that an active business enterprise with a tangible net worth between $50,000 and $250,000 should have as a maximum not more than two-thirds of its tangible net worth in fixed assets. Where the tangible net worth is in excess of $250,000, not more than 75% of the tangible net worth should be represented by fixed assets. When these percentages are greatly exceeded, annual depreciation charges tend to be too heavy, the net working capital too moderate, and liabilities expand too rapidly for the good health of the business. Alternative leasing should be considered.

The capital expenditures budget should include estimates not only for the budget period, but long-range estimates covering a period of many years. The ideal situation is where machinery is purchased at a time when prices are low. A long-range capital expenditures budget will indicate what machinery will be of use in the future. Then, machinery may be acquired when prices are considered low. Inefficient or obsolete machines can sometimes be made into satisfactory units by rebuilding them. If it is estimated that gains derived from rebuilding machinery will exceed the costs, then provision should be made in the capital expenditures budget to incur these expenses. Such expenditures are frequently called betterments and prolong the useful life of the machines. The preparation of detailed and accurate records is an essential part of the capital expenditures budget. The following information should be included in such a record:

(1) Description of machines;

(2) Date of requisition;

(3) Cost for depreciation rate.

From the above information, it is a simple matter to complete the depreciation for the budget period.

As with other budgets, actual expenditures should be compared with the estimates, and any variation should be analyzed. In addition, a statement should be prepared showing the extent to which actual results obtained from the use of certain capital expenditures are in line with expectations. This is particularly important where substantial investments are made in labor-saving equipment, new processes or new machines.

[¶4106] **THE CASH BUDGET**

The cash budget is a composite reflection of all the operating budgets in terms of cash receipts and disbursements. Its purpose is to determine the cash resources that will be available during the entire budget program so that the company will know in advance whether it can carry out its program without borrowing or obtaining new capital or whether it will need to obtain additional capital from these sources. Thus, the company can arrange in advance for any necessary borrowing, avoiding emergencies and, more importantly, a cash crisis caused by a shortage.

A knowledgeable financial man goes into the market to borrow money when he can get the cheapest rate. The cash budget will tell the manager when he will need to borrow so he can plan accordingly. In a like manner, he can foresee when he will have sufficient funds to repay loans.

A cash budget is very important to a firm which does installment selling. Installment selling ties up cash resources, and a careful analysis of estimated future collections is needed to forecast the cash position of the company.

Other purposes of the cash budget are: (1) to provide for seasonal fluctuations in business which make heavy demands on funds to carry large inventories and receivables; (2) to assist the financial executive in having funds available to meet maturing obligations; (3) to aid in securing credit from commercial banks; the bank is more likely to lend funds for a definite plan that has been prepared, indicating when and how the funds will be repaid; and (4) to indicate the amount of funds available for investments, when available and for what duration.

[¶4106.1]   Preparation of the Cash Budget

The main difference between a cash budget and other budgets is that in the cash budget all estimates are based on the dates when it is expected cash will be received or paid. Other budgets are prepared on the basis of the accrual of the different items (for accrual-basis companies). Therefore, in the cash budget, the budget executive cannot base the estimate of cash receipts directly on the sales budget for the obvious reason that all the cash will not be received from such sales in the same month in which they are billed. This, of course, is not true in the case of a business on a strictly cash basis. Depreciation is another item handled differently in the cash budget. Depreciation is a cost of doing business and as such increases expenses and reduces net income for financial reporting purposes. It is not, however, a cash item and is ignored in preparing the cash budget. On the other hand, the amount paid for a new plant or equipment in a single year or budget period is included in full in the cash budget.

Cash receipts of a typical firm come from cash sales, collections on accounts and notes receivable, interest, dividends, rent, sale of capital assets and loans. The cash sale estimate is taken from the sales budget. The estimate of collections on accounts should be based on the sales budget and company experience in making collections. With concerns whose sales are made largely on account, the collection experience should be ascertained with considerable care. As an illustration, assume the March account sales have actually been collected as follows:

Month	%
March	6.4
April	80.1
May	8.5
June	3.6
Cash Discount Taken	1.1
Bad Debts Loss	.3
Total	100.00

If the same experience is recorded for each month of the year, it is possible to resolve the sales estimates into a collection budget. It is sometimes desirable to develop the experience separately for different classes of customers for different geographical areas. Once these figures are ascertained, they should be tested from time to time.

Cash disbursements in a typical firm are made for payroll, materials, operating expenses, taxes, interest, purchases of equipment, repayment of loans, payment of dividends, etc. With a complete operating budget on hand, there is little difficulty in estimating the amount of cash that will be required and when it will be required. Wages and salaries are usually paid in cash and on definite dates. For purchases of material (from the materials budget), the purchasing department can readily indicate the time allowed for payments. Operating expenses must be considered individually. Some items, such as insurance, are prepaid. Others, such as commissions, are accrued. So, cash payments may not coincide with charges on the operating budget.

[¶4107] MANUFACTURING EXPENSE BUDGET

In preparing the manufacturing expense budget, estimates and probable expenses should be prepared by persons responsible to authorize expenditures. The general responsibility for variable expenses lies with the production manager. But the immediate responsibility for many of these expenses lies with the foremen of the several departments. Generally, expenses are estimated by those who control them. Each person who prepares a portion of the manufacturing expense budget is furnished with data of prior periods and any plans for the budget period which may affect the amount of expenses. With these data we can decide:

(1) Which, if any, of present expenses can be eliminated.

(2) Probable effect of the sales and production forecasts on those expenses which must be incurred.

No plans for the elimination or reduction of variable expenses should be made unless it is certain that the plan can be enforced.

The responsiblilty for many fixed manufacturing expenses is with the general executives. Such fixed expenses include long-term leases, pension plans, patents, amortization, salaries of major production executives, etc.

In preparing the budget estimates of manufacturing expenses, a common practice is to use percentages. Each expense is taken as a percent of sales or production costs. For, example, if a certain expense is estimated to be 5% of sales, this percentage is applied to the sales estimate to obtain the amount of this expense. The fallacy with this method is that all expenses do not vary proportionately with sales or production. A sounder method of estimating manufacturing expenses is to give individual expenses separate treatment. In estimating the indirect labor expense, it is important to first analyze the expense for the period preceding the budget period. The requirements for additional help or the possibility of eliminating some of the help should be considered, along with plans for increasing or decreasing any of the rates of compensation. Detailed schedules should be prepared, showing the nature of each job and the amount to be paid. By summarizing these schedules, an aggregate estimate can be determined. Indirect materials expense should be estimated by first analyzing the amount consumed in prior periods. This, together with the production budget showing the proposed volume for the period budget, serves as a basis for estimating the quantities of the indirect material requirements. The probable cost of such requirements estimated by the purchasing department is the amount to be shown in the manufacturing expense budget. Repairs and maintenance estimates are based on past experience data, supplemented by a report on the condition of the present equipment. If any additional equipment is to be installed during the budget period, recognition must be given to the prospect of additional repairs and maintenance charges. Electric power expense is in direct proportion to the production volume. The charges for depreciation of equipment can be estimated with considerable accuracy. Insurance expense for the budget period is estimated on the basis of the insurance in force charged to production with adjustments made for contemplated changes in equipment, inventories, or coverage of hazard incident to manufacturing.

To budget manufacturing expenses effectively it is important to establish standard overhead rates.

At frequent intervals during the budget period, comparision should be made between the actual expenses in each department and the amount estimated to be spent for actual production during the period. Variations should be investigated and steps taken to correct weaknessses in the production program.

A distinction should be made between controllable and uncontrollable expenses so that the responsibility of individuals can be more closely determined. To facilitate the estimating of expenses, a further distinction is made between fixed and variable expenses. Fixed expenses are those which remain the same regardless of the variations in sales or production. Variable expenses are those which increase or decrease proportionally with changes in volume, sales or production. Maintenance is seldom treated in a separate budget. It is usually regarded as part of the manufacturing expense budget.

Here is an example of a Schedule of Estimated Manufacturing Expenses for each operation of a particular product:

Y CORPORATION
FOR THE YEAR ENDED 12/31/xx

	Total	Operation 1	Operation 2	Operation 3
Variable expenses:				
Indirect materials	$ 20,000	$ 5,000	$ 10,000	$ 5,000
Indirect labor	100,000	10,000	15,000	75,000
Light and power	30,000	5,000	13,000	12,000
Telephone	5,000	3,000	—0—	2,000

	Total	Operation 1	Operation 2	Operation 3
Fixed and semivariable:				
Factory rent	50,000	14,000	18,000	18,000
Superintendence	100,000	30,000	35,000	35,000
Depreciation	100,000	20,000	60,000	20,000
General and				
administrative expense	50,000	12,000	17,000	21,000
Total	$455,000	$ 99,000	$168,000	$188,000

After estimates of materials, direct labor and manufacturing expenses have been prepard, a Schedule of Estimated Cost of Production may be prepared as follows:

Z CORPORATION
FOR THE YEAR ENDED 12/31/xx

	Total	Product A	Product B	Product C
Cost Element:				
Materials	$200,000	$ 80,000	$ 50,000	$ 70,000
Labor	340,000	100,000	80,000	160,000
Manufacturing expenses	70,000	30,000	30,000	10,000
Total	$610,000	$210,000	$160,000	$240,000

[¶4108] BREAK-EVEN POINT ANALYSIS

One type of budget which provides useful supplementary statistics is the break-even analysis. Although a complete and adequate budget may be developed without using a break-even analysis, its use adds to the understanding of estimates.

The break-even point is that amount of sales necessary to yield neither income nor loss. If sales should be less than indicated by the break-even point, a loss would result.

Where the total cost of goods sold and other expenses is less than sales and if this total varied in direct proportion to sales, operations would always result in net income. For example, in a company in which the cost of goods sold and expenses amounts to $1.80 per unit sold and the sale price is $2, on the first unit there would be net income of 20°. On a million items, the net income would amount to $200,000.

As a practical matter, the simple example cited above is not realistic. The reason is that although some expenses may vary with volume of sales (e.g., salesmen's commissions, traveling expenses, advertising , telephone, delivery costs, postage, supplies, etc.), there are many other types of expenses which are not affected by the variations in sales. These expenses are called "fixed" expenses. Examples are depreciation, rent, insurance, heat, etc.

If, going back to the above illustration, we assume that fixed costs and expenses amount to $40,000, we have at least $40,000 of costs and expenses before even one unit is sold. If we sell a million units, however, we have an income before deducting fixed expenses of $200,000. After fixed expenses, our net income is $160,000. So, our income picture goes from a loss of $40,000 (where no units are produced) to a profit of $160,000 (where one million units are produced). Somewhere between these, however, is a point represented by a certain number of units at which we will have neither income nor loss— the break-even point.

[¶4108.1]   How to Compute the Break-Even Point

Here is how we determine the break-even point. Let S equal the sales at the break-even point. Since sales at this point are equal to the total fixed costs and expenses ($40,000) plus variable costs and expenses ($1.80 per unit or 90% of sales),

$$S = \$\ 40,000 + .9S$$
$$S - .9S = \$\ 40,000$$
$$.1S = \$\ 40,000$$
$$S = \$400,000$$

Even the above illustration oversimplifies the problem. It makes the assumption that all costs and expenses can be classified as either *fixed* or *variable*. However, in actual operations, expenses classified as fixed expenses may become variable where sales increase beyond a certain point, and some variable expenses may not vary in direct proportion to the sales.

Rent expense, for example, may not always be a fixed expense. A substantial increase in sales may create a need for additional showroom or salesroom space or, perhaps, salesmen's offices, or salesmen's commissions may rise unexpectedly when they have gone above a certain quota.

Then, there are types of hybrid expenses which may be classified as *semifixed*. For example, executives' salaries, association dues, subscriptions to periodicals and many other expenses are not in proportion to sales. Another unreality in the above problem is that as sales increase, there is a likelihood that sale prices will decrease because of larger orders. Now let's take a look at another situation:

Net sales		$2.500,000
Costs and expenses:		
Fixed	$ 250,000	
Variable	1,500,000	1,750,000
Net income		$ 750,000

This company currently has under consideration an investment in a new plant which will cause an increase in its fixed expenses of $200,000.

The present break-even point is as follows:

$$S = \$ \ 250,000 + .6S$$
$$S - .6S = \$ \ 250,000$$
$$.4S = \$ \ 250,000$$
$$S = \$ \ 625,000$$

If the company builds the plant, the break-even calcuation will be:

$$S = \$ \ 450,000 + .6S$$
$$S - .6S = \$ \ 450,000$$
$$.4S = \$ \ 450,000$$
$$S = \$1,125,000$$

If the plant expansion is undertaken, then the sales must be increased by $500,000 for the company to maintain its net income of $750,000, as follows:

$$S = \$450,000 + .6S + \$750,000$$
$$S - .6S = \$1,200,000$$
$$.4S = \$1,200,000$$
$$S = \$3,000,000$$
$$\text{Increase} = \$500,000 \ (\$3,000,000 \ \text{less} \ \$2,500,000)$$

Now let's analyze the situation under two alternatives. The maximum production with the present plant is 1,500,000 units. At an average sale price of $2 per unit, sales would be $3,000,000. With the new plant, sales are estimated to hit $5,000,000 (2,500,000 units @ $2 per unit).

	Without New Plant	With New Plant
Net sales	$3,000,000	$5,000,000
Less: Fixed costs and expenses	250,000	450,000
	2,750,000	4,550,000
Less: Variable costs and expenses (60% of sales)	1,800,000	3,000,000
Net income	$ 950,000	$1,550,000

If the sales do not increase, the increase in fixed costs and expenses of $200,000 would cut the net income to $550,000. The break-even point will have been boosted $500,000, and the sales will have to be increased by this amount to produce the current $750,000 of income. Alternatively, the net income can be increased by $600,000 if the sales figure is increased by $2,000,000. Although these figures are based on an assumption that all costs and expenses are fixed or variable, the break-even analysis focuses attention on the factors involved in costs and income and provides a basis for consideration of various problems.

42

Financial Statement Analysis

[¶4201]

Analysis techniques applied to financial statements are of interest to the corporate financial officer in a number of instances. For one thing, his own company's financial statements will be subject to analysis by creditors, credit grantors, and investors. Furthermore, he will want to analyze his own company's statements for internal management use. Also, he may be called upon to analyze other companies' financial statements for credit purposes and perhaps for investment purposes (where an acquisition is being considered).

[¶4202] **BASIC ANALYSIS TECHNIQUES**

Much of the analytical data obtained from the statements are expressed in terms of ratios and percentages. (Usually carrying calculations to one decimal place is sufficient for most analysis puposes.) The basic analysis technique is to use these ratios and percentages in either a *horizontal* or *vertical* analysis, or both.

Horizontal Analysis: Here, we compare similar figures from several years' financial statements. For example, we can run down two years' balance sheets and compare the current assets, plant assets, current liabilities, long-term liabilities, etc., on one balance sheet with the similar items on the other and note the amount and percentage increases or decreases for each item. Of course, the comparison can be for more than two years. A number of years may be used, each year being compared with the base year or the immediate preceding year.

Vertical Analysis: Here, we compare component parts to the totals in a single statement. For example, we can determine what percentage each item of expense on the income statement is of the total net sales. Or we can determine what percentage of the total assets the current assets comprise.

324

Ratios: Customarily, the *numerator* of the equation is expressed first, then the denominator. For example, fixed assets to equity means fixed assets *divided by* equity. Also, whenever the numerator is the larger figure, there is a tendency to use the word "turnover" for the result.

As indicated above, these techniques are widely used, generally in the course of one analysis.

[¶4203] BALANCE SHEET ANALYSIS

The significance of the balance sheet is that it shows relationships between classes of assets and liabilities. From long experience, businessmen have learned that certain relationships indicate the company is in actual or potential trouble or is in good financial shape. For example, they may indicate that the business is short of working capital, is undercapitalized generally, or has a bad balance between short- and long-term debt.

It must be emphasized that there are no fixed rules concerning the relationships. There are wide variations between industries and even within a single industry. It is often more valuable to measure these relationships against the past history of the same company than to use them in comparison with other businesses. If sharp disparities do show, however, it is usually wise not to ignore them. Many of the so-called "excesses" that in the past have led to recessions often show up in the balance sheets of individual companies. The most important balance sheet ratios and their implications for the business are discussed below.

[¶4203.1] Ratio Of Current Assets to Current Liabilities

This ratio (the *current ratio*) is probably the best known. It measures the ability of the business to meet its current liabilities. The current ratio indicates the extent to which the current liabilities are covered. For example, if current assets total $400,000 and current liabilities are $100,000, the current ratio is 4 to 1.

Good current ratios will range from about 2 to almost 4 to 1. However, the ratio will vary widely in different industries. For example, companies which collect quickly on their accounts and do not have to carry very large inventories can usually operate with a smaller current ratio than those companies whose collections are slower and inventories larger.

If current liabilities are subtracted from current assets, the resulting figure is the *working capital* of the company — in other words, the amount of free capital which is immediately available for use in the business. Probably the most significant reason for the failure of small businesses is the lack of working capital, which makes it difficult or impossible for the business to cope with sudden changes in economic conditions.

The details of working capital flow are presented in the two-year comparative Statement of Changes in Financial Position which is now a mandatory part of the financial statements.

An important feature of the ratios to remember:
When you *decrease* both factors by the *same* amount, you *increase* the ratio:

	OLD	CHANGE	NEW
Current Assets	$100,000	$(25,000)	$75,000
Current Liabilities	50,000	(25,000)	25,000
Working Capital	$ 50,000	0-	$50,000
Ratio	2 to 1		3 to 1

By paying off $25,000 worth of liabilities (depleting Cash), you have increased the ratio to *3 to 1* from *2 to 1*. Note that the *dollar* amount of *working capital* remains the same $50,000.

Conversely, should you borrow $50,000 on short-terms (increasing Cash and Current Liabilities), you would *reduce* the ratio to *1½ to 1* ($150,000/100,000), again with the dollar amount of working capital remaining at $50,000.

A variation of the current ratio is the *acid test*. This is the ratio of *quick assets* (cash, marketable securities, and accounts receivable) to *current liabilities*. This ratio eliminates the inventory from the calcuation, since inventory may actually not have ready convertibility to cash.

[¶4203.2] Ratio of Current Liabilities to Stockholders' Equity

This ratio measures the relationship between the short-term creditors of the business and the owners. Heavy short-term debt is frequently a danger sign, since it means that the short-term creditors are providing much or all of the company's working capital. If anything happens to frighten the short-term creditors, they will demand immediate repayment and thus create the risk of insolvency. Short-term creditors are most often suppliers of the business, and the company's obligation to them is listed under accounts payable. However, short-term creditors may also include short-term lenders.

A general rule occasionally cited for this ratio is that for a business with a tangible capital and earnings (net worth) of less than $250,000, current liabilities should not exceed two-thirds of this tangible net worth. For companies having a tangible net worth over $250,000, current liabilities should not exceed three-fourths of tangible net worth.

Tangible net worth is used instead of total net worth because intangible assets (such as patents and copyrights) may have no actual market value if the company is forced to offer them in distress selling.

[¶4203.3] Ratio of Total Liabilities to Stockholders' Equity

The ratio differs from the preceding one only in that it includes long-term liabilities. Since the long-term creditors of a company are normally not in a position to demand immediate payment, as are short-term creditors, this ratio may be moderately greater than the preceding one without creating any danger for the company. However, the ratio should never exceed 100%. If it did, this would mean that the company's creditors have a larger stake in the enterprise than the owners themselves. Under such circumstances, it is very likely that credit would not be renewed when the existing debts matured.

[¶4203.4] Ratio of Fixed Assets to Stockholder's Equity

The purpose of this ratio is to measure the relationship between fixed and current assets. The ratio is obtained by dividing the book value of the fixed assets by the tangible value of stockholders' equity. A rule sometimes used is that if tangible net worth is under $250,000, fixed assets should not exceed two-thirds of tangible net worth. If tangible net worth is over $250,000, fixed assets should not exceed three-fourths of tangible net worth.

[¶4203.5] Ratio of Fixed Assets to Long-Term Liabilities

Since long-term notes and bonds are often secured by mortgages on fixed assets, a comparison of the fixed assets with the long-term liabilities reveals what "coverage" the note or bondholders have — i.e., how much protection they have for their loans by way of security. Furthermore, where the fixed assets exceed the long-term liabilities by a substantial margin, there is room for borrowing additional long-term funds on the strength of the fixed asset position.

[¶4203.6] Ratio of Cost of Goods Sold to Inventory— Inventory Turnover

One of the most frequent causes of business failure is lack of inventory control. A firm, optimistic about future business, may build up its inventory to greater than usual amounts. Then, if the expected business does not materialize, the company will be forced to stop further buying and may also have difficulty paying its creditors. In addition, if a company is not selling off its inventory regularly, that item, or part of it, is not really a *current* asset. Also, there may be a considerable amount of unsalable inventory included in the total. For all these reasons, a business is interested in knowing how often the inventory "turns over" during the year. In other words, how long will the current inventory be on the shelves, and how soon will it be turned into money?

To find out how often inventory turns over, we compare the average inventory to the cost of goods sold shown on the income statement. (Typically, average is computed by adding opening and closing inventories and dividing the total by two.) For example, if average inventory is $2,000,000 and cost of goods sold adds up to $6,000,000, we have in the course of the year paid for three times the average inventory. So we can say the inventory turned over three times. In other words, at year-end we had about a four months' supply of inventory on hand.

Another way to measure the same results is by using the ratio of net sales to inventory. In this ratio, net sales is substituted for cost of goods sold. Since net sales will always be a larger figure (because it includes the business's profit margin), the resulting inventory turnover will be a higher figure.

[¶4203.7]   Ratio of Inventory to Working Capital

This is another ratio to measure over- or under-inventory. Working capital is current assets minus current liabilities. If inventory is too high a proportion of working capital, the business is short on quick assets — cash and accounts receivable. A general rule for this ratio is that businesses of tangible net worth of less than $250,000 should not have an inventory which is more than three-fourths of net working capital. For a business with tangible net worth in excess of $250,000, inventory should not exceed net working capital. The larger-size business can tolerate a condition where there are no quick assets because its larger inventory can be borrowed against; and, in addition, it presumably has fixed assets which can be mortgaged if necessary.

[¶4203.8]   Average Collection Period

An important consideration for any business is the length of time it takes to collect its accounts receivable. The longer accounts receivable are outstanding, the greater the need for the business to raise working capital from other sources. In addition, a longer collection period increases the risk of bad debts. A general rule for measuring the collection period is that it should not be more than one-third greater then the net selling terms offered by the company. For example, if goods are sold on terms of 30 days net, the average collection period should be about 45 days, though this varies from industry to industry. Special rules apply in the case installment selling.

Another way of measuring the collection rate of accounts receivable is to divide the net sales by the average accounts receivable. This gives us the accounts receivable turnover; i.e., how many times during the year the average accounts receivable were collected. A comparison with prior years reveals whether the company's collection experience is getting better or worse.

[¶4203.9]   Ratio of Net Sales to Stockholders' Equity

A company acquires assets in order to produce sales which yield a profit. If tangible assets yield too few sales, the company is suffering from underselling; i.e., the under-utilization of its assets. On the other hand, the company may suffer from overtrading; i.e., too many sales in proportion to its tangible net worth. In other words, there is too heavy a reliance on borrowed funds to generate sales.

Another way of measuring the effective utilization of assets is to determine the ratio of net sales to total assets (excluding long-term investments).

In either case, comparisons of these ratios with similar ratios of other companies in the same industry can indicate the relative efficiency in utilization of assets of the company being analyzed.

¶4203.10]   Ratio of Net Sales to Working Capital

This is similar to the preceding ratio, since it measures the relationship between sales and assets. In this case, the ratio measures whether the company has sufficient net current assets to support the volume of its sales or, on the other hand, if the capital invested in working capital is working hard enough to produce sales.

[¶4203.11]   Book Value of the Securities

This figure represents the value of the outstanding securities according to the values shown on the company's books. This, of course, may have little relationship to market value — especially in the case of common stock. Nevertheless, book value is an important test of financial strength. It is computed by simply subtracting all liabilities from total assets. The remaining sum represents the book value of the equity interest in the business. In computing this figure, it is a good idea to include only tangible assets — land, machinery, inventory, etc. A patent right or other tangible may be given a large dollar value on the balance sheet but in the event of liquidation may not be salable at all. The theory underlying the measurement of book value is that it is a good measure of how much cash and credit the company may be able to raise if it comes upon bad times. Book value is usually expressed per share outstanding.

Book value is also an important measure for the bondholders of the company. For them, the value has the significance of telling them how many dollars per bond outstanding the company has in available assets. Since they have a call on the company's assets before either the preferred stockholders or the common stockholders, a substantial book value per bond in excess of the face amount of the bond offers relative assurance of the safety of the bond — assurance that funds will be available to pay off the bonds when they become due. To find the book value of the bonds, add together the total stockholders' equity and the amount of the bonds outstanding.

For example, stockholders' equity totals $5 million. Bonded indebtedness is $2 million. From this $7 million total we subtract $1 million of intangibles. That leaves $6 million. This represents a coverage of three times the total bond indebtedness, usually a fairly substantial coverage.

[¶4203.12]   Ratio of Long-Term Debt to Equity

This ratio measures the leverage potential of the business; that is, the varying effects which changes in operating profits will have on net profits. The rule is that the higher the debt ratio, the greater will be the effect on the common stock of changes in earnings because of increased interest expenses.

Many security analysts feel that in an industrial company equity should equal at least half the total of all equity and debt outstanding. Railroads and utilities, however, are likely to have more debt (and preferred stock) than common stock because of the heavy investments in fixed assets, much of which is financed by the use of debt and preferred stock.

[¶4203.13]   Earnings Per Share (EPS)

Probably, the most important ratio used today is the earnings per share (EPS) figure. It is a *mandatory* disclosure on all annual financial (income) statements (for both public and non-public companies) and mandatory for all interim statements (though unaudited) for public companies. Moreover, the EPS must be broken out separately for extraordinary items. The standards of calculation are quite complex where preferred stock, options and convertibility are involved.

The Accounting Section of this book goes into the factors involved in the computation and disclosure of a complex stock structure.

Basically, the EPS is the net income divided by the number of outstanding shares (including equivalent shares which are treated on an ''as-if-issued'' basis).

Investor reaction to the EPS figure — how it compares with other companies, with its own prior history, with the other investment choices (bonds, commodities, bank accounts, treasury notes, etc.) — is probably one of the largest factors in setting the market price of the stock, second only to dividends actually paid.

[¶4203.14]   Return on Equity

This ratio is another method of determining earning power. Here, the opening Equity (Capital Stock plus Retained Earnings, plus or minus any other equity-section items) is divided into the net income for the year to give the percentage earned on that year's investment.

[¶4203.15]   Return to Investors

This is a relatively new ratio used mostly by financial publications, primarily for comparison of many companies in similar industires. The opening equity is divided into the sum of (the dividends paid plus the market price appreciation of the period). In addition, the ratio is sometimes extended to cover five years, ten years or more.

[¶4204]   INCOME STATEMENT ANALYSIS

Just as with the balance sheet, most of the figures obtained from the income statement acquire real meaning only by comparison with other figures — either with similar figures of previous years of the same company or with the corresponding figures of other companies in the same or similar business.

For example, we could compare each significant item of expense and cost with net sales and get a percentage of net sales (vertical analysis) which we could then compare with other companies. Percentages are more meaningful to compare than absolute dollar amounts since the volume of business done by other companies in the same industry may vary substantially from the volume of our company.

We could also compare each of the significant figures on the income statement with the same figures for prior years (horizontal analysis). Here, too, comparisons of percentages rather than absolute dollar amounts might be more meaningful if the volume of sales has varied substantially from year to year.

Other significant comparisons are covered in the following paragraphs.

[¶4204.1] Sales Growth

The raw element of profit growth is an increase in sales (or revenues when the company's business is services). While merely increasing sales is no guarantee that higher profits will follow, it is usually the first vital step. So in analyzing a company, check the sales figures for the past four or five years. If they have been rising and there is no reason to believe the company's markets are near the saturation point, it is reasonable to assume that the rise will continue.

When a company's sales have jumped by the acquisition of another firm, it is important to find out if the acquisition was accomplished by the issuance of additional common stock, by the assumption of additional debt, or for cash. If the company paid by common stock and if the acquired firm's earnings are the same on a per-share basis as those of the acquiring firm, the profit picture remains exactly as it was before. The additional sales growth is balanced by the *dilution of the equity* — that is , the larger number of shares now sharing in the earnings.

The situation is quite different if the purchase was for cash or in exchange of bonds or preferred stock. Here, no dilution of the common stock has occurred. The entire profits of the new firm (minus the interest which must be paid on the new debt or the interest formerly earned on the cash) benefit the existing shareholders.

In any event, acquisitions of new companies often require a period of consolidation and adjustment and frequently are followed by a decreased rate of sales growth.

Consideration should be given to the effect of inflation on sales. A situation can exist where the increase in sales may be caused by the increase in prices. The result may be that unit sales have dropped in relation to the previous year's, but the dollar sales have increased. Comparing unit sales may be a better method of ascertaining the sales increase under certain circumstances.

[¶4204.2] Computing Operating Profit

A company's costs of operations fall into two groups: *cost of goods sold* and *cost of operations*. The first relates to all the costs of producing the goods or services matched to the revenues produced by those costs. The second includes all other costs not directly associated with the production costs, such as selling and administrative costs (usually called period expenses).

Subtracting both of these groups of costs from sales leaves *operating profit*.

Various special costs and special forms of income are then added or subtracted from operating income to get *net income before taxes*. After deducting state and federal income taxes, the final figure (which is commonly used for computing the profit per share) is *net income*. When analyzing a company, however, you will often be most interested in the operating profit figure, since this reflects the real earning capacity of the company.

The best way to look at cost figures is as a percentage of sales. Thus a company may spend 90 cents out of every dollar in operating costs. We say its cost percentage is 90% or, more commonly, its operating profit margin is 10%. Profit margins vary a great deal among industries, running anywhere from 1% to 20% of sales, so don't compare companies in different industries. The trend of the operating profit margin for a particular company, however, will give an excellent picture of how well management is able to control costs. If sales increases are obtained only by cutting prices, this will immediately show as a decrease in the margin of profit. Of course, in introducing a new product it is sometimes necessary to incur special costs to make initial market penetration, but this should be only temporary.

The most used, examined and discussed ratio within a company is the Gross Profit Ratio. More significance is probably attached to this ratio than to any other, because increases usually indicate improved performance (more sales, more efficient production) and decreases indicate weaknesses (poor selling effort, waste in production, weak inventory controls).

The terminology in the gross profit percentages is sometimes confusing and misinterpreted, especially when the word "markup" is used. As an example:

	$	%
Sales	$ 100	100%
Cost of Sales	80	80%
Gross Profit	$ 20	20%

In conventional usuage, there is a 20% Gross Profit or Margin on the sale (20/100)

However, if we were to determine the *markup,* the Cost of Sales is the denominator and the Gross Profit is the numerator (20/80 equals a 25% markup)

Sometimes, we start with Gross Profit *percentage desired*; we want to gross 20%, so what should the selling price be? (The only known factor is Cost).

	%	Known	As calculated
Selling price	100%	?	$ 150
Cost	80%	$ 120	120
Gross Profit	20%	?	$ 30

Selling price is always 100%. If cost is $120 and is equal to 80% of the selling price (it must be 80% because we've set a gross of 20%), divide $120 *by* 80% to get the 100% selling price of $150.

Another aspect of cost is salaries and special benefits to executives of the company. This is an area of abuse, particularly in smaller firms. If salaries seem unusually low, investigation may reveal that the executives have been given large options to buy corporate stock at favorable prices. While this is an excellent incentive to them, it may mean that constant dilution of the common stock (by issuance of new stock below the market price) will eliminate a good deal of the benefit from increased earnings.

[¶4205] EVALUATION OF FINANCIAL RATIOS

While most ratios are valuable in measuring the financial excellence of a business, certain ratios will be emphasized for particular purposes. The more common purposes for which ratios are used are the following:

[¶4205.1] Management Evaluation

Management's primary interest is in how efficiently the assets of the company are being used. Thus it will be particularly interested in the turnover ratios, such as the inventory turnover and the relationship of working capital to total sales. To the extent that assets are not being used efficiently, the company is overinvesting and consequently is realizing a smaller return than possible on its equity. On the other hand, excessive turnover is dangerous because it puts the company in an extremely vulnerable position. Management will also be particularly interested in trend relationships shown in the income statement for the past few years. Excessive selling expenses may indicate that commissions or other payments are out of line with the market. Management will also make a comparison between the company and its competitiors in all areas to indicate where improvement in operations should be expected.

[¶4205.2] Short-Term Creditors

A lender from whom short-term loans are sought will be particularly interested in the current ratio, since this is a measure of the borrower's ability to meet current debt and his margin of working capital. Also important is the net-worth-to-debt ratio, which shows the relationship of the stockholders' investments to funds contributed by trade creditors and others. It shows ability to stand up under pressure of debt. The sales-to-receivables ratio (net annual sales divided by outstanding trade receivables) shows the relationship of sales volume to uncollected receivables and indicates the liquidity of the receivables on the balance sheet. Another important ratio to the short-term lender is cost of sales to inventory, which shows how many times the company turns over its inventory. Among other things, this shows whether inventories are fresh and salable and helps evaluate the liquidation value of such inventory.

[¶4205.3] Long-Term Creditors

Since the long-term lender is looking some periods ahead, he wants to be convinced above all that the company's earnings will continue at least at the same level. In addition, he will study the various working capital ratios to determine if the company will have sufficient cash when needed to amortize the debt. The ratio of total liabilities to the stockholders' equity is important because the long-term lender wants to be sure that the shareholder has a sufficient stake in the business. One ratio which is used almost solely by the long-term lender is the number of times fixed charges are earned. Fixed charges represent the interest payments on the lender's debt as well as any debt which has priority over it. When total earnings of the company are divided by total fixed charges, the resulting figure represents the number of times fixed charges are earned.

[¶4205.4]   Stockholders

While stockholders are interested in the excellence of the company as a whole, they will tend to think in terms of per-share figures. Of these, probably the most important is the dividend return, since this represents the actual income which the stockholder will receive. For many years now, there has been greater emphasis on growth companies and capital appreciation, and far less emphasis on dividends. Consequently, to a stockholder in a growth company, earnings per share is a far more important figure than dividends. Investors who seek "bargain" situations will be on the lookout for stocks which sell at a price equal to or lower than book value per share. In theory, the liquidating value of such a company is at least equal to the price paid for the stock. An even more restrictive test is a stock which is selling at a price equal to net working capital per share. In such a company, the liquid assets alone are equal to the market value of the shares.

[¶4206]   CASH FLOW

The term "cash flow" refers to a variety of concepts, but its most common meaning in financial literature is the same as "funds derived from operations." The *concept* of cash flow can be used effectively as one of the major factors in judging the ability to meet debt retirement requirements, to maintain regular dividends, to finance replacement and expansion costs, etc.

In no sense, however, can the amount of cash flow be considered to be a substitute for or an improvement upon the net income, properly determined, as an indication of the results of operations or the change in financial position.

[¶4206.1]   Importance of Cash Flow

The concept of cash flow seems to have been originated by security analysts. It has been stated that in evaluating the investment value of steel company stocks, cash flow is frequently regarded as more meaningful than net income as a measure of the company's ability to finance expansion without undue borrowing or holding back payment of dividends.

In using cash flow as an analytic tool, care is required. For example, Corporation X has been capitalized with straight common stock. Corporation Y, the same size as Corporation X and comparable in other respects, has been capitalized 25% with common stock and 75% with debt. A cash flow equivalent to, say, 20% of each corporation's gross sales will seem to be four times as large in relation to Corporation Y's stock when compared with the common stock of Corporation X. Cash flow as a meaningful tool, therefore, will have more significance when related to industries and companies in which long-term debt is limited.

One valid point in using cash flow is to put the profit margin squeeze into proper perspective. One of the most rapidly increasing costs is the depreciation charged against newly acquired plants and equipment. The use of accelerated methods of depreciation has created huge depreciation deductions which reduce profits. At the same time, the depreciation creates enormous cash flow and encourages further spending for facilities. In the opinion of some financial authorities, a showing of relatively high cash flow per dollar of capitalization is some compensation for a poor showing of net income per dollar of capitalization.

High cash flow is also the reason that some companies with relatively poor earnings per share are able to continue paying cash dividends per share; sometimes in excess of earnings. In addition to profits, oil companies get cash flow through depletion allowances, drilling writeoffs and amortization of development costs and depreciation.

Cash flow also helps analysts judge whether debt commitments can be met without refinancing, whether the regular cash dividend can be maintained despite ailing earnings, whether the extractive industries (i.e., oils and mining) will be able to continue exploration without raising additional capital, or whether additional facilities can be acquired without increasing debt or present capital.

Relative cash flow is an important factor in deciding whether to buy or lease. But it's not necessarily true that owning property creates funds for use in expansion. The cash made available to a corporation through operations will be similar whether the business property is owned or leased. Owned property acquired by borrowed capital will require periodic payments on the debt which will have to be met before funds are available for expansion.

43

Going Public

[¶4301]

Some of the factors to be considered in "going public" (having your stock listed on a stock exchange, being traded in the open market):

1) You will have to make public certain information about the company and its officers and owners which has heretofore been private.

2) The prior 3-year audited financial statements will have to be presented (plus other information usually covering seven years) and should ordinarily show a progressively increasing sales/profit growth picture (in substantial amounts) to be attractive to potential investors.

3) You will need an underwriter, an SEC attorney, a bank as a registrar and transfer agent and an independent auditor to guide you in preparing the prospectus for making the public offering of stock — to meet the standards required by the Securities and Exchange Commission (SEC) and the listing requirements of the stock exchanges.

4) Be prepared for some initial high fees (the printing costs for the prospectus might alone reach $100,000).

5) If you make it and become a public corporation, your corporate life (financial and management) will henceforth be on display publicly, subject to the scrutiny and regulation of the SEC on behalf of the protection of the public investor.

Some of the details of your operations which will then be under close observation will be:

1) Accounting methods and practices

2) Capital structure

3) Affiliates, controlled or in which you have some controlling interests

4) Indebtedness to shareholders and vice versa

5) Insider dealings.

[¶4301.1]   SEC REPORTS

The reporting procedure for filings of accounting information with the SEC is found in two types of rules published by the SEC:

1) Regulation S-X

2) Accounting Series Releases

The following reports are required to be filed:

One-time reports:
Form S-1   — upon registration.
Form 10   — also upon registration.

Regular reports:
Form 10-K — detailed *annual* audited financial reports covering two years (plus other information) — within 90 days of year-end;
Form 10Q   summary quarterly unaudited financial reports — 45 days after quarter-end;
Proxy Statements — usually prior to each annual or special stockholders' meeting,

Form 4   — ''Insider'' reports about 10% owners; other information about directors, officers — with 10 days after month-end of ownership changes;
Form 8-K — required whenever certain particular material changes occur (legal proceedings, defaults, major asset acquisitions or dispositions, etc.) — within 10 days after month-end;
Form 11-K — employee stock plans — annual report.

The Proxy Statement filings also include data about officer remuneration, retirement plans, incentive plans, etc.

Anyone who has been involved with SEC work will readily recognize the importance of keeping updated on the latest requirements and changes. Also, there are many topics constantly being discussed among the regulatory agency and business management, attorneys and the accounting profession, as well as the listing stock exchanges. One notable area of conflict and argument is the possible extent of an accountant's liability for a clean opinion issued for a financial operation or status which later proves to be fraudulent, deceptive or grossly erroneous. Individual accountants should be guided by the pronouncements of both the AICPA and the SEC.

44

Letter Stock

The holders of restricted stock, often called "letter stock," used to need SEC permission before they could sell their stock. Now, if they meet certain requirements, they can sell without SEC permission.

The term "Letter stock" has come to be used because the individual to whom the stock is issued normally writes a letter to the issuer stating that he is buying the stock for investment purposes, not for resale.

The practice had been to apply to the SEC in each individual case for a no-action letter, saying that the SEC would take no action if the holder sold. In making a determination on the application, the SEC would take into account the holding period and/or whether there had been sufficient change in the circumstances of the holder to justify a sale consistent with his original intention to buy and hold the stock for investment. Medical emergencies, financial reverses, and other unanticipated needs might or might not be sufficient, depending on all the circumstances presented.

Under the rules which became effective April 15, 1972, letter stock may be resold without registration if these requirements are met:

(1) The stock has been owned and "fully" paid for by the seller for at least two years. Stock not actually fully paid for may be deemed to be "fully paid" on certain conditions; for example, a loan fully collateralized by other stock;

(2) The amount of stock sold over a six-month period does not exceed 1% of the issuer's outstanding stock or the average weekly trading volume, if sold on an exchange, over a four-week period before the sale;

(3) The stock is sold to the public via a normal, brokerage transaction;

(4) Adequate current information about the issuer is available;

(5) The SEC is given notice of the sale concurrent with the placing with a broker of an order for the sale of the securities.

[¶4401.1]   Utility and Value

The present rules increase the utility and value of restricted stock and at the same time protect members of the general public purchasing such stock from the original holder.

Basically, the rules provide an objective test which makes it certain that the owner will be able to sell his letter stock at the end of two years. In practical terms, this means that issuers of letter stock will no longer have to offer such deep discounts on the initial sale of letter stock and that the holder of such stock will no longer be confronted with the necessity, expense and delay formerly involved in getting a no-action letter because of uncertainty about the sufficiency of his holding period.

In another aspect, the elimination of the no-action letter and putting the burden of proof on the holder, when he sells before the two-year holding period in reliance on a change of circumstances, injects a new element of uncertainty. This new uncertainty should be taken into account in fixing the discount on the initial sale of the stock.

SECTION FOUR

APPENDIXES

Appendix A

INDEX FOR JOURNAL ENTRIES

References Are to Journal Entry Numbers

DISCs — deemed distributions: (Parent's Entry)

> For 1975 — under old law — 118
> For 1976 — under new law — 119

Equity method:

> Original investment — 93
> Adjust underlying equity at purchase — 94
> Receipt of cash dividend — 95
> Pick up share of investee income
> (including extraordinary item) — 96
> Set up deferred taxes — 97
> Set up actual tax liability — 98

Federal income tax — netting extraordinary item — 54

Foreign currency translation:

> Year 1 — adjust payable — 87
>   set up deferred tax — 88
> Year 2 — payment on account — 89
>   adjust payables, year-end — 90
>   set up actual tax expense — 91
>   adjust deferred tax — 92

Fund accounting:

> See Municipal accounting
> Membership-type organization:
>> initial dues received — 105
>> purchase of building with mortgage — 106
>> first mortgage payment — 107
>> to close year's income — 108
>> transfer building and mortgage to plant fund — 109
>> in plant fund — set up building and mortgage — 110

Goodwill:

> In consolidation — 99 & 100
> In purchase method — 102
> In equity method — 94

Imputed interest on notes receivable:

> Original receipt of note — 48
> Set up imputed interest — 49
> Year 2 — amortize interest income — 50

Installment sales method:

> Original sale — 30
> Payment on account — 31
> Profit entry — 32

Inventory — year-end entries:

> See Sampling — 67 & 68
> Adjusting standard figures:
>> to physical count — 69
>> to actual cost — 70
>> Year 2 — to new actual — 71

Investment tax credit — deferral method:

> Initial deferral — 34
> Year 2 — amortization of — 35

. Lease — for lessee:

> Capitalizing present value, with contra liability — 55
> First rental payment — 56
> Interest entry, first payment — 57
> Amortizing asset (depreciation) — 58

Marketable securities:

> As current asset:
>> Adjust to year 1 market — 77
>> Year 2 — selling part of stock — 78
>> — adjust to market — 79

> As non-current asset:
>> Adjust to year 1 market — 80
>> Year 2 — selling part of stock — 81
>> — adjust to market — 82

Muncipal accounting:

> Booking the budget — 111
> Actual year's transactions:
>> Issue purchase orders — 112
>> Invoices received — 113
>> Tax levy — 114
>> Actual revenues received — 115 & 116
>> To zero budget accounts and adjust fund balance — 117

Notes receivable discounted — 22

> Note paid by customer — 23

Officer life insurance:

> Paying premium on — 59
> Set up cash surrender value — 60
> Loan taken on policy — 61

Partnership dissolution:

> First sale of assets — 72
> Cancel one partner's overdrawn account — 73

Stock acquisitions:

>Equity method — 93 to 98
>Consolidation — 99 to 101

Stock dividend:

>3% taxable dividend (to recipient) — 41
>Nontaxable dividend (to recipient) — 42

Stock options — employee compensation entries — see Chapter 15

Stock split-up — 44

Stock split-up effected in the form of a stock dividend — 43

Sub-Chapter S corporation:

>First year's net income — 27
>Retitling prior retained earnings — 28
>New distribution — 29

Summary monthly entries:

>Purchase journal — 7
>Cash disbursements — regular account — 8
>Cash disbursements - payroll account — 9
>Sales book — 10
>Cash receipts book — 11
>Petty cash box — 12

Tax loss carryback — 26

Treasury stock:

>Purchase of — 83
>Sale of — 84

Voiding own check — 33

SAMPLE JOURNAL ENTRIES

OPENING INVESTMENT — Sole Proprietorship:
[1]

Cash	5,000	
Building (fair value)	45,000	
A. Able, Net Worth		50,000

OPENING INVESTMENT — Partnership:
[2]

Cash	30,000	
Inventory	30,000	
B. Baker (50%), Capital		30,000
C. Charles (50%), Capital		30,000

PARTNERSHIP INVESTMENT — With Goodwill
[3]

Building (fair value)	45,000	
Goodwill	15,000	
A. Able (50%), Capital		60,000

Able contributes building for
½ share of partnership.

PARTNERSHIP INVESTMENT — Skill, no funds:
[4]

A. Able, Capital	3,000	
B. Baker, Capital	3,000	
C. Charles, Capital	6,000	
D. Dog, Capital		12,000

Dog gets 10% of partnership
for the skill he'll contribute.
Ratios will now be:

Able	(25% less 10%)	22.5%
Baker	(same)	22.5%
Charles	(50% less 10%)	45.0%
Dog	(as granted)	10.0%
		100.0%

PARTNERSHIP INCORPORATES:
[5]

Cash	30,000	
Inventory — Raw Material	30,000	
Building (fair value)	45,000	
Capital Stock (par $10; 10,000		
shares issued; 100,000 auth.)		100,000
Additional Paid-in Capital		5,000

Shares issued: A. 2250; B, 2250;
C, 4500; D, 1,000. Note that
partnership goodwill is not carried
over to corporation.

CORPORATE INVESTMENT — with Goodwill:
[6]

Machinery & Equipment (fair value)	9,000	
Goodwill	1,000	
Capital Stock (1,000 shares)		10,000
Issuing 1,000 shares to E. Easy		
@ $10 par for machinery contributed.		

CORPORATION MONTHLY ENTRIES — The corporation books all entries into the general ledger *through* summary entries made in the general journal from the books and sources of original entry:

[7] *Summary of Purchase Journal,* where all vendor invoices are entered:

Purchases — Raw Material	10,000	
Shop Supplies	2,000	
Office Supplies	1,000	
Office Equipment	3,000	
Utilities	1,000	
Freight Out	2,000	
Advertising	1,000	
Accounts Payable		20,000

[8] *Summary of Cash Disbursements, Regular Cash A/C:*

Cash — Payroll A/C	13,000	
Petty Cash	200	
Accounts Payable	14,500	
Federal Tax Deposits Made	5,100	
Bank Charges	2	
Cash — Regular A/C		32,602
Cash Discounts Taken		200

[9] *Summary of Cash Disbursements, Payroll A/C:*

Direct Labor — Shop	12,500	
Indirect Labor — Shop	1,500	
Salaries — Sales Dept.	2,000	
Salaries — G & A	4,000	
Cash — Payroll A/C (net pay)		13,000
W/H Tax Pay — Federal		4,400
FICA Tax Withheld		1,200
SUI & Disability W/H		300
State Income Taxes W/H		600
Savings Bonds W/H		500

[10] *Summary of Sales Book:*

Accounts Receivable	35,000	
Sales Returns & Allowances	500	
Sales — Product L		18,000
Sales — Product M		16,600
Sales Taxes Payable		900

[11] *Summary of Cash Receipts Book:*

Cash — Regular A/C	30,500	
Cash Discounts Allowed	500	
Accounts Receivable		30,000
Machinery and Equipment		1,000

[12] *Summary of Petty Cash Box:*

Postage	40	
Entertainment	60	
Travel Expense	30	
Misc. Expense	20	
Petty Cash		150

[13] *General Journal Entries during month:*

Depreciation — M & E	10	
Machinery and Equipment	400	
Gain on Sale of Machinery		410

To correct entry from cash receipts:

Basis	$ 600	
Deprec.	10	(1/60th)
	590	
S.P.	1000	
Gain	$ 410	

[14]

Depr. — Bldg (1/40x45,000x1/12)	94	
Depr. — M&E (1/5 x 8, 400x1/12)	140	
Depr. — OE (1/5 x 3,000x1/12)	50	
Amortization (1/40x1,000x1/12)	2	
Accum Depr. — Bldg		94
Accum Depr. — M&E		140
Accum Depr. — OE		50
Goodwill		2

[15]

Real Estate Taxes	300	
Accrued Taxes — RE		300
1/12th of estimated $3,600 for yr		

[16]

Direct Labor (3125)	2,500	
Indirect Labor (375)	300	
Salaries — Selling (500)	400	
Salaries — G & A (1000)	800	
Accrued Salaries (5000)		4,000
To accrue 4/5 of last payroll in month.		

[17]

W/H Tax Payable — Federal	3,300	
FICA Tax Withheld	900	
FICA Tax Expense — employer	900	
Federal Tax Deposits Made		5,100

FICA Tax Expense — employer	300	
SUI & DISAB Expense	600	
FUI Expense	100	
Accrued Taxes — Payroll		1,000

To zero deposit account against
withholding accounts and to book
employer FICA expense and estimated
unemployment tax for month.

[18]

Overhead	6,106	
Depr. — Bldg (60% of 94)		56
Depr. — M&E (all)		140
Indirect Labor (all)		1,800
Payroll Tax Exp (70% of 1900)		1,330
Shop supplies (all considered used)		2,000
Utilities (60% of 1000)		600
Taxes — RE (60% of 300)		180

To allocate expenses to overhead.
Taxes based on payroll proportion.
Other allocations based on space occupied.

[19]

Inventory — Raw Materials	(15,000)	
Inventory — Work in Process	none	
Inventory — Finished Goods	15,369	
Cost of Production — Inventory Change		369

To increase or (decrease) inventory
accounts to reflect new month-end
inventory as follows:

Raw Material:

Opening Inventory	$30,000
Purchases	10,000
Less used in production	(25,000)
Closing inventory	15,000
To adjust opening	$(15,000)

Finished Goods:

Materials used (above)	$ 25,000
Direct labor costs	15,000
Overhead costs	6,106
3 units produced	46,106
1 unit unsold (⅓)	$ 15,369

(none at hand at beginning)
No work in process this month.

(The entries through here are all related with respect to the dollars shown. From here on,
they are independent with respect to each CAPITAL HEADING, but related within the
headed area.)

CUSTOMER'S CHECK BOUNCES
[20]

| Accounts Receivable (Mr. A.) | 100 | |
| Cash (Disbursements) | | 100 |

To record bank charge for
Mr. A's check return — insufficient
funds.

[21]

Cash (Receipts)	100	
Accounts Receivable (Mr. A.)		100

For re-deposit of above, per
customer's instructions.

NOTES RECEIVABLE DISCOUNTED

[22]

Cash	9,900	
Interest Expense	250	
Notes Receivable Discounted		10,000
Interest Income		150

For proceeds from customer note discounted,
due 90 days @ 6%, discount rate 10%.

[23]

Notes Receivable Discounted	10,000	
Notes Receivable		10,000

To offset. Customer note paid,
per bank notice.

FIRST-YEAR DEPRECIATION

[24]

Depreciation Expense — M & E	2,000	
Accumulated Depr — M & E		2,000

For maximum first-year depreciation
taken on 6/30 purchase of extruder.
See next entry for regular deprec.

[25]

Depreciation — M &E	400	
Accumulated Depr — M & E		400

To take straight-line on above:

Cost	$	10,000
Less 1st yr. Depr		(2,000)
S/L basis		8,000
Over 10 yrs — per yr	$	800
Six months this yr (no salvage value)	$	400

TAX LOSS CARRYBACK

[26]

FIT Refund and Interest Receivable	106,000	
Income Tax (Current Yr. Income Statement)		100,000
Interest Income		6,000

To set up receivable for carryback tax
refund due, plus interest.

SUB-CHAPTER S EQUITY ENTRIES

End of Year 1:

[27]

Net income for Current Year	30,000	
Undistributed Earnings — Post-Election		30,000

To close year's net income into
new Sub-S undistributed earnings
Equity account.

[28]

Retained Earnings	55,000	
Retained Earnings — Pre-Election		55,000

To retitle opening retained earnings
account and keep it separate from
earnings after Sub-S election.

[29]

Post-Election Dividends	10,000	
Cash		10,000

For cash distributions made of current earnings. (NOTE: State law may require a *formal*
declaration of a dividend for corporations. If
this is true, and there is no such declaration,
this must be treated as a *loan receivable* from
stockholders.)

INSTALLMENT SALES METHOD

[30]

Accounts Receivable	1,000	
Cost of Installment Sale		700
Deferred Gross Profit on Installment Sales		300

For original sale. (GP% is 30%)

[31]

Cash	300	
Accounts Receivable		300

For payment on account.

[32]

Deferred Gross Profit on Installment Sales	90	
Realized Gross Profit		90

To amortize 30% of above collection
to realized income.

VOIDING YOUR OWN CHECK (Issued in a prior period)

[33]

Cash (Ck #1601)	1,500	
Rent Expense		1,500

To void check #1601 (last month).
Check reported lost. Payment
stopped. Replaced with this month's
check #1752. (See CD book)

INVESTMENT TAX CREDIT — THE DEFERRAL METHOD

[34]

Taxes Payable	7,000	
Deferred Investment Tax Credits		7,000

To set up investment tax credit under
the deferred method. *Note:* The tax
expense for this year on the income
statement does *not* reflect the use
of this credit.

Year 2:

[35]

Deferred Investment Tax Credits	700	
Income Tax Expense		700
To amortize 1/10th, based on 10-year		
life of asset to which applicable.		

ACCUMULATED PREFERRED STOCK DIVIDENDS
[36]

Dividends (Income Statement)	30,000	
Dividends Payable (Liability)		30,000
To accrue this year's commitment,		
6% of $500,000. *Note:* There was		
no "only as earned" provision attached		
to this issue.		

DIVIDEND DECLARATION — COMMON STOCK
[37]

Retained Earnings	100,000	
Common Stock Extra Dividend		
Declared — (show in Equity Section)		100,000
To segregate common stock extra dividend		
from accumulated earnings (until paid),		
10ᶜ per share, 1,000,000 shares.		

PAYMENT OF ABOVE TWO DIVIDENDS
[38]

Dividends Payable •	30,000	
Common Stock Extra Dividend Declared	100,000	
Cash		130,000
For payment of dividends.		

APPROPRIATION OF RETAINED EARNINGS
[39]

Retained Earnings	50,000	
Reserve Appropriation for Inventory		
Declines (Equity Section)		50,000
To set aside retained earnings for possible		
inventory losses — per Board resolution.		

PRIOR PERIOD ADJUSTMENT
[40]

Retained Earnings — (1/1 opening)	150,000	
Cash		150,000
To record settlement of litigation		
heretofore held uncertain and qualified		
in last auditor's report.		

STOCK DIVIDEND

Usually:

[41]

Retained Earnings (at market)	45,000	
Common Stock (par $10, 3,000 shares)		30,000
Additional Paid-in Capital		15,000

For 3% stock dividend distributed on
100,000 shares — 3,000 shares issued.
Market value $15 at dividend date.

Sometimes:
[42]

Additional Paid-in Capital	30,000	
Common Stock (par $10, 3,000 shares)		30,000

For non-taxable distribution out of
Paid-in Capital.

SPLIT-UP EFFECTED IN THE FORM OF A STOCK DIVIDEND
[43]

Retained Earnings (at par)	1,000,000	
Common Stock (par $10, 100,000 shs)		1,000,000

For split in the form of a stock dividend
(to conform with state law). One share
issued for each share outstanding.
100,000 shares at par of $10.

STOCK SPLIT-UP
[44]

Common Stock (100,000 shares @ 10.)	memo	
Common Stock (200,000 shares @ $ 5.)		memo

Memo entry only. To record stock split-up
by showing change in par value and in
number of shares outstanding. One share
issued for each outstanding. Par changed
from $ 10 to $ 5.

STOCK OPTIONS FOR EMPLOYEES AS COMPENSATION

See Entries shown in Chapter 15.

PARTNERSHIP WITHDRAWALS
[45]

S. Stone, Withdrawals	15,000	
T. Times, Withdrawals	5,000	
Cash		20,000

For cash withdrawals.

PARTNERSHIP PROFIT ENTRY
[46]

Net Income — P & L a/c	100,000	
S. Stone, Capital (50%)		50,000
T. Times, Capital (50%)		50,000

To split profit as follows:

Per P & L closing account	$ 80,000
Add back above included	
in P & L accont	20,000
Profit to distribute	$100,000

[47]

S. Stone, Capital	15,000	
T. Times, Capital	5,000	
S. Stone, Withdrawals		15,000
T. Times, Withdrawals		5,000

To close withdrawal accounts
to capital accounts.

IMPUTED INTEREST (ON NOTES RECEIVABLE)

[48]

Notes Receivable (Supplier A — 6 yrs)	1,000,000	
Cash		1,000,000

For loan made to supplier. Received
non-interest bearing note, due 6 yrs.

[49]

Cost of Merchandise (from supplier A)	370,000	
Unamortized Discount on Notes Receiv.		370,000

To charge imputed interest of 8% on
above note, due in 6 years, to cost
of merchandise bought from A.

Year 2:

[50]

Unamortized Discount on Notes Receiv.	50,000	
Interest Income		50,000

To amortize this year's applicable
imputed interest on note.

BOND DISCOUNT, PREMIUM AND ISSUE COSTS

[51]

Cash	2,025,000	
Unamortized Bond Issue Costs	15,000	
Bonds Payable (8%, 10 yrs)		2,000,000
Unamortized Premium on Bonds		40,000

To set up face value of bonds, issue
costs and net cash proceeds received.

Year 2:

[52]

Unamortized Premium on Bonds	4,000*	
Unamortized Bond Issue Cost		1,500*
Interest Expense (difference)		2,500

To set up approximate amortization.
(*Should actually be based on present
values.)

[53]

Interest Expense	160,000	
Cash		160,000

To record actual payment of bond
interest. 8% of $2,000,000.

FEDERAL INCOME TAX — INTERIMS — AND EXTRAORDINARY ITEM

[54]

Income Tax (on continuing operations)	350,000	
Extraordinary Loss (tax effect)		50,000
Taxes Payable		300,000

To set up FIT at end of First Quarter
based on full year's 50% rate and
to segregate tax applicable to
extraordinary item.

Statement should show:

Net from continuing operations	$700,000
Less FIT	(350,000)
	350,000
Extraordinary loss	
(net of $50,000 tax effect)	50,000
Net Income	$300,000

CAPITALIZING A LEASE (LESSEE)

At contracting:

[55]

Capitalized Leases	1,920,000	
Long-Term Lease Liability		3,600,000
Unamortized Discount on Lease		(1,680,000)

To capitalize lease of $ 25,000 per
month for 12 years @ 12% imputed
interest rate. Estimated life of asset
is 15 years. Present value used, since
fair value is higher at $2,000,000.

(Note: The two credit items shown are
netted and shown as *one net liability*
on the balance sheet. The liability
(at present value) should always equal
the asset value, also at present value.
Future lease payments are broken out,
effectively, into principal and interest.)

Month-end 1:

[56]

Long-Term Lease Liability	25,000	
Cash		25,000

First payment on lease.

[57]

Interest Expense	18,950	
Unamortized Discount on Lease		18,950

For one month's interest.
1% of $3,600,000 less $1,680,000,
less initial payment on signing of
contract of $25,000 *(entry not shown)* or
$1,895,000.

[58]

Depreciation Expense	10,667	
Accumulated Depr of Capitalized Lease		10,,667

One month:
$1,920,000 x1/15x1/12

CASH SURRENDER VALUE — OFFICER LIFE INSURANCE

[59]

Officer Life Insurance — expense	1,500	
Cash		1,500

For payment of premiun. *Note:* Expense
is not deductible for tax purpose and
is a *permanent* difference.

[60]

Cash Surrender Value-Officer Life Ins.	1,045	
Officer Life Ins. expense		1,045

To reflect increase in C.S.V. for year

[61]

Cash	5,000	
Loans Against Officer Life Insurance		5,000
(Displayed against the asset "C.S.V.")		

To record loan against life policy. No intent
to repay within the next year.

STANDARD COST VARIANCES

[62]

Purchases — Raw Mat (at stand)	200	
Accounts Payable — actual		188
Variance — material price		12

[63]

Direct Labor — at standard	50	
Variance — Direct Labor rate	10	
Payroll — actual direct labor		58
Variance — Labor Time		2

[64]

Overhead — at Standard	75	
Variance — overhead	15	
Overhead itemized actual accounts		90

Adjusting Inventories:

[65]

Inventory — Raw Materials at standard	100	
Finished Goods — at standard	75	
Cost of Production — at standard		175

To adjust inventory accounts to reflect
end-of-month on-hand figures at standards.

[66]

Variance — material price	xx	
Variance — labor time	xx	
Variance — direct labor rate		xx
Variance — overhead		xx
Contra Inventory Asset a/c (variances		
to offset standard and reflect cost)		xx

To pull out of variance accounts that
portion which is applicable to inventory,
in order to keep an isolated contra account,
which in offset to the "standard" asset
account, reflects approximate cost.
The portion is based on an overall ratio
of variances to production and inventory
figures (at standard). (If normal, apply
to cost of sales for interims.)

ADJUSTING INVENTORY FOR SAMPLING RESULTS

[67]

Cost of Sales	50,000	
Inventory		50,000

To reduce inventory by $50,000 based
on sampling results:

Inventory per computer run	$ 1,000,000	
Estimated calculated		
inventory per sample	950,000	
Reduction this year	$ 50,000	

Year 2:

[68]

Inventory	10,000	
Cost of Sales		10,000

To adjust inventory to actual
based on actual physical count
of entire inventory. Last year-end
sample error proved to be 4%,
not 5%.

ADJUSTING CLOSING INVENTORY FROM CLIENT'S STANDARD COST TO
AUDITOR'S DETERMINED (AND CLIENT AGREED) ACTUAL COST, AND TO
REFLECT PHYSICAL INVENTORY VS. BOOK INVENTORY DIFFERENCES

[69]

Inventory — Finished Goods (Standard)	25,000	
Cost of Sales		25,000

To adjust general ledger inventory
(at standard) to actual physical
inventory count, priced out at
standard. Actual is $ 25,000 more.

[70]

Cost of Sales	80,000	
Inventory — Finished Goods		
(Asset Contra Cost account)		80,000

To set up a contra account reducing
asset account, which is at standard
costs, effectively to audited actual
cost or market, whichever lower.

Year 2: (End of Year)

[71]

Inventory — Finished Goods (Asset		
Contra Cost account)	50,000	
Cost of Sales		50,000

To reduce the contra account to
the new year-end difference between
the ''standard'' asset account and the
actual cost determined for this new
year-end inventory.

PARTNERSHIP DISSOLUTION:

Balance Sheet

Cash	$ 20,000
Assets other	35,000
Liabilities	(25,000)
A Capital (50%)	(20,000)
B Capital (30%)	(14,000)
C Capital (20%)	4,000
	-0-

[72]

Cash	15,000	
Assets other		15,000

For sale of some assets at book value.

[73]

A Capital (⅝)	2,500	
B Capital (⅜)	1,500	
C Capital		4,000

C cannot put in his overdraw —
to apportion his deficit.

[74]

Liabilities	25,000	
Cash		25,000

To pay liabilities

[75]

Cash	10,000	
Loss on Sale of Assets other	10,000	
Assets other		20,000
A Capital (⅝)	6,250	
B Capital (⅜)	3,750	
Loss on Sale of Assets other		10,000

Selling remaining assets and apportioning loss

[76]

A Capital (remaining balance)	11,250	
B Capital (remaining balance)	8,750	
Cash		20,000

To distribute remaining cash
and zero capital accounts.

NOTE THE SHARING OF C'S DEFICIT
AND OF THE LOSS ON ASSET SALE
BEFORE DISTRIBUTING REMAINING
CASH.

MARKETABLE SECURITIES

Shown as Current Assets:
[77]

Unrealized Loss — to P & L	1,500	
Marketable Securities — Current		1,500

To write down 100 U.S. Steel:

Cost 1/1	$ 10,000
Market 12/31	8,500
Unrealized Loss	$ 1,500

Year 2:
[78]

Cash	4,500	
Marketable Securities — Current		4,250
Realized Gain — to P & L		250

Sold 50 @ 90	$ 4,500
At 12/31 priced at	4,250
Financial gain	$ 250

(Note: For tax purposes, there
is a loss of $500)

[79]

Marketable Securities — Current	500	
Unrealized Gain — to P & L		500

To adjust asset account to market:

12/31 market 50 sh @ 95	$ 4,750
Booked to last year end	4,250
Unrealized gain	$ 500

Shown as Non-Current Asset:

[80]

Unrealized Loss (Equity Section)	1,000	
Marketable Securities — Non-Current		1,000

To write-down 100 shares GM from
cost to 12/31 market price:

Cost 1/1 100 sh @ 60	$ 6,000
Market 12/31 100 @ 50	5,000
Unrealized (Equity) Loss ´	$ 1,000

Year 2:

[81]

Cash	2,900	
Realized Loss — P & L	100	
Marketable Securities — Non-Current		2,500
Unrealized Loss (Equity Section)		500

Sold 50 sh @ 58	$ 2,900
Cost at purchase 50 @ 60	3,000
Realized Loss for P & L	$ 100

And to cancel that portion sitting
now in asset account and unrealized
equity loss account (½ of 5,000; and
½ of 1,000 respectively for 50 shares
out of 100 shares)

[82]

Marketable Securities — Non-Current	500	
Unrealized Loss (Equity Section)		500

To adjust 50 shares of GM to
cost or market, whichever lower:
(Market value at yearend 2 is $65;
Cost was $60; adjust to no higher
than cost — this is the only stock in the
non-current portfolio). (If there were
additional stocks and the *net*
of all stocks was still below cost after
using current *market* value for *all* stocks
in the portfolio), a higher-than-cost
market value could be used for this one
out of an entire portfolio.)

Cost 50 sh @ $60	$ 3,000
Booked to last year end	
50 @ $50	2,500
Unrealized Gain	$ 500

TREASURY STOCK

Purchase of:
[83]

Treasury Stock — at Cost	125,000	
Cash		125,000
Purchase of 1,000 shares @ 125		
market. Par value $ 50.		
No intent to cancel the stock.		

Sale of:
[84]

Cash	140,000	
Treasury Stock — at Cost		125,000
Additional Paid — in Capital		15,000
For sale of treasury stock @ 140.		

APPRAISAL WRITE-UPS
[85]

Building	350,000	
Appraisal Capital (Equity Section)		350,000
To raise building from cost of $400,000 to		
appraised value of $750,000 per require-		
ment of the lending institution.		

Year 2:
[86]

Depreciation — Building	21,667	
Accumulated Depreciation — Building		21,667
To depreciate based on appraised value:		
(400,000 for 40 years; 350,000 for 30 yrs)		
Building was 10 years old at appraisal.		

FOREIGN CURRENCY EXCHANGE
[87]

Unrealized Loss (income statement)	10,000	
Accts Payable — Foreign		10,000
To adjust liabilities payable in		
Swiss Francs to US Dollars at 12/31:		

Exchange rate at 12/31 .40	$40,000	
Booked at (100,000 frs) .30	30,000	
More dollars owed	$10,000	

[88]

Deferred Taxes	5,000	
Income Tax Expense		5,000
To show deferred tax effect (50% rate		
times $10,000 above)		

Year 2:
[89]

Accounts Payable — Foreign	20,000	
Cash		19,000
Realized Gain (Books, not Tax)		1,000
For payment of 50,000 Swiss Francs at ex-		
change rate of .38		

[90]

Accounts Payable — Foreign	500	
Unrealized Gain		500

To restate liability at year-end:

50,000 Frs @ .39	$ 19,500
Booked to last yr	20,000
(Gain)	$ (500)

[91]

Taxes Payable	2,000	
Income Tax Expense	500	
Deferred Taxes		2,500

To transfer to actual taxes payable (from deferred) that portion applying to the payment of $19,000. Original debt in dollars was $15,000. 50% tax rate on $4,000 or $2,000, plus $500 — to offset 2,500 booked to last 12/31.

[92]

Income Tax Expenses	250	
Deferred Taxes		250

To adjust deferred taxes to equal ½ of 4,500 (19,500 liability now, less original liability of 15,000) for $2,250 tax deferral.

THE EQUITY METHOD

[93]

Investment — Oleo Co.	275,000	
Cash		275,000

Purchase of 25% of Oleo's stock, at cost (25,000 shares @ $11)

[94]

Investment — Oleo Co.	40,000	
Deferred Good Will in Oleo		40,000

To set up additional underlying equity in Oleo Co. at date of acquisition — to write-off over 40 years.

[95]

Cash	5,000	
Investment — Oleo Co.		5,000

For receipt of 20ᶜ per share cash dividend from Oleo.

[96]

Investment — Oleo Co.	27,500	
Income from Equity Share of Undistributed Earnings of Oleo continuing operations		25,000
Income from Equity Share of Undistributed Extraordinary Item of Oleo		2,500

To pick up 25% of the following reported Oleo annual figures:

Net income after taxes, but before Extraordinary item	$100,000
Extraordinary Income (net)	10,000
Total net income reported	$110,000

[97]

Income Tax Expense — Regular	12,500	
Income Tax Expense — Extra' Item	1,250	
Deferred Taxes		13,750

To set up 50% of above income as accrued taxes. Expectation is that Oleo *will* continue paying dividends.

[98]

Deferred Taxes	2,500	
Income Taxes Payable		2,500

To set up actual liability for tax on cash dividends received.

CONSOLIDATION

Trial Balances
Now-at
12/31-End of Year

	A Co.	B Co.	Fair Value Excess at Acquisition
Cash	10,000	6,000	
A/R	20,000	10,000	
Inventory	30,000	5,000	
Equip	50,000	30,000	5,000
Investment Cost	40,000		
Liabilities	(30,000)	(5,000)	(1,000)
Common Stock	(20,000)	(10,000)*	
Retained Earnings	(50,000)	(20,000)*	
Sales	(80,000)	(40,000)	
Costs of Sale	20,000	14,000	
Expenses	10,000	10,000	
	-0-	-0-	
	(Parent)	(Sub)	

*Unchanged from opening balances.

At year-end there were $5,000 intercompany receivables/payables. The parent had sold $5,000 worth of product to the subsidiary. The inventory of the subsidiary was $1,000 over the parent's cost.

Consolidating
Entries:

[99]

Excess Paid over Book Value	10,000	
Investment Cost		10,000

To reduce investment cost to that of the subsidiary's equity at time of purchase (unchanged at 12/31).

[100]

Equipment	5,000	
Liabilities		1,000
Excess Paid over Book V lue		4,000

To reflect fair value corrections at time of
consolidation for the combination of current year-end trial bal nces.

[101]

B Co. Equity	30,000	
Investment Cost		30,000
Sales	5,000	
Costs of Sale		5,000
Costs of Sale	1,000	
Inventory		1,000
Liabilities	5,000	
Accounts Receivable		5,000
Excess paid over book value (expense)	150	
Goodwill		150

To eliminate intercompany dealings, debt,
investment, and to amortize goodwill.

Consolidated figures will then be:

Cash	16,000	
A/R	25,000	
Inventories	34,000	
Equipment	85,000	
Investment cost	---	
Goodwill	5,850	
Liabilities	(31,000)	
Common Stock	(20,000)	(Opening)
Ret. Earnings	(50,000)	(Opening)
Sales	(115,000)	
Cost of sales	30,000	
Expenses	20,150	
	-0-	

The year's consolidated net income (before
provision for income taxes) is $64,850.

PURCHASE METHOD OF BUSINESS COMBINATION

[102]

Accounts Receivable (present value)	50,000	
Inventory (current cost or market, lowest)	40,000	
Building (fair value)	110,000	
Equipment (fair Value)	30,000	
Investments, non-current securities-market	5,000	
Goodwill	16,200	
Accounts Payable — (present value)		25,000
Long-term Debt — (face value)		30,000
Unamortized discount on long-term debt		
(to reflect present value)		(3,800)
Common Stock (Par $10; 10,000 shares)		100,000
Additional Paid-in Capital		100,000

To reflect, by the purchase method, the
purchase of Diablo Company assets and

liabilities for 10,000 shares of common stock; total purchase price of contract $200,000 based on market price of stock at date of consummation of $20 per share (1/1)

[103]

Amortization of Goodwill (1/40)	405	
Goodwill		405
Unamortized discount on long-term debt	760	
Discount Income (approx 1/5th)		760*

To amortize pertinent Diablo items, first yearend. Goodwill on straight-line basis — 40 years. *Should be calculated present value computation.

POOLING METHOD OF BUSINESS COMBINATION
[104]

Inventory	43,000	
Cash	5,000	
Accounts Receivable	60,000	
Reserve for Doubtful Accounts		7,000
Building	75,000	
Accumulated Depreciation — Building		15,000
Equipment	100,000	
Accumulated Depreciation — Building		60,000
Investments — non-current securities	4,000	
Accounts Payable		25,500
Long-Term Debt		30,000
Common Stock (10,000 shs @ par $10)		100,000
Additional Paid-in Capital		49,500

To reflect the pooling of Diablo items, per *their book value* on date of consummation.

FUND ACCOUNTING

Initial transactions:

[105]

Cash	100,000	
Dues Income		100,000

For initial membership dues received.

[106]

Building	50,000	
Mortgage Payable		40,000
Cash		10,000

Purchase of building for cash and mortgage.

[107]

Interest Expense	2,400	
Mortgage Payable	2,000	
Cash		4,400

For first payment on mortgage.

[108]

Net Income (100,000 less 2,400)	97,600	
Current Fund Balance		97,600

To close year's income

[109]

Mortgage Payable	38,000	
Current Fund Balance	12,000	
Building		50,000

To transfer building and mortgage to plant fund.

Plant Fund Entry:

[110]

Building	50,000	
Mortgage Payable		38,000
Plant Fund Balance		12,000

To set up building in plant fund.

Note that interest expense is to be borne by the current fund every year as a current operating expense used in the calculation of required dues from members. Also, the principal sum-payments against mortgage are to come out of current fund assets, with no interfund debt to be set up, until such time as a special drive is held for plant fund donations for improvements and expansion.

MUNICIPAL ACCOUNTING — CURRENT OPERATING FUND

To book the budget:

[111]

Estimated Revenues	600,000	
Appropriations		590,000
Fund Balance		10,000

Actual year's transactions:

[112]

Encumbrances	575,000	
Reserve for Encumbrances		575,000

To enter contracts and purchase orders issued.

[113]

Expenditures — itemized (not here)	515,000	
Vouchers Payable		515,000
Reserve for Encumbrances	503,000	
Encumbrances		503,000

To enter actual invoices for deliveries received and service contracts performed and to reverse applicable encumbrances.

[114]

Taxes Receivable — Current	570,000	
Revenues		541,500
Estimated Current Uncollectible Taxes		28,500

To enter actual tax levy and to estimate uncollectibles at 5%.

[115]

Cash	55,000	
Revenues		55,000

For cash received from licenses, fees,
fines and other sources.

[116]

Cash	549,500	
Estimated Current Uncollectible Taxes	8,000	
Taxes Receivable		549,500
Revenues		8,000

For actual taxes collected for this year.

To close out budget accounts:
[117]

Revenues	604,500	
Appropriations	590,000	
Estimated Revenue		600,000
Expenditures		515,000
Encumbrances		72,000
Fund Balance		7,500

To zero budget accounts and adjust
fund balance.

DISCS — DEEMED DISTRIBUTIONS (Parent's Books)

1975 — under old law
[118]

DISC Dividends Receivable (previously taxed)	110,000	
Deemed Distribution from DISC (income)		110,000

To pick up ½ of DISC's net of $220,000.

1976 — under the new law
[119]

DISC Dividends Receivable (previously taxed)	189,375	
Deemed Distribution from DISC (income)		189,375

As follows:
Facts:

Gross export receipts average for 1972-1975	$1,100,000
Gross export receipts - 1976	$1,300,000
Net DISC income - 1976 only	$ 250,000

Since the 1976 net income is over
$150,000, the graduated relief in the 1976
law does not apply, and the calculation is:

67% of 1,100,000 = 670,000

670,000 ÷ 1,300,000 = 51.5%

51.5% × 250,000 =	$	128,750
250,000 − 128,750 = 121,250		
121,250 × 50% =		60,625
Total Deemed Distribution	$	189,375

Appendix B
Guide to Record Retention Requirements

Office of the Federal Register
GUIDE TO RECORD RETENTION REQUIREMENTS
REVISION AS OF JANUARY 1, 1976

This is a Guide in digest form to the provisions of Federal laws and regulations relating to the keeping of records by the public. It tells the user (1) what records must be kept, (2) who must keep them, and (3) how long they must be kept.

The Guide is derived from the regulations published in the Code of Federal Regulations, as amended in the daily issues of the FEDERAL REGISTER through December 31, 1975. Authority for the regulations is derived from the laws published in the United States Code, as amended by laws enacted during 1975.

This Guide was prepared under the editorial direction of Rose Steinman, with Roy Nanovic and Carol Blanchard as Chief Editors. INQUIRIES, telephone 202–523–5227. SUGGESTIONS concerning this publication may be sent to Fred J. Emery, Director, Office of the Federal Register, National Archives and Records Service, Washington, D.C. 20408.

Coverage

In preparing the Guide it was necessary to establish boundaries in order to keep it from going beyond its intended purpose.

The Guide adheres strictly to the retention of records. It does not cover such matters as the furnishing of reports to Government agencies, the filing of tax returns, or the submission of supporting evidence with applications or claims.

The Guide is limited to provisions which apply to a class. Requirements applying only to named individuals or bodies have been omitted.

The Guide is confined to requirements which have been expressly stated. In many laws and regulations there is an implied responsibility to keep copies of reports and other papers furnished to Federal agencies, and to keep related working papers. Such implied requirements have not been included in the Guide.

The following types of requirements have also been excluded from the Guide:

(1) Requirements as to the keeping of papers furnished by the Government, such as passports, licenses, permits, etc., unless they are closely related to other records which must be kept.

(2) Requirements as to the display of posters, notices, or other signs in places of business.

(3) Requirements contained in individual Government contracts, unless the contract provisions are incorporated in the Code of Federal Regulations.

368

Income, Estate, Gift and Employment Taxes

4. Internal Revenue Service

NOTE: The following items refer to requirements issued under the Internal Revenue Code of 1939 and the Internal Revenue Code of 1954 which were in effect as of January 1, 1975. All regulations applicable under any provision of law in effect on August 16, 1954, the date of enactment of the 1954 Code, are applicable to the corresponding provisions of the 1954 Code insofar as such regulations are not inconsistent with the 1954 Code, and such regulations remain applicable to the 1954 Code until superseded by regulations under such Code. The Internal Revenue Service points out that the omission from this compilation of any record retention requirement provided for by law or regulation issued thereunder shall not be construed as authority to disregard any such requirement. The Service also points out that persons subject to income tax are bound by the retention requirement given in item 4.1 regardless of other requirements which for other purposes allow shorter retention periods.

The record retention requirements of the Internal Revenue Service are divided into the following categories: Income, Estate, Gift, Employment, and Excise Taxes.

INCOME TAX

4.1 Persons subject to income tax.

(a) *General.* Except as provided in paragraph (b), any person subject to tax, or any person required to file a return of information with respect to income shall keep such permanent books of account or records, including inventories, as are sufficient to establish the amount of gross income, deductions, credits, or other matters required to be shown by such person in any return of such tax or information.

(b) *Farmers and wage-earners.* Individuals deriving gross income from the business of farming, and individuals whose gross income includes salaries, wages, or similar compensation for personal services rendered, are required to keep such records as will enable the district director to determine the correct amount of income subject to the tax, but it is not necessary that these individuals keep the books of account or records required by paragraph (a).

(c) *Exempt organizations.* In addition to the books and records required by paragraph (a) with respect to the tax imposed on unrelated business income, every organization exempt from tax under section 501(a) of the Code shall keep such permanent books of account or records, including inventories,

as are sufficient to show specifically the items of gross income, receipts, and disbursements, and other required information.

Retention period: So long as the contents thereof may become material in the administration of any internal revenue law. 26 CFR 1.6001-1

4.1a Section 38 property; computation of investment credit and qualified investment.

(a) *Component members of a controlled group on a December 31 apportionment of $25,000 amount.* To keep as a part of its records a copy of the statement containing all the required consents to the apportionment plan. 26 CFR 1.46-1

(b) *Persons computing qualified investment in certain depreciable property.* Maintain sufficient records to determine whether section 47 of the Internal Revenue Code, relating to certain dispositions of section 38 property, applies with respect to any asset. 26 CFR 1.46-3

(c) *Recomputation of credit and qualified investment.* Maintain records which will establish with respect to each item of section 38 property, the following facts: (1) The date the property is disposed of or otherwise ceases to be section 38 property, (2) the estimated useful life which was assigned to the property for computing qualified investment, (3) the month and the taxable year in which property was placed in service, and (4) the basis (or cost), actually or reasonably determined, of the property.

Taxpayers who, for purposes of determining qualified investment, do not use a mortality dispersion table with respect to section 38 assets similar in kind but who consistently assign to such assets separate lives based on the estimated range of years taken into consideration in establishing the average useful life of such assets, must, in addition to the above records, maintain records which will establish to the satisfaction of the district director that such asset has not previously been considered as having been disposed of. 26 CFR 1.47-1

(d) *Disposition or cessation of section 38 property.* Any taxpayer who seeks to establish his interest in a trade or business, a former electing small business corporation, an estate or trust, or a partnership, shall maintain adequate records to demonstrate his indirect interest after any such transfer or transfers. 26 CFR 1.47-3, 1.47-4, 1.47-5, 1.47-6

(e) *Persons selecting used section 38 property, $50,000 cost limitation.* To maintain records which permit specific identification of any item of used section 38 property selected, which was placed in service by the person selecting the property. Each member, other than the filing member, of a controlled group shall retain as part of its records a copy of the apportionment statement which was attached to the filing member's return. 26 CFR 1.48-3

(f) *Election of lessor of new section 38 property to treat lessee as purchaser.* The lessor and the lessee shall keep as a part of their records the statements filed with the lessee, signed by the lessor and including the written consent of the lessee. 26 CFR 1.48-4

Retention period: See Item 4.1

4.1b Apportionment of the first $25,000 of the work incentive program (WIN) credit among members of a controlled group of corporations.

Each component member of the group shall keep a copy of the statement containing all the required consents. 26 CFR 1.50A-1

Retention period: See Item 4.1.

4.1c Persons claiming that a recomputation of the work incentive program (WIN) credit is not required by the early termination of a participating employee.

To maintain sufficient records to support claim that a termination of employment falls within the exceptions specified in the section cited.

Retention period: Expiration of the pertinent period of limitations. 26 CFR 1.50A-4

4.1d Persons maintaining that the transfer of an interest in a former small business corporation, estate or trust, or partnership for an interest in another entity does not result in a diminution requiring a recapture of the work incentive program (WIN) credit.

To maintain adequate records to demonstrate their indirect interest after any such transfer or transfers. 26 CFR 1.50A-5, 1.50A-6, 1.50A-7

Retention period: See Item 4.1.

4.1e Persons participating in employer accident or health plans. [Added]

To maintain records as are necessary to substantiate amount treated as their investment in their annuity contract. 26 CFR 1.72-15

Retention period: See Item 4.1.

4.1f Persons not totally blind claiming the additional exemption for blindness. [Renumbered]

To retain a copy of the certified opinion of the examining physician skilled in the disease of the eye that there is no reasonable probability that his visual acuity will ever improve beyond the minimum standards described in section 1.151-1 (d) (3) of the regulations. 26 CFR 1.151-1(d) (4)

Retention period: See Item 4.1.

4.2 Persons paying travel or other business expenses incurred by an employee in connection with the performance of his services.

To maintain adequate and detailed records of ordinary and necessary travel, transportation, entertainment, and other similar business expenses, including identification of amount and nature of expenditures, and to keep supporting documents, especially in connection with large or exceptional expenditures. 26 CFR 1.162-17

Retention period: See Item 4.1.

4.3 Persons claiming allowance for depreciation of property used in trade or business or property held for the production of income.

To keep records and accounts with respect to basis of property, depreciation rates, reserves, salvage, retirements, adjustments, elections, property excluded from elections, cost of repair, maintenance or improvement of property, agreements with respect to estimated useful life, rates and salvage, and other factors. 26 CFR 1.167(a)-7, 1.167(a)-11, 1.167(a)-12, 1.167(d)-1

Retention period: See Item 4.1.

4.3a Persons changing method of depreciation of section 1245 or section 1250 property.

To maintain records which permit specific identification of section 1245 or section 1250 property in the account with respect to which the election is made, and any other property in such account. The records shall also show for all the property in the account the date of acquisition, cost or other basis, amounts recovered through depreciation and other allowances, the estimated salvage value, the character of the property, and the remaining useful life of the property. 26 CFR 1.167(e)-1, 1.167(j)-1

Retention period: See Item 4.1.

4.3b Persons claiming depreciation with respect to residential rental property.

To maintain a record of the gross rental income derived from a building, and the portion thereof which constitutes gross rental income from dwelling units, in addition to records required under section 1.167(a)–7(c) with respect to property in a depreciation account. 26 CFR 1.167(j)–3

Retention period: See Item 4.1.

4.3c Persons claiming depreciation of expenditures to rehabilitate low-income rental housing.

To maintain detailed records which permit specific identification of the rehabilitation expenditures that are permitted to be allocated to individual dwelling units under the allocation rules and income certifications that must be obtained from tenants who propose to live in rehabilitated dwelling units after the close of the certification year. 26 CFR 1.167(k)–2, 1.167(k)–3

Retention period: See Item 4.1.

4.3d Persons claiming a deduction for amounts expended in maintaining certain students as a member of household.

To keep adequate records of amounts actually paid in maintaining a student as a member of the household. For certain items, such as food, a record of amounts spent for all members of the household, with an equal portion thereof allocated to each member, will be acceptable. 26 CFR 1.170–2, 1.170A–2

Retention period: See Item 4.1.

4.4 Persons electing to treat trademark or trade name expenditures as deferred expenses.

To make an accounting segregation on his books and records of trademark and trade name expenditures, for which the election has been made, sufficient to permit an identification of the character and amount of each expenditure and the amortization period selected for each expenditure. 26 CFR 1.177–1

Retention period: See Item 4.1.

4.5 Persons electing additional first-year depreciation allowance for section 179 property.

To maintain records which permit specific identification of each piece of "section 179 property" and reflect how and from whom such property was acquired. 26 CFR 1.179–4

Retention period: See Item 4.1.

4.5a Persons electing to deduct reha- bilitation expenditures with respect to certain railroad rolling stock.

To maintain a separate section 263(e) record, as specified in the section cited, for each unit for which rehabilitation expenditures are deducted, and to maintain records for expenditures deducted as incidental repairs and maintenance. 26 CFR 1.263(e)–1

Retention period: See Item 4.1.

4.6 Persons receiving any class of exempt income or holding property or engaging in activities the income from which is exempt.

To keep records of expenses otherwise allowable as deductions which are directly allocable to any class or classes of exempt income and amounts of items or parts of items allocated to each class. 26 CFR 1.265–1

Retention period: See Item 4.1.

4.7 Taxpayer substantiation of expenses for travel, entertainment, and gifts related to active conduct of trade or business.

A taxpayer must substantiate each element of an expenditure by adequate records or sufficient evidence corroborating his own statements. 26 CFR 1.274–1, 1.274–5

Retention period: See Item 4.1.

4.7a Persons who file a waiver of attribution agreement with respect to a redemption of stock in termination of their interest.

To retain copies of income tax returns and any other records indicating fully the amount of tax which would have been payable had the redemption been treated as a distribution subject to section 301. 26 CFR 1.302–4

Retention period: See Item 4.1.

4.7b Corporations using different methods of depreciation for taxable income and earnings and profit.

To maintain records which show the depreciation taken each year and which will allow computation of the adjusted basis of the property in each account using depreciation taken. 26 CFR 1.312–15(d)

Retention period: See Item 4.1.

4.8 Corporations receiving distributions in complete liquidation of subsidiaries.

To keep records showing information with respect to the plan of liquidation and its adoption. 26 CFR 1.332–6

Retention period: See Item 4.1.

4.9 Qualified electing shareholders receiving distributions in complete liquidation of domestic corporations other than collapsible corporations.

To keep records in substantial form showing all facts pertinent to the recognition and treatment of the gain realized upon shares of stock owned at the time of the adoption of the plan of liquidation. 26 CFR 1.333–6

Retention period: See Item 4.1.

4.10 Persons who participate in a transfer of property to a corporation controlled by the transferor.

To keep records in substantial form showing information to facilitate the determination of gain or loss from a subsequent disposition of stock or securities and other property, if any, received in the exchange. 26 CFR 1.351–3

Retention period: See Item 4.1.

4.11 Persons who participate in a taxfree exchange in connection with a corporate reorganization.

To keep records in substantial form showing the cost or other basis of the transferred property and the amount of stock or securities and other property or money received (including any liabilities assumed upon the exchange, or any liabilities to which any of the properties received were subject), in order to facilitate the determination of gain or loss from a subsequent disposition of such stock or securities and other property received from the exchange. 26 CFR 1.368–3

Retention period: See Item 4.1.

4.12 Persons who exchange stock and securities in corporations in accordance with plans of reorganizations approved by the courts in receivership, foreclosure, or similar proceedings, or in proceedings under chapter X of the Bankruptcy Act.

To keep records in substantial form showing the cost or other basis of the transferred property and the amount of stock or securities and other property or money received (including any liabilities assumed upon the exchange), in order to facilitate the determination of gain or loss from a subsequent disposition of such stock or securities and other property received from the exchange. 26 CFR 1.371–2

Retention period: See Item 4.1.

4.13 Corporations which are parties to reorganizations in pursuance of court orders in receivership, foreclosure, or similar proceedings, or in proceedings under chapter X of the Bankruptcy Act.

To keep records in substantial form showing the cost or other basis of the transferred property and the amount of stock or securities and other property or money received (including any liabilities assumed upon the exchange), in order to facilitate the determination of gain or loss from a subsequent disposition of such stock or securities and other property received from the exchange. 26 CFR 1.371–1

Retention period: See Item 4.1.

4.14 Railroads participating in a taxfree reorganization.

Records in substantial form must be kept by every railroad corporation which participates in a tax-free exchange in connection with a reorganization under section 374(a) of the Internal Revenue Code, showing the cost or other basis of the transferred property and the amount of stock or securities and other property or money received, including any liabilities assumed upon the exchange, in order to facilitate the determination of gain or loss from a subsequent disposition of such stock or securities and other property received from the exchange.

Retention period: Permanent. 26 CFR 1.374–3

4.15 Records required in computing depreciation allowance carryovers of acquiring corporations in certain corporate acquisitions.

Records shall be maintained in sufficient detail to identify any depreciable property to which section 1.381(c)(6)–1 of the regulations applies and to establish the basis thereof. 26 CFR 1.381(c)(6)–1

Retention period: See Item 4.1.

4.16 Corporations and shareholders for whom elections are filed with respect to the tax treatment of corporate reorganizations.

To keep permanent records of all relevant data in order to facilitate the determination of gain or loss from a subsequent disposition of stock or securities or other property acquired in the

transaction in respect of which the election was filed. 26 CFR 1.393–3
Retention period: See Item 4.1.

4.16a   Qualified pension or annuity plans with provisions for certain medical benefits.

To keep a separate account for record-keeping purposes with respect to contributions received to fund medical benefits described in section 401(h) of the Internal Revenue Code. 26 CFR 1.401–14
Retention period: See Item 4.1.

4.17   Employers maintaining a pension, annuity, stock bonus, profit-sharing, or other funded plan of deferred compensation.

To keep records substantiating all data and information required to be filed with respect to each plan. 26 CFR 1.404(a)–2, 1.404(a)–2A
Retention period: See Item 4.1.

4.18   Persons required to seek the approval of the Commissioner in order to change their annual accounting period.

To keep adequate and accurate records of their taxable income for the short period involved in the change and for the fiscal year proposed. 26 CFR 1.442–1
Retention period: See Item 4.1.

4.19   Persons selling by the installment method.

(a) *Installment method.* In adopting the installment method of accounting the seller must maintain such records as are necessary to clearly reflect income. A dealer who desires to compute income by the installment method shall maintain accounting records in such a manner as to enable an accurate computation to be made by such method.

(b) *Revolving credit plan.* The percentage of charges under a revolving credit plan which will be treated as sales on the installment plan shall be computed by making an actual segregation of charges in a probability sample of the revolving credit accounts in order to determine what percentage of charges in the sample is to be treated as sales on the installment plan. The taxpayer shall maintain records in sufficient detail to show the method of computing and applying the sample. 26 CFR 1.453–1, 1.453–2
Retention period: See Item 4.1.

4.19a   Prepaid dues income.

A taxpayer who makes an election with respect to prepaid dues income shall maintain books and records in sufficient

detail to enable the district director to determine upon audit that additional amounts were included in the taxpayer's gross income for any of the three taxable years preceding such first taxable year. 26 CFR 1.456–7
Retention period: See Item 4.1.

4.20   Persons engaged in the production, purchase, or sale of merchandise.

(a) *General.* To keep a record of inventory, properly computed and summerized, conforming to the best accounting practices in the trade or business which clearly reflects income, enables inventories to be verified, and is consistent from year to year.

(b) *Manufacturers—full absorption method.* To maintain records and working papers to support burden rate calculations; and to preserve at his principal place of business all records, data, and other evidence relating to the full absorption values of inventory resulting from an election to change to the full absorption method. 26 CFR 1.471–1, 1.471–2, 1.471–11
Retention period: See Item 4.1.

4.20a   Persons permitted or required to use the LIFO method of inventory valuation.

(a) *General.* To maintain such supplemental and detailed inventory records as will enable the District Director to verify the inventory computations.

(b) *Dollar-value method.* To maintain adequate records to support the appropriateness, accuracy, and reliability of the index or link-chain method. 26 CFR 1.472–2, 1.472–8
Retention period: See Item 4.1.

4.20b   Controlled entities arm's length charges.

To maintain adequate books and records to permit verification of costs or deductions when a factor in determining the arm's length charge for services rendered to other members of a controlled group. 26 CFR 1.482–2(b)(3)
Retention period: See Item 4.1.

4.20c   Supplemental Unemployment Benefit Trusts.

To maintain records indicating the amount of separation benefits and sick and accident benefits which have been provided to each employee. If a plan is financed, in whole or in part, by employee contributions to the trust, the trust must maintain records indicating the amount of each employee's total contributions allocable to separation benefits. 26 CFR 1.501(c)(17)–2(j)
Retention period: See Item 4.1.

4.20d Farmer's cooperative marketing and purchasing associations.

To keep permanent records of the business done both with members and nonmembers, which show that the association was operating during the taxable year on a cooperative basis in the distribution of patronage dividends to all producers. While under the Code patronage dividends must be paid to all producers on the same basis, this requirement is complied with if an association, instead of paying patronage dividends to nonmember producers in cash, keeps permanent records from which the proportionate shares of the patronage dividends due to nonmember producers can be determined, and such shares are made applicable toward the purchase price of a share of stock or of a membership in the association. 26 CFR 1.521–1
Retention period: See Item 4.1.

4.21 Corporations claiming deduction for dividends paid.

To keep permanent records necessary (a) to establish that dividends with respect to which the deduction is claimed were actually paid during the taxable year, and (b) to supply the information required to be filed with the income tax return of the corporation. To also keep canceled dividend checks and receipts obtained from shareholders acknowledging payment. 26 CFR 1.561–2
Retention period: See Item 4.1.

4.21a Mutual savings banks, etc., maintaining reserves for bad debts.

To maintain as a permanent part of its regular books of account, an account for: (1) a reserve for losses on nonqualifying loans, (2) a reserve for losses on qualifying real property loans, and (3) if required, a supplemental reserve for losses on loans. A permanent subsidiary ledger containing an account for each of such reserves may be maintained. 26 CFR 1.593–7
Retention period: See Item 4.1.

4.21b Mutual savings banks, etc., making capital improvements on land acquired by foreclosure.

To maintain such records as are necessary to reflect clearly, with respect to each particular acquired property, the cost of each capital improvement and whether the taxpayer treated minor capital improvements with respect to such property in the same manner as the acquired property. 26 CFR 1.595–1
Retention period: See Item 4.1.

4.22 Persons claiming allowance for cost depletion of natural gas property without reference to discovery value or percentage depletion.

To keep accurate records of periodical pressure determinations where the annual production is not metered. 26 CFR 1.611–2
Retention period: See Item 4.1.

4.23 Persons claiming an allowance for depletion and depreciation of mineral property, oil and gas wells, and other natural deposits.

To keep a separate account in which shall be accurately recorded the cost or other basis of such property together with subsequent allowable capital additions to each account and all other required adjustments; and, to assemble, segregate, and have readily available all the supporting data which is used in compiling certain summary statements required to be attached to returns and such other records as indicated in sections cited. 26 CFR 1.611–2, 1.611–5, 1.613–6
Retention period: See Item 4.1.

4.23a Mineral property, taxable income computation, allocation of section 1245 gain.

Taxpayer shall have available permanent records of all the facts necessary to determine with reasonable accuracy the portion of any gain recognized under section 1245(a)(1) of the Code which is properly allocable to the mineral property in respect of which the taxable income is being computed. In the absence of such records, none of the gain recognized under section 1245(a)(1) shall be allocable to such mineral property. 26 CFR 1.613–5
Retention period: See Item 4.1.

4.23b Persons computing gross incomes from mining by use of representative market or field price.

To keep records as to the source of his pricing information and relevant supporting data. 26 CFR 1.613–4(c)(5)
Retention period: See Item 4.1.

4.24 Persons claiming an allowance for depletion of timber property.

To keep accurate ledger accounts in which shall be recorded the cost or other basis of the property and land together with subsequent allowable capital additions in each account and all other adjustments. In such accounts there shall be set up separately the quantity of timber, the quantity of land, and the quantity of other resources, if any, and a proper part of the total cost or value shall be allocated to each after proper provision for immature timber growth. The timber accounts shall be credited each year with the amount of the charges to the depletion accounts or the amount of the charges to the depletion accounts shall be credited to depletion reserves accounts. 26 CFR 1.611-3

Retention period: See Item 4.1.

4.25 Persons electing to aggregate separate operating mineral interests.

To maintain adequate records and maps that shall contain a description of the aggregation and the operating mineral interests within the operating unit which are to be treated as separate properties apart from the aggregation. A general description, accompanied by appropriately marked maps, which accurately circumscribes the scope of the aggregation and identifies the properties which are to be treated separately will be sufficient. There shall also be included a description of the operating unit in sufficient detail to show that the aggregated operating mineral interests are properly within a single operating unit. 26 CFR 1.614-2

Retention period: See Item 4.1.

4.26 Persons with separate operating mineral interests in the case of mines.

To maintain adequate records and maps and statements of election as indicated in the section cited. 26 CFR 1.614-3

Retention period: See Item 4.1.

4.26a Persons aggregating operating mineral interests in oil and gas wells in a single tract or parcel of land.

To obtain accurate and reliable information, and keep records with respect thereto, establishing all facts necessary for making the computations prescribed for the fair market value method of determining basis on the aggregation. 26 CFR 1.614-6

Retention period: See Item 4.1.

4.26b Persons electing to treat separate operating mineral interests in oil and gas wells in a single tract or parcel of land as separate properties.

To maintain and have available records and maps sufficient to clearly define the tract or parcel and all of the taxpayer's operating mineral interests therein. 26 CFR 1.614-8

Retention period: See Item 4.1.

4.26c Trustee of trust claiming charitable remainder interest deduction, incompetent grantor. [Added]

To retain certificate of incompetency or a copy of the judgment or decree and any modification thereof. 26 CFR 1.642 (c)-2(b)(3)

Retention period: See Item 4.1

4.26d Pooled income fund investing or reinvesting any portion of its properties jointly with other properties. [Renumbered]

To maintain records which identify the portion of the total fund which is owned by the pooled income fund and the income earned by, and attributable to, such portion. 26 CFR 1.642(c)-5

Retention period: See Item 4.1.

4.26e Trusts-accumulation distribution allocated to preceding years. [Renumbered]

For all taxable years of a trust, the trustee must retain copies of the trust's income tax return as well as information pertaining to any adjustments in the tax shown as due on the return. Trustee shall also retain trust's records required by section 6001 of the Internal Revenue Code and the regulations thereunder for each taxable year for which the period of limitations on assessment of tax under section 6501 of the Code has not expired. 26 CFR 1.666(d)-1A

Retention period: See Item 4.1.

4.26f Life insurance companies issuing contracts with reserves based on segregated asset accounts. [Renumbered]

To keep such permanent records and other data relating to such contracts as is necessary to enable the District Director to determine the correctness of the application of the separate accounting rules and the accuracy of the computations. 26 CFR 1.801-8(c)

Retention period: See Item 4.1.

4.27 Life insurance companies distributing dividends to policyholders.

Every life insurance company claiming a deduction for dividends to policyholders shall keep such permanent records as are necessary to establish the amount of dividends actually paid during the taxable year. Such company shall also keep a copy of the dividend resolution and any necessary supporting data relating to the amounts of dividends declared and to the amounts held or set aside as reserves for dividends to policyholders during the taxable year.

Retention period: Permanent. 26 CFR 1.811–2

4.28 Life insurance companies with respect to the optional treatment of policies reinsured under modified coinsurance contracts.

The reinsured and reinsurer shall maintain as part of their permanent books of account any subsequent amendments to the original modified coinsurance contract between the reinsured and reinsurer. 26 CFR 1.820–2

Retention period: See Item 4.1.

4.29 Regulated investment companies. [Revised]

(a) To maintain records showing the information relative to the actual owners of its stock contained in the written statements to be demanded from the shareholders.

(b) To maintain records showing the maximum number of its shares (including the number and face value of securities convertible into stock) to be considered as actually or constructively owned by each of the actual owners of its stock during the last half of its taxable year.

(c) To maintain a list of persons failing or refusing to comply in whole or in part with its demand for statements respecting ownership of its shares.

(d) To keep a record of the proportion of each capital gain dividend which is gain described in section 1201(d) (1) or (2) of the Internal Revenue Code of 1954 for taxable years ending after 1969, and beginning before 1975.

(e) To keep a record of the proportion of undistributed capital gains which are gains described in section 1201(d) (1) or (2) of the Code for taxable years ending after 1969, and beginning before 1975. 26 CFR 1.852–4(c) (3), 1.852–6, 1.852–9 (a) (1) (iii) and (c) (3).

Retention period: See Item 4.1.

4.29a Shareholders of regulated investment companies.

To keep copy C of Form 2439 furnished for the regulated investment company's taxable years ending after 1969, and beginning before 1975, to show increases in the shareholder's adjusted basis of shares of such company. 26 CFR 1.852–9

Retention period: See Item 4.1.

4.30 Real estate investment trust [Revised]

(a) To keep a record of the proportion of each capital dividend which is gain described in section 1201(d) (1) or (2) of the Internal Revenue Code of

1954 for taxable years ending after 1969, and beginning before 1975.

(b) To maintain records showing the information relative to the actual owners of its stock contained in the written statements to be demanded from its shareholders.

(c) To maintain records showing the maximum number of its shares (including the number and face value of securities convertible into stock) to be considered as actually or constructively owned by each of the actual owners of its stock during the last half of its taxable year.

(d) To maintain a list of persons failing or refusing to comply in whole or in part with its demand for statements respecting ownership of its shares. 26 CFR 1.857–4(e) (2), 1.857–6

Retention period: See Item 4.1

4.31 Persons claiming credit for taxes paid or accrued to foreign countries and possessions of the United States.

To keep readily available for comparison on request the original receipt for each such tax payment, or the original return on which each such accrued tax was based, a duplicate original, or a duly certified or authenticated copy, in case only a sworn copy of a receipt or return is submitted. 26 CFR 1.905–2

Retention period: See Item 4.1.

4.32 Western Hemisphere trade corporations.

To keep records substantiating income tax statement showing that its entire business is done within the Western Hemisphere and if any purchases are made outside the Western Hemisphere, the amount of such purchases, the amount of its gross receipts from all sources, and any other pertinent information. 26 CFR 1.921–1

Retention period: See Item 4.1.

4.32a Persons or corporations seeking to come within the exception to the limitation on reduction in income tax liability incurred to the Virgin Islands, under section 934 of the Internal Revenue Code of 1954.

Must maintain such records and other documents as are necessary to determine the applicability of the exception. 26 CFR 1.934–1

Retention period: See Item 4.1.

4.32b United States shareholders of controlled foreign corporations.

To provide permanent books of account or records which are sufficient to verify for the taxable year subpart F, export

trade, and certain other classes of income; gross income excluded from base company income and the increase in earnings invested in United States property; also, if the Commissioner has issued a determination letter granting authority for excluding certain income from foreign base company income, a copy of the letter shall be retained. 26 CFR 1.954–1(b)(4)(v), 1.964–3, 1.964–4
Retention period: See Item 4.1.

4.32c Domestic international sales corporations (DISCs); foreign investment attributable to producer's loans.

To keep permanent books or records as are sufficient to establish the transactions, amounts, and computations described in the section cited. 26 CFR 1.995–5 (f) and (g)
Retention period: See Item 4.1.

4.32d Election to use the average basis method for certain regulated investment company stock.

To maintain records as are necessary to substantiate the average basis (or bases) used on an income tax return in reporting gain or loss from the sale or transfer of shares. 26 CFR 1.1012–1
Retention period: See Item 4.1.

4.33 Executors or other legal representatives of decedents, fiduciaries of trusts under wills, life tenants and other persons to whom a uniform basis with respect to property transmitted at death is applicable.

To make and maintain records showing in detail all deductions, distributions, or other items for which adjustment to basis is required to be made. 26 CFR 1.1014–4
Retention period: See Item 4.1.

4.34 Persons making or receiving gifts of property acquired by gift after December 31, 1920.

To preserve and keep accessible a record of the facts necessary to determine the cost of the property and, if pertinent, its fair market value as of March 1, 1913, or its fair market value as of the date of the gift, to insure a fair and adequate determination of the proper basis. 26 CFR 1.1015–1
Retention period: See Item 4.1.

4.35 Persons participating in exchanges or distributions made in obedience to orders of the Securities and Exchange Commission.

To keep records in substantial form showing the cost or other basis of the property transferred and the amount of stock or securities and other property (including money) received. 26 CFR 1.1081–11
Retention period: See Item 4.1.

4.36 Stock or security holders records of distribution pursuant to the Bank Holding Company Act of 1956.

Each stock or security holder who receives stock or securities or other property upon a distribution made by a qualified bank holding corporation under section 1101 of the Internal Revenue Code shall maintain records of all facts pertinent to the nonrecognition of gain upon such distribution. 26 CFR 1.1101–4
Retention period: See Item 4.1.

4.36a Gain upon sale or exchange of obligations issued at an original issue discount after December 31, 1954.

Taxpayer shall keep a record of the issue price and issue date upon or with each such obligation (if known or reasonably ascertainable by him). If the obligation held is an obligation of the United States received from the United States in an exchange upon which gain or loss is not recognized because of section 1037(a) of the Code (or so much of section 1031 (b) or (c) as relates to section 1037(a)), the taxpayer shall keep sufficient records to determine the issue price of such obligations for purposes of applying section 1.1037–1 of the regulations upon the disposition or redemption of such obligations. 26 CFR 1.1232–3(f)
Retention period: See Item 4.1.

4.37 Persons engaged in arbitrage operations in stock and securities.

To keep records that will clearly show that a transaction has been timely and properly identified as an arbitrage operation. Such identification must ordinarily be entered in the taxpayer's records on the day of the transaction. 26 CFR 1.1233–1
Retention period: See Item 4.1.

4.37a Grantors of straddles.

In the case of a multiple option where the number of options to sell and the number of options to buy are not the same or if the terms of all the options are not identical, the grantor must indicate in his records the individual serial number of, or other characteristic symbol imprinted upon, each of the two individual options which comprise the straddle, or by adopting any other method of identification satisfactory to the Commissioner. Such identification must be made before the expiration of the fifteenth day after the day on which the multiple option is granted and is applicable to multiple options granted after January 24, 1972, 26 CFR 1.1234-2

Retention period: See Item 4.1.

4.38 Record retention requirements for corporations and shareholders with respect to the substantiation of ordinary loss deductions on small business corporation stock.

(a) *Corporations.* The plan to issue stock which qualifies under section 1244 of the Internal Revenue Code must appear upon the records of the corporation. In addition, in order to substantiate an ordinary loss deduction claimed by its shareholders, the corporation should maintain records as indicated in section cited.

(b) *Shareholders.* Any person who claims a deduction for an ordinary loss on stock under section 1244 of the Code shall file with his income tax return for the year in which a deduction for the loss is claimed a statement setting forth information indicated in section cited.

In addition, a person who owns "section 1244 stock" in a corporation shall maintain records sufficient to distinguish such stock from any other stock he may own in the corporation. 26 CFR 1.1244(e)-1.

Retention period: See Item 4.1.

4.38a Foreign investment companies.

To maintain and preserve such permanent books of account, records, and other documents as are sufficient to establish what its taxable income would be if it were a domestic corporation. Generally, if the books and records are maintained in the manner prescribed by regulations under section 30 of the Investment Company Act of 1940, the requirements shall be considered satisfied. 26 CFR 1.1247-5

Retention period: See Item 4.1.

4.38b Recomputed basis of section 1245 property and additional depreciation adjustments to section 1250 property when such property is sold, exchanged, transferred, or involuntarily converted.

To maintain permanent records which include (1) the date and manner in which the property was acquired, (2) the basis on the date the property was

acquired and the manner in which the basis was determined, (3) the amount and date of all adjustments to basis, and (4) similar information with respect to other property having an adjusted basis reflecting depreciation or amortization adjustments by the taxpayer, or by another taxpayer on the same or other property. 26 CFR 1.1245-2, 1.1250-2

Retention period: See Item 4.1.

4.39 Persons involved in the liquidation and replacement of lifo inventories.

To keep detailed records such as will enable the Commissioner, in his examination of the taxpayer's return for the year of replacement, readily to verify the extent of the inventory decrease claimed to be involuntary in character and the facts upon which such claim is based, all subsequent inventory increases and decreases, and all other facts material to the replacement adjustment authorized. 26 CFR 1.1321-1, 1.1321-2

Retention period: See Item 4.1.

4.40 Unincorporated business electing to be taxed as a domestic corporation.

To keep records, render statements, and make returns in the same manner as a domestic corporation and maintain such other records as indicated in the sections cited. 26 CFR 1.1361-10, 1.1361-14

Retention period: See Item 4.1.

4.41 Records by small business corporations of (1) distributions of previously taxed income and (2) undistributed taxable income.

A small business corporation must keep records of (1) distributions of the net share of the previously taxed income of each shareholder and (2) each person's share of undistributed taxable income. In addition, each shareholder of such corporation shall keep a record of his own net share of previously taxed income and undistributed taxable income and shall make such record available to the corporation for its information. 26 CFR 1.1375-4; 1.1375-6

Retention period: See Item 4.1.

4.41a Persons required to withhold tax on nonresident aliens, foreign corporations, and tax-free covenant bonds on payments of income made on and after January 1, 1957.

To keep copies of Forms 1042 and 1042S. 26 CFR 1.1461-2

Retention period: See Item 4.1.

4.41b Affiliated group; (1) intercom-

pany transactions, accounting for deferred gain or loss, and (2) alocation of Federal income tax liability.

(1) Maintain permanent records (including work papers) which will properly reflect the amount of deferred gain or loss and enable the group to identify the character and source of the deferred gain or loss to the selling member and apply the applicable restoration rules. (2) If an affiliated group elects to use the method of allocating Federal income tax liability provided in section 1.1502–33(d) (2)(i) of the regulations, it must maintain specific records to substantiate the tax liability of each member on a separate return basis for purposes of paragraphs (a)(1) and (b)(1) of such subdivision (i). In addition, allocations of tax liability may be made in accordance with any other method approved by the Commissioner, but a condition of such approval shall be that the group maintain specific records to substantiate its computations pursuant to such method. 26 CFR 1.1502–13(c)(5), 1.1502–33, 1.1552–1

Retention period: See Item 4.1.

4.41c Withholding agents making payment to nonresident aliens, foreign partnerships, or foreign corporations after December 31, 1971, which are subject to a reduced rate or an exemption from tax pursuant to a tax treaty.

To maintain Form 1001, Ownership, Exemption, or Reduced Rate Certificate.

Retention period: *Coupon bond interest* at least 4 years after the close of the calendar year in which the interest is paid; *Income other than coupon bond interest or dividends* at least 4 years after the close of the calendar year in which the interest is paid; *Noncoupon bond interest* at least 4 years after the interest is paid. 26 CFR 1.1441–6, 1.1461–1

4.42 Tax-exempt organizations.

(a) *General.* To keep records and books of account pertaining to information included in the annual return, including items of gross income, receipts, disbursements, and contributions and gifts received, and to keep other pertinent information which will enable the district director to inquire into the organization's exempt status. An organization claiming an exception from the filing of an information return must maintain adequate records to substantiate such claim. 26 CFR 1.6001–1, 1.6033–1, 1.6033–2

(b) *Employees' trusts.* To keep as a part of its records for taxable years beginning after December 31, 1969, and ending before December 31, 1971, written notification, or a copy thereof, from an employer to the trustee that the employer has or will timely file the information required under section 404 of the Internal Revenue Code. 26 CFR 1.6033–2

(c) *Group returns.* The central organization shall retain the certified statements of those local organizations authorizing their inclusion in a group return. 26 CFR 1.6033–1, 1.6033–2

Retention period: (a) and (b) See Item 4.1; (c), for taxable years prior to January 1, 1970, permanent; for taxable years after December 31, 1969, until the expiration of 6 years after the last taxable year for which a group return includes the local organization.

4.42a Banking institutions, trust companies, or brokerage firms, who elect to file Form 1087, Nominee's Information Return, for each actual owner for whom it acts as nominee.

Must maintain such records as will permit a prompt substantiation of each payments of dividends made to the actual owner. 26 CFR 1.6042–1

Retention period: See Item 4.1.

4.42b Any trustee, insurance company, or other person, which is notified under section 6047(b) of the Code that contributions to a trust or under a retirement plan have been made on behalf of an owner-employee.

Shall maintain a record of such notification.

Retention period: Until all funds of the trust or under the plan on behalf of the owner-employee have been distributed. 26 CFR 1.6047–1

4.42c Nonbank trustees, pension and profit-sharing trusts benefiting owner-employees. [Added]

To maintain separate and distinct fiduciary records, permanent records of all fiduciary assets deposited or withdrawn from vault, full information relative to each account, and an adequate record of all pending litigation in connection with exercise of fiduciary powers. 26 CFR 11.401(d)(1)–1(f)

Retention period: See Item 4.1

4.42d Persons making payments of estimated tax installments in foreign currency. [Renumbered]

Maintain a copy of the statement certified by the foundation, commission, or other person having control of the payments to the taxpayer in nonconvertible foreign currency which are expected to be received during the taxable year for the purpose of exhibiting it to the disbursing officer when making installment deposits of foreign currency. 26 CFR 301.6316–6

Retention period: See Item 4.1.

4.43 Persons engaged in construction of aircraft for the Army and the Air Force.

To keep books, records, and original evidences of costs pertinent to the determination of the true profit, excess profit, deficiency in profit, or net loss from the performance of a contract or subcontract.

Retention period: So long as the contents thereof may become material in the administration of the act of March 27, 1934, as amended. 26 CFR 16.13 (see 26 CFR 1.1471–1)

4.44 Persons engaged in construction of naval vessels or aircraft for the Navy.

To keep books, records, and original evidences of costs pertinent to the determination of the true profit, excess profit, deficiency in profit, or net loss from the performance of a contract or subcontract.

Retention period: So long as the contents thereof may become material in the administration of the act of March 27, 1934, as amended. 26 CFR 17.14 (see 26 CFR 1.1471–1)

4.44a Domestic building and loan associations.

To maintain adequate records to establish to the satisfaction of the district director that various assets tests are met for taxable years beginning after October 16, 1962, and ending before November 1, 1964. 26 CFR 301.7701–13

Retention period: See Item 4.1.

4.44b Organizations seeking classification as private nonoperating foundations.

To maintain adequate records substantiating that all contributions received in taxable years ending in either 1970 or 1971 were distributed not later than the 15th day of the third month after the close of the taxable year or by the 30th day after final regulations under section 170(b)(1)(E)(ii) are published in the Federal Register, whichever is later. 26 CFR 13.15

Retention period: See Item 4.1.

ESTATE TAX

4.45 Executors of estates.

To keep detailed records of the affairs of the estate as will enable the district director to determine the amount of the estate tax liability, including copies of documents relating to the estate, appraisal lists of items included in the gross estate, copies of balance sheets or other financial statements relating to value of stock, and any other information necessary in determining the tax.

Retention period: Not specified. 26 CFR 20.6001–1

GIFT TAX

4.46 Persons making transfers of property by gift.

To maintain books of account or records as are necessary to establish the amount of the total gifts together with the deductions allowable in determining the amount of taxable gifts, and other information required to be shown in their gift tax returns.

Retention period: Permanent. 26 CFR 25.6001–1

EMPLOYMENT TAX

4.47 General record retention requirement for employment taxes.

(a) Persons required by regulations or instructions shall keep copies of any return, schedule, statement, or other document as part of their records.

(b) Any person who claims a refund, credit, or abatement shall keep records as indicated in the section cited.

(c) While not mandatory (except in the case of claims) it is advisable for each employee to keep permanent accurate records as indicated in the section cited.

Retention period: 4 years after the due date of such tax for the return period to which the records relate or the date such tax is paid, whichever is later. In the case of claimants, at least 4 years after the date the claim is filed. 26 CFR 31.6001–1

4.48 Vow-of-poverty religious orders electing social security coverage for its members.

To maintain records of the details relating to the retirement of each of its members.

Retention period: Not specified. 26 CFR 31.3121(r)–1

4.49 Employers required to deduct and withhold income tax on wages which include sick pay.

To keep records with respect to payments (sick pay) made directly to employees under a wage continuation plan, and other informaton specified in the sections cited.

Retention period: 4 years after the due date of such tax for the return period to which the records relate or the date such tax is paid, whichever is later. 26 CFR 31.3401(a)-1, 31.6001-5 (retention: 31.6001-1)

4.50 Employers liable for tax under the Federal Insurance Contributions Act.

To keep records of all remuneration, whether in cash or in a medium other than cash, paid to his employees after 1954 for services (other than agricultural labor which constitutes or is deemed to constitute employment, domestic service in a private home of the employer, or service not in the course of the employer's trade or business) performed for him after 1936; and records of all remuneration in the form of tips received by employees after 1965 and reported to him. Records shall include information specified in section cited.

Retention period: 4 years after the due date of such tax for the return period to which the records relate, or the date such tax is paid, whichever is the later. 26 CFR 31.6001-2 (retention: 31.6001-1)

4.51 Employers and employee representatives subject to the Railroad Retirement Tax Act.

To keep records of all remuneration (whether in money or in something which may be used in lieu of money) other than tips, paid to his employees after 1954 for services rendered to him (including "time lost") after 1954 and such other records as specified in section cited.

Retention period: 4 years after the due date of such tax for the return period to which the records relate, or the date such tax is paid, whichever is the later. 26 CFR 31.6001-3 (retention: 31.6001-1)

4.52 Employers and persons who are not employers for purposes of the Federal Unemployment Tax Act.

To maintain records as specified in the section cited to determine the correct liability or nonliability for the tax.

Retention period: 4 years after the due date of such tax for the return period to which the records relate or the date such tax is paid, whichever is later. 26 CFR 31.6001-4 (retention: 31.6001-1)

4.53 Employers required to deduct and withhold income tax on wages paid. [Revised]

(a) To keep records of all remuneration paid to such employees and tips received by employees and reported to him. Such records shall show with respect to each employee the information specified in the section cited.

(b) To retain the Internal Revenue Service copy and the employee copy of all undeliverable annual withholding statements.

Retention period: 4 years after the due date of such tax for the return period to which the records and statements relate, or the date such tax is paid, whichever is later. 26 CFR 31.6001-5, 31.6051-1(f)(3) (retention: 31.6001-1)

4.54 Employers claiming a refund, credit, or abatement of tax under the Federal Insurance Contributions Act or Railroad Retirement Tax Act.

Every employer who has filed a claim for refund, credit, or abatement of employee tax under section 3101 or section 3201 of the Internal Revenue Code, or a corresponding provision of prior law, collected from an employee shall retain as part of his records the written receipt of the employee showing the date and amount of the repayment, or the written consent of the employee, whichever is used in support of the claim. Where employee tax was collected under section 3101 of the Code, or a corresponding provision of prior law, from an employee in a calendar year prior to the year in which the credit or refund is claimed, the employer shall also retain as part of his records a written statement from the employee (a) that the employee has not claimed refund or credit of the amount of the overcollection, or if so, such claim has been rejected, and (b) that the employee will not claim refund or credit of such amount.

Retention period: 4 years after the date the claim is filed. 26 CFR 31.6402(a)-2, 31.6404(a)-1 (retention: 31.6001-1)

4.55 Repayment by employer of tax erroneously collected from employee under the Federal Insurance Contributions Act or the Railroad Retirement Tax Act and of income tax withheld from wages.

(a) *Before employer files return.* To obtain and keep as part of his records the written receipt of the employee showing the date and amount of the repayment.

(b) *After employer files return.* If the amount of an overcollection is repaid to an employee, the employer shall obtain and keep as part of his records the written receipt of the employee, showing the date and amount of the repayment. If in any calendar year, an employer repays or reimburses an employee in the amount of an overcollection of employee tax under section 3101 of the Internal Revenue Code, or a corresponding provision of prior law, which was collected from the employee in a prior calendar year, the employer shall obtain from the employee and keep as part of his records a written statement (a) that the employee has not claimed refund or credit of the amount of the overcollection, or if so, such claim has been rejected, and (b) that the employee will not claim refund or credit of such amount.

Retention period: 4 years after the due date of such tax for the return period to which the records relate, or the date such tax is paid, whichever is the later. The records of claimants shall be maintained for a period of at least 4 years after the date the claim is filed. 26 CFR 31.6413(a)–1 (retention: 31.6001-1)

Appendix C
Financial Planning Tables

The following tables, involving the effects of interest factors, are useful in various forms of future business planning.

SIMPLE INTEREST TABLE

SIMPLE INTEREST TABLE

Example of use of this table:
Find amount of $500 in 8 years at 6% simple interest.
From table at 8 yrs. and 6% for $1   1.48
Value in 8 yrs. for $500 (500 x 1.48) $740

Number of Years	Interest Rate							
	3%	4%	5%	6%	7%	8%	9%	10%
1	1.03	1.04	1.05	1.06	1.07	1.08	1.09	1.10
2	1.06	1.08	1.10	1.12	1.14	1.16	1.18	1.20
3	1.09	1.12	1.15	1.18	1.21	1.24	1.27	1.30
4	1.12	1.16	1.20	1.24	1.28	1.32	1.36	1.40
5	1.15	1.20	1.25	1.30	1.35	1.40	1.45	1.50
6	1.18	1.24	1.30	1.36	1.42	1.48	1.54	1.60
7	1.21	1.28	1.35	1.42	1.49	1.56	1.63	1.70
8	1.24	1.32	1.40	1.48	1.56	1.64	1.72	1.80
9	1.27	1.36	1.45	1.54	1.63	1.72	1.81	1.90
10	1.30	1.40	1.50	1.60	1.70	1.80	1.90	2.00
11	1.33	1.44	1.55	1.66	1.77	1.88	1.99	2.10
12	1.36	1.48	1.60	1.72	1.84	1.96	2.08	2.20
13	1.39	1.52	1.65	1.78	1.91	2.04	2.17	2.30
14	1.42	1.56	1.70	1.84	1.98	2.12	2.26	2.40
15	1.45	1.60	1.75	1.90	2.05	2.20	2.35	2.50
16	1.48	1.64	1.80	1.96	2.12	2.28	2.44	2.60
17	1.51	1.68	1.85	2.02	2.19	2.36	2.53	2.70
18	1.54	1.72	1.90	2.08	2.26	2.44	2.62	2.80
19	1.57	1.76	1.95	2.14	2.33	2.52	2.71	2.90
20	1.60	1.80	2.00	2.20	2.40	2.60	2.80	3.00
21	1.63	1.84	2.05	2.26	2.47	2.68	2.89	3.10
22	1.66	1.88	2.10	2.32	2.54	2.76	2.98	3.20
23	1.69	1.92	2.15	2.38	2.61	2.84	3.07	3.30
24	1.72	1.96	2.20	2.44	2.68	2.92	3.16	3.40
25	1.75	2.00	2.25	2.50	2.75	3.00	3.25	3.50
26	1.78	2.04	2.30	2.56	2.82	3.08	3.34	3.60
27	1.81	2.08	2.35	2.62	2.89	3.16	3.43	3.70
28	1.84	2.12	2.40	2.68	2.96	3.24	3.52	3.80
29	1.87	2.16	2.45	2.74	3.03	3.32	3.61	3.90
30	1.90	2.20	2.50	2.80	3.10	3.40	3.70	4.00
31	1.93	2.24	2.55	2.86	3.17	3.48	3.79	4.10
32	1.96	2.28	2.60	2.92	3.24	3.56	3.88	4.20
33	1.99	2.32	2.65	2.98	3.31	3.64	3.97	4.30
34	2.02	2.36	2.70	3.04	3.38	3.72	4.06	4.40
35	2.05	2.40	2.75	3.10	3.45	3.80	4.15	4.50
36	2.08	2.44	2.80	3.16	3.52	3.88	4.24	4.60
37	2.11	2.48	2.85	3.22	3.59	3.96	4.33	4.70
38	2.14	2.52	2.90	3.28	3.66	4.04	4.42	4.80
39	2.17	2.56	2.95	3.34	3.73	4.12	4.51	4.90
40	2.20	2.60	3.00	3.40	3.80	4.20	4.60	5.00

COMPOUND INTEREST TABLE

Example of use of this table:

Find how much $1,000 now in bank will grow to in 14 years at 6% interest.

From table 14 years at 6%   2.2609

Value in 14 years of $1,000 $2,260.9

Interest Rate

Number of Years	6%	7%	8%	9%	10%	11%	12%	13%
1	1.0600	1.0700	1.0800	1.0900	1.1000	1.1100	1.1200	1.1300
2	1.1236	1.1449	1.1664	1.1881	1.2100	1.2321	1.2544	1.2769
3	1.1910	1.2250	1.2597	1.2950	1.3310	1.3576	1.4049	1.4428
4	1.2624	1.3107	1.3604	1.4115	1.4647	1.5180	1.5735	1.6304
5	1.3332	1.4025	1.4693	1.5386	1.6105	1.6350	1.7623	1.8424
6	1.4135	1.5007	1.5868	1.6771	1.7715	1.8704	1.9738	2.0819
7	1.5030	1.6057	1.7138	1.8230	1.9487	2.0761	2.2106	2.3526
8	1.5938	1.7181	1.8509	1.9925	2.1435	2.3045	2.4759	2.6584
9	1.6894	1.8384	1.9990	2.1718	2.3579	2.5580	2.7730	3.0040
10	1.7908	1.9671	2.1589	2.3673	2.5937	2.8394	3.1058	3.3945
11	1.8982	2.1048	2.3316	2.5804	2.8531	3.1517	3.4785	3.8358
12	2.0121	2.2521	2.5181	2.8126	3.1384	3.4984	3.8959	4.3345
13	2.1329	2.4098	2.7196	3.0658	3.4522	3.8832	4.3634	4.8980
14	2.2609	2.5785	2.9371	3.3417	3.7974	4.3104	4.8871	5.5347
15	2.3965	2.7590	3.1721	3.6424	4.1772	4.7845	5.4735	6.2542
16	2.5403	2.9521	3.4259	3.9703	4.5949	5.3108	6.1303	7.0673
17	2.6927	3.1588	3.7000	4.3276	5.0544	5.8950	6.8660	7.9860
18	2.8543	3.3799	3.9960	4.7171	5.5599	6.5435	7.6899	9.0242
19	3.0255	3.6165	4.3157	5.1416	6.1159	7.2633	8.6127	10.1974
20	3.2075	3.8696	4.6609	5.6044	6.7274	8.0623	9.6462	11.5230
21	3.3995	4.1405	5.0338	6.1088	7.4002	8.9491	10.8038	13.0210
22	3.6035	4.4304	5.4365	6.6586	8.1402	9.9335	12.1003	14.7138
23	3.8197	4.7405	5.8714	7.2578	8.9543	11.0262	13.5523	16.6266
24	4.0489	5.0723	6.3411	7.9110	9.8497	12.2391	15.1786	18.7880
25	4.2918	5.4274	6.8484	8.6230	10.8347	13.5854	17.0000	21.2305
26	4.5493	5.8073	7.3963	9.3991	11.9181	15.0793	19.0400	23.9905
27	4.8223	6.2138	7.9880	10.2450	13.1099	16.7386	21.3248	27.1092
28	5.1116	6.6488	8.6271	11.1671	14.4209	18.5799	23.8838	30.6334
29	5.4183	7.1142	9.3172	12.1721	15.8630	20.6236	26.7499	34.6158
30	5.7434	7.6122	10.5582	13.2676	17.4494	22.8922	29.9599	39.1158
31	6.0881	8.1451	10.8676	14.4617	19.1943	25.4104	33.5551	44.2009
32	6.4533	8.7152	11.7370	15.7633	21.1137	28.2055	37.5817	49.9470
33	6.8408	9.3253	12.6760	17.1820	23.2251	31.3082	42.0915	56.4402
34	7.2510	9.9781	13.6901	18.7284	25.5476	34.7521	47.1425	63.7774
35	7.6860	10.6765	14.7853	20.4139	28.1024	38.5748	52.7996	72.0685
36	8.1479	11.4239	15.9681	22.2512	30.9128	42.8180	59.1355	81.4374
37	8.6360	12.2236	17.2456	24.2538	34.0039	47.5280	66.2318	92.0242
38	9.1542	13.0792	18.6252	26.4366	37.4048	52.7561	74.1796	103.9874
39	9.7035	13.9948	20.1152	28.8159	41.1447	58.5593	83.0812	117.5057
40	10.2857	14.9744	21.7245	31.4094	45.2592	65.0008	93.0509	132.7815

PERIODIC DEPOSIT TABLE

Example of use of this table:
How much is $1,000 a year invested at 6% worth in 20 years?
At 6% for 20 years, the figure is   38.993
For $1,000 a year, the amount is $38,993

Interest Rate

Number of Years	6%	7%	8%	9%	10%	11%	12%	13%
1	1.060	1.070	1.080	1.090	1.100	1.110	1.120	1.130
2	2.183	2.215	2.246	2.278	2.310	2.342	2.374	2.407
3	3.375	3.440	3.506	3.573	3.641	3.710	3.779	3.850
4	4.637	4.751	4.867	4.985	5.105	5.228	5.353	5.480
5	5.975	6.153	6.336	6.523	6.716	6.913	7.115	7.323
6	7.394	7.654	7.923	8.200	8.487	8.783	9.089	9.405
7	8.897	9.260	9.637	10.028	10.436	10.859	11.300	11.757
8	10.491	10.978	11.488	12.021	12.579	13.164	13.776	14.416
9	12.181	12.816	13.487	14.193	14.937	15.722	16.549	17.420
10	13.972	14.784	15.645	16.560	17.531	18.561	19.655	20.814
11	15.870	16.888	17.977	19.141	20.384	21.713	23.133	24.650
12	17.882	19.141	20.495	21.953	23.523	25.212	27.029	28.985
13	20.015	21.550	23.215	25.019	26.975	29.095	31.393	33.883
14	22.276	24.129	26.152	28.361	30.772	33.405	36.280	39.417
15	24.673	26.888	29.324	32.003	34.950	38.190	41.753	45.672
16	27.213	29.840	32.750	35.974	39.545	43.501	47.884	52.739
17	29.906	32.999	36.450	40.301	44.599	49.396	54.750	60.725
18	32.760	36.379	40.446	45.018	50.159	55.939	62.440	69.749
19	35.786	39.995	44.762	50.160	56.275	63.203	71.052	79.947
20	38.993	43.865	49.423	55.765	63.002	71.265	80.699	91.470
21	42.392	48.006	54.457	61.873	70.403	80.214	91.503	104.491
22	45.996	52.436	59.893	68.532	78.543	90.148	103.603	119.205
23	49.816	57.177	65.765	75.790	87.497	101.174	117.155	135.831
24	53.865	62.249	72.106	83.701	97.347	113.413	132.334	154.620
25	58.156	67.676	78.954	92.324	108.182	126.999	149.334	175.850
26	62.706	73.484	86.351	101.723	120.100	142.079	168.374	199.841
27	67.528	79.698	94.339	111.968	133.210	158.817	189.699	226.950
28	72.640	86.347	102.966	123.135	147.631	177.397	213.583	257.583
29	78.058	93.461	112.283	135.308	163.494	198.021	240.333	292.199
30	83.802	101.073	122.346	148.575	180.943	220.913	270.293	331.315
31	89.890	109.218	133.214	163.037	200.138	246.324	303.848	375.516
32	96.343	117.933	144.951	178.800	221.252	274.529	341.429	425.463
33	103.184	127.259	157.627	195.982	244.477	305.837	383.521	481.903
34	110.435	137.237	171.317	214.711	270.024	340.590	430.663	545.681
35	118.121	147.913	186.102	235.125	298.127	379.164	483.463	617.749
36	126.268	159.337	202.070	257.376	329.039	421.982	542.599	699.187
37	134.904	171.561	219.316	281.630	363.043	469.511	608.831	791.211
38	144.058	184.640	237.941	308.066	400.448	522.267	683.010	895.198
39	153.762	198.635	258.057	336.882	441.593	580.826	766.091	1012.704
40	164.048	213.610	279.781	368.292	486.852	645.827	859.142	1145.486

COMPOUND DISCOUNT TABLE

Example of use of this Table

    Find how much must be put at interest now to equal $10,000 in 12 years at a net rate of 4%

       From table for 12 years 4%   .6246
       Invest now for $10,000 (10,000 x .6246) $ 6246

Number of Years	Interest Rate							
	1-1/2%	2%	2-1/2%	3%	3-1/2%	4%	4-1/2%	5%
1	0.9852	0.9804	0.9756	0.9709	0.9662	0.9615	0.9569	0.9524
2	0.9707	0.9612	0.9518	0.9426	0.9335	0.9246	0.9157	0.9070
3	0.9563	0.9423	0.9286	0.9151	0.9019	0.8890	0.8763	0.8638
4	0.9422	0.9238	0.9060	0.8885	0.8714	0.8548	0.8386	0.8227
5	0.9283	0.9057	0.8839	0.8626	0.8420	0.8219	0.8025	0.7835
6	0.9145	0.8880	0.8623	0.8375	0.8135	0.7903	0.7679	0.7462
7	0.9010	0.8706	0.8413	0.8131	0.7860	0.7599	0.7348	0.7107
8	0.8877	0.8535	0.8207	0.7894	0.7594	0.7307	0.7032	0.6768
9	0.8746	0.8368	0.8007	0.7664	0.7337	0.7026	0.6729	0.6446
10	0.8617	0.8203	0.7812	0.7441	0.7089	0.6756	0.6439	0.6139
11	0.8489	0.8043	0.7621	0.7224	0.6849	0.6496	0.6162	0.5847
12	0.8364	0.7885	0.7436	0.7014	0.6618	0.6246	0.5897	0.5568
13	0.8240	0.7730	0.7254	0.6810	0.6394	0.6006	0.5643	0.5303
14	0.8118	0.7579	0.7077	0.6611	0.6178	0.5775	0.5400	0.5051
15	0.7999	0.7430	0.6905	0.6419	0.5969	0.5553	0.5167	0.4810
16	0.7880	0.7284	0.6736	0.6232	0.5767	0.5339	0.4945	0.4581
17	0.7764	0.7142	0.6572	0.6050	0.5572	0.5134	0.4732	0.4363
18	0.7649	0.7002	0.6412	0.5874	0.5384	0.4936	0.4528	0.4155
19	0.7536	0.6864	0.6255	0.5703	0.5202	0.4746	0.4333	0.3957
20	0.7425	0.6730	0.6103	0.5537	0.5026	0.4564	0.4146	0.3769
21	0.7315	0.6598	0.5954	0.5375	0.4856	0.4388	0.3968	0.3589
22	0.7207	0.6468	0.5809	0.5219	0.4692	0.4220	0.3797	0.3418
23	0.7100	0.6342	0.5667	0.5067	0.4533	0.4057	0.3634	0.3256
24	0.6995	0.6217	0.5529	0.4919	0.4380	0.3901	0.3477	0.3101
25	0.6892	0.6095	0.5394	0.4776	0.4231	0.3751	0.3327	0.2953
26	0.6790	0.5976	0.5262	0.4637	0.4088	0.3607	0.3184	0.2812
27	0.6690	0.5859	0.5134	0.4502	0.3950	0.3468	0.3047	0.2678
28	0.6591	0.5744	0.5009	0.4371	0.3817	0.3335	0.2916	0.2551
29	0.6494	0.5631	0.4887	0.4243	0.3687	0.3207	0.2790	0.2429
30	0.6398	0.5521	0.4767	0.4120	0.3563	0.3083	0.2670	0.2314
31	0.6303	0.5412	0.4651	0.4000	0.3442	0.2965	0.2555	0.2204
32	0.6210	0.5306	0.4538	0.3883	0.3326	0.2851	0.2445	0.2099
33	0.6118	0.5202	0.4427	0.3770	0.3213	0.2741	0.2340	0.1999
34	0.6028	0.5100	0.4319	0.3660	0.3105	0.2636	0.2239	0.1904
35	0.5939	0.5000	0.4214	0.3554	0.3000	0.2534	0.2143	0.1813
36	0.5851	0.4902	0.4111	0.3450	0.2898	0.2437	0.2050	0.1727
37	0.5764	0.4806	0.4011	0.3350	0.2800	0.2343	0.1962	0.1644
38	0.5679	0.4712	0.3913	0.3252	0.2706	0.2253	0.1877	0.1566
39	0.5595	0.4619	0.3817	0.3158	0.2614	0.2166	0.1797	0.1491
40	0.5513	0.4529	0.3724	0.3066	0.2526	0.2083	0.1719	0.1420

PRESENT WORTH TABLE — SINGLE FUTURE PAYMENT

Example of use of this table:
Find how much $10,000 payable in 12 years is worth now at an interest rate of 6%.
From table for 12 years 6% .4970
Present value of $10,000 in 12 years (10,000 x .6246) $4,970

Interest Rate

Number of Years	6%	7%	8%	9%	10%	11%	12%	13%
1	0.9434	0.9346	0.9259	0.9174	0.9091	0.9009	0.8929	0.8850
2	0.8900	0.8734	0.8573	0.8417	0.8264	0.8116	0.7972	0.7831
3	0.8396	0.8163	0.7938	0.7722	0.7513	0.7312	0.7118	0.6931
4	0.7921	0.7629	0.7350	0.7084	0.6830	0.6587	0.6355	0.6133
5	0.7473	0.7130	0.6806	0.6499	0.6209	0.5935	0.5674	0.5428
6	0.7050	0.6663	0.6302	0.5963	0.5645	0.5346	0.5066	0.4803
7	0.6651	0.6227	0.5835	0.5470	0.5132	0.4816	0.4523	0.4251
8	0.6274	0.5820	0.5403	0.5019	0.4665	0.4339	0.4039	0.3762
9	0.5919	0.5439	0.5002	0.4604	0.4241	0.3909	0.3606	0.3329
10	0.5584	0.5083	0.4632	0.4224	0.3855	0.3522	0.3220	0.2946
11	0.5268	0.4751	0.4289	0.3875	0.3505	0.3173	0.2875	0.2607
12	0.4970	0.4440	0.3971	0.3555	0.3186	0.2858	0.2567	0.2307
13	0.4688	0.4150	0.3677	0.3262	0.2897	0.2575	0.2292	0.2042
14	0.4423	0.3878	0.3405	0.2992	0.2633	0.2320	0.2046	0.1807
15	0.4173	0.3624	0.3152	0.2745	0.2394	0.2090	0.1827	0.1599
16	0.3936	0.3387	0.2919	0.2519	0.2176	0.1883	0.1631	0.1415
17	0.3714	0.3166	0.2703	0.2311	0.1978	0.1696	0.1456	0.1252
18	0.3503	0.2959	0.2502	0.2120	0.1799	0.1528	0.1300	0.1108
19	0.3305	0.2765	0.2317	0.1945	0.1635	0.1377	0.1161	0.0981
20	0.3118	0.2584	0.2145	0.1784	0.1486	0.1240	0.1037	0.0868
21	0.2942	0.2415	0.1987	0.1637	0.1351	0.1117	0.0926	0.0768
22	0.2775	0.2257	0.1839	0.1502	0.1228	0.1007	0.0826	0.0680
23	0.2618	0.2109	0.1703	0.1378	0.1117	0.0907	0.0738	0.0601
24	0.2470	0.1971	0.1577	0.1264	0.1015	0.0817	0.0660	0.0532
25	0.2330	0.1842	0.1460	0.1160	0.0923	0.0736	0.0588	0.0471
26	0.2198	0.1722	0.1352	0.1064	0.0829	0.0663	0.0525	0.0417
27	0.2074	0.1609	0.1252	0.0976	0.0763	0.0597	0.0470	0.0369
28	0.1956	0.1504	0.1159	0.0895	0.0693	0.0538	0.0420	0.0326
29	0.1846	0.1406	0.1073	0.0822	0.0630	0.0485	0.0374	0.0289
30	0.1741	0.1314	0.0994	0.0754	0.0573	0.0437	0.0334	0.0256
31	0.1643	0.1228	0.0920	0.0691	0.0521	0.0394	0.0298	0.0226
32	0.1550	0.1147	0.0852	0.0634	0.0474	0.0354	0.0266	0.0200
33	0.1462	0.1072	0.0789	0.0582	0.0431	0.0319	0.0238	0.0177
34	0.1379	0.1002	0.0730	0.0534	0.0391	0.0288	0.0212	0.0157
35	0.1301	0.0937	0.0676	0.0490	0.0356	0.0259	0.0189	0.0139
36	0.1227	0.0875	0.0626	0.0449	0.0323	0.0234	0.0169	0.0123
37	0.1158	0.0818	0.0580	0.0412	0.0294	0.0210	0.0151	0.0109
38	0.1092	0.0765	0.0536	0.0378	0.0267	0.0189	0.0135	0.0096
39	0.1031	0.0715	0.0497	0.0347	0.0243	0.0171	0.0120	0.0085
40	0.0972	0.0668	0.0460	0.0318	0.0221	0.0154	0.0107	0.0075

PRESENT WORTH TABLE — PERIODIC FUTURE PAYMENTS

Example of use of this table:
To find the cost now of $1,000 of income per year for 20 years at 7%.
From table for 20 years at 7% 10.5940
Cost of $1,000 per year ($1,000 × 10.5940) $10,594

Interest Rate

Number of Years	6%	7%	8%	9%	10%	11%	12%	13%
1	0.9434	0.9346	0.9259	0.9174	0.9091	0.9009	0.8929	0.8850
2	1.8334	1.8080	1.7833	1.7591	1.7355	1.7125	1.6901	1.6681
3	2.6730	2.6243	2.5771	2.5313	2.4869	2.4437	2.4018	2.3612
4	3.4651	3.3872	3.3121	3.2397	3.1699	3.1024	3.0373	2.9745
5	4.2124	4.1002	3.9927	3.8897	3.7908	3.6959	3.6048	3.5172
6	4.9173	4.7665	4.6229	4.4859	4.3553	4.2305	4.1114	3.9975
7	5.5824	5.3893	5.2064	5.0330	4.8684	4.7122	4.5638	4.4226
8	6.2098	5.9713	5.7466	5.5348	5.3349	5.1461	4.9676	4.7988
9	6.8017	6.5152	6.2469	5.9952	5.7590	5.5370	5.3282	5.1317
10	7.3601	7.0236	6.7101	6.4177	6.1446	5.8892	5.6502	5.4262
11	7.8869	7.4987	7.1390	6.8052	6.4951	6.2065	5.9377	5.6869
12	8.3838	7.9427	7.5361	7.1607	6.8137	6.4924	6.1944	5.9176
13	8.8527	8.3577	7.9038	7.4869	7.1034	6.7499	6.4235	6.1218
14	9.2950	8.7455	8.2442	7.7862	7.3667	6.9819	6.6282	6.3025
15	9.7122	9.1079	8.5595	8.0607	7.6061	7.1909	6.8109	6.4624
16	10.1059	9.4466	8.8514	8.3126	7.8237	7.3792	6.9740	6.6039
17	10.4773	9.7632	9.1216	8.5436	8.0216	7.5488	7.1196	6.7291
18	10.8276	10.0591	9.3719	8.7556	8.2014	7.7016	7.2497	6.8399
19	11.1581	10.3356	9.6036	8.9501	8.3649	7.8393	7.3658	6.9380
20	11.4699	10.5940	9.8181	9.1285	8.5136	7.9633	7.4694	7.0248
21	11.7641	10.8355	10.0168	9.2922	8.6487	8.0751	7.5620	7.1016
22	12.0416	11.0612	10.2007	9.4424	8.7715	8.1757	7.6446	7.1695
23	12.3034	11.2722	10.3711	9.5802	8.8832	8.2664	7.7184	7.2297
24	12.5504	11.4693	10.5288	9.7066	8.9847	8.3481	7.7843	7.2829
25	12.7834	11.6536	10.6748	9.8226	9.0770	8.4217	7.8431	7.3299
26	13.0032	11.8258	10.8100	9.9290	9.1609	8.4881	7.8957	7.3717
27	13.2105	11.9867	10.9352	10.0266	9.2372	8.5478	7.9426	7.4086
28	13.4062	12.1371	11.0511	10.1161	9.3066	8.6016	7.9844	7.4412
29	13.5907	12.2777	11.1584	10.1983	9.3696	8.6501	8.0218	7.4701
30	13.7648	12.4090	11.2578	10.2737	9.4269	8.6938	8.0552	7.4957
31	13.9291	12.5318	11.3498	10.3428	9.4790	8.7331	8.0850	7.5183
32	14.0840	12.6466	11.4350	10.4062	9.5264	8.7686	8.1116	7.5383
33	14.2302	12.7538	11.5139	10.4644	9.5694	8.8005	8.1354	7.5560
34	14.3681	12.8540	11.5869	10.5178	9.6086	8.8293	8.1566	7.5717
35	14.4982	12.9477	11.6546	10.5668	9.6442	8.8552	8.1755	7.5856
36	14.6210	13.0352	11.7172	10.6118	9.6765	8.8786	8.1924	7.5979
37	14.7368	13.1170	11.7752	10.6530	9.7059	8.8996	8.2075	7.6087
38	14.8460	13.1935	11.8289	10.6908	9.7327	8.9186	8.2210	7.6183
39	14.9491	13.2649	11.8786	10.7255	9.7569	8.9357	8.2330	7.6268
40	15.0463	13.3317	11.9246	10.7574	9.7791	8.9511	8.2438	7.6344

SINKING FUND REQUIREMENTS TABLE

Example of use of this table:
To find the amount of money which must be deposited at the end of each year to grow to $10,000 in 19 years at 8%.
From table for 19 years at 8%   .02413
Amount of each deposit ($10,000 × .02413) $241.30

Interest Rate

Number of Years	6%	7%	8%	9%	10%	11%	12%	13%
1	1.00000	1.00000	1.00000	1.00000	1.00000	1.00000	1.00000	1.00000
2	.48544	.48309	.48077	.47847	.47619	.47393	.47169	.46948
3	.31411	.31105	.30803	.30505	.30211	.29921	.29635	.29352
4	.22859	.22523	.22192	.21867	.21547	.21233	.20923	.20619
5	.17740	.17389	.17046	.16709	.16379	.16057	.15741	.15431
6	.14336	.13979	.13632	.13292	.12961	.12638	.12323	.12015
7	.11913	.11555	.11207	.10869	.10541	.10222	.09912	.09611
8	.10104	.09747	.09401	.09067	.08744	.08432	.08130	.07839
9	.08702	.08349	.08008	.07679	.07364	.07060	.06768	.06487
10	.07587	.07238	.06903	.06582	.06275	.05980	.05698	.05429
11	.06679	.06336	.06008	.05695	.05396	.05112	.04846	.04584
12	.05928	.05590	.05269	.04965	.04676	.04403	.04144	.03899
13	.05296	.04965	.04652	.04357	.04078	.03815	.03568	.03335
14	.04758	.04434	.04129	.03843	.03575	.03323	.03087	.02867
15	.04206	.03979	.03683	.03406	.03147	.02907	.02682	.02474
16	.03895	.03586	.03298	.03030	.02782	.02552	.02339	.02143
17	.03544	.03243	.02963	.02705	.02466	.02247	.02046	.01861
18	.03236	.02941	.02670	.02421	.02193	.01984	.01794	.01620
19	.02962	.02675	.02413	.02173	.01955	.01756	.01576	.01413
20	.02718	.02439	.02185	.01955	.01746	.01558	.01388	.01235
21	.02500	.02229	.01983	.01762	.01562	.01384	.01224	.01081
22	.02305	.02041	.01803	.01590	.01401	.01231	.01081	.00948
23	.02128	.01871	.01642	.01438	.01257	.01097	.00956	.00832
24	.01968	.01719	.01498	.01302	.01129	.00979	.00846	.00731
25	.01823	.01581	.01368	.01181	.01017	.00874	.00749	.00643
26	.01690	.01456	.01251	.01072	.00916	.00781	.00665	.00565
27	.01570	.01343	.01145	.00973	.00826	.00699	.00590	.00498
28	.01459	.01239	.01049	.00885	.00745	.00626	.00524	.00439
29	.01358	.01145	.00962	.00806	.00673	.00561	.00466	.00387
30	.01265	.01059	.00883	.00734	.00608	.00502	.00414	.00341
31	.01179	.00979	.00811	.00669	.00549	.00451	.00369	.00301
32	.01100	.00907	.00745	.00609	.00497	.00404	.00328	.00266
33	.01027	.00841	.00685	.00556	.00449	.00363	.00292	.00234
34	.00960	.00779	.00630	.00508	.00407	.00326	.00260	.00207
35	.00897	.00723	.00580	.00464	.00369	.00293	.00232	.00183
36	.00839	.00676	.00534	.00424	.00334	.00263	.00206	.00162
37	.00786	.00624	.00492	.00387	.00303	.00236	.00184	.00143
38	.00736	.00579	.00454	.00354	.00275	.00213	.00164	.00126
39	.00689	.00539	.00419	.00324	.00249	.00191	.00146	.00112
40	.00646	.00501	.00386	.00296	.00226	.00172	.00130	.00099

Appendix D — Accounting Methods — Advantages and Disadvantages

Who May Use	When Income Is Taxed	When Expenses Are Deductible	Advantages	Disadvantages
Cash Method				
Any taxpayer — unless inventories necessary to reflect income.	In year cash or property is received. For property, use fair market value.	Year in which payment is made in cash or property. Giving note is not payment; payment can be made with borrowed funds.	You don't pay taxes until you get the income.	You don't always match related income and expenses in one year, thus creating distortions.
Must be used if no records or incomplete ones.	Taxed in year of *constructive receipt*— even if there's no actual receipt (i.e., year income was available to you although you didn't take it).	Certain prepaid expenses must be spread over periods to which they apply even though full amount has been paid: *e.g.*, insurance premiums, rent. But payment for supplies bought in advance is currently deductible.	You can control each year's receipts and payouts and even out income over the years.	You may not have full control over receipts and income may pile up in one year.
Can use in one business although other method is used in other business.			You can keep simple records.	Liquidation or sale of business may create income bunching — all accounts receivable may have to be picked up at one time.
Accrual Method				
Anyone except those with no — or incomplete — books or records.	In year income is earned — i.e., year in which right to income becomes fixed, regardless of year of receipt.	In the year all events have occurred which fix the fact and the amount of your liability, regardless of the year of payment.	It matches income and related expenses and tends to even out your income over the years.	Have less leeway than cash-basis taxpayer to defer or accelerate income or deductions.

Who May Use	When Income Is Taxed	When Expenses Are Deductible	Advantages	Disadvantages
You must use if inventories are necessary to reflect income clearly — unless you can use one of the methods discussed below.	You do not accrue contingent, contested, or uncollectable items. Prepaid amounts are income when received — even if not yet earned. However, some relief is available by a special election to defer the income (see *Rev. Proc. 71-21*).	You do not accrue contingent or contest- of liabilities. But if you pay a liability and still contest it, you deduct it when you pay it. If you get a recovery later, it's income when recovered. *Special rule:* accruals to certain related taxpayers must be paid within 2½ months of close of taxable year of accrual or deduction is lost.		Can still accelerate deductions, however, by: advancing repairs and advertising expenditures within desired period, purchasing supplies, getting bills for professional services before year-end.

"Hybrid" Method (*see Reg.* §1.446-(c)(1)(iv))

Who May Use	When Income Is Taxed	When Expenses Are Deductible	Advantages	Disadvantages
Any taxpayer if method clearly reflects income and is consistently used.	Accrual method is used in respect of purchases and sales, while cash method is used for all other items of income and expense.		Method is simple: it's not necessary to accrue income items such as interest, dividends. And the bother of accruing small expenses is removed.	Method is not entirely accurate. Since it is a "hybrid" it does not reflect *true* income. However, if consistently used, it gives a fairly good idea of how business is doing.

Who May Use	When Income Is Taxed	When Expenses Are Deductible	Advantages	Disadvantages
Installment Method				
Installment dealers who elect this method. Seller in casual sale of personal property of more than $1,000 or of real property — provided, in either case, no more than 30% of selling price is received in year of sale.	Each year that collections are made, a proportionate amount of each collection (equal to percentage of gross profit on entire sale) is picked up as gross income in the year of collection.	Dealer deducts expenses when paid (cash basis) or incurred (accrual basis). On casual sales, expense of sale reduces sales price, thereby having effect of spreading deduction over period of reporting income.	Income is spread over period of collection—so you do not pay taxes on amounts not yet received. If tax rates decline in future, part of profits will bear a lower tax.	Dealers who switch from accrual to installment basis may have to pay a double tax on some receivables — unless they sell off all receivables before the switch. Tax rates may go up; in which case some profits will bear a higher tax.
Deferred Payment Sales Method				
Any cash-basis taxpayer on sale of personal property. Any cash or accrual taxpayer on sale of real estate.	At time of sale, seller picks up cash and *fair market value* of buyer's obligations. If total exceeds basis of sold property, difference is taxable. In later years, as obligations are collected, difference between amount received and value at which obligations were picked up originally is taxable at time of collection.	Used generally with casual sales, so expense of sale reduces sale price and is thus spread out over period of collection.	Can use where installment sale reporting is not possible — i.e., where more than 30% of sales price is received in year of sale. Useful in somewhat speculative deals where value of buyer's obligations are contingent on future operations and have little or no ascertainable present value.	You may be in for a long and costly argument with IRS as to value of obligations. Even though original sale gave capital gain, gain on collection of the obligations in future years will be taxable as ordinary income.

Long-Term Contract Methods

Percentage of Completion Method

Who May Use	When Income Is Taxed	When Expenses Are Deductible	Advantages	Disadvantages
Taxpayers who have long-term contracts more than a year to complete — usually construction contracts. There are two long-term contract methods — (1) percentage of completion and (2) completed contract — and IRS permission is needed to switch to or from either.	A portion of the total contract price is taken into account each year according to the percentage of the contract completed that year. Architects' or engineers' certificates are required.	All expenses made during the year allocable to that contract are deducted — with adjustments made for inventories and supplies on hand at the beginning and end of the year.	Income from long-term contract is reflected as earned. Income bunching in one year is avoided.	Accurate estimates of completion are difficult to make in some cases. If expenses are irregular as compared with income, there may be distortion of income in the interim years— although the final total will work out accurately.

Completed Contract Method

	When Income Is Taxed	When Expenses Are Deductible	Advantages	Disadvantages
	The entire contract price is picked up as income in the year the contract is completed and accepted.	Expenses allocable to specific contracts (that would exclude general administrative cost) are not deductible until year of completion — when income is picked up.	Income can be reflected more accurately — all the figures are in when the computation is made. Avoids estimates in interim years which may turn out to be wrong.	Bunching of income or losses in one year is possible if a number of profitable or unprofitable contracts are all finished in one year. A steady flow of completed contracts from year to year overcomes this problem. There may be some argument with IRS as to proper year of completion in some cases.

Appendix E — Installment Method Examples

(1) ADJUSTMENTS IN TAX ON CHANGE TO
    INSTALLMENT METHOD

(2) COMPUTATION BY DEALER UNDER
    INSTALLMENT METHOD

(3) UNCOLLECTED INSTALLMENTS AND
    UNREALIZED GROSS PROFITS

ADJUSTMENTS IN TAX ON CHANGE TO INSTALLMENT METHOD

	Taxable Years Prior to Change		Adjustment Years After Change		
	Year 1	Year 2	Year 3	Year 4	
Gross profit from installment sales (receivable in periodic payments over 5 years)	$100,000	$ 50,000	$ 20,000 [1] 10,000 [2] 80,000 [3]	$ 12,000 [4] 8,000 [5] 40,000 [6] 90,000 [7]	
Other income	80,000	200,000	90,000	90,000	
Gross income	$180,000	$250,000	$200,000	$240,000	
Deductions	60,000	50,000	50,000	60,000	
Taxable income	120,000	200,000	150,000	180,000	
Tax rate assumed	30%	50%	40%	40%	
Tax would be	$ 36,000	$100,000	$ 60,000	$ 72,000	

Computation of Adjustment in Year 3

Year 1 Items

			Lesser Tax Portion
In Year 3 Portion of tax	20,000/200,000 × 60,000 = $6,000		
In Year 1 Portion of tax	20,000/180,000 × 36,000 = 4,000		$4,000

Year 2 Items

In Year 3 Portion of tax	10,000/200,000 × 60,000 = 3,000		
In Year 2 Portion of tax	10,000/250,000 × 100,000 = 4,000		3,000
Adjustment to tax of Year 3			$7,000

Computation of Adjustment in Year 4

Year 1 Items

			Lesser Tax Portion
In Year 4 Portion of tax	12,000/240,000 × 72,000 = $3,600		
In Year 1 Portion of tax	12,000/180,000 × 36,000 = 2,400		$2,400

Year 2 Items

In Year 4 Portion of tax	8,000/240,000 × 72,000 = 2,400		
In Year 2 Portion of tax	8,000/250,000 × 100,000 = 3,200		2,400
Adjustment to tax of Year 4			$4,800

---

[1] and [4] from Year 1 Sales
[2] and [5] from Year 2 Sales
[3] and [6] from Year 3 Sales
[7] from Year 4 Sales

COMPUTATION BY DEALER UNDER INSTALLMENT METHOD

	First Year		Second Year		Third Year	
	(a) Cash Sales	(b) Installment Sales	(a) Cash Sales	(b) Installment Sales	(a) Cash Sales	(b) Installment Sales
(1) Unit sales	40	80	60	100	70	120
(2) Gross sales	$16,000	$40,000	$24,000	$50,000	$28,000	$60,000
(3) Cost of goods sold	12,000	24,000	18,900	31,500	20,300	34,800
(4) Gross profit	$ 4,000	$16,000	$ 5,100	$18,500	$ 7,700	$25,200
(5) Gross profit accrual basis	$20,000		$23,600		$32,900	
(6) Rate of gross profit	40%		37%		42%	
(7) Receipts from installment sales:						
First year	$15,000		$24,000		$ 1,000	
Second year			15,000		27,500	
Third year					22,500	
(8) Gross profit from installment sales:						
First year 40%	$ 6,000		$ 9,600		$ 400	
Second year 37%			5,550		10,175	
Third year 42%					9,450	
Total	$ 6,000		$15,150		$20,025	
Gross profit from cash and installment sales (4a) plus (9b)	$10,000		$20,250		$27,725	

(3) UNCOLLECTED INSTALLMENTS AND UNREALIZED GROSS PROFITS

An example showing how the dealer computes his profit if he uses the installment method follows. Our dealer runs an appliance store and has been selling refrigerators on the installment plan. The price is $400 cash or $500 on an 18-month installment basis, $50 down and $25 a month thereafter. Average cost per unit sold is $300 for the first year, $315 for the second, and $290 for the third.

If an installment account becomes uncollectible, there is no deduction for uncollected gross profit; but the portion of the uncollected balance that represents unrecovered cost is a bad debt. To use an extreme case, suppose the entire $45,000 in the example below became uncollectible. There would be no deduction for the $18,525 of unrealized gross profit; however, the balance of $26,475 would be deductible as a bad debt. Repossessions would reduce the deduction by an amount equal to the fair market value of the repossessed items. If the value of the repossessions exceeds the basis for the installment obligation, the difference, in the case of a dealer, is ordinary income.

Here are the uncollected installments and unrealized gross profits at the end of the third year:

	Uncollected Installments	Rate	Unrealized Gross Profit
2nd year's sales	$ 7,500	37%	$ 2,775
3rd year's sales	37,500	42%	15,750
Total	$45,000		$18,525

Appendix F —
Illustrated Depreciation Methods

STRAIGHT-LINE METHOD

The depreciation expense is the same from period to period. The formula followed for this method is:

$$\text{Depreciation expense} = \frac{(\text{Cost - Salvage Value})}{\text{Estimated Life}}$$

For example, if the asset costs $10,000, has a salvage value of $100, and an estimated life of ten years, the depreciation expense for the year would be computed as follows:

$$\frac{(\$10,000—\$100)}{10} = \$990.$$

The straight-line method depends upon the hypothesis that depreciation will be at a constant rate throughout the estimated life.

200%-DECLINING-BALANCE METHOD

Under this method (also called the double-declining-balance method), the amount of depreciation expense decreases from period to period. The largest depreciation deduction is taken in the first year. The amount then declines steeply over succeeding years until the final years of estimated useful life when the depreciation charge becomes relatively small. Code §167 restricts the taxpayer to a rate not in excess of twice the straight-line rate if the straight-line method had been employed.

While true declining-balance method requires the application of a complex formula, if you are going to use the maximum declining-balance depreciation — i.e., the 200% method — you need not go through these mathematical computations. Just do this: (1) determine the straight-line percentage rate; (2) double it; (3) apply it against your full basis (undiminished by salvage value) to get your first year's deduction. In the second year, (1) reduce your basis by the previous year's depreciation deduction; (2) apply the same percentage rate to the new basis you arrived at in step (1). In the third year and later years, repeat the same process.

Example: You buy a truck for the business. It costs $5,500 and has a five-year useful life. We'll assume you bought it January 1, 1975. Since it has a five-year life, the percentage of depreciation by the straight-line method is 20%. Using 200%-declining-balance, you'll use a 40% rate. So, for 1975, you'd deduct $2,200 (40% of $5,500). For 1976 , you'd reduce your $5,500 basis (original cost) by the $2,200 1975 depreciation deduction. That gives you a basis for 1976 of $3,300. For 1976, your depreciation deduction would be 40% of that $3,300, or $1,320. That cuts your basis for 1977 to $1,980 and your depreciation deduction for that year becomes $792 (40% of $1,980). This process continues on for the future years you continue to hold this truck.

SUM-OF-YEARS-DIGITS METHOD

Here, diminishing rates, expressed fractionally, are applied to the total depreciable value (cost — salvage).

Under sum-of-the-digits, the annual depreciation charge decreases rapidly; since maintenance charges, on the other hand, increase rapidly, the effect is to level off the annual costs of depreciation and maintenance.

To use sum-of-the-digits, you proceed as follows. Using, for purposes of illustration, a depreciation account of $5,500 with a 10-year life and ignoring salvage, add the numbers of the years: $10 + 9 + 8 + 7 + 6 + 5 + 4 + 3 + 2 + 1 = 55$. Depreciation the first year will be 10/55 of $5,500, or $1,000. For the remaining years, you can follow one of two practices. Either you continue to base depreciation on original cost, using 55 as the denominator of your fraction and the number of the year as the numerator — 9/55 of $5,500, 8/55 of $5,500, and so on, or you apply a fraction with a diminishing denominator to unrecovered cost — 9/45 of $4,500, 8/36 of $3,600, and so on.

Note that in the second method, the amount by which the denominator for a given year diminishes is always the amount of the numerator for the preceding year. Denominator 45 in the second year is denominator 55 for the first year, less numerator 10 for the first year; denominator 36 for year 3 is denominator 45 for year 2, less numerator 9 for year 2.

Regardless of which method is used, annual depreciation will be the same: 9/55 of $5,500 and 9/45 of $4,500 both give $900 of depreciation; 8/55 of $5,500 and 8/36 of $3,600 both give depreciation of $800.

SINKING-FUND METHOD

The sinking-fund method of computing depreciation has been generally preferred by independent businessmen. An imaginary sinking fund is established by a uniform end-of-year annual deposit throughout the useful life of the asset.

The assets are assumed to draw interest at some stated rate, e.g., 6%, sufficient to balance the fund with the cost of the asset minus estimated salvage value. The amount charged to depreciation expense in any year consists of sinking fund plus the interest on the imaginary accumulated fund. The book value of the asset at any time is the initial cost of the asset minus the amount accumulated in the imaginary fund.

Assume that an asset cost $1,000 and has no salvage value but has an estimated life of 25 years. The interest rate is assumed to be 6%. By using conversion tables, the sinking fund deposit is $1,000 × .01823 or $18.23. In the second year, the depreciation charge will be $18.23 + ($18.23 × .06) = $19.32; in the third year, it will be $18.23 + ($18.23 + $19.32) × .06 = $20.48, and so forth. The $18.23 represents the sinking fund deposit and remains the same for the period of depreciation. In other words, under this method the business man anticipates earnings and profits on his capital investment and thus increases his capital.

This method is permissible for Federal income tax purposes provided it does not exceed the rate as computed under the declining-balance method, during the first two-thirds of the asset life.

UNIT-OF-PRODUCTION METHOD

This method is used for the depreciation of assets used in production. Under this method, an estimate is made of the total number of units the machine may be expected to produce during its life. Cost less salvage value, if any, is then divided by the estimated total production to determine a depreciation charge for each unit of production. The depreciation for each year is obtained by multiplying the depreciation charge per unit by the number of units produced. Here's how it works on a $10,600 machine good for 300,000 units of output:

$$R = \frac{\text{Cost - Salvage Value}}{\text{Estimated Units}}$$

$$R = \frac{\$10,600 - \$600}{300,000}$$

$$R = \$.03\tfrac{1}{3}$$

Units produced for 1 year = 24,000
Depreciation = 24,000 × $.03⅓ = $800

A severe obstacle to the use of this method is the difficulty of ascertaining the total number of units which the asset will produce. The production method is most applicable to fixed assets like airplane engines, automobiles, and machinery where wear is such an important factor. It is useful for fixed assets that are likely to be exhausted prematurely by accelerated or abnormal use.

Appendix G —
Tax Factors in Equipment
and Plant Acquisition

BIRD'S-EYE VIEW OF THE EFFECT OF
THE TAX FACTORS
ON VARIOUS FORMS OF ACQUISITION

The following chart shows how the various tax factors come into play in various types of acquistions. Covered here are these tax factors: availability of regular depreciation, the investment credit, the special first-year writeoff, accelerated depreciation, depreciation recapture, and the possibility of recapture of part of the investment credit should the disposition take place within certain time limits.

The impact of these tax factors is considered in the following situations: the rental of business property, the purchase of property (outright or financed), involuntary conversions, trade-in purchases, separate sales of old equipment and repurchase of new or second-hand equipment, and abandonments followed by acquisitions of new equipment. The chart does not take into account real property and recapture of depreciation thereon.

	Investment Credit	Regular Depreciation	First-Year Additional Depreciation	Accelerated Depreciation	Investment Credit Recapture	Depreciation Recapture
Rent — business rent always deductible if reasonable.	A lessor may elect to pass through the credit to the lessee. But the pass-through only applies to new property, not to a credit allowed for used or reconstructed property.		Not available to lessee.		Applicable only to lessee.	Not applicable.
Outright purchase — cost recovered through depreciation.	Available where the useful life is at least 3 years. Maximum per year is $25,000 plus one-half of liability in excess of $25,000. For used property, purchases up to $100,000 per year qualify.	Available; basis reduced by first-year depreciation.	Available where useful life is 6 years or more—$2,000 maximum, $4,000 on joint return (20% of $10,000 or $20,000) —based on cost.	Available where useful life is 3 years or more — basis reduced by first-year depreciation — new property only for double-declining-ba and sum-of-the-years-digits; used property use 150% declining balance — prorate over year.	Applicable.	Applicable to gain.
Financed purchase — interest on loan is deductible.	Available under the limits indicated above.	Available; same as previous item.	Available; same as previous item.	Available; same as previous item.	Applicable; same as previous item.	Applicable; same as previous item.

	Investment Credit	Regular Depreciation	First-Year Additional Depreciation	Accelerated Depreciation	Investment Credit Recapture	Depreciation Recapture
Involuntary conversion and reinvestment of proceeds of insurance.	Available to the extent of the amount reinvested reduced by smaller of insurance recovery or adjusted basis of destroyed property.	Available on new basis — (a) if gain is recognized, new basis is cost; (b) if gain not recognized, new basis is old basis plus additional amounts reinvested.	Available to extent of reinvestment of proceeds.	Available on new basis.	Applicable — but in the case of a reinvestment, applies only if loss under recapture rule is greater than under "reduction" rule.	Not applicable if all reinvested — if not, applicable to smaller of gain recognized or §1245 potential.
Trade-in on purchase.	Available to the extent of the cash paid for the new property; if used property is acquired the $100,000 limitation applies.	Available; basis same for new or old.	Available on cost — without regard to carryover basis of old property.	Available on new basis (including the carryover basis of old property) after reduction by first-year depreciation.	Applicable.	Applicable only to boot received on trade (rare): §1245 potential carries over to replacement asset and can be taxed on later sale at a gain.
Separate sale of old equipment and purchase of new equipment. (Gain, if any, recognized on sale.)	Available on full amount paid for the property.	Available.	Available.	Available.	Applicable.	Applicable to gain.

	Investment Credit	Regular Depreciation	First-Year Additional Depreciation	Accelerated Depreciation	Investment Credit Recapture	Depreciation Recapture
Separate sale and purchase of secondhand equipment.	Available on the same basis as a trade-in if the disposition and replacement occur within 60 days.	Available.	Available.	Only 150%-declining-balance available.	Applicable.	Applicable.
Abandonment of present equipment and purchase of new equipment.	Available on the full purchase price of the new equipment without regard to the basis of the old property.	Available.	Available.	Available.	Is abandonment a disposition? (If not, no recapture and deduct remaining basis as abandonment loss.)	Not applicable — no gain if abandoned.

Appendix H

SOURCES OF AC SECTIONS QUOTED IN THE ACCOUNTING SECTION OF THIS TEXT*

AC
Section

100 —	ARB 43
510 —	ARB 43
520 —	Rule of Conduct 203
1010 —	APB Stmt 1
1020 —	APB Stmt 4
1021 —	same, Chap 1 as amended
1022 —	same, Chap 2 as amended
1023 —	same, Chap 3 as amended
1024 —	same, Chap 4 as amended
1025 —	same, Chap 5
1026 —	same, Chap 6 as amended
1027 —	same, Chap 7 as amended
1028 —	same, Chap 8 as amended
1029 —	same, Chap 9 as amended
1041 —	APB Op 29
1051 —	APB Op 20 as amended
1051-1 —	FASB Int. 1
1071 —	APB Stmt 3 as amended
1081 —	ARB 43, Chap 12 as amended
1083 —	FASB Stmt 8
1083-1	FASB Int 15
1091 —	APB Op 16 as amended
1091-1 —	FASB Int 9
1092 —	FASB Stmt 10
2010 —	APB Op 9 as amended
2011 —	APB Op 15 as amended
2012 —	APB Op 30 as amended
2013 —	FASB Stmt 4
2021 —	APB Op 19 as amended
2031 —	ARB 43, Chap 3A as amended
2032 —	APB Op 10, Par 7
2033 —	FASB Stmt 6
2033-1 —	FASB Int 8

*Through December 15, 1976

AC
Section

2041 —	ARB 43, Chap 2A as amended
2042 —	APB Op 12, Pars 9 & 10
2043 —	APB Op 12, Pars 4 & 5
2044 —	APB Op 12, Pars 2 & 3
2045 —	APB Op 22, as amended
2051 —	ARB 43 Chap 1A Par 3 and
	ARB 51 as amended
2061 —	APB Stmt 2
2062 —	FASB Stmt 7
2062-1 —	FASB Int 7
2071 —	APB Op 28 as amended
2072 —	FASB Stmt 3
4010 —	ARB 43, Chap 1A, Par 1
4020 —	APB Op 10, Par 12
4031 —	ARB 45
4041 —	ARB 43, Chap 11A
4042 —	ARB 43, Chap 11B as amended
4043 —	ARB 43, Chap 11C
4053 —	FASB Stmt 13
4061 —	ARB 43, Chap 13B as amended
4062 —	APB Op 25
4063 —	APB Op 8
4063-1 —	FASB Int 3
4064 —	APB Op 12, Pars 6-8
4071 —	ARB 43, Chap 9A
4072 —	APB Op 6, Par 17
4073 —	ARB 43, Chap 9C as amended
4074 —	ARB 44 (Revised) as amended
4081 —	ARB 43, Chap 10A as amended
4091 —	APB Op 11 as amended
4092 —	APB Op 10, Par 6
4093 —	APB Op 1, as amended
4094 —	APB Ops 2 & 4, as amended
4095 —	APB Op 23 as amended
4096 —	APB Op 24
4097 —	FASB Stmt 9
4111 —	APB Op 21
4111-1 —	FASB Int 2
4211 —	FASB Stmt 2
4211-1 —	FASB Int 4
4211-3 —	FASB Int 6
4311 —	FASB Stmt 5 as amended
4311-1 —	FASB Int 14
4312 —	FASB Stmt 11
5111 —	ARB 43, Chap 1A Par 5
5121 —	ARB 43, Chap 4 as amended
5131 —	APB Op 18 as amended
5132 —	FASB Stmt 12
5132-1 —	FASB Int 10
5132-2 —	FASB Int 11
5132-3 —	FASB Int 12
5132-4 —	FASB Int 13

AC
Section

5141 —	APB Op 17 as amended
5361 —	APB Op 12, Pars 16 & 17
5362 —	APB Op 26 as amended
5511 —	ARB 43, Chap 1A, Par 2
5512 —	ARB 43, Chap 1A, Par 6
5515 —	APB Op 10, Pars 10 & 11 as amended
5516 —	APB Op 14
5541 —	ARB 43, Chap 1A, Par 4
5542 —	ARB 43, Chap 1B, as amended
5561 —	ARB 43, Chap 7B as amended
5581 —	ARB 43, Chap 7A
5582 —	ARB 46
6011 —	APB Op 2 addendum

BIBLIOGRAPHY

Publications by the AICPA: The following publications (with the exception of those parts of Volumes 3 and 4 which are copyrighted by the FASB as listed in the acknowledgments following) are copyrighted © in the year indicated by the American Institute of Accountants, Inc., 1211 Avenue of the Americas, New York, N.Y. 10036.

Professional Standards, Vol 1 — Auditing, Management
                                    Advisory Services, Tax Practice
(same)   , Vol 2 — Ethics and Bylaws
(same)   , Vol 3 and Vol 4 — Accounting

Technical Practice Aids — including Statements of Position

NOTE: the above 5-volume loose-leaf service is published for the AICPA by Commerce Clearing House, Inc. on updating continuous service. The service is available either through the AICPA (for members) or Commerce Clearing House.

For this Fifth Edition of the Accounting Desk Book, the standards reflected cover the period through December 15, 1976.

The Accounting Basis of Inventories, Horace G. Barden, B.S., CPA, Accounting Research Study #13, © 1973, 189 pages.

Accounting For Depreciable Assets, Charles W. Lamden, CPA, Ph. D.; Dale L. Gerboth, CPA; and Thomas W. McRae, CPA, Accounting Research Monograph #1, © 1975, 189 pages.

Accounting For Income Taxes, Donald J. Bevis and Raymond E. Perry, © 1969, 70 pages.

Accounting For Retail Land Sales, Prepared by the Committee on Land Development Companies of the AICPA, Kenneth A. Mounce, Chairman, © 1973, 41 pages.

Accounting Trends & Techniques 1974 (Twenty-Eighth Edition), Edited by George Dick, CPA, and Richard Rikert, © 1974, 450 pages.

APB Accounting Principles, Volume Two — (Soft cover) as of June 30, © 1973. Pages 6001 through 9755. (Used for Accounting Terminology references)

Audits of State and Local Governmental Units, prepared by the Committee on Governmental Accounting and Auditing of the AICPA, An Industry Audit Guide, © 1974, 160 pages.

Objectives of Financial Satements — Volume 2/Selected Papers, compiled and edited by Joe J. Cramer; Jr. and George H. Sorter, © 1974. 395 pages.

Practical Accounting and Auditing Problems — (A three-volume set), by Edmund F. Ingalls, © 1966, 2,250 total pages

Stockholders' Equity — by Beatrice Melcher, CPA, An Accounting Research Study #15, © 1973, 355 pages.

Tax Planning Techniques For Individuals — by Stuart R. Josephs, CPA, Studies in Federal Taxation #2, © 1971, 417 pages.

Working With The Revenue Code — 1974 — edited by Mario P. Borini, CPA, © 1974, 358 pages.

Handbook for Auditors, James A. Cashin, Editor-in-Chief, New York, McGraw-Hill Book Company; 1971, 52 Chapters (not numbered by pages)

Montgomery's Auditing, Ninth Edition, by Philip L. Defliese, CPA; Kenneth P. Johnson, CPA: and Roderick K. Macleod, CPA, New York, The Ronald Press Company, 1975, 869 pages.

Principles of Accounting, Introductory (Sixth Edition), by H.A. Finney and Herbert E. Miller, Englewood Cliffs, N.J., Prentice-Hall, Inc. 1963, 688 pages.

Finney and Miller's Principles of Accounting, Advanced, by James A. Gentry, Jr., Ph.D., CPA, and Glenn L. Johnson, Ph.D., Englewood Cliffs, N.J., Prentice-Hall, Inc., 1971, 578 pages.

Guide to Record Retention Requirements, revised as of Jan. 1, 1976, Office of the Federal Register, National Archives and Records Service, General Services Administration, U.S. Government Printing Office, Washington, D.C., Stock Number 022-003-00915-9, Price, $1.50, Vol. 41; No. 93, May 12, 1976, 96 pages.

The Following Publications by Commerce Clearing House, Inc.: (Chicago, Illinois)

1976 U.S. Master Tax Guide, 544 pages. (#5956)

Internal Revenue Code (As of July 20, 1976), pages 3865 through 5443. (#5465)

Income Tax Regulations (Final and Proposed as of July 8, 1976), a three-volume set, pages 30,001 through 45,054. (#5464)

Tax Reform Act of 1976 (Law and Explanation), 1596 pages (#5442)

The Following Publications by The Institute for Business Planning, Inc., Englewood Cliffs, New Jersey:

Forms of Business Agreements and Resolutions, a three-volume loose-leaf service, updated through December 31, 1976.

Tax Planning, a two-volume loose-leaf service, updated through December 31, 1976.

SUBJECT INDEX

(References are to paragraph [¶] numbers)

412

ACKNOWLEDGMENTS

To the FASB:

We thank the Financial Accounting Standards Board for permission to quote and paraphrase FASB Statements Nos. 1 - 13 and FASB Interpretations Nos. 1 - 15, as published in the AICPA FINANCIAL STANDARDS — *Financial Accounting,* Volumes 3 and 4 of the loose-leaf service. All quoted material is indicated either through stylistic differentiation in the text or through the use of quotation marks, and all material is referenced to the codified paragraph numbers of the "Standards" volumes.

Because of our use of codified section numbers, a cross-reference to the *original pronouncement* is included in APPENDIX H. Listed below, in issuance order, are the FASB Statements and FASB Interpretations (and the codified sections to which they pertain), which are copyrighted © by the Financial Accounting Standards Board, High Ridge Park, Stamford, Connecticut 06905, U.S.A. and which (in part) are reprinted with permission. Copies of the complete documents are available from the FASB:

Statement 1 — (Replaced by Statement #8)	Interpretation 1 — AC 1051-1
	Interpretation 2 — AC 4111-1
Statement 2 — AC 4211	Interpretation 3 — AC 4063-1
Statement 3 — AC 2072	Interpretation 4 — AC 4211-1
Statement 4 — AC 2013	Interpretation 5 — Replaced by Statement #7
Statement 5 — AC 4311	Interpretation 6 — AC 4211-3
Statement 6 — AC 2033	Interpretation 7 — AC 2062-1
Statement 7 — AC 2062	Interpretation 8 — AC 2033-1
Statement 8 — AC 1083	Interpretation 9 — AC 1091-1
Statement 9 — AC 4097	Interpretation 10 — AC 5132-1
Statement 10 — AC 1092	Interpretation 11 — AC 5132-2
Statement 11 — AC 4312	Interpretation 12 — AC 5132-3
Statement 12 — AC 5132	Interpretation 13 — AC 5132-4
Statement 13 — AC 4053	Interpretation 14 — AC 4311-1
	Interpretation 15 — AC 1083-1

To the AICPA:

We thank the American Institute of Certified Public Accountants, Inc., for permission to quote and paraphrase from the additional material in Volumes 3 and 4 of the AICPA FINANCIAL STANDARDS — *Financial Accounting* loose-leaf service, which is copyrighted by the American Institute of Accountants, Inc., 1211 Avenue of the Americas, New York, New York 10036. The Institute's copyright in Volumes 3 and 4 covers all the codified sections *not* enumerated above under FASB copyright. APPENDIX H cross-references the codified sections to the original APB Opinions and Statements, Accounting Research Bulletins and Accounting Interpretations, updated as pertinent through December 15, 1976. Volume 1 — *Auditing, Management Advisory Services* and *Tax Practice; Volume 2 — Ethics* and *By-Laws;* and the TECHNICAL PRACTICE AIDS volume (including *Statements of Position)* are all entirely copyrighted by the AICPA, and we gratefully acknowledge the permission granted their use and quotation.

In addition, within the text, permitted direct quotations are used from the following copyrighted AICPA publications, more fully described and credited in the preceding BIBLIOGRAPHY: *"Accounting for Depreciable Assets;" "Objectives of Financial Statements;" "Accounting for Retail Land Sales;"* and *"APB Accounting Principles — Volume Two* (softcover) (for terminology).

Additional AICPA copyrighted publications, as indicated in the BIBLIOGRAPHY, are used with permission.

All quoted material is indicated within the text either by quotation marks, stylistic type-differences or specific preceding source-referencing.

Copies of the complete publications are available from the AICPA.

To Others:

Chapter 19 contains the CONSOLIDATED STATEMENT OF CHANGES IN FINANCIAL POSITION of the Hilton Hotels Corporation and Subsidiaries, from their 1975 (public) Annual Report. This illustration encompasses an extensive variety of the disclosure requirements and format suggested by the Standards for this type of statement, and we acknowledge its use and recommend its study by our readers.

To the other publishers listed in the BIBLIOGRAPHY, we acknowledge the use of their material which was so helpful in the preparation of this edition.